NEW DIMENSIONS OF URBAN MANAGEMENT IN INDIA

NEW DIMENSIONS OF URBAN MANAGEMENT IN INDIA

NISHITH RAI
AWADHESH KUMAR SINGH

Regional Centre for Urban & Environmental Studies, Lucknow

SERIALS PUBLICATIONS
NEW DELHI (INDIA)

First Published – 2010

ISBN: 978-81-8387-232-4

Published by

SERIALS PUBLICATIONS
4830/24, 1st Floor, Ansari Road
Darya Ganj, New Delhi-110002 (India)
Phone : 23245225. Fax : 91-11-23272135
E-mail: serials@sify.com

CONTENTS

FOREWORD

India entered into the new millennium with much awaited change in development paradigm. The focus of development planning has shifted to participatory development and inclusive growth with social justice and equity. It calls for decentralized governance ensuring people's participation in decision making and their involvement in development process. The historic and revolutionary 73'd and 74th (Amendment) Acts, 1992, to the Constitution initiated a new era of empowering grass root governments in the country. Though, India is experiencing steady growth in level of urbanization, the growing importance of urban sector as 'engines of growth' is reflected in its immense contribution to country's Gross Domestic Product. Urban governance in the country therefore is no more confined to the provision of infrastructure and civic services and, there is increasing felt need of a prudent and efficient strategy for financial and asset management with strong administrative and democratic framework of local governments to increase the efficiency of governance and management of civic affairs.

The concentration of population especially in larger urban centres in the country has put immense pressure on existing infrastructure and civic services. The gap between demand and supply of urban infrastructure and services has widened to an extent which calls for massive investment and effective system for managing resources. Cities need to develop a long term planning framework with people's participation and stakeholder's commitment. Despite many major initiatives in past, the existing institutional arrangement for the provision of urban services is unlikely to be adequate in the face rapid increase in demand for urban services. In the context of new economic policies and market based economy, urban sector assumes even greater significance and efforts would be needed to improve urban infrastructure, productivity and employment. The growing fiscal stress on municipal governments will require fiscal corrections, effective fiscal management and resource mobilization through initiating municipal financial reforms as well as introducing public private partnership initiatives in managing urban affairs.

In order to bridge the growing deficit in infrastructure and services, Jawaharlal Nehru National Urban Renewal Mission was launched in December 2005 by Government of India which envisages creation of infrastructure in cities along with implementation of reforms. This initiative has opened up an unparalleled window of opportunity in urban space in the country. The scheme emphasizes strengthening urban local bodies and re-engineering their process of service delivery besides creating conducive environment for urban infrastructure investment. This innovative approach with significant central assistance has enthused the governments at state and local levels by ushering in a new era of development.

I am happy that Prof. Nishith Rai and Dr. A.K. Singh have brought out the "New Dimensions of Urban Management in Indian" which would be of help to urban managers in the context of new policy regime and changed environment. The book has actively touched upon some of the crucial dimensions of urban development and management in the country. The analysis of data and critical appreciation of pertinent literature, in my view, may be of importance for understanding the ever-changing dynamics of urban development and governance. I hope that the book will prove to be yet another much desired step in ushering in a new culture in urban governance in the country.

15-12-08

Dr. M. Ramachandran, IAS
Secretary,
Ministry of Urban Development,
Government of India, New Delhi

PREFACE

Cities play a vital role in economic growth and development. Sustainable development of cities largely depends upon their physical, social and institutional infrastructure, while urban centres may be viewed as engines of growth, the cities are at the crossroads of change. In India, the process of urbanization is at critical juncture. India is among the countries at low level of urbanization. However, structure of urbanization is changing in India. There has been change in the pattern of urban growth. During 1951 to 1991, urban growth was generally high in relatively less developed states and developed states experienced low urban growth. However, a significant departure of this pattern in 199s's from the earlier decades as the developed states registered urban growth above the national average. The increasing population and urbanization have put pressure on existing infrastructure, services and amenities. Large investment in infrastructure and services are required for accelerating the growth rate of economy. The gap between the availability and demand for urban infrastructure and services has widened over the years. This has resulted in deterioration of space, environment, and quality of life in urban centres. The provisions for infrastructure facilities required for support to large concentration of population is lagging far behind the pace of urbanization. Though the Indian economy is booming, but the public sector seems to be deteriorating. The service sector is booming while the employment opportunities in organized sector and particularly public sector are declining. This has called for inclusive economic growth and holistic development. Healthy, inclusive economic growth needs faster urban growth to reduce the economic burden on rural areas.

There has been paradigm shift in urban governance in India. Decentralization as envisaged by 74th Constitutional Amendment Act, 1994 has led the process of municipal reforms and ensuring urban governance, however, the task of devolution of powers, functions, and finances to local bodies is still showing unfinished agenda. The escalating demand for urban infrastructure and services has called for mobilization of resources through public private partnership initiatives and introducing municipal reforms in urban local governments. The urban infrastructure development schemes - JNNURM, UIDSSMT and IHSDP have shown the new path of infrastructure development and its maintenance since the schemes are reforms oriented and seek public private partnership, community participation, resources mobilization and focus on augmenting efficiency of urban local governments. The urban governance is also experiencing a paradigm shift. The policy on urban housing and habitat intends to promote sustainable development of human settlements with a view to ensuring equitable supply of land, shelter, and services at affordable prices to all section of society. The strategies for empowering urban poor are also changing.

India is a large, diverse and poor country that faces severe environmental problems. The environmental problems are vast and mitigation measures are expensive. Many of the urban environmental problems have their genesis in the growth strategies adopted in post independence era. There are three major sources of pollution viz. domestic sewage, industrial effluents and agricultural run off. The untreated sewage and waste water is thrown into water bodies while most of local bodies do not have sewer line for disposal of waste water and sewage. The urban centres also produce about 50 million tonnes of solid waste annually and most of the local bodies don't have adequate resources and technical capacity to deal with the gigantic problem. The increasing concern about natural disasters in urban areas has also called for multipronged approaches and strategies to mitigate, and manage the growing vulnerability of natural disasters.

The present volume is out come of research projects and capacity building programmes conducted by Regional Centre for Urban and Environmental Studies, Lucknow during the recent period. Most of the papers were prepared for the purpose of organizing programmes while a few were prepared as working papers. Some of the papers of the volume were already published in edited volumes and journals; however, these are updated and revised. The inclusion of these papers is with the view of understanding the dynamics of urban problems and emerging issues for their effective management.

The volume is the result of cooperation, support, inspiration and assistance extended by several persons. We place on records the sincere appreciation of all Faculty Members for suggesting modifications in the papers for enhancing the quality. Thanks are due to our colleague Dr. U.B. Singh and Dr. Richa Varmani for their thoughtful observations and suggesting valuable modifications in the volume. We are thankful to Ms. N. Kamala Kumari and Mr. K.D. Pandey for taking pains in composing of the papers and giving them to this shape. Lastly we are thankful to Mr. S. K. Jha, for showing his interest in publishing the manuscript and giving it to book shape.

1

URBANIZATION

TRENDS OF URBANIZATION

Widespread urbanization is a twentieth century phenomenon. Rome was probably the first settlement to reach one million population in 5 BC while London become the second such city in 1800. In 1900, the total urban population of the world was not more than 250 million, less than 15 per cent of the total population. The Indian urban population today is itself greater than this number. In 2000, the world's urban population had increased to almost 2.9 billion, about 47 per cent of the total population. Today Asian countries have emerged as most populous countries. According to United Nations Study (1995), by the year 2015 ten of the world's fifteen largest cities will be in Asia, three of these will be in India. Of the 10 most populous countries, 6 are in Asia (Table 1).

The structural reforms and the associated development strategies launched in 1991 are expected to accelerate rural urban migration and boost the pace of urbanization. The demographic and economic growth in India is likely to be concentrated in and around fifty to sixty large cities with population of about a million or more. There is migration from villages to town and cities which results in growth of metropolitan cities since they provide multiple avenues, services and amenities viz. education, health care, employment, business and entertainment options etc. People also migrate for economic opportunities and urban life styles. Though urbanization brings about development in the social, economic and cultural spheres of life but some times it disturbs the ecological system. Rapid and unplanned growth of urban agglomeration generates a series of negative environmental and social effects. Today urban India presents a very pathetic scene. Cities have become a site of rotting garbage, degrading drainage system and shocking night soil removal system. Besides, poor have practically no access to covered toilets and in many towns and cities, the majority have to defecate in the open. The untreated sewage being dumped into the nearest water body leads to health hazards.

Table 1
Urban Population of Most Populous Countries

Country	*1950*		*2000*		*2030*	
	Percentage of Urban Population	*Population (Million)*	*Percentage of Urban Population*	*Population (Million)*	*Percentage of Urban Population*	*Population (Million)*
China	12.5	555	35.8	1275	59.5	1485
India	17,3	357	29.0	1009	40.9	1409
USA	64.2	158	77.2	283	84.5	358
Brazil	36.5	54	81.2	170	90.5	226
Indonesia	12.4	79	41.0	212	63.7	283
Nigeria	10.1	30	44.1	114	63.6	220
Pakistan	17.5	40	33.1	141	48.9	273
Mexico	42.7	28	74.4	99	81.9	135
Japan	50.3	84	78.8	127	84.8	121
Bangladesh	4.3	42	25.0	137	44.3	223

Source: United Nations, 2002

India is one of the least urbanized countries in the world because between 1951 and 2001, the level of urbanization increased by 13 percentage points only. However, it has the second largest urban population in the world and more than two third of it lives in the 393 cities that have population of over one lakh. The four mega cities viz., Mumbai, Kolkata, Delhi and Chennai with a population of more than 6 millions each in 2001 account for almost one fourth of population living in cities. As per 2001 census, 285 million population i.e. 27.8 per cent of 1027 million total population of India is residing in

5161 cities and towns in the country, where as in 1991, 25.7 per cent population lived in urban areas. The decadal growth in urban population during 1991-2001 has been 31.2 per cent whereas at the beginning of the 20th century, only 10.8 per cent of total 218 million population of the country resided in cities and towns. The number of million plus cities has increased to 35 in 2001 from 12 in 1981 and 23 in 1991. These 35 million plus cities account for 107.9 million urban population of the country (Table 2). As per projections of Government of India, the urban population of the country in 2011 will be 405.26 million and 553.04 million in 2021. Thus, around one third population is expected to live in urban areas.

There has been phenomenon growth in the number of towns and urban agglomerations over the period of 1981 to 2001, however, annual exponential growth rate of urban population is low. Even, in the recent the growth has been reported to be declining. There has been just 2.06 percentage points increase in proportion of urban population to total population during 1991 to 2001.

Table 2
Urbanization in India

Year	*Percentage of Urban Population*	*Number of Towns*	*Total Population (Million)*	*Urban Population (Million)*
1901	10.8	1827	238.39	25.85
1911	10.3	1815	252.09	25.95
1921	11.2	1949	251.32	28.09
1931	12.0	2072	278.98	33.46
1941	13.9	2250	318.66	44.16
1951	17.3	2843	361.23	62.44
1961	18.0	2365	439.23	78.13
1971	19.9	2590	548.15	109.11
1981	23.3	3378	159.46	159.56
1991	25.7	3762	846.30	217.61
2001	27.8	5161	1048.15	296.97

Source: Census, 2001

An analysis of the distribution of urban population by size categories reveals that the process of urbanization in India has been large city oriented. This is proved that a high proportion of urban population being concentrated in Class I cities, which has gone up systematically over the decades in the last century, the massive increase in proportion of Class I cities from 26 per cent in 1901 to 85.20 per cent in 1991 while it declined to 61.48 per cent in 2001, has been attributed to faster growth of large cities. The number of class one cities has grown to 423 in 2001 from 24 in 1901. There has been more than five fold increase in the number of class one cities since 1951 (Table 3).

Table 3
Number of Towns and Percentage of Urban Population in Different Size Categories

Year	*Class I*	*Class II*	*Class III*	*Class IV*	*Class V*	*Class VI*	*Total*
1901	24	43	130	391	744	479	1827
	(26.00)	(11.29)	(15.64)	(20.83)	(20.14)	(6.10)	
1911	23	40	135	364	707	485	1815
	(27.48)	(10.51)	(16.4)	(19.73)	(19.31)	(6.57)	
1921	29	45	145	370	734	571	1949
	(29.70)	(10.39)	(15.92)	(18.29)	(18.67)	(7.03)	
1931	35	56	183	434	800	509	2072
	(31.20)	(11.65)	(16.8)	(18.00)	(17.14)	(5.21)	
1941	49	74	242	498	920	407	2250
	(38.23)	(11.42)	(16.35)	(15.78)	(15.08)	(3.14)	
1951	76	91	327	608	1124	569	2365
	(44.63)	(9.96)	(15.72)	(13.63)	(12.97)	(3.09)	
1961	102	129	437	719	711	172	2365
	(51.42)	(11.27)	(16.94)	(12.77)	(6.87)	(0.77)	
1971	148	173	558	827	623	147	2590
	(57.24)	(10.92)	(16.01)	(10.94)	(4.45)	(0.44)	
1981	218	270	743	1059	758	253	3378
	(60.37)	(11.63)	(14.33)	(19.54)	(3.50)	(0.50)	
1991	300	345	947	1167	740	197	3768
	(65.20)	(10.95)	(13.19)	(7.77)	(2.60)	(0.29)	
2001	423	498	1386	1560	1057	227	5161
	(61.48)	(12.30)	(15.00)	(8.08)	(2.85)	(0.29)	(100.00)

Source: India Infrastructure Report, 2006.

The startling fact is that the proportion of population living in smaller towns has shown declining trend over the period while there is massive growth in population of larger towns. Importantly, growth of population in smaller towns has been reported negative while the growth of population in large cities and towns has been found massive. During 2001, the high proportion of urban population has been reported to be in Delhi, Pondicherry, Goa, Chandigarh, Mahrashtra, Mizoram, Lakshadweep, Tamil Nadu, Karnataka, Gujarat etc. (Table – 4). The high rate of growth of urban population during 1991-2001 has been reported high in Dadra & Nagar Haveli (14.59 per cent) followed by Arunachal Pradesh (7.0 per cent), Andaman and Nicobar Islands (4.14 per cent), Sikkim (4.83 per cent), and Delhi (4.14 per cent).

Table 4
Patterns of Urbanization and Growth of Urban Population Across the States

State	*Percentage of Urban Population*				*Annual Exponential Growth Rate*		
	1971	*1981*	*1991*	*2001*	*1971-81*	*1981-91*	*1991-2001*
Andhra Pradesh	19.31	23.25	26.84	27.08	3.94	3.55	1.37
Arunachal Pradesh	3.70	6.32	12.21	20.41	8.32	9.28	7.00
Assam	8.82	9.88	11.09	12.72	3.29	3.29	3.09
Bihar	7.97	9.84	10.40	10.47	4.27	2.66	2.57
Chhatisgarh	10.38	14.69	17.40	20.08	5.33	4.00	3.09
Delhi	89.70	92.84	89.93	93.01	4.56	3.79	4.14
Goa	26.44	32.46	41.02	49.77	4.37	3.96	3.32
Gujarat	28.08	31.08	34.40	37.55	3.42	2.92	2.80
Haryana	17.66	21.96	24.79	29.00	4.65	3.58	4.11
Himachal Pradesh	6.99	7.72	8.70	9.79	3.02	3.11	2.81
Jammu & Kashmir	18.59	21.05	22.76	24.88	3.80	3.44	3.44
Jharkhand	16.01	20.09	21.25	22.25	4.51	2.61	2.55
Karnataka	24.31	28.91	30.91	33.98	4.08	2.55	2.53
Kerala	16.24	18.78	26.44	25.97	3.19	4.76	0.74
Madhya Pradesh	18.58	22.34	25.27	26.67	4.25	3.63	2.71
Maharashtra	31.17	35.03	38.73	42.4	3.35	3.27	2.95
Manipur	13.19	26.44	27.69	23.88	9.70	2.98	1.21
Meghalaya	14.55	18.03	18.69	19.63	4.84	3.10	3.16
Mizoram	11.36	25.17	46.2	49.5	11.79	9.57	3.27
Nagaland	9.95	15.54	17.28	17.74	8.49	5.58	5.27
Orissa	8.41	11.82	13.43	14.97	5.21	3.08	2.61
Punjab	23.73	27.72	29.72	33.95	3.62	2.55	3.19
Rajasthan	17,63	20.93	22.88	23.38	4.52	3.31	2.71
Sikkim	9.37	16.23	9.12	11.1	9.55	-3.23	4.83
Tamil Nadu	30.26	32.98	34.2	43.86	2.45	1.76	3.56
Tripura	10.43	10.98	15.26	17.02	3.26	6.19	2.53
U.P.	14.02	18.01	19.89	20.78	4.78	3.27	2.84
Uttrakhand	NA	NA	NA	25.59	NA	NA	2.84
West Bengal	24.75	26.49	27.39	28.03	2.75	2.54	1.84
All India	20.22	23.73	25.72	27.78	3.79	3.09	2.73

Source: Census of India, 2001

During 2002, there were 3641 urban local bodies. Out of total urban local bodies in India, 107 ULB's, were Municipal Corporations, 1443 Municipal Councils, and 2091 Nagar Panchayats. The highest number of local bodies were reported in Tamil Nadu (719) followed by Uttar Pradesh, Madhya Pradesh and Maharastra (Table 5). State-wise number of elected representatives in urban local bodies is shown in Table 6. There were 68554 people's representatives in urban local bodies in 1991. The composition of people's representatives significantly varies in the state of Bihar since it has already implemented 50% reservation for women councillors in urban local bodies as against the statutory norm of 33 per cent. Similarly Madhya Pradesh government has announced a reservation of 50% seats for women councillors in local bodies.

Table 5
State-Wise No. of Urban Local Bodies in India

State	*Municipal Corporations*	*Municipal Councils*	*Nagar Panchayats*	*Total*
Andhra Pradesh	7	109	1	117
Arunachal Pradesh	–	–	–	–
Assam	1	29	38	68
Bihar	5	32	80	117
Chhattisgarh	6	20	49	75
Delhi	1	1	–	2
Goa	–	13	–	13
Gujarat	6	85	58	149
Haryana	1	21	46	68
Himachal Pradesh	1	20	31	52
Jammu & Kashmir	–	3	67	90
Jharkhand	2	16	22	40
Karnataka	6	124	87	217
Kerala	5	53	–	58
Madhya Pradesh	14	86	234	334
Maharastra	19	224	2	245
Manipur	–	8	21	29
Meghalaya	–	6	03	9
Mizoram	–	1	1	1
Nagaland	–	–	8	8
Orissa	2	33	68	103
Punjab	4	97	30	131

Contd...

State	*Municipal Corporations*	*Municipal Councils*	*Nagar Panchayats*	*Total*
Rajasthan	3	11	169	183
Sikkim	–	–	8	8
Tamil Nadu	–	102	611	719
Tripura	6	1	12	13
Uttar Pradesh	12	193	423	628
Uttarakhand	1	31	28	60
West Bengal	16	112	4	422
India	108	1492	2011	3641

Source: Nagarpalika Network Newsletter, July 2001.

Table 6
State-Wise Elected Representatives in Urban Local Bodies (1999)

State	*Municipal Corporations*	*Municipal Councils*	*Nagar Panchayats*	*Total*
Andhra Pradesh	395	2833	314	3542
Assam	NA	353	204	557
Bihar	–	–	–	–
Goa	–	155	–	155
Gujarat	468	2745	1260	4473
Haryana	NA	NA	NA	1359
Himachal Pradesh	25	183	221	429
Karnataka	410	3196	1355	4961
Kerala	298	1597	–	1895
Madhya Pradesh	1067	2527	4537	8131
Maharastra	1417	4901	–	6318
Manipur	–	NA	NA	NA
Orissa	70	560	1056	1686
Punjab	NA	NA	NA	1699
Rajasthan	NA	NA	NA	4412
Tamil Nadu	480	3494	9794	13768
Tripura	–	NA	NA	2706
Uttar Pradesh	841	5970	5518	12329
West bengal	NA	NA	NA	2706
Delhi	134	–	–	134
Total	5605	28534	24259	68554

Source: Nagarpalika Network Newsletter (July 2001) and UNESCAP, 2000

The task of improving urban services is constantly more challenging due to the large increase in population. This will put a strain on the present management and delivery systems. In many cases delivery mechanisms would need to be redesigned to meet the large demand. If urban population growth is to be accelerated, it will need even greater acceleration in urban infrastructure investment. With the rapid urbanization that is now expected in ensuing decades in India, it would be better to decentralize the instruments of infrastructure provision so that the agencies providing such infrastructure services are able to finance themselves and can respond flexibly to the changing demand of growing city. It would be better if private agencies are given more opportunities to perform the functions of financing, planning and management of urban infrastructural services and amenities. There is strong demand for (I) wider coverage of urban infrastructure services, which is a daunting task given in the expected huge growth in urban population and (II) improvement in the quality of urban infrastructure services especially in large cities, making the demand for urban infrastructure more heterogeneous than what has been witnessed in the past. The Tenth Plan had in the context of urban development, laid stress on improving the functional and financial autonomy of urban local bodies, strengthening of their finances through smooth implementation of SFC's awards, rationalization of property taxation system and levy of user charges. The Plan advocated broad based urban sector reform measures and emphasized that public private partnership should be brought on urban agenda in order to improve the efficiency and delivery of services. The growth of population has put urban infrastructure and services under severe stress. Smaller cities have found it particularly difficult to cope with the increasing demands on services because of inadequate financial resources.

2

DECENTRALIZED GOVERNANCE

Decentralization has become a buzz word today. Numerous definitions of decentralization emerge from the literature. The term refers to changes which occur within political systems. This, rules out three of six things which are sometimes discussed. The first type of change to be excluded is sometimes called decentralization by default. This happens when government institutions become so ineffective that they fail almost entirely to make the influence of central authorities penetrate down to lower level arenas, and people at the gross roots become heartily cynical about government. When this occurs in countries, voluntary organizations or NGO's, take part in development projects and share resources with government. The second thing to be excluded is privatization, the handover of task formerly performed by state agencies to the private sector. Privatization often involves a shift of power and resources from one major, centralized power centre to another. We also set aside one further type of decentralization, namely, delegation of some responsibilities for development programmes or projects to parastatal agencies. This leaves us with three key definitions: (i) decentralization or administrative decentralization; (ii) fiscal decentralization; (iii) devolution or democratic decentralization. Decentralization refers to the dispersal of agents of higher levels of government into lower level arenas. It may be described as administrative decentralization. Second, the term decentralization some times refers to downward fiscal transfers, by which higher levels in a system code influence over budgets and financial decisions to lower levels. This authority may pass to decentralized bureaucrats who are accountable only to superior at higher levels, or to unelected appointees selected from higher level. Finally there is devolution - the transfer of resources and power (and often tasks) to lower level authorities which are largely or wholly independent of higher levels of government, and which are democratic in some way and to some degree. It is recognized that decentralization of resources and responsibilities without (democratizing) political reforms would have been incomplete and probably, not conducive to society effective results.

DECENTRALIZATION

Democratic decentralization can take varied forms. It clearly includes cases in which the persons in authority within institutions at intermediate and or local levels are elected by secret ballots. Elections may be direct or indirect. The persons who are elected may be the members of a council, or the executive head of an authority, or both. Elections are usually on a first-past-the-post basis, but they some times make use of some form of proportional representation. Decentralization can entail transfers of power to different levels within political systems. It can be bestowed or one or more intermediate levels. When it involves the creation of fully blown governments at the regional level, it qualifies as federalism. But more limited powers may go to intermediate levels, in experiments which fall short of outright federal restructuring.

The causes of decentralization differ substantially from one place to another. The multiplicity of theories and the diversity of experiences suggest the possible validity of the following propositions:

- No single factor is sufficient to explain decisions to decentralize in all countries or in a single country.
- No single factors are necessary to decisions or decentralize in all countries.

- Decentralization in each country is the result of a combination of causes.
- The combination of causes producing decentralization varies from country to country.

The degeneration of patronage systems and the ruling parties in less developed countries played a role. The regimes faced mounting demands from organized interests, yet sluggish economic growth and increasing corruption by political activities at all level, undermined their ability to respond to those demands. The oil shocks of the mid and late 1970's compounded that problem and caused others. Many national leaders over centralized power in the interests of personal rule and that undermined the autonomy resources, effectiveness and responsiveness of ruling parties and formal institutions. By 1970's, it was becoming increasingly possible for small enterprises in many sectors to compete with larger companies - including state owned enterprises. This was partly resulting of technological innovations. This impelled all manner of decision makers towards greater decentralization. The two paradigms which had long dominated political analyses of less developed countries and the political development/modernization school and dependency theory become increasingly less convincing during the 1980's. New modes of analysis gained popularity in their place and helped to prepare the ground for experiments with decentralization. During the 1980's some donor agencies also began to shift their emphasis away from large scale development programmes to more modest, micro level projects into which grass roots communities could be drawn as participants, in the hope of making development more sustainable. This helped open the way to decentralization. The collapses of the Soviet System and the end of the cold war have also played a role. It lead to the globalization and restructuring of society, economy and polity. The influence of Gandhian ideas in India has always ensured a some what wider constituency for decentralization than in most other countries. But the lack of enthusiasm for such views in Nehru's circle and among India's constitution makers ensured that the elected councils which were created during the 1950's at local and intermediate levels had only very limited powers. Thereafter, national leaders preoccupations with large scale development projects and state level politician's aversion to sharing power with elected members of lower level councils largely thwarted decentralization. Decentralization assists in tackling the low collective action potential of small farmers and of other, even poorer groups. It has genuine promise in fostering, over time, a more equitable balance of power both between local communications and higher levels of government, and between more and less prosperous groups within local arenas. Decentralization strengthens civil society. It integrates pre-existing, informal arrangements and processes at the local level for managing resources and local affairs into the official political process. This can enhance the sustainability of development programmes and policies. Decentralization makes rural dwellers more aware of government policies, and better able to differentiate between those which are beneficial and those which are not. Decentralization now helps ordinary people to develop their analytical capacities and to make use of them. Decentralization promotes the flow of information from people at lower level to the upper reaches of government. Thus it enables government to become more responsive. It increases hugely the numbers of people at lower level in political systems who know how much public money is available for development. This promotes political stability. Decentralization can enhance political stability more responsive to people at lower levels, it can break down popular cynicism about politics and increase the legitimacy of political system. Second, by creating a large number of elected posts in authorities at lower levels, it generates opportunities for political activities at those levels who aspire to a role in government. This eases their frustrations which can threaten stability. Third, it eases the frustrations of opposition parties by increasing the number of arenas in which there are political prizes to be won. After decentralization, elections occur not just to the national presidency or legislature, but to authorities at regional and local levels. This helps to persuade opposition parties and interests, whose candidates lose elections for one of those bodies, to remain engaged with the democratic process, since they may win in another arena at the next opportunity.

The imperatives of decentralized planning in India have been repeatedly emphasized in the Five Year Plan documents in our country. However, the progress in this direction remained slow and faltering despite frequent changes in the policy prescriptions. Indian economy has reached a stage in the process of development wherein the existence and survival of democratic politicization calls for immediate implementation of the process of decentralized planning. The structural, technological, institutional and organizational impediments to development can be effectively dealt only when the process of planning is approached and viewed in the proximity of the specific areas and the local public.

As we approach 21st century Indian polity has been striving for establishing democratic goals through modernizing its political and administrative institutions. With a change in development paradigms, the focus of development planning has shifted to participatory development with social justice and equity. It called for decentralized administration ensuring people's participation in decision making and giving priorities to their local needs. The 73rd and 74th Constitutional Amendment Acts, 1992 made the provision for ensuring local self governance through empowering local bodies. Thus, the units of the local self governments were given statutory status and state governments were given the mandatory provisions for establishing three tiers of local governments both in rural and urban areas. Importantly, the local bodies have become the units of the governments to have a share in decision making and active participation in development process for social-economic development of the region. The constitution of 74th Amendment Act, 1992, has marked the beginning of a historical reform to decentralize power at the grass root level in urban areas of the country. This act has provided a constitutional form to the structure and mandate of municipalities to enable them to function as an effective democratic institution of local self government. One of its important objectives is to promote people's participation in planning, provision and delivery of civic services. It introduced some fundamental changes in the system of municipal governance with a new structure, additional devolution of functions, planning responsibilities, new system of fiscal transfers and empowerment of women and the weaker sections of the society. There have been significant changes in the institutional structure for the financing and management of basic services in the post decentralization period. Prior to 1994, the central government was not involved in any transfer of resources to the ULB's. This provision was made by 74th Constitution Amendment Act. The Tenth Finance Commission had recommended the transfers of resources to the local (both rural and urban) bodies in India. It recommended an amount of Rs. 1000 crores for the municipalities for the period of 1996-2000. The inter-se allocations were made on the basis of the ratio of slum population to urban population of seventies. This transfer was conditional upon the municipalities making matching contribution and was useable for properly identified projects. The Eleventh Finance Commission has recommended a grant of Rs. 2000 crores for the urban local bodies for the period 2000-2005. This would supplement the funds flowing from the states to the ULB's as also the resources accruing to municipalities, as a result of the implementation of the recommendations of State Finance Commissions. It has allocated the grants to the states on the basis of a set of multiple criteria, which includes (a) urban population based on (1991 population census) (40 per cent); (b) index of decentralization (20 per cent), (c) distance from highest per capita income (20 per cent); (d) revenue efforts (10 per cent), and (e) geographical area (10 per cent). The Twelfth Finance Commission has recommended for the 2005-10 period, a sum of Rs. 5000 crores for municipalities (Table 1).

This is an ad hoc amount. The commission refined the criteria for allocating recommended devolution of revenue from both tax and non taxes sources.

Table 1
Shares of States in Allocation to Municipalities

States	*11th Finance Commission*		*12th Finance Commission*	
	(Percentage)	*(Rs. Crores)*	*(Percentage)*	*(Rs. Crores)*
Andhra Pradesh	8.23	164.66	7.480	374
Arunachal Pradesh	0.03	68.00	0.060	3
Assam	1.08	21.54	1.100	55
Bihar	4.69	93.90	2.840	142
Chhatisgarh	–	–	1.760	88
Goa	0.23	4.64	0.240	12
Gujarat	6.63	132.52	8.280	414
Haryana	1.83	36.84	1.820	91
Himachal Pradesh	0.19	3.89	0.16	8
Jammu & Kashmir	0.78	15.66	0.760	38
Jharkhand	–	–	1.960	98
Karnataka	6.24	124.82	6.460	323
Kerala	3.76	75.25	2.980	149
Madhya Pradesh	7.80	156.01	7.220	361
Maharashtra	1.81	316.25	15.820	791
Manipur	0.22	4.40	0.180	9
Meghalaya	0.13	2.70	0.160	8
Mizoram	0.19	3.84	0.200	10
Nagaland	0.09	2.70	0.160	8
Orissa	2.00	39.96	2.080	104
Punjab	2.74	54.73	3.420	171
Rajasthan	4.97	99.42	4.400	220
Sikkim	0.01	0.21	0.020	1
Tamil Nadu	9.67	193.37	11.440	572
Tripura	0.20	4.02	0.160	8
Uttar Pradesh	12.58	251.63	10.340	517
Uttaranchal	–	–	0.680	34
West Bengal	9.87	197.49	7.860	393
Total	100.0	2000	100.00	5000

Source: Twelfth Finance Commission, Government of India

Provision of basic services such as water supply, sewerage, sanitation, solid waste disposal and street lighting has traditionally been the responsibility of the local governments. These services are being provided through state government departments, state level boards, corporations etc. Public Health Engineering Department, Public Works Department, Urban Development Department, Housing Boards, Department of Local Self Government, Water Supply and Sewerage Boards etc. are some of the departments of the state government which performs municipal functions. With the passing of 74th Constitutional Amendment Act, Metropolitan Planning Committee and District Planning Committee have been formed to take up developmental activities in the concerned region in place of the parastatals. The ULB's have also been empowered to take up development functions. States have responded in diverse manner with regard to the status of parastatal agencies in the post decentralized period. Many state governments like Kerala and Karnataka have recommended the abolition of the parastatals while some have recommended for a change in their functional role like in Tamil Nadu, Uttar Pradesh, Maharashtra, West Bengal and Andhra Pradesh. Government of India has also recommended to modify the Municipal Act of the states in the lines of Modern Municipal Act, incorporating the Rajya Nagar Bill. Bihar is the first and only state who has adopted Modern Municipal Act in toto in order to ensure complete decentralization process. The parastatal agencies have also been merged with Urban Development Department.

The 74th Constitutional Amendment Act has also transferred administrative and financial process and created an enabling environment for the local bodies to under take planning and development responsibility. Local bodies are simply not equipped to take up the responsibility of planning, especially of launching capital projects. Ahmadabad is one of the few lucky cities that have been able to mobilize funds from capital markets in the mid nineties, through credit rating done by CRISIL. Bangalore, Ludhiana, Nagpur, Nashik, Indore, Madurai, Ahmadabad, Hyderabad and Chennai have issued Municipal Bonds in the tune of Rs. 5185 million. (Table 2).

Table 2
Municipal Bonds in India

City	*Amount (Rs. Million)*	*Interest (%)*	*Guarantee*	*Purpose*
Ahmadabad	1000	14	No	Water supply and sanitation
Bangalore	1250	13	State Govts.	City roads, Street, drainage
Ludhiana	100	13.5-14	No	Water supply and Sanitation
Nagpur	500	13	No	Water supply

Contd...

City	Amount (Rs. Million)	Interest (%)	Guarantee	Purpose
Nashik	1000	14.75	No	–
Indore	100	NA	Yes	City road
Madurai	300	12.25	No	Water supply and sanitation
Ahmadabad (Tax Free)	1000	9	No	Road construction and widening
Hyderabad (Tax Free)	825	8.5	No	Water supply and sanitation
Tamil Nadu (Pooled Financing)	110	9.20	USAID Provided backup guarantee of 50% of the bonds	–

Source: India Infrastructure Report, OUP, Delhi, 2006.

The JNNURM, UIDSSMT and IHSDP like infrastructure development schemes of Government also focus on financial and functional aspects of decentralization. The schemes aimed at strengthening ULBs through provision of mandatory and obligatory municipal reforms agenda. World Bank in India is mainly contributing in urban water and sanitation project. The Bank has also initiated training programmes in Tamil Nadu, Karnataka and Uttar Pradesh with focus on developing the basic capacity of the staff of ULB's and the state governments. Asian Development Bank has developed its urban lending operation by supporting state-wise urban development projects and credit lines for housing and urban infrastructure through domestic financial intermediaries. DFID and UNICEF have entered the urban scene in India relatively recently. Both the agencies focus on poverty reduction and improving the living conditions of slum dwellers. USAID through its FIRE project has been promoting commercially viable infrastructure projects and City Managers Associations. It is also assisting state and local officials in introducing changes at the local level in the operation of water systems. UNDP through its project on capacity building has helped local bodies in introducing Report Card System and strengthening the local bodies in Uttar Pradesh and Uttaranchal. Recently in another project on capacity building for decentralized governance, it is assisting state governments in strengthening local bodies in financial sector and resource mobilization through introducing GIS and Double Entry Accounting System. Japan Bank for International Cooperation is also entering in the urban sector through providing financial assistance in the development of urban water and sanitation infrastructure.

Several academics, administrative and constitutional experts have reviewed the 74th Constitutional Amendment Act, 1992. The following issues can be highlighted:

(1) The XIIth Schedule is not mandated and it is up to the state governments to decide as to which of the functions may be devolved to the ULB's. Most states have amended their Acts to include part or in some cases all of these. Studies show that only marginal changes that were regarded as mandatory have been carried out. Only a few states have implemented fully the vision of the Act in order to avoid overlapping institutional functional and geographic jurisdictions.

(2) In almost all states with the exception of West Bengal and Kerala, political decentralization has not been backed by enough financial devolution. Thus, ULB's have to depend upon the state government's political and bureaucratic set up to access funds. This reinforces the lack of financial devolution. In many states, the ULB's find themselves in difficult situation to provide their share in infrastructure development projects under JNNURM, UIDSSMT and IHSDP programmes of Central Government.

(3) While provisions for reservation for Scheduled Castes/ Scheduled Tribes and women have been made accordance with the provision of 74th Constitutional Amendment Act, however, reservation criteria is being used for political purposes by the ruling party. Bihar become the first state to provide 50 per cent reservation for women in the ULB's against the mandatory provision of one third seats for women. Recently, Madhya Pradesh has also amended the Act to provide 50 per cent reservation for women in ULB's. This will change the political landscape of the ULB's in the coming years.

(4) While legal provisions for the constitution of ward committees have also been made in most states, the actual spirit of the Amendment is fully realized. Government of India has introduced Rajya Nagar Bill which makes provision for realistic formation and functioning of ward committees, however, except in Bihar, nowhere it has been introduced. Even in Bihar it has been recently introduced and for effective implementation it requires introducing of manual and bylaws.

(5) All the states have established State Finance Commission and most of the SFC's have submitted their reports to their respective state governments. There has been however, a substantial time lag between the submission of the SFC report and its approval by the government. There is no similarity in the preparation of reports and their recommendations.

(6) Most of the states have conducted elections in all the ULB's and provided representation of weaker sections, however, they could not ensure adequate training and grounding of new councilors in matters of municipal administration, conduct and functioning of municipalities.

(7) District Planning Committer's and Metropolitan Planning Committees have been set up only in a few states - Kerala, Madhya Pradesh and West Bengal. Separate legislation has not been enacted for the constitution of MPC's and DPC's in most of the states.

(8) No state has been able to take specific action on the situation of Development Authorities except Bihar where Department of Housing Development has been merged with Department of Urban Development and Housing Department. Now Department is called as Urban Development and Housing Department. Kerala has also attempted to bring various line agencies under the ULB's.

(9) Short duration of the terms of Mayors and Presidents make for poor programme implementation and

tighten state government control over ULB's. Mayor's in Karnataka have a term of only one year, while presidents of TMC, for two and a half years. Kerala and West Bengal in contrast provide a longer term for Mayors/Presidents.

NATURE AND SCOPE OF URBAN GOVERNMENT

Municipal government and administration is no longer a simple affair rather it has become quite complicated and complex with phenomenal growth in the pace and process of urbanization resulting in the spurt of urban problems and consequential increase in their functions. It was envisaged in the post independence era that the new set of local bodies as instruments of national policy would progressively be used with steady increase in their functions. Accordingly, they were called upon not only to provide civic amenities like, water supply, sanitation, medical health, transport and sewerage but also to carry out the programmes of national development. Therefore, their responsibilities have increased many-fold for providing better conditions of living, ameliorating the urban poor etc. and to ensure adequate infrastructure and appropriate administrative structure to cope with urban problems of unprecedented nature and magnitude. Thus scope of urban government has become very wide and diversified as well.

The history of a nation is created by the milestone events, which drastically change the way society is governed, organized and bequeathed to the new generation. The 74th Constitution Amendment Act, 1992 has become the milestone in the history of urban administration in India. It recognized municipalities as Constitutional bodies forming the third tier of the federal polity of India. The decentralization initiative in urban areas was first mooted by the Rural-Urban Relationship Committee, constituted by the Government of India in 1963, however it took nearly 30 years to concretize in the shape of the Constitutional Amendment in 1992. The Constitutional 74th Amendment Act, envisaged a systematic change in the pattern of municipal government in the country with a view to enabling cities and towns to play a critical role in economic and social development and signified the beginning of a historic reform to decentralize power to the people. The Act prescribes a common legal institutional frame work for the efficient and effective delivery of municipal services and comprises of the following mandatory institutions:

(1) State Election Commission (Article 243k)

(2) Elected Municipalities: Municipal Corporation (for larger urban areas), Municipal Councils (Smaller Urban areas); and Nagar Panchayats (for transitional areas) (Article 243Q).

(3) Ward committees and other committers (Article 243R)

(4) State Finance Commission (Article 243I),

(5) District Planning Committee (Article 243ZE)

(6) Metropolitan Planning Committee (Article 243ZE)

Until recently, local government in India was organized on the basis of the ultra-virus principle and the state governments were free to extend or control the functional sphere of the local bodies through executive decisions without amendments to the legislative provisions. Through the 74th Amendment Act an attempt has been made to improve the performance and ability of ULBs. The important provisions of the Act include constitution of three types of municipalities, devolution of greater functional responsibilities and financial powers to them, adequate representation of weaker sections and women, regular and fair conduct of elections, and constitution of Wards Committees, District Planning Committee, Metropolitan Planning Committee and State Finance Commission. It further provided a basis for the state legislature to guide the state government in the assignment of various responsibilities to ULBs and strengthening of municipal governance. Accordingly, state governments have amended their municipal laws so as to bring them in conformity with the 74th Constitutional Amendment Act (Chart 1).

Recent years have witnessed an increasing interest in and growing consciousness of the need and importance of local

Chart 1
State-Wise Compliance of 74th CAA Provisions

State	Composition of ULBs	Reservation of Seats	Regular Conducted of Elections	Constitution of Ward Committees	Constitution of DPC	Constitution of SFCs
Andhra Pradesh	✓	✓	✓	✓	–	✓
Arunachal Pradesh	–	–	–	–	✓	✓
Assam	✓	✓	✓	–	✓	✓
Bihar	✓	✓	✓	–	✓	✓
Chhattisgarh	✓	✓	–	✓	✓	✓
Delhi	✓	✓	✓	✓	–	✓
Goa	✓	✓	✓	–	–	✓
Gujarat	✓	✓	✓	–	–	✓
Haryana	✓	✓	✓	–	″	✓
Himachal Pradesh	✓	✓	✓	–	–	✓
Jharkhand	✓	✓	–	–	–	✓
Karnataka	✓	✓	✓	✓	✓	✓
Kerala	✓	✓	–	–	–	
Madhya Pradesh	✓	✓	✓	✓	✓	✓
Maharashtra	✓	✓	✓	✓	–	✓
Manipur	✓	✓	✓	–	–	✓
Meghalaya	–	–	–	–	–	–
Mizoram	–	–	–	–	–	–
Nagaland	–	–	–	–	–	–
Orissa	✓	✓	✓	–	✓	✓
Punjab	✓	✓	✓	–	–	✓

Rajasthan	✓	✓	✓	–	✓	✓
Sikkim	✓	✓	✓	–	–	✓
Tamil Nadu	✓	✓	✓	✓	✓	✓
Tripura	✓	✓	✓	–	–	✓
Uttaranchal	✓	✓	✓	–	–	✓
Uttar Pradesh	✓	✓	✓	–	DPC/MPC	✓
West Bengal	✓	✓	✓	✓		✓

Source: India Infrastructure Report, 2006

self government as provider of services to the community and as instrument of democratic self government. Urban local bodies (ULBs) are mandated to be formed as democratic institutions based on the principle of self government and should represent people's expectations. Due to massive urban growth during the last decade, quality of urban life has deteriorated creating an urgent need for effective and efficient urban local bodies that can deliver services and improve living conditions of urban dwellers. The urban local governments offer enhanced opportunity for people's participation, bottom up planning, and effective implementation by enhancing coordination and responsiveness to users. The 74th Constitutional Amendment Act seeks to introduce fundamental changes in urban local bodies. Its salient features are:

(1) introduction of the 12th Schedule which lists the functions of urban local bodies, covering planning, regulation and developmental aspects;

(2) establishment of District and Metropolitan Planning Committees responsible for the preparation of development plans at district and metropolitan levels;

(3) establishment of ward committees in areas having a population of over 300,000;

(4) specification by law of the powers and responsibilities to be entrusted to municipalities and ward committees;

(5) holding of periodical and timely elections, if municipality is dissolved for any reason it should be reconstituted within 6 months;

(6) Specifying by law the sources of municipal finance and their periodic review by a statutorily constituted SFC and by making it obligatory on the part of the Central Finance Commission to recommend measures needed to augment state resources to assist the municipal governments;

(7) restrictions on the power of state governments to do away with democratically elected municipal governments;

(8) Reservation of one third seats for women and weaker sections (SC/ST/OBC's as proportion of reservations) in municipal bodies.

The mandates of various local government institutions as prescribed by the Constitutional Amendment Act 1992 are as follows:

(1) State Election Commissioner to superintend, direct and control the preparation of electoral rolls and conduct all elections to the rural and urban local bodies (Article 2430);

(2) Municipalities to function as institutions of self government, prepare plans for economic development and social justice, perform functions and implement schemes as may be entrusted to them by the state government including those related to the Twelfth Schedule [Article 243 (W) (a)];

(3) Ward Committees and Special Committees to take municipal government physically closer to the people and carry out the responsibilities conferred upon them including those in relation to the Twelfth Schedule [243 (w) (b)];

(4) State Finance Commission to review the financial position of the rural and urban local bodies, and make recommendations regarding the principles of devolution of resources from the state to the local bodies and the measures needed to improve their finances and functioning [Article 243(1)];

(5) District Planning Committee to consolidate the plans prepared by the Panchayats and the municipalities in the district and to prepare a draft development plan for the district as a whole [Article 243 D(1)];

(6) Metropolitan Planning Committee to prepare draft development plan for the Metropolitan area as a whole [Article 2432E(1)].

STRUCTURE AND COMPOSITION OF MUNICIPALITIES

The 74th Constitution Amendment Act, 1992 envisages the following types of municipalities:

Municipal Corporation

The Act made a provision for the constitution of Municipal Corporation in the metropolitan cities which have population of one million and above. The Governor generally takes the following points into the account while notifying municipal corporation: (i) the population of the area; (ii) the density of population; (iii) the percentage of employment in non-agricultural activities; (iv) the economic importance of the area: (v) such other factors as the Governor may deem fit.

Table 3

Population Criteria for Formation of Urban Local Bodies across States

State Corporation	*Municipal Council*	*Municipal Panchayat*	*Nagar*
Andhra Pradesh	4 lakh and above	40,000 and above	25000 to 40,000
Gujarat	Size of municipality is depend on the elected councillors	Size of municipality is depend on the elected counillors	5000 and above
Haryana	5 lakh and above	50,000 to 5 lakhs	50,000 to 5 lakhs
Karnataka	Not less than 3 lakhs	20,000 to 3 lakhs	10,000 to 20,000
Kerala	Not specified	Not specified	Not specified
Madhya Pradesh	Not specified	Not specified	Not specified
Punjab	More than 3 lakh	15000 to 3 lakhs	5000 to 15000
Tamil Nadu	As defined in clause (2) of Article 243Q	As defined in clause (2) of Article 243Q	Not less than 5000
Uttar Pradesh	5 lakh and above	1 lakh to 5 lakhs	30,000 to 1 lakh
West Bengal	Not specified	Not less than 20,000	State Government will classify on population

Source: Nagarpalika Network (2002)

Population criteria for formation of urban local bodies across the states are shown in Table 3. There is no uniform criteria of population for formation of the local bodies across the states. Generally the municipal corporation is formed in larger cities having population above 3 lakhs. Similarly Municipal Corporation is formed in the small and medium size cities having the population size in between 40,000 to 3 lakhs. The Nagar Panchayats is formed in the transitory cities having population of less than 40,000.

Table 4
Elections held in Post Decentralization Period in Different States

State	*Number of Elections held since 1994*	*Municipal Corporations*	*Municipal Councils*	*Nagar Panchayats*
Andhra Pradesh	2	1995, 2000-02	1995, 2000-02	1995, 2000
Gujarat	2	1994-95, 2000	1994-95, 1999, 2000-02	1994, 2000
Haryana	2	1994, 2000	1994, 2000	1994, 2000
Karnataka	2	1996, 2001	1996, 2001	1994, 2000
Kerala	2	1995, 2000	1995, 2000	1995,2000
Madhya Pradesh	2	1994, 1999	1994, 1999	1994,1999
Maharastra	2	1997-98, 2002	1997-98, 2002	1997-98, 2002
Punjab	2	1998,2002	1998	1998
Rajasthan	2	1994-95, 1999	1994-95, 1999	1994-95, 1999
Tamil Nadu	2	1996, 2001	1996, 2001	1996, 2001
Uttar Pradesh	3	1995, 2001, 2006	1995, 2001, 2006	1995, 2001,2006
West Bengal	2	1993-94, 1999-2000	1993-94, 1999-2000	1993-94, 1999-2000
Bihar	2	2002, 2007	2002, 2007	2002, 2007

Source: NIUA, 2004.

The criteria for formation of Municipal Corporation across major states is shown in Chart 2. Population, its density, percentage of population engaged in non-agricultural activities, revenue generation and economic importance are some of the important criteria for formation of Municipal Corporations in Andhra Pradesh, Karnataka and Gujarat while other states have provision of population criteria only. The population of a corporation ranges in between 3 lakh and 5 lakh. Karnataka has made provision for formation of corporation in a city which has not less than 3 lakh population and 50 per cent of it is engaged in non-farm activities, however density of population should not be less than 3000 persons per sq. km. Andhra Pradesh has the provision for formation of corporation in a city which has population of 4 lakh and above with population density of 10,000 persons, however 85

Chart 2
Criteria for Formation of Municipal Corporation across Major States

State	*Population*	*Density (Persons per sq. km.)*	*Percentage of Population engaged in non-agricultural activities*	*Likely Revenue generated per annum (Rs.)*	*Economic Importance*	*Other Criteria*
Andhra Pradesh	4 lakh and above	10,000 and above	Not less than 85%	4 crores and above	Potential for growth of industries commerce, higher education and adequate infrastructure	The number of peripheral villages in the proposed larger urban area.
Gujarat	Size of the municipality is dependent on the elected councilors	400 persons per sq. km.	75%	Not specified	Not specified	Not specified
Haryana	5 lakh and above	Not specified	Not specified	Not specified	Not specified	Not specified
Karnataka	Not less than 3 lakh	Not less than 3000	Not less than 50%	6 crores or Rs. 200/- per capita per annum which ever is higher		
Kerala	Not specified	Not specified	Not specified	Not specified	Not specified	Not specified
Madhya Pradesh	Not specified	Not specified	Not specified	Not specified	Not specified	Not specified
Maharashtra	Not less than 3 lakh	Not specified	Not specified	Not specified	Not specified	Not specified
Punjab	More than 3 lakh	Not specified	Not specified	More than 2 crores	Not specified	Not specified

Source: NIUA, 2004

per cent population should be engaged in non-agricultural activities.

Mode of elections of Mayors/Chairpersons and their term across major states is shown in Table 5. Except in the state of Uttar Pradesh, Tamil Nadu, Madhya Pradesh, Maharashtra and Andhra Pradesh the Mayor/Chiarpersons are indirectly elected. In the States of Gujarat, Haryana, Karnataka and Maharashtra the term of Mayors/Chairpersons is ranging in between one year and 2 and half years.

Table 5
Mode of Election of Mayors/ Chairpersons and their term across Major States

State	*Election*	*Term*
Andhra Pradesh	Direct	5 years
Gujarat half years	Indirect	Two and
Haryana	Indirect	One year
Karnataka	Indirect	One year
Kerala	Indirect	Five years
Madhya Pradesh	Director	Five yars
Maharashtra	Direct for Municipal Councils and Nagar Panchayats and Indirect for Municipal Corporations	Two and half years
Punjab	Indirect	Five years
Rajasthan	Indirect	Five Years
Tamil Nadu	Direct	Five Years
Uttar Pradesh	Direct	Five years
West Bengal	Indirect	Five years

Source: Nagarpalika Network (2002).

Municipal Council

A smaller urban area is notified by the Governor taking into account the above factors as municipal council. The criterion for formation of Municipal Council across major states is shown in Chart 3. In most of the states population ranges in between 15000 to 5 lakh. Andhra Pradesh, Gujarat, Karnataka and West Bengal have provision of population density while only Andhra Pradesh, and Karnataka have made criteria of revenue generation.

Chart 3
Criteria for Formation of Municipal Council across Major States

State	*Population*	*Density (Persons per sq. km.)*	*Percentage of population engaged in non-agricultural activities*	*Likely revenue generated per annum (Rs.)*	*Economic Importance*	*Other Criteria*
Andhra Pradesh	40,000 and above	1,000 and above	60% and above	60 lakh and above	Availability of market facilities and potential for industrial development	Local area acquiring urban characteristics
Gujarat	Size of the municipality is dependent on the elected councilors	400 persons per sq. km.	75%	Not specified	Not specified	Not specified
Haryana	50,0000 to 5 lakh	Not specified	Not specified	Not specified	Not specified	Not specified
Karnataka	20,000 to 3 lakh	1,500 and above	Not less than	9 lakhs and 50%	above or Rs.45 per capita	Not specified
Kerala	Not specified	Not specified	Not specified	Not specified	Not specified	Not specified
Madhya Pradesh	Not specified	Not specified	Not specified	Not specified	Not specified	Not specified
Maharashtra	25,000 and above	Not specified	Not less than 75%	Not specified	Not specified	Not specified
Punjab	15,000 to 3 lakh	Not specified	Not specified	Not specified	Not specified	Not specified
Rajasthan	1 lakh to 5 lakh	Not specified	Not specified	Not specified	Not specified	Not specified
Tamil Nadu	As defined in Clause (2) of Article 243Q	Not specified	Not specified	Not specified	Not specified	Not specified
Uttar Pradesh	1 lakh to 5 lakh	Not specified	Not specified	Not specified	Not specified	Not specified
West Bengal	Not less than 20,000	Not less than 750 persons	50% and above	Not specified	Not specified	Not specified

Source: NIUA, 2004

Nagar Panchayats

Transitional area is to be known as the Nagar Panchayat. This has also been left to the Governor's notification taking into account the same considerations as in case of larger area in transition from a rural to urban. Criteria for formation of Nagar Panchayats across the major states is shown in Chart 4. Population, population density, percentage of population engaged in non farm activities and economic importance are important criterion for its formation. The population of Nagar Panchayat varies from state to state. It ranges in between 5000 to 5 lakh. Andhra Pradesh, Gujarat, Karnataka and Maharashtra have made provision for formation of Nagar Panchayat in a city or town if 50 to 75 per cent population is engaged in non-agricultural activities.

The urban local bodies shall have three types of members elected, nominated and ex-officio. Every urban local body shall have a chairperson, but the manner of his/her selection has been left to be decided by the state legislature. As regards the composition or membership of municipalities, Act provides that every municipality shall have two categories of councilors, viz. directly elected councillors and nominated councillors. The number of elected councillors varies according to size of the population of the territorial area of the Municipal Corporation or Municipal Council concerned. In case of nominated councillors, the state law has to specify the conditions and procedure for their nomination. Variations are found in the amended legislation of various states in fixing the minimum number of elected councilors in a municipality or a corporation. Maharashtra's amended municipal laws provide that the minimum number of elected councillors in a Municipal Corporation should be 65. This number, however, is to increase progressively to 221, commensurate with the progressively larger population of the city. Similarly, the minimum number of elected councillors in a Municipal Council is 7 and maximum is 65. The range of minimum and maximum number of elected councillors in a municipality is 10-25 in Andhra Pradesh, 10-37 in Bihar, 21-51 in Gujarat, 7-19 in Himachal Pradesh, 11-35

Chart 4
Criteria for Formation of Nagar Panchayat across Major States

State	*Population*	*Density (Persons per sq. km.)*	*Percentage of population engaged in non-agricultural activities*	*Likely revenue generated per annum (Rs.)*	*Economic Importance*	*Other Criteria*
Andhra Pradesh	25,000 to 40,000	1,000 and above	50% and above	40 lakh and above	Availability of market facilities and potential for industrial development	Local area acquiring urban characteristics
Gujarat	5000 and above	400 persons per sq. km.	75%	Not specified	Not specified	Not specified
Haryana	50,000 to 5 lakh	Not specified	Not specified	Not specified	Not specified	Not specified
Karnataka	10,000 to 20,000	Not less than 400 per sq. km.	Not less than 50%	Not specified	Not specified	All Taluka HQs irrespective of population
Kerala	Not specified	Not specified	Not specified	Not specified	Not specified	Not specified
Madhya Pradesh	Not specified	Not specified	Not specified	Not specified	Not specified	Not specified
Maharashtra	10,000 to 35,000	Not specified	Not less than 50%	Not specified	Not specified	Such area is not more than 16 kms away from the territorial limits of MC
Punjab	5000 to 15,000	Not specified	Not specified	Not specified	Not specified	Not specified
Rajasthan	Less than 1 lakh	Not specified	Not specified	Not specified	Not specified	Not specified
Tamil Nadu	Not less than 5,000	Not specified	Not specified	Not specified	Not specified	Not specified
Uttar Pradesh	30,000 to 1 lakh	Not specified	Not specified	Not specified	Not specified	Not specified
West Bengal	State Govt. will classify on population	Not specified	Not specified	Not specified	Not specified	Not specified

Source: NIUA, 2004

in Karnataka, 15-40 in Madhya Pradesh, 11-40 in Orissa and 25-55 in Uttar Pradesh. In case of nominated and co-opted members, many state Municipal Laws have made provisions with regard to their number and categories. According to Article 243 RC2 special knowledge or experience in municipal administration is a precondition for their nomination. Besides a member of the state legislative Assembly (MLA), State Legislative Council (MLC) and Parliament (MP) representing a constituency comprising wholly or partly of a municipal corporation/municipality, becomes its members in ex-officio capacity. These members, however, do not have the rights to vote. In order to provide for adequate representation of the Scheduled Castes/Scheduled Tribes and women in the municipal bodies, provisions have been made for reservation of seats for them in all the categories of positions under Article 243T. Most of the states have amended their laws to conform to this provision. Reservation of Other Backward Classes (OBC's) has been made in some states like Andhra Pradesh, Mahrastra, Bihar, and Karnataka, U.P. etc. Interestingly, the amended Municipal Law of Himachal Pradesh does not mention anything about reservation of seats in a municipality in the state. Similarly, no provision has been made in the amended law of Andhra Pradesh and Punjab regarding reservation of seats for Scheduled Castes and Scheduled Tribes. Bihar and Madhya Pradesh have made provision for 50 per cent reserved seats for women, beyond 30 per cent statutory norms in the municipalities. Thus, the political shape and scape of the municipal bodies in India is likely to change. The election of Mayors and Chairpersons varies from state to state. Andhra Pradesh, Uttar Pradesh and Tamil Nadu provide for direct election to these positions. Similarly, their term of office also varies significantly. In Andhra Pradesh it is five years, in Karnataka and Madhya Pradesh, it is two and a half years and in Gujarat it is one year only.

State-wise reservation of seats and the criteria adopted for reservation are shown in Chart 5. In all the states one third seats are reserved for women. However, Bihar and Madhya Pradesh have made provision for 50 per cent reserved seats.

Chart 5
State-wise Reservation of Seats and the Criteria adopted for Reservation

State	Category	Responsibility	Reservation Basis			
			SC	ST	BC	Women
Andhra Pradesh	Councillors	State Government	In proportion to population and allotted by rotation; 1/3rd of seats so reserved is for women belonging to SC ST and allotted by rotation		1/3rd of the seats and allotted by rotation; 1/3rd of seats so reserved is for women belonging to BC allotted by rotation	1/3rd of the total number of seats including the reserved ones
Gujarat	Councillors	State Election Commission	In proportion to population and allotted by rotation; 1/3rd of seats so reserved is for women belonging to SC/ST and allotted by rotation.		1/10th of the seats and allotted by rotation; 1/3rd of seats so reserved is for womenbelonging to BCs, allotted by rotation.	1/3rd of the total number of seats including the reserved ones.
	Mayors/ Chairpersons	State Election Commissioner				
Haryana	Councillors	State Government	In proportion to population and allotted to such wards having maximum population of persons belonging to SC; 1/3rd of seats so reserved is for women belonging to SC and allotted by rotation and by lots.	–	2 seats in Municipal Corporation and Municipal Council and 1 seat in Municipal Committee and allotted in territorial constituencies having maximum population of persons belonging to BCs.	1/3rd of the total number of seats including the reserved ones and allotted by rotation and by lots
	Mayors/ Chairpersons	State Government	Reserved for SC by rotation and by lots in			

			the manner prescribed	–	–	Reserved for women by rotation and by lots in the manner prescribed.
Karnataka	Councillors	State Government	In proportion to population and allotted by rotation		1/3rd of total number of seats and allotted by rotation.	
	Mayors/ Chairpersons		State Government		In proportion to population	
Kerala	Councillors	State Election Commissioner	In proportion to population and allotted by rotation 1/3rd of seats so reserved is for women belonging to SC/St and allotted by rotation.	–		1/3rd of the total number of seats including the reserved ones and allotted by rotation.
	Mayors/ Chairpersons	State Election Commissioner	In proportion to population: 1/3rd of the seats reserved for SC/St women			
Madhya Pradesh	Councillors	State Government	In proportion to Population; 1/3d of seats reserved for SC/St women		25% of the total number of wards reserved for other BCs in such municipalities where 50% or less seats are reserved for SC/St, allotted by rotation;1/3rd of the seats reserved for other BCs women.	1/3rd of the total number of seats including the reserved ones for women, allotted by rotation.
	Mayors / Chairperson	State Government	In proportion to Population; 1/3d of seats reserved for SC/ST women		1/4th of the States	1/rd of the seats

Maharashtra	Councillors	State Election Commissioner	In proportion to population and allotted by rotation; 1/3rd of the seats reserved for SC/ST women, allotted by rotation; where only one seat is reserved for SC/ST and where only two seats are reserved for SC/ST, one of the two seats shall be reserved		27% of the total seats and allotted by rotation; 1/3rd of the seats reserved for women belonging to BC and allotted by rotation	1/3rd of the total number of seats including the reserved ones for women and allotted by rotation
	Mayors / Chairperson	State Election Commissioner				
Punjab	Councillors	State Government	In proportion to population and allotted by rotation 1/3rd of seats so reserved is for women belonging to SC	–	2 seats for in Municipal Corporations and 1 seat in Municipalities allotted by rotation.	1/3rd of the total number of seats including the reserved ones for women and
Mayors /	State Chairperson	Government	5% of seats	–	2% of seats	5% of seats including SC women
Rajasthan	Councillors	State Government	In proportion to population and allotted by rotation 1/3rd of the reserved seats for SC women allotted by rotation	In proportion to population and allotted by rotation; 1/3rd of so reserved seats for ST women, allotted by rotation	In proportion to population and allotted by rotation; 1/3rd of so reserved seats for BCs women, allotted by rotation	1/3rd of the total number of seats including the reserved ones for women allotted by rotation
	Mayors / Chairpersons	State Government				
Tamil Nadu	Councillors	State Government	In proportion to population; 1/3rd of so reserved seats for SC and ST women		–	1/3rd of the total number of seats including the reserved ones.
	Mayors /	State	In proportion to population		–	1/rd of the total

	Chairpersons	Government	and allotted by rotation; 1/3rd of so reserved seats for SC women allotted by rotation			number of seats including the reserved ones allotted by rotation
Uttar Pradesh	Councillors	State Government	In proportion to population; 1/3rd of the reserved seats for Sc and ST women	In proportion to population; 1/3rd of the reserved seats for ST women	27% of seats; 1/3rd of the reserved seats for BC women	1/3rd of the total number of seats including the reserved ones allotted by rotation
West Bengal	Councillors	State Government	In proportion to population and allotted by rotation; 1/3rd of the reserved seats for SC and ST women, allotted by rotation		–	1/3rd of the total number of seats including the reserved ones allotted by rotation
	Mayors / Chairpersons	State Government	The office of the Chairperson of municipality shall be reserved for a women for the 1st term if at least 50% of the total number of elected members are women; shall be reserved for a SC for the next term if at least 50% of the elected members belong to SC and ST; shall be reserved for a ST for the next term where at least 50% of the elected members belong to the SC and ST.			

Source: NIUA, 2004

Chart 6

Procedures for Removal of Mayors/ Chairpersons of Municipal Corporation across Major States

State	*Name of the Act*	*Procedure for removal of the Mayor/ Chairperson*
Andhra Pradesh	The Hyderabad Municipal Corporation Act, 1955	The State Government may, by notification remove the Mayor or the Deputy Mayor who in their opinion willfully omits or refuses to carry out or disobeys any provisions of the act, or any rule, by-laws, regulation, or regulations or lawful order made issued under the Act or abuses his position of power vested in him
Gujarat	Gujarat Municipalities Act, 1963	Motion of No-Confidence: written notice of the intention signed by not less than 1/3rd of the total number of Councillors to the municipality as prescribed by the State Government. It will be carried by majority of not less than 2/3rd of the total number of Councillors.The State Government may remove the President who has been guilty of misconduct in the discharge of his duties or of any disgraceful conduct or has become incapable of performing his duties under the Act.
Haryana	The Haryana Municipal Corporation Act, 1994	Motion of No-Confidence: Mayor or Senior Deputy Mayor or Deputy Mayor may be removed by a resolution of the Corporation passed by a majority of not less than 2/3rd of the total members of the Corporation.
Karnataka	The Karnataka Municipalities Act 1964	No such provision in the Karnataka Municipal Corporation Act, 1976. Motion of No-Confidence: notice of resolution is signed by not less than 1/3rd of the total number of Councillors and at least 10 days notice has been given of the intention to move the resolution. A similar resolution in respect of same President or Vice-President or Vice President shall not be removed from the office by the Government for misconduct in the discharge of his duties or for neglect of or incapacity to perform his duties or if he is unable to pay dues he owes to the municipal council or has suffered an order for commitment to civil prison for non payment of any decretal debt and shall not be eligible for re-election during the remainder of his term of office.

Kerala	The Kerala Municipality Act, 1994	Motion of No-Confidence: Written notice of the intention signed by not less than 1/3rd of the sanctioned strength of the Council submitted to the officer authorized by the Government. The officer convenes a meeting of the elected Councillors notice of not less than 10 days of such meeting. If the motion is carried with the support of more than one half of the strength of the Councillors, the Chairperson or the Deputy Chairperson or the Chairman of the Standing Committee as case may be shall cease to function and the Government shall notify his removal from the office. If the notion is not carried by majority or if the meeting could not be held for want of quorum, no motion of any subsequent motion shall be entertained until after expiry of 6 months from the date of meeting. No motion shall be entertained within 6 months of the assumption of the office.
Madhya Pradesh	The Madhya Pradesh Municipalities Act 1961	The State Government may remove President or Vice-President if his continuance as such is not in the opinion of the State Government desirable in public interest or in the interest of the Council or if it is found that he is incapable of performing his duties or is working against the provisions of the Act or any rules made there under.Motion of No-Confidence: A motion of no-confidence may be moved at a meeting by a majority of more than 3/4th of the elected Councillors present and voting by more than 2/3rd of the total number of Councillors. No such motion shall lie within a period of 2 years from the President enters the office within a period of 1 year on which previous motion was rejected or if the remaining period of the council is less than 6 months and shall be signed by not less than one half of the total number of Councillors.
Maharashtra	The Maharashtra Municipal Councils, Nagar Panchayats and Industrial Township Act, 1965	Motion of No-Confidence: A President shall ceased if the Council by resolution passed by a majority of not less than 2/3rd of the total number of Councillors and shall be signed by not less than one half of the total number of Councillors.The State Government may remove the President who has been guilty of misconduct in the discharge of his duties or of neglect of or incapacity to perform his duties or for being guilty of any disgraceful conduct and shall not be eligible for re-election for re-election or re-appointment during the number of the term.

Punjab	Punjab Municipal Corporation Act, 1976	Motion of No-Confidence: A Councillor holding the office as a Mayor or Senior Deputy Mayor or Deputy Mayor may be removed from his office by a resolution of the Corporation passed by a majority of the total membership of the Corporation and by majority of not less than 2/3rd of the members of the Corporation present and voting in a meeting of the Corporation in a prescribing manner.
Rajasthan	The Rajasthan Municipalities Act, 1959	State Government may remove the Chairperson or Vice-Chairman from the office if he has been guilty of misconduct in the discharge of his duties or any disgraceful conduct or become incapable of performing his duties, otherwise flagrantly abused in any manner his position.
Tamil Nadu	Tamil Nadu District Municipalities Act, 1920	No such provision in the Madras City Municipal Corporation Act Motion of No-confidence. The Councillors constitute 1/3rd of the sanctioned strength, by a written notice, to the Regional Inspector, express their intention to make a motion against the chairman that the chairman willfully omits or refuse to carry out or disobeys any provision of the Act, or any rule, by law, regulation, or lawful order made issued under the Act or abuses any power vested in him not before six months of assumption of office. The Regional Inspector convene a special meeting for the consideration of the motion. The motion shall be deemed to have passed by the council if 2/3rd of sanctioned strength present and voting by 2/3rd of the strength present.
Uttar Pradesh	Uttar Pradesh Municipal Corporation Act, 1959	Motion of No-Confidence: Notice written by not less than one-half of the total number of Councillors and passed by more than one-half of elected Councillors.
West Bengal	The Calcutta Municipal Corporation Act, 1980	Motion of No-Confidence: The Mayor may be removed by resolution carried by a majority of the total number of elected members of the Corporation at a special meeting of the Corporation called for this purpose upon a requisition made in writing by not less than 1/3rd of the elected member of a period of 6 months from the date of assumption. No further resolution shall be moved before the expiry of a period of 6 months from the date on which the former resolution was moved.

Source: Nagarpalika Network (2002) and SFC Reports

The seats are being reserved on the basis of rotation in most of the states.

The procedures for removal of Mayors/Chairpersons of Municipal Corporations across major states are shown in Chart 6. The state Acts have made provision for removal of Mayors/Chairpersons. In most of the states, there is provision of motion of non-confidence; however, it is not mentioned in the state Acts of Andhra Pradesh, Karnataka, Madhya Pradesh, Rajasthan and Tamil Nadu.

DISTRICT/ METROPOLITAN PLANNING COMMITTEE

Considering the importance of integrated area planning at the district and metropolitan level, the 74th Amendment Act has provided for the obligatory constitution of District Planning Committees (DPC's) and Metropolitan Planning Committees (MPC's). However, only a few states have set up, these authorities in pursuance of the Constitutional provision.

The 74th Amendment Act, has provided that there shall be constituted in every state at the district level a District Planning Committee to consolidate the plans prepared by the Panchayats and the Municipalities in the district and to prepare a draft development plan for the district as a whole. The legislature of a state may by law, make provision with respect to (a) the composition of the District Planning Committees; (b) the manner in which the seats in such committees shall be filled. The Act further made provision that not less than four fifth of the total number of members of such committee shall be elected by and from amongst the elected members of the Panchayat at the district level and of the Municipalities in the district in proportion to the ratio between the population of the rural areas and urban areas. The functions assigned to such committees are as follows: Every D.P.C. shall, in preparing the draft development Plan have regard to (i) matters of common interest between Panchayat and the Municipalities including spatial planning, sharing of water and other physical and natural resources, the integrated development of infrastructure and environmental conservation; (ii) the extent and type of available resources whether financial or otherwise; (b) consult such institutions and organizations as the Governor may by order, specify. There is no provision of DPC in the state Acts of Andhra Pradesh, Gujarat while in Haryana, Tamil Nadu and Uttar Pradesh the provisions exist. (Chart 7).

The 74th Amendment Act directs the constitution of a Metropolitan Planning Committee in every metropolitan area. While its composition and the manner of filling seats has been left to be finalized by the state legislature, the Amendment Act specifically lays down that not less than two thirds of the members of the Metropolitan Planning Committee shall be elected by and from amongst, the elected members of urban local bodies and chairpersons of the rural local bodies in the metropolitan area in proportion to the ratio between the population of the urban and rural local bodies in that metropolitan area. Moreover, the state legislature may also provide for the representation in the Metropolitan Planning Committee of the officials of the central and state governments as also of such organizations and institutions as it may deem necessary. The Metropolitan Planning Committee has been given the task to prepare a draft development plan for the metropolitan area as a whole. The functions relating to planning and coordination for the metropolitan area shall be worked out by the state legislature. While preparing the draft development plan the Metropolitan Planning Committee must have regard to (a) plans prepared by the urban and the rural local bodies in the metropolitan area; (b) matters of common interest between the urban and the rural local bodies, including coordinated spatial planning of the area, sharing of water and other physical and natural resources, the integrated development of infrastructure and environmental conservation; (c) the overall objectives and priorities set up by the central and state governments; (d) the extent and nature of investments likely to be made in the metropolitan area by agencies of the central and state government and other available resources whether financial or otherwise. The Metropolitan Planning Committee is also expected to consult such institutions and organizations as the state Governor may by order specify.

Chart 7
District Planning Committee (DPC)

State	*Whether the provision of the committee (in the Act) is made or not*	*Composition**	*Secretary Chairperson*	*Remarks*	*If any*
Andhra Pradesh	No mention in the Act				
Assam	Provided	MPs, MLAs, President of Zila Parishad, Mayor or Chairperson of Municipal Corporation / Municipal Board / Town Committee having jurisdiction over Head Quarters of the District. Elected members as prescribed under the Amendment	CEO of the Zila Parishad	President of the Zila Parishad	Deputy Commissioner is permanent invitee of the committee at an ex-officio member
Bihar	Provided	MPs, MLAs, MLCs, Adhyaksha Zila Parishad, Mayor/President of Municipal Corporation/ Municipal Council having jurisdiction over Head quarter of the Distt. Elected members as prescribed under the Amendment.	CEO	Adhyaksha of Zila Parishad	D.M., Chairman of the District Corporative Bank and Chairman of Bhumi Vikas Bank as permanent invitee
Gujarat		Not mentioned in the Act Constituted			
Haryana		Shall be constituted as per the provisions of Article 243 Z.D (details not given)			
Himachal Pradesh	Provided	MP, Chairman of Zila Parishad, President of the Municipality having jurisdiction over the H.Q. of the district, Elected members as prescribed under the Amendment	The Secretary of Z.P.	To be chosen as prescribed	MLAs, DC/DM, representatives of cooperative bank and LDB are permanent invitee.

Karnataka	Provided	MPs, MLAs, MLCs, Adhyaksha, Zila Parishad, Mayor/ President of the Municipal Corporation/ Municipal Council having jurisdiction over the H.Qs. of the district.	CEO	To be chosen as prescribed
Kerala	Not mentioned in the Act			
Madhya Pradesh	Not mentioned in the Act			
Mahara-shtra	Not mentioned in the Act			
Orissa	Not mentioned in the Act			
Punjab	Provided	Details not provided in the Act		
Rajasthan	Provided	Persons representing the State Government, MPs, MLAs, Members representing such organizations and institutions as may be deemed necessary by the Government, elected members as prescribed under the Amendment	Appointed by the Government	As may be prescribed
Tamil Nadu	Provided	MPs, MLAs, Chairman, District Panchayat, Mayor/Chairman of the Municipal Corporation / Municipal Council having jurisdiction over the H.Qs. of the district, elected members as prescribed under the Amendment		
Uttar Pradesh	Provided	Separate Act		
West Bengal	Provided	Separate Act		

FUNCTIONS AND FINANCES

The Constitutional Amendment Act, 1992 assigned a critical role in urban development and governance. The Act inserted the Twelfth Schedule (Article 243 W) to the Constitution of India providing for an illustrative list of legitimate municipal functions (Chart 8).

Chart 8
Twelfth Schedule of the Constitution

Functions

- Urban Planning, including town planning
- Regulation of land use and constitution of buildings
- Planning for economic and social development Roads and bridges
- Water supply for domestic, industrial and commercial purposes
- Public health, sanitation conservancy and solid waste management
- Fire services
- Urban forestry, protection of environment and promotion of ecological aspects
- Safeguarding the interests of wealth sections of society, including the disabled and mentally retarded
- Slum improvement and upgrading
- Urban poverty alleviation
- Provision of urban amenities and facilities such as parks, gardens, play grounds
- Promotion of cultural, educational and aesthetic aspects
- Burials and burial grounds, cremation, cremation grounds and electric cremations
- Cattle pounds, prevention of cruelty to animals
- Vital statistics including registration of births and deaths
- Public amenities including street lighting, parking lots, bus stops and public conveniences
- Regulation of slaughter houses and tanneries.

The state list in the Constitution empowers the state governments to lay down the functions, powers and responsibilities of municipal governments. Accordingly out of powers and responsibilities enumerated in the state list, the state governments have assigned certain functions and duties to municipalities. Typically, these have consisted of public health and sanitation, burials and cremations and cremation grounds, libraries, museums and other similar institutions controlled and funded by the state; communications, i.e. roads and bridges, water supplies, drainage, and embankments subject to the provision of list, and markets and fairs. The main functions which the municipalities are associated and which are generally, though not uniformly, performed by them include services that have the characteristics of private goods, for example, water supply, sewerage and drainage, and conservancy and sanitation and others that are in the nature of public goods, for example, street lighting and municipal roads. In addition, the municipalities are vested with a number of regulatory duties such as development of markets, commercial complexes, and the like. Several municipal corporations have a larger functional domain, which consists of running hospitals and dispensaries, electricity generation, and distribution and bus transport services. The functional domain of municipalities has witnessed periodic shifts and changes, on account of the withdrawal of certain functions and creation of development authorities such as PHE, Land Development Authorities, State Road Transport Corporation, etc. There is mismatch between the functions and finances.

The incorporation of schedule 12 into the Constitution has been understood that the municipal functional domain has acquired some sort of a discrete character, apart from an expansion of its portfolio. However, the functions and duties enumerated in schedule 12 are not in addition to what the municipalities were responsible for in the pre-1992 period. There is substantial overlap between the functions of municipalities in pre-1992 period and those that are listed in Schedule 12. Of the 18 functions enumerated in Schedule 12, 11 formed part of the municipal domain even in pre-1992 period. These are regulation of land use and construction of buildings, roads and bridges; water supply for domestic, industrial and commercial purposes; public health, sanitation, conservancy, and solid waste management; fire services; provision of urban amenities and facilities such as parks, gardens and play grounds; burials and burial grounds; and cremation grounds and electric cremations; cattle ponds, prevention of cruelty to animals; vital statistics including registration of births and deaths; public amenities including street lighting, bus stop and public conveniences, and regulation of slaughter houses and tanneries. The remaining functions incorporated in the Schedule 12 are part of the state list and concurrent list.

In order to strengthen the fiscal base of the urban local bodies, the 74th Amendment empowers the state legislature to enact law in order to:

(1) authorize an urban local body to levy, collect and appropriate taxes, duties, tolls, and fees;

(2) assign to an urban local body taxes, duties, tolls and fees levied and collected by the state government; and

(3) Provide for making grant in aid to the urban local bodies from the Consolidated Fund of the state.

The principles which shall govern the above fiscal resources have been left to be recommended by the State Finance Commission. The commission shall lay down principles which should govern:

(1) the distribution between the state and the urban local bodies of the net proceeds of the taxes, duties and fees leviable by the state, which may be divided between them and the allocation between the urban local bodies at all levels of their respective shares of such proceeds;

(2) the determination of the taxes, duties, tolls and fees which may be assigned to or appropriated by the urban local bodies; and

(3) the grants in aid to the urban local bodies from the Consolidated Fund of the state.

Urban local bodies derive finances from tax and non tax sources. They also receive funds from the state governments in the form of grants in aid as also a share in taxes collected by the state government. There is some variation among the states in the matter of taxation powers entrusted to the ULB's. However, significant variations exist across states in the application of taxation powers and the rate structure of taxes. Octroi is levied only in a few states while professions tax is limited to few others.

The Constitution of India does not lay down the revenue base for municipalities. The powers to determine their revenue base be it tax authority, tax base, tax rate setting, local tax autonomy, or even the grants in aid and other forms of transfers rests with the state governments. Within this framework, the state governments have specified the taxes that the municipalities can levy and collect, which historically have comprised of taxes on land and buildings; taxes on entry of goods into a local area for consumption, use or sale therein; taxes on advertisements other than advertisements published in newspapers; taxes on professions, trades, callings and employment, and taxes on entertainment. In addition, there are charges, fees and fines forming the non-tax base of municipalities. Taxes on property and taxes on the entry of goods into a local area for consumption, use or sale therein (octroi) firm the backbone of municipal tax base in India. The revenue base of municipalities in Indian states has shown little change. Octroi, a major source of revenue for municipalities has been abolished without being substituted by any other local source and has substantially shrunk the revenue base of municipalities in such states as Haryana, Orissa, and Rajasthan. In 2001-02, the size of the municipal revenues was estimated at Rs. 12748 crores. The revenues formed 3.07 per cent of publicly raised resources, the share of central government and all state governments combined being 57.5 per cent and 39.5 per cent, respectively. Over the period of 1997-8 to 2001-02, the size of the municipal sector has registered a marginal expansion. However, many states have changed the system of property taxation and are in process of shifting from a single entry, cash based system to an accrual based accounting system. Some corporations have raised funds in the capital markets for financing city based infrastructure activities by using credit enhancement instruments.

REVENUE ASSIGNMENT

Most common revenue sources available to the municipalities to discharge various local government functions in India can be divided into the following broad categories: (i) Taxes; (ii)

Non-Taxes; (iii) User Charges, fees and sale % hire purchase; (iv) assigned revenues; (v) grants and contribution; (vi) debt and (vii) other revenues (Table 6).

Table 6
Revenue Assignment of Urban Local Bodies

Category	*Particulars*
Taxes	Property Tax, Advertisement Tax, Tax on Animals, Vacant Land Tax, Taxes or Carriages and Carts, Octroi
Non Taxes, User Charges & Fees	Water Charges, Water Supply Donations, Trade Licensing Fee, Building Permit Fees, Development Charges/Betterment Charges, Mutation Fee, Magisterial Fines, Market Fee, Slaughter House Fee, Encroachment Fee, Parking Fee etc.
Sales & Hire Charges	Sale of Rubbish, Certificate Fees, Sale of Forms, Staff Raters Rents, Shop Room Rents
Assigned Revenues	Entertainment Tax, Surcharge on Stamp Duty, Profession Tax, Motor Vehicles Tax, Entry Tax Grants & Contributions
(a) Non Plan Grants	Animal and Vehicle Tax Compensation, Toll Compensation (Octroi Compensation), Property Tax Compensation, Per Capita Grant.
(b) Plan Grants	Road Grants, School Building Grants, Master Plan Grants Integrated Development of Small and Medium Towns (UIDSSMT), SJSRY, NSDP, ILCS, EIVS, UBSP, JNNURM, IHSDP etc.
Debt	Water Supply Schemes, Sewerage Schemes, Roads, ILCs, UIDSSMT, IHSDP, JNNURM, other civic Infrastructure Projects and Capital Works.

Source: P.K. Mohanty, 2005

Table 7
Major Sources of User Charges and Fees of Municipal Corporations in India

State	*Municipal Corporation*	*User Charges and Cess*
Maharastra	Greater Mumbai	Water charges, sewerage charges, Building License Fees
West Bengal	Kolkata	Planning Fees, Car Parking Fees, Mutation Fees
Karnataka	Bangalore	Betterment Charges, Building License Fees, Penalty for late Tax Payment
Orissa	Bhubaneswar	Building License Fees, Market Fees, Water Charges, Building related Fees

Contd...

State	*Municipal Corporation*	*User Charges and Cess*
Gujarat	Surat	Water Charges, Building related Fees, Betterment Charges
Tamil Nadu	Chennai	Building License Fees, Market Fees, Other License Fees, Parking Fees
Andhra Pradesh	Hyderabad	Dangerous and Offensive Trade License Fees, Market Fees, Slaughter House Fees
Uttar Pradesh	Kanpur	Building License Fees, Market Fees

Property tax is the most important source of taxation in majority of the urban local bodies in the country. A few states like Maharastra and Gujarat do still have octroi, considered to be an obnoxious tax and needed to be phased out. The major sources of municipal user charges and fees levied by selected municipal corporations in the country are shown in Table 7.

Table 8 shows the major sources of assigned or shared revenues in selected municipal corporations in the country.

Table 8
Shared Municipal Revenue in India

State	*Municipal Corporation*	*Shared Municipal Taxes*
Maharastra	Greater Mumbai	Non-agricultural Assessment Tax, Entertainment Tax
West Bengal	Kolkata	Motor Vehicles Tax, Entertainment Tax
Karnataka	Bangalore	Entertainment Tax, Surcharge on Stamp Duty
Tamil Nadu	Chennai	Surcharge on Sales Tax, Duty on Transfer of Property, Entertainment Tax
Gujarat	Surat	Transfer of Immovable Property Tax, Professional Tax, Entertainment Tax

The major sources of grants in aid provided to municipalities is octroi compensation, development grants and urban infrastructure projects based grants (Table 9).

Table 9
Major Sources of Grants in Aid to Municipal Corporations in India

State Corporation	*Municipal Corporation*	*Grants in Aid to Municipal*
Maharastra	Greater Mumbai	Primary Education Grant, Secondary Education Grant
West Bengal	Kolkata	Dearness Allowance Grant, Great to Implement Recommendations of Pay Commission, Water Supply, Sewerage and Drainage Grants
Karnataka	Bangalore	Octroi Compensation, Motor Vehicle Tax Compensation, Family Planning Schemes Grants
Orissa	Bhubaneswar	Salary and Dearness Allowance Grants, Road Development Grant, Primary Education Grant, Secondary Education Grant
Gujarat	Surat	Education Grant, Family Planning Grant, Small Savings Grant
Tamil Nadu	Chennai	Revenue Grant, Contributions, Compensation for Toll
Andhra Pradesh	Hyderabad	Dearness Allowance Grant, Property Tax Compensation, Octroi Compensation, Per Capita Grant, Motor Vhicle Tax Compensation, Road Grant, Education Grant (Primary & Secondary)
Uttar Pradesh	Kanpur	Octroi Compensation, Salary Grant, Education Grant (Primary & Secondary), Medical Grant, Road Grant

Internal resource mobilization is principal criterion for measuring the performance of municipalities. Internal resource generation shows 10.5 per cent annual growth during the period of 1997-8 to 2001-02. The highest growth was recorded in the Karnataka followed by Jammu & Kashmir, Tripura, Punjab, Goa, Andhra Pradesh and Himachal Pradesh. During 2001-02 municipal revenue as percentage of GSPP was reported 0.71 per cent at the national average. It was found more pronouncing in Maharastra, Gujarat, Punjab, Tamil Nadu, and Karnataka (Table 10).

Table 10
Internal Resource Generation

State	*Internally Resources Generated (Rs. Lakh 2001-2)*	*Per Capita (Rs. 2001-2)*	*ACGR 1997-98 to 2001-2*	*As Percent GSDP*	
				1997-98	*2001-02*
Andhra Pradesh	71745.7	386.8	14.5	0.42	0.48
Assam	3825.8	153.3	9.10	0.12	0.12
Bihar	3408.4	39.5	-2.7	0.07	0.07
Chhatisgarh	12555.3	321.6	11.3	–	0.41
Goa	1858.7	510.6	15.9	0.20	0.26
Gujarat	144849.2	809.4	5.1	1.30	1.16
Haryana	12106.9	207.8	3.6	0.27	0.20
Himachal Pradesh	1978.9	335.6	14.5	0.13	0.15
Jammu & Kashmir	1199.0	48.2	21.5	0.05	0.05
Jharkhand	1496.2	39.5	10.7	–	0.05
Karnataka	56349.7	322.0	25.7	0.29	0.51
Kerala	22432.8	371.1	11.2	0.29	0.29
Madhya Pradesh	29437.0	188.7	-4.1	0.44	0.36
Maharastra	587058.3	1493.3	11.9	1.88	2.16
Manipur	224.0	41.6	-3.7	0.12	0.06
Orissa	10176.8	194.5	3.8	0.27	0.24
Punjab	75381.2	932.4	20.2	0.69	1.07
Rajasthan	10339.7	80.7	-27.8	0.49	0.12
Tamil Nadu	92013.0	355.5	9.9	0.60	0.62
Tripura	217.7	58.9	19.6	0.03	0.04
Uttaranchal	2320.6	113.7	10.0	–	–
Uttar Pradesh	26551.0	79.5	11.2	0.12	0.14
West Bengal	42201.7	215.8	8.1	0.31	0.27
Total	1209727.8	482.1	10.5	0.65	0.71

Source: O.P. Mathur, 2006.

Municipalities in Bihar having an annual per capita revenue generation of Rs. 39.5 compared with Rs. 1493 generated by municipalities in Maharastra. There are states - Goa, Gujarat, Mahrastra, and Punjab whose per capita own revenue averages are excess to the national average. Many states - Andhra Pradesh, Karnataka, Kerala, Mahrastra, Punjab and Uttar Pradesh witnessed high annual growth in our revenues. The per capita out revenues of municipalities in Bihar, Madhya Pradesh, Manipur, and Rajasthan witnessed a decline due to division of state abolition of octroi etc.

Table 11
Municipal Own Resources

State	*Share in Urban Population (Percent) 2001*	*Share in own Resources (Percent) 2001-2*	*Share in net Addition to own Revenues over 1997-98 to 2001-2*
Andhra Pradesh	7.39	5.93	7.62
Assam	0.99	0.32	0.28
Bihar	3.44	0.28	-0.10
Chhatisgarh	1.56	1.04	3.03
Goa	0.15	0.15	0.21
Gujarat	7.13	11.97	6.40
Haryana	2.32	1.00	0.39
Himachal Pradesh	0.24	0.16	0.21
Jammu & Kashmir	0.99	0.10	0.17
Jharkhand	1.51	0.12	0.36
Karnataka	6.98	4.66	8.64
Kerala	2.41	1.85	1.96
Madhya Pradesh	6.22	2.43	-1.27
Maharastra	15.67	48.53	53.74
Manipur	0.21	0.02	-0.01
Orissa	2.08	0.84	0.34
Punjab	3.22	6.23	10.08
Rajasthan	5.4	0.85	-5.08
Tamil Nadu	10.32	7.61	7.29
Tripura	0.15	0.02	0.03
Uttarakhand	0.81	0.19	2.31
Uttar Pradesh	13.30	2.19	0.56
West Bengal	7.8	3.49	2.83

Source: O.P. Mathur, 2006.

Table 11 shows municipal own revenues. Only in a few states such as Andhra Pradesh, Gujarat, Karnataka, Maharastra, Punjab and Tamil Nadu have the own revenues GSDP ratios in excess of 0.40 Per cent. These ratios have shown a marginal improvement in these states over the 5 years period. Disparities in municipal performance across the states are extraordinary large. Mahrastra, Punjab, Andhra Pradesh, Gujarat, Karnataka and Tamil Nadu account for 93.77 percent in municipal own revenues of the country as against their share of 50.71 per cent in urban population. In 2001-2, the non tax component was 25 per cent of the total own revenues of municipalities. In Andhra Pradesh and Karnataka, municipal effort in accelerating revenues has been higher than the other states as shown in annual average growth rates. In other states such as Assam, Bihar, Madhya Pradesh, Tamil Nadu, Uttar Pradesh and West Bengal, little effort has been made to make use of charges, fees etc.

Transfers in municipal finances are shown in Table 12. During 2001-02, Rs. 562958 lakh were transferred by state governments to municipalities. Transfers as percentage of total municipal revenues was recorded highest in Jammu & Kashmir (83.7%) and lowest in Punjab (10.1%). Bihar, Jammu & Kashmir, Jharkhand, Rajasthan, Tripura and Uttar Pradesh witnessed a larger share of transfers in their municipal resource base. The annual growth of transfers during 1997-98 to 2001-02 was reported to be 13.5 per cent at the national average, however, it was recorded high in Rajasthan (38.6%) and Orissa (22.4%). Per capita transfers were reported high in Himachal Pradesh, Rajasthan, Chhattisgarh and Karnataka.

Table 12
Role of Transfers in Municipal Finances

State	*Transfers (Rs. lakh 2001-02*	*Percent of Total Municipal (Revenue) 2001-02*	*AAGR percent (1997-98 to 2001-02)*	*Per capita Transfers (Rs. 2001-02)*
Andhra Pradesh	31784	30.7	12.4	171.4
Assam	1624	29.7	16.7	65.1
Bihar	5559	62.0	-0.5	64.4
Chhattisgarh	12624	50.1	–	323.3
Goa	941	33.6	11.0	258.6
Gujarat	31395	17.8	14.6	175.5
Haryana	7892	39/5	18.6	135.5
Himachal Pradesh	27.87	58.5	0.7	472.6
Jammu & Kashmir	6162	83.7	16.2	247.6
Jharkhand	2440	62.0	–	64.4
Karnataka	60859	57.9	14.5	347.7
Kerala	17949	44.5	3.4	296.9
Madhya Pradesh	37663	54.8	-2.1	241.4
Maharastra	94177	13.8	22.8	239.6
Manipur	195	56.5	33.1	36.1
Orissa	8047	44.2	22.4	153.8
Punjab	8489	10.1	9.7	105.1
Rajasthan	51703	83.3	38.6	403.5
Tamil Nadu	46770	33.7	-2.8	180.7

Contd...

State	Transfers (Rs. lakh 2001-02	Percent of Total Municipal (Revenue) 2001-02	AAGR percent (1997-98 to 2001-02)	Per capita Transfers (Rs. 2001-02)
Tripura	1100	83.5	5.6	297.8
Uttarakhan	5105	63.7	–	250.1
Uttar Pradesh	77488	74.5	14.4	232.1
West Bengal	50203	54.3	14.1	256.7
Total	562958	31.7	13.5	224.4

Source: O.P. Mathur, 2006

Expenditure on establishment (salaries and wages) accounts for 54.2 per cent of the total municipal expenditure. In several states, however, it is high as 80.4 per cent (Madhya Pradesh), Haryana (69.7%), Orissa (50.6%), West Bengal (65.0%), Rajasthan (63.2%) and Uttar Pradesh (60%). During 2001-02, per capita revenue expenditure was recorded highest in Maharastra, Punjab, Himachal Pradesh and Gujarat while it was reported least in Manipur. Annual growth of revenue expenditure was reported as high as 17.22 per cent in Punjab while it showed declining trend in Madhya Pradesh (Table 13).

Table 13
Per Capita Revenue Expenditure

State	Per Capita Revenue Expenditure (2001-02)	Annual Growth Rate (percent) (1997-98 to 2001-02)	Percent of GSDP (2001-02)
Mahrastra	1253.71	6.51	1.82
Punjab	1008-12	17.22	1.15
Himachal Pradesh	955.45	13.02	0.38
Gujarat	865.12	7.11	1.24
Goa	604.18	13.24	0.31
Andhra Pradesh	508.88	14.47	0.63
Kerala	493.17	10.65	0.39
West Bengal	487.49	10.33	0.61
Tamil Nadu	481.79	0.96	0.84
Madhya Pradesh	427.66	-2.59	0.82
Karnataka	418.29	11.32	0.67
Uttaranchal	399.77	–	–
Jammu & Kashmir	392.69	19.86	0.52
Rajasthan	390.36	7.30	0.56
Chhattisgarh	376.07	–	0.49
Tripura	356.75	7.09	0.37

Contd...

State	Per Capita Revenue Expenditure (2001-02)	Annual Growth Rate (percent) (1997-98 to 2001-02)	Percent of GSDP (2001-02)
Orissa	355.06	13.87	0.43
Uttar Pradesh	275.18	9.54	0.49
Haryana	255.23	1.45	0.25
Assam	211.79	5.21	0.16
Jharkhand	87.20	–	0.11
Bihar	87.20	5.53	0.15
Manipur	81.03	4.90	0.85
Total	576.71	7.36	0.85

Source: O.P. Mathur, 2006

An analysis of the structure of municipal revenues-mix of taxes, user charges and fees, transfers and loans-in the country suggested that it varies considerably between states and suffer from the following problems:

Horizontal Imbalance

Most of the local governments suffer from inadequate own resources leading to heavy dependence on transfers from state governments.

State Government Control

Municipalities suffer from uneven access to resources. This gives rise to imbalances between Municipalities of various population sizes and even within the same population size, with similar tax base.

State Government Control

Generally the state Government control the municipal authority to levy taxes and user charges, set rates, grant exemptions, borrow funds, etc. and may also determine the pattern of transfers to Municipalities. Mostly high yielding and buoyant sources of revenue are not with the local government, excepting in the case of octroi levying states. Grants in aid are in often discretionary.

Municipal Revenue Mix

Taxes and transfers constitute the predominant sources of municipal revenues. Property tax is the most comnion and often the single most important municipal tax. User charges, though becoming increasingly popular are yet to dominate the municipal scene. Borrowing constitutes a relatively small source.

Systematic Inefficiency

Municipalities generally suffer from under exploitation of own revenue sources and high administrative and revenue collection costs.

The above issues need to be addressed carefully as a part of a holistic municipal finance reforms programme. Municipal revenue reforms are complex and depend on a number of factors. There is no optional tax structure. Useful principles may guide tax reforms in a given situation. Broadening the tax base may avoid reliance on relatively high tax rates which are opposed by the tax payers. In order to promote specific economic and social objectives, tax preference and exemptions need to be eliminated or reduced. Tax rates should be moderate to ensure better tax compliance and to prevent tax evasion.

JAWAHARLAL NEHRU NATIONAL URBAN RENEWAL MISSION

Cities and towns have a vital role in India's socio-economic transformation and change. Cities in India are the centre point of innovations and hub of many activities. However, most of the cities and towns are severely stressed in terms of infrastructure and services availability. The inner areas of cities face widespread dereliction, decadence and neglect, with significant negative consequences. Municipalities and other institutions responsible for delivery of municipal services are facing acute resource crunch. In view of the above, Government of India has launched Jawahar Lal Nehru National Renewal Mission (JNNURM). The mission aimed at creating economically productive, efficient, equitable and responsive cities, with focus on (i) improving and augmenting the economic and social infrastructure of cities; (ii) ensuring basic services to the urban poor including security of tenure at affordable prices; (ii) initiating wide ranging urban sector reforms whose primary aim is to eliminate legal, institutional and financial constraints that have impeded investment in urban infrastructure and services; (iv) strengthening municipal governments and their functioning in accordance with the provisions of the 74th Constitution Amendment Act, 1992. It provides for public disclose of local spending decisions together with earmarking of budgetary allocations for basic services to the poor. The mission is designed to make effective use of the potential the private sector in service delivery and management of the infrastructure. It is estimated that over a seven years period (2005-06 to 2011-12), the urban local bodies would require a total investments of Rs. 120536 crores. This includes investment in basic infrastructure and services i.e. annual funding requirement of Rs. 17219 crores. In order to mobilize these resources, a national level initiative is called for that would bring together the state governments and strengthen ULBs to catalyze investments flow in the urban infrastructure sector.

While several reforms initiatives have been taken e.g. the 74th constitutional Amendment Act and model municipal law, there is potential for further reform oriented steps in order to meet the development objectives. Reform initiatives also need to be articulated by the state governments in order to create an investor friendly environment. There is need to integrate the reforms initiatives and scale up the effort to catalyze investment in urban infrastructure sector. There is also need for sustainable infrastructure development. Moreover, there is urgent need to take measures to enhance efficiencies in urban services delivery through introducing reforms and institutional restructuring. The mission is inconformity with National Common Minimum Programme of the Government of India as well as Millennium Development Goals of United Nations. The objectives of mission include:

(i) to integrate development of infrastructure services in cities covered under the mission;

(ii) to establish linkages between asset creation and asset management through a slew of reforms for long term project sustainability;

(iii) to ensure adequate funds to meet the deficiencies in urban infrastructural services;

(iv) to plan development of identified cities including peri-urban areas, out growths, and urban corridors leading to dispersed urbanization;

(v) to scale up delivery of civic amenities and provision of utilities with emphasis on universal access to the urban poor;

(vi) to focus on urban renewal programme for the old city areas to reduce congestion; and

(vii) to make provision of basic services to the urban poor including security of tenure at affordable prices, improved housing, water supply and sanitation and ensuring delivery of other existing universal services of the government for education, health and social security.

The mission has two sub missions, namely:

- Sub-mission for Urban Infrastructure and Governance which laid main thrust on infrastructure projects relating to water supply and sanitation, sewerage, solid waste management, road network, urban transport and re-development of old city areas with a view to upgrading infrastructure therein shifting industrial and commercial establishments to other areas, etc.
- Sub-mission for Basic Services to the urban poor which laid emphasis on integrated development of slums through projects for providing shelter, basic services and other related civic amenities with a view to providing utilities to the urban poor.

The mission duration would be seven years beginning from the year 2005-06. It is expected that the following outcome will be achieved after completion of the mission:

(i) Modern and transparent budgeting, accounting financial management systems, designed and adopted for all urban services and governance functions;

(ii) City wise framework for planning and governance will be established and become operational;

(iii) All urban residents will be able to obtain access to a basic level of urban services;

(iv) Financially self sustaining agencies for urban governance and services delivery will be established through reforms to major revenue instruments;

(v) Local service and governance will be conducted in a manner that is transparent and accountable to citizens;

(vi) E-governance applications will be introduced in core functions of ULB's/parastatals resulting in reduced cost and time of service delivery processes.

The JNNURM shall provide assistance for infrastructure development in the 63 cities across states in the country. The criteria for selection of the cities has been based on population, state capital, religious historical and tourism importance etc. The following projects are eligible for the mission:

Sub-Mission I

(i) Urban renewal i.e. development of inner city

(ii) Water supply and sanitation

(iii) Sewerage and solid waste management

(iv) Construction and improvement of drains and storm water drains

(v) Urban transportation including roads, highways express ways, MRTS and metro-projects

(vi) Parking lots and spaces on public private partnership basis

(vii) Development of heritage areas

(viii) Prevention and rehabilitation of soil erosion and landslides only in case of special category states where such problems are common and

(ix) Preservation of water bodies.

Sub-Mission II

(i) Integrated development of slums, housing and development of infrastructure projects in slums in the identified cities

(ii) Projects involving development, improvement, and maintenance of basic services to the urban poor;

(iii) Slum improvement and rehabilitation projects

(iv) Projects on water supply, sewerage, drainage, community toilets, and baths etc.

(v) Projects for providing houses at affordable cost for slum dwellers, urban poor, economically weaker sections and lower income group categories

(vi) Construction and improvement of drains and storm water drains

(vii) Environment improvement of slums and solid waste management

(viii) Street lighting

(ix) Civic amenities, civic community halls, child care centres etc.

(x) Operation and maintenance of assets created under this component.

(xi) Convergence of health, education and social security schemes for the urban poor.

The following components are not admissible under the mission:

I. Power

II. Telecom

III. Health

IV. Education

V. Wage employment programme and staff components

VI. Creation of fresh employment opportunities.

The thrust of the mission is to ensure improvement in urban governance and service delivery so that ULB's become financially sound and sustainable for undertaking new programmes. The mission has tried emphasis on reforms agenda to be implemented by both the local bodies and state governments. There are two types of reforms: (i) mandatory reforms at the level of ULB's and parastatal agencies; and state level; (ii) optional reforms for states local bodies and parastatal agencies.

MANDATORY REFORMS

For ULB's and Parastatal Agencies

(a) Adoption of modern accrual based double entry accounting system

(b) Introduction of a system of e-governance using IT applications, such as GIS. and MIS for various services

(c) Reforms of property tax through introducing GIS technology

(d) Levy of reasonable user charges

(e) Internal earmarking budget for basic services to the urban poor

(f) provision of basic services to the urban poor including security of tenure at affordable prices, improved housing, water supply and sanitation.

For State Governments

(a) Implementation of decentralization measures as envisaged in 74th Constitutional Amendement Act

(b) Repeal of ULCRA

(c) Reform of Rent Control Laws

(d) Rationalization of stamp duty to bring it down to not more than 5 per cent

(e) Enactment of Public Discloser Law

(f) Enactment of Community Participation Law

(g) Assigning elected ULB's with city planning function.

OPTIONAL REFORMS (COMMON TO STATES, ULB'S AND PARASTATAL AGENCIES)

(a) Revision of bye-laws to streamline the approval process for construction of buildings, development of sites etc.

(b) Simplification of legal and procedural frameworks for conversion of land from agricultural to non-agricultural purposes

(c) Introduction of Property Title Certification system in ULB's

(d) Earmarking at least 20-25 per cent of developed land in all housing projects for EWS and LIG category with a system of cross subsidization.

(e) Introduction of computerized process of registration of land and property

(f) ·Revision of bye-laws to make rain water harvesting mandatory in all buildings and adoption of water conservation measures

(g) Bye-laws for reuse of recycled water

(h) Reduction in establishment costs by adopting the voluntary Retirement Scheme, not-filling posts falling vaant due to retirement etc.; structural reforms, and encouraging public private partnership.

Urban Infrastructure Development Scheme for Small and Medium Towns (UIDSSMT) has been launched in small and medium towns which are not covered under JNNURM. The scheme has been merger of Integrated Development of Small and Medium Towns (IDSMT) and Accelerated Urban Water Supply Programme (AUWSP). The objectives of the scheme include (i) improving infrastructural facilities and helping to create durable public assets and quality oriented services; (ii) enhancing public private partnership in infrastructural development and; (iii) promoting planned integrated development of towns and cities. The duration of the scheme is also for 7 years beginning from 2005-06. The components covered under the scheme are same as mentioned in the JNNURM. It has equally laid emphasis on reforms both for local bodies and parastatal agencies, as well as state governments. The reform agenda is same as mentioned in the JNNNURM.

Integrated Housing & Slum Development Programme (IHSDP) also aims at combining the existing schemes of VAMBAY and NSDP under the new IHSDP scheme for having an integrated approach in ameliorating the conditions of the urban slum dwellers who do not posses adequate shelter and reside in dilapidated conditions. The scheme is applicable to all cities and towns except cities covered under JNNURM. The scheme seeks to enhance public and private investments in housing and infrastructural development in urban areas. The components for assistance under the scheme will include all slum improvement, upgradation, relocation projects including upgradation, new construction of houses and infrastructural facilities, like water supply, and sewerage. The scheme is also reforms linked.

The government of India has allocated Rs. 50,000 crores as central assistance under the JNNURM, UIDSSMT and IHSDP. However, states and local bodies have to provide their share (20 and 10 per cent, respectively) besides mobilization of funds through public private partnership. Out of total budgetary allocation, Rs. 40,000 crores have been earmarked for JNNURM, Rs. 6000 crores for UIDSSMT and Rs. 4000 crores for IHSDP. The financing and release of funds under these schemes are linked with reforms.

In the context of growing cities and urbanization, there is need for effective governance. Urban governance is no more limited to the provision of infrastructure and operation of civic services. The traditional approaches of urban governance are proved to be inappropriate and restrictive. Good urban governance is called for which is characterized by sustainability, equity, efficiency, transparency, accountability, civic engagement, security development of partnerships, etc. There is a need for prudent and efficient financial and asset management to increase their capacity to facilitate market borrowings for investment in urban development. In view of the emerging challenges of urban development, Government of India launched JNNURM with three interrelated and complimentary components i.e. governance, infrastructure development and provision of basic services to poor. Implementation of governance reforms like enactment of community participation and public disclosure laws, earmarking of funds for poverty alleviation by local bodies, levy and collection of user charges, simplification of procedures etc. in identified areas is a precondition for accessing funds under JNNURM.

It is estimated that over a seven year period (2005-12), the urban local bodies would require a total investment of Rs. 120536 crores. This includes investment in basic infrastructure and services i.e. annual fund requirements in the tune of Rs. 17219.5 crores. The larger amount of funding is required for larger cities above one million population (Table 14).

Table 14
Urban Sector Investment Requirement

(Rs. crores)

Category	*Number of cities*	*Investment Requirement (over 7 years starting 2005-06)*	*Annual Funds Requirement*
Cities with over 4 million Population	7 (11.11)	57,143 (47.41)	8163.3 (47.41)
Cities with 1-4 million Population	28 (44.44)	57,143 (47.41)	8613.3 (47.41)
Selected cities with less than one million Population	28 (44.44)	6,250 (5.18)	892.9 (5.18)
Total	63 (100.00)	1,20,536 (100.00)	17,219.5 (100.00)

Source: Ministry of Urban Development, Government of India, Delhi, 2007

The Government of India has proposed substantial assistance through JNNURM over the seven years period. During the period, funds will be provided for proposals that would meet the Mission's requirements. Under JNNURM financial assistance will be made available to the urban local bodies and parastatal agencies, which could deploy these funds for implementing the projects themselves or through the special purpose vehicles that may be expected to be set up. Assistance under the Mission is additional central assistance, which would be provided as grant to the implementing agencies. Further, assistance from JNNURM is expected to facilitate further investment in the urban sector.

One of the objectives of Mission is to facilitate and ensure participatory urban development to contribute to sustainability. The community development programmes by the cities are the result of stakeholder consultations. One of the mandatory reforms for the participation of the community of stakeholders is decision making and governance at ward and sub-ward level. The projects under Community Participation Fund are eligible to a maximum funding of Rs. 10 lakhs and there should be a community contribution of 10 per cent which may be relaxed to 5 per cent in case of projects involving the poor.

The JNNURM is under implementation for over two years and the Mission has made substantial progress over the period. All the Mission cities have formulated city development plans which were appraised and approved by the Ministry, 58 cities signed MOA; with the Ministry for implementation of reforms several projects have been approved and their implementation is in different stages of progress in the Mission cities. As on 30th September, 2007, 248 projects with values of Rs. 21403 crores were sanctioned in 46 cities of 22 states (Table 15). Most of the projects were from the states of Gujarat, Andhra Pradesh, Maharastra, and Tamil Nadu. The share of Project values was reported highest in Maharastra (29.88 per cent) followed by Gujarat (11.67 per cent), Andhra Pradesh (10.53 per cent) and Tamil Nadu (9.92 per cent).

Table 15
Projects Sanctioned Under JNNURM
(As on 30th September 2007)

State	*Projects*	*Value (Rs. crores)*	*Percentage*
Andhra Pradesh	33	2253.91	10.53
Arunachal Pradesh	02	89.19	0.42
Assam	01	35.16	0.16
Bihar	01	36.95	0.17
Chandigarh	02	56.98	0.27
Chattisgarh	01	303.64	1.42
Gujarat	44	2497.69	11.67
Haryana	03	210.97	0.99
Himachal Pradesh	02	26.13	0.12
Jammu & Kashmir	02	262.15	1.22
Karnataka	30	1654.62	7.73
Kerala	06	680.05	3.18
Madhya Pradesh	13	987.99	4.61
Maharastra	47	6396.19	29.88
Manipur	01	25.80	0.12

Contd...

State	*Projects*	*Value (Rs. crores)*	*Percentage*
Orissa	02	504.93	2.36
Pondicherry	01	203.40	0.95
Punjab	02	328.83	1.54
Rajasthan	06	474.53	2.21
Tamil Nadu	22	2123.00	9.92
Uttar Pradesh	09	988.06	4.62
West Bengal	19	1263.80	5.90
Total	248	21,403.80	100.00

Source: Ministry of Urban Development, Government of India, New Delhi, 2007.

Out of total projects sanctioned, most of the projects were related with water supply (29.84 per cent) followed by Roads/ Flyovers (18.95 per cent) and Sewerage (18.15 per cent). The share of value involved in the sanctioned projects was reported high in case of water supply (33.02 per cent) followed by sewerage (26.45 per cent) and drainage/storm water drains (12.28 per cent) (Table 16).

Table 16
Nature of Projects Sanctioned

Sector	*Projects*	*Percentage*	*Value (Rs. cores)*	*Percentage*
Water Supply	74	29.84	7067.98	33.02
Sewerage	45	18.15	5660.82	26.45
Drainage/Storm Water Drains	33	13.31	2527.71	12.28
Solid Waste Management	23	9.27	1187.07	5.55
Mass Rapid Transport System	11	4.43	2427.41	11.34
Roads/Flyovers/RoB	47	18.95	1995.18	9.32
Other Urban Transport	08	3.22	270.47	126
Urban Renewal	06	2.42	124.03	0.58
Heritage Development	01	0.48	43.13	0.20
Total	248	100.00	21403.80	100.00

Source: Ministry of Urban Development, Government of India, New Delhi, 2007.

STATUS OF URBAN REFORMS

Central and State Governments as well as ULB's have made efforts to improve the organization and working of the local governments. During the last two decades, the reform process in the urban sector has been intensive. 74th Constitutional Amendment Act is itself a major reform effort to strengthen urban administration. Ministry of Urban Development, Government of India initiated several reforms, including urban Reforms Incentive Fund (URIF), City Challenge Fund etc. The URIF itself consisted of several reforms like repeal of ULCPA, rationalization of stamp duty and rent control laws, implementation of commercial accounting, simplification of procedures, etc. Some state Governments like Tamil Nadu, Andhra Pradesh, Karnataka, Uttar Pradesh and Gujarat also initiated reforms through issues of municipal bonds, introduction of e-governance, double entry accounting system, streamlining and simplification of issue of building permission and introduction of self assessment system of property taxation. However, most of these reforms were ad-hoc and project based. The JNNURM synthesized these reforms initiatives and designed a package to be implemented at the state and local levels. The reforms under JNNURM aim at strengthening urban governments and to decentralize and devolve functions, finances, and functionaries to them in order as enable them to function to self governing institutions.

The Constitution Act, 1992 is an important initiative of the Government of India to strengthen municipal governance and to provide them constitutional status. The important provisions of the Act include constitution of three types of municipalities, devolution of functional and financial powers, adequate representation of weaker sections and women, regular and fair conduct of elections, constitution of ward committees, District Planning Committees, Metropolitan Planning Committees, State Finance and Election Commissions. Table 16 shows the status of implementation of decentralization measures as per 74th Constitutional Amendment Act in states. All the States amended their municipal Acts and Laws in conformity with the constitutional provisions. There are variations between the states in the constitution and working of ward committees, DPC', and MPC's as seen in the table.

Table 17
Implementation of Decentralization Measures as per 74th Constitutional Amendment Act

State	*Ward Committees*	*District Planning Committees*	*Metropolitan Planning Committees*
Andhra Pradesh	Y	Y	N
Assam	N	Y	N
Chhattisgarh	Y	Y	N
Gujarat	Y	N	N
Haryana	N	N	N
Himachal Pradesh	N	Y	NA
Karnataka	Y	Y	N
Kerala	Y	Y	N
Madhya Pradesh	Y	Y	N
Maharastra	Y	Y	N
Manipur	N	N	N
Nagaland	N	Y	N
Orissa	Y	Y	N
Punjab	Y	N	N
Rajasthan	Y	Y	N
Chennai	Y	Y	N
Uttarakhand	Y	N	NA
Uttar Pradesh	Y	N	N

Source: Ministry of Urban Development, Government of India, New Delhi, 2007

Implementation of state level municipal reforms is shown in Table 18.

Table 18
State Level Municipal Reforms

Reforms	*States which have accomplished reforms*
• 74th CAA (Transfer of 12th Schedule Functions)	Bihar, Chhattisgarh, Gujarat, Kerala, Madhya Pradesh, Mahrastra, Tipura, West Bengal.
• 74th CAA (Constitution of DPC)	Andhra Pradesh, Assam, Bihar, Chhattisgarh, Himachal Pradesh, Kerala, Madhya Pradesh, Mahrastra, Orissa, Rajasthan, Tamil Nadu, West Bengal.
• 74th CAA (Constitution of MPC) Transfer-City Planning Function	Assam, Chhattisgarh, Gujarat, HImachal Pradesh, Madhya Pradesh, Mahrastra, Tamil Nadu, West Bengal.
• Transfer Water Supply and Sanitation	Chandigarh, Chhattisgarh, Gujarat, Haryana, Himacha; Pradesh, Madhya Pradesh, Mahrastra, Tamil Nadu, West Bengal.

Contd...

Reforms	*States which have accomplished reforms*
• Reforms in Rent Control	Nagaland, Rajasthan.
• Stamp Duty Rationalization to 5 per cent.	Maharastra, Sikkim.
• Repeal of ULCRA	Assam, Bihar, Chandigarh, Chhattisgarh, Gujarat, Haryana, Madhya Pradesh, Punjab, Orissa, Rajasthan, Sikkim, Tamil Nadu, West Bengal.
• Enactment of Public Disclose Law	Gujarat

Source: Centre for Good Governance, Hyderabad, 2007.

Bihar has already implemented the Modern Municipal Act with the transfer of functions under 12th Schedule. While Chhattisgarh, Gujarat, Kerala, Madhya Pradesh, Maharastra, Tripura, and West Bengal have transferred functions under 12th Schedule of 74th Constitutional Amendment Act. DPC's have been constituted in Andhra Pradesh, Assam, Bihar, Chhattisgarh, Himachal Pradesh, Kerala, Madhya Pradesh, Maharastra, Orissa, Rajasthan, Tamil Nadu and West Bengal. Only West Bengal has constituted Metropolitan Planning Committees. Similarly, only Gujarat has introduced Public Disclosure Law. While most states have made enabling acts to constitute District Planning Committees, they have not been actually constituted in all states and where constituted are not functional. In Assam, Karnataka, Kerala, Rajasthan and West Bengal, the state laws envisage the DPC as a part of the Zilla Parishad. The Chairperson of the Parishad is also designated as Chairperson of the DPC. In Madhya Pradesh, a Minister of the state Government is the chairperson of the DPC and is expected to had and guide district planning with the help of the district administration. The Chairperson of the Zilla Parishad is a Vice Chairman. Gujarat and Maharastra have long had District Planning and Development Committees with a Minister of the state Government as the Chairperson. Thus, designation of a Minister as the President of DPC virtually makes it an extension of the state Government and goes against the spirit of constitution. In Rajasthan, DPC's have been formed in all districts with the President of the Zilla Parishad as the

Chairperson and the Chief Planning Officer of the Zilla Parishad as the Secretary. In Uttar Pradesh and Karnataka, the DPC's have been set up but they are not functional (Table 19). The DPC's have been constituted in 10 states viz. Bihar, Chhattisgarh, Haryana, Karnataka, Kerala, Madhya Pradesh, Orissa, Rajasthan, Tamil Nadu, and West Bengal.The number of members' of DPC's varies between states. They generally comprise the Minister in-charge of the district Mayor of Corporation, Chairperson of Council, Chairpersons of Zilla Parishad/Panchayat, elected members of local bodies, special invitees, nominated members, divisional commissioners, deputy commissioners, district collectors, district planning officer, etc.

Table 19
Composition of District Planning Committees

State	*Total Members*	*Elected Members*	*Nominated Members*	*Chairperson*	*Secretary*
Kerala	15	12	03	President of Zilla Parishad	DM
Madhya Pradesh	15-25	Four fifths	one fifth	Minister nominated by State Government	DM
Maharas-tra	30-50	Four fifths	one fifth	Minister nominated by State Government	DM
West Bengal	10-100 (depending on size of district)	Four fifths	one fifth	President of Zilla Parishad	Chief Planning Officer of Zilla Parishad
Rajasthan	25	20	5	Minister nominated by State Government	CDO of Distt.
Uttar Pradesh	20-40	Four fifths	one fifth	Minister nominated by state government	CEO of ZP
Karnataka	–	Four fifths	one fifth	President of the Zilla Parishad	CEO of Zilla Parishad
Tamil Nadu	–	Four fifths	one fifth	Collection , Zilla Parishad, President Vice Chairman	CEO of Distt. Panchayat

Source: Centre for Good Governance, Hyderabad, 2007

Metropolitan cities are the engines of growth. Urban transport water supply, waste management, public health etc.

require metropolitan level planning, implementation and coordination. Constitution of a Metrpolitan Committee is a constitutional requirement, however, except West Bengal, no state has setup MPC's. In the composition for MPC it is envisaged that one third of its members are to be elected by and from amongst the elected representatives of urban and rural local bodies in the metropolitan areas. The Kolkata Metropolitan Planning Committee comprise 60 members, including Chief Minister of state, Minister in charge of Municipal Affairs and urban development, elected members of local bodies and nominated members of the 60 members, 2/3rd members are elected and 1/3rd are nominated. Chief Minister of the state is the Chairman of the Committee and the Minister incharge of Municipal Affairs and Urban Development Department of the state is the Vice Chairman of the Committee. As per the 74th Constitutional Amendment Act, Wards Committees have to be formed in all urban local bodies with more than three lakhs population to bring greater decentralization of functions. The constitution of Wards Committees varies considerably in states. In states like Kerala and West Bengal, Wards Committees are constituted for each Ward and in others for a group of wards. In Kerala, there is a Ward Committee for every ward with the Councillor as Chairman. The Committee consists of about 50 persons nominated by the Chairperson of the Municipality in consultation with the Councillor and drawn from residents association, NGO', CBO', etc. The functional domain of ULBs as per the 12th Schedule of 74th Constitution Amendment Act is given in Table 20. Gujarat, Maharastra, Uttarakhand are defaulters in transferring functions to ULBs as per schedule.

Cities which have accomplished reforms are shown in Table 27. E-governance has been set up in Hyderabad, Vishakhapattanam, Raipur, Vijayawada, Bhopal, Coimbatore and Madurai, Double entry accounting system has been introduced in Indore, Jaipur, Coimbatore, Madurai, Nagpur, Bhubaneshwar, Chennai, and Kolkata. Chandigarh, and Madurai have introduced property title certification system in ULB's while Ahmadabad, Vadodara and Bhopal have

Table 20
Functional Domain of ULB's as per 12th Schedule

State	*1*	*2*	*3*	*4*	*5*	*6*	*7*	*8*	*9*	*10*	*11*	*12*	*13*	*14*	*15*	*16*	*17*	*18*
Andhra Pradesh	y	y	y**	y	y	y	–	y**	y**	y	y	y	y	y	y	y	y	y
Chhatis-garh	y	y	y	y	y	y	y	y	y	y	y	y	y	y	y	y	y	y
Gujarat	y	–	–	–	y	y	–	–	–	–	–	–	–	–	–	–	–	–
Karnataka	y	y	y	y	y	y	y	y(P)	y	y	y	y	y	y	y	y	y	y
Kerala	y	y	y	y	y(P)	y	y	y	y	y	y	y	y	y	y	y	y	y
Maharastra	y	–	–	–	y	y	–	–	–	–	–	–	–	–	–	–	–	–
Orissa	y(P)	N	y	y(P)	N	y	N	N	N	y	y	y	y	y	y	y	y	y
Tamil Nadu	N	y	y	y	y	y	N	y*	y*	y	y	y	y	y	y*	y	y	y
Uttar Pradesh	y(P)	y(P)	N	y(P)	y(P)	y(P)	N	y(P)	y(P)	y(P)	y(P)	y	y	y	y	y	y	y
Uttarakhand	y	y	y	–	y	–	y	y	y	–	–	–	y	–	–	–	–	–
Madhya Pradesh	y	y	y	y	y	y	y	y	y	y	y	y	y	y	y	y	y	y
Haryana	y	y	y	y	y	y	y	y	y	y	y	y	y	y	y	y	y	y
Assam	y	y	y	y	y	y	N	N	N	y	y	y	y	y	y	y	y	y
Manipur	y	y	y	y	y	y	y	y	y	y	y	y	y	y	y	y	y	y
Rajasthan	N	y	y	y	y	y	y	y	y	y	y	y	y	y	y	y	y	y
Jammu & Kashmir	y	y	y	y	y	y	y	N	y	y	y	y	y	y	y	y	y	y
Nagaland	N	y	y	N	N	y	N	y	y	y	N	y	y	y	y	y	y	y
Punjab	y	y	y	y	y	y	y	y	y	y	y	y	y	y	y	y	y	y
Himachal Pradesh	y	y	y	y	y	y	y	y	y	y	y	y	y	y	y	y	y	y

Source: Ministry of Urban Development, Government of India, New Delhi, 2007
y = Assigned to Municipalities
N = Not assigned to Municipalities
P = Partly
* = Data varies within cities in the state
** = Services transferred only by executive order.

revised building bye laws for streamlining the approval process. Similarly, Shimla, Jaipur, Coimbatore, Madurai, Chennai, and Vijayawada have introduced computerized process of registration of land and property.

The State Finance Commissions (SFC's) have attempted a detailed review of the financial position of ULB's and local level issues of governance and made recommendations to overcome the prevailing constraints confronting ULB's. Bihar is an exception, where the report could not be submitted due to various reasons. Most of the states have accepted recommendations of SFC's. In some states the SFC's have given importance to devolution of functions, functionaries and powers alongwith transfer of funds. Integration of city planning and delivery functions is expected to bring about the process of planning and delivery of all urban infrastructure provision and management functions and services coverage with the functions of ULB's. In the management of city, several state government agencies and parastatals play a very significant role along with local bodies. Often these organizations work independent of the ULB's. Thus, 74th Constitutional Amendment Act envisages, transferring the function of local bodies as listed in 12th Schedule. The performance of functions and delivery of services by different organizations continues even after 15 years of enactment of the 74th Constitutional Amendment Act. Therefore, the JNNURM incorporated a reform making it mandatory for the integration of city planning and delivery functions. The local bodies are expected to play a critical role in decision making in relation to these functions while other parastatals should be integrated with the local bodies. Presently, eight states have transferred city planning functions to ULBs.

Rent control is imposing a ceiling on rents in housing markets. Rent control refers to laws that limit the amounts of rent and the amounts that rent can be increased. It prevents the landlords from charging exorbitant rents and evicting. Housing is a state subject and enactment and enforcement of the rent control legislations is the responsibility of the concerned state government. In view of the increasing importance of rent control, reform has been identified as one of the mandatory reforms at the state level. Assam, Bihar, Chandigarh, Chhatisgarh, Gujarat, Haryana, Madhya Pradesh, Punjab, Orissa, Rajasthan, Sikkim, Tamil Nadu and West Bengal have initiated the repealing of Urban Land Ceiling Rent Act. While Nagaland and Rajasthan have started reforming in rent control.

The stamp duty framework has not kept pace with changes. Laws relating to rates of stamp duties, registration charges etc. were initially governed by the main objectives of revenue mobilization, without considering the market needs. The maximum stamp duty rate levied in most developed countries ward-wise is in the range of 1-4 per cent, however, in some states of India, it is in double digit. Thus, there is urgent need to rationalize it, only Mahrastra and Sikkim have rationalized stamp duty upto 5 per cent while other states could not initiate the reform.

Reforms to streamline administration, mobilize resources, improve efficiency in service delivery, provision of basic services to the poor, etc. have been on the priority list and are being undertaken both by state and local governments. The JNNURM has also identified administrative reforms as critical and need to be achieved during the mission period. The administrative reforms include right sizing the personnel structure, reducing establishment expenditure, capacity building of institutions and individuals, providing longer tenure to senior functionaries etc. Importantly, structural reforms were also planned under the Mission. These include institutional strengthening, citizen charters, e-governance, charges in planning process encouraging partnership, participatory processes etc. E-governance, Public Private Partnership initiatives, application of GIS in resource mobilization etc. have been taken in some of the local bodies. Significantly, in most cases citizen must have access to proper information on municipal affairs. As a result they do not follow proper procedures in their access to functionaries for redressal of problems to overcome these constraints. Citizen charters are useful in discriminating information and educating citizens.

Public Discloser Law along-with the provisions of Right to Information Act may also be useful instrument to ensure public participation in civic affairs. Only Gujarat has enacted Public Director Law while rest of the states does not have such type of arrangement. Moreover, Report Card System is also important mechanism to get feedback regarding the quality and coverage of services and improving governance, however it is limited in operation.

Table 21
Cities Having Accomplished Reforms

Reforms	*Cities/ States*
Mandatory Reforms	
• E-governance set up	Hyderabad, Vishakhapattanam, Raipur, Vijayawada, Bhopal, Coimbatore, Madurai
• Shift to Double Entry Accounting	Indore, Jaipur, Coimbatore , Madurai, Nagpur, Bhubaneshwar, Chennai, Kolkata
• Property Tax (85% coverage)	Vijayawada, Chandigarh, Agra, Allahabad, Lucknow, Vishakhapatnam, Chennai
• Property Tax (90% collection efficiency)	Vijayawada, Chandigarh, Agra, Allahabad, Lucknow, Vishakhapattanam, Chennai
• 100% cost Recovery of O&M for water supply	Chennai, Vishakhapattanam
• 100% cost Recovery for Solid Waste Management	Vishakhapattanam
• Internal Earmarking of Funds for Services to Urban Poor	Hyderabad, Vijayawada, Vishakhapattanam, Chandigarh, Raipur, Ahmadabad, Surat, Vadodara, Nagpur, Nanded, Nashik, Pune, Mumbai, Kohima, Jaipur, Ajmer, Coimbatore, Madurai, Jabalpur, Bhopal, Indore, Allahabad, Varanasi, Kanpur, Mathura, Agra, Lucknow
Optional Reforms	
• Introduction of Property • Title Certification System in ULB's	Chandigarh, Madurai
• Revision of Building • Bye-Laws-Streamlining the Approval Process	Ahmadabad, Vadodara, Bhopal
• Revision of Building Bye-Laws- • Mandatory Rainwater Harvesting in all buildings	Faridabad, Shimla, Kochin, Thiruvananthapuram, Bangalore, Nagpur, Chennai, Agra, Allahabad, Kanpur, Lucknow, Mathura, Meerut, Varanasi, Vijayawada, Bhopal

Contd...

Reforms	*Cities/ States*
• Earmarking 25 per cent developed land in all Housing Projects for EWS/LIG	Ajmer
• Bye laws on Reuse of Recycled Water	Chandigarh
• Introduction of Computerized Process of Registration of Land and Property	Shimla, Jaipur, Coimbatore, Madurai, Chennai, Vijayawada

Source: Centre for Good Governance, Hyderabad, 2007.

PUBLIC FINANCIAL MANAGEMENT AND ACCOUNTABILITY

Improved public financial management and accountability environment is crucial for effective urban governance. The increasing urbanization and dynamics of urban development require higher capital investment and better management of resources. The recent legislations, policies and programmes such as JNNURM, IHSDP, UIDSSMT, Right to Information Act, Public Discloser Law, Community Participation Law, Modern Municipal Act, 74th Constitutional Amendment Act, etc. have placed greater responsibility on urban local bodies to become more accountable for management and use of public money. The Government of India recognizes the need to make urban local bodies self reliant and responsive. In India, urban governance is a state level subject. Governance includes both the administration of urban areas as well as the requirements of control and transparency on public spending.

The 74th Constitution (Amendment) Act, 1992 recognizes urban local bodies on the third tier of government in India and envisages that they be made autonomous through devolution of resources, powers and functions. With respect to public financial management, the 11th Finance Commission recommended that Comptroller and Auditor General of India be entrusted with technical guidance and supervision of ULB's audit in all states having implemented 74th Constitutional Amendment Act under this support, C&AG has proposed accounting and auditing formats for urban local bodies.

Presently, only 18 states have given full entrustment of technical guidance and supervision to C&AG.

The Ministry of Urban Development, Government of India formulated a Model Municipal Law in 2003 to serve as template for states to revise their municipal legal framework. Key provisions of the law include:

(1) Acknowledgement of role and recommendations of State Finance Commission in municipal finances;

(2) A form of administrative receivership for cities that default in performance of their duties;

(3) Mandatory framing of ULB debt limitation policy;

(4) Development of standards municipal accounting manual and practices;

(5) Creation of municipal accounts committee and preparation of annual financial statements;

(6) Mandatory requirement for urban local bodies to prepare inventory of all municipal assets;

(7) Encouragement for urban local bodies to prepare their own development plans; and

(8) Enabling private sector participation in the construction, financing and delivery of urban services.

The Right to Information Act, 2005 has also implications for public accountability system in India. It requires government bodies to provide information sought on its operations within specified timeframe. It also promotes disclosure of certain information by government bodies. Urban Local Government Disclosure Bill, 2006 envisages to enhance transparency and accountability in local government functioning. Each local body is required to maintain adequate records and make disclosure of key information at regular intervals to the public. Disclosure of information (both related to financial and services matters) may be made through newspapers, internet, notice boards, ward offices, public hearings, group meetings, etc. Bill also envisages voluntary sharing of information by the ULB's and it is a step forward from the RTI Act, 2005.

In order to mobilize resources and financial management by ULB's, certain Municipal Bonds and Pooled Financing has been introduced, the Ahmadabad Municipal Corporation is the pioneer in launching municipal bonds in 1998. There after, several corporations have issued municipal bonds. The Government of India has also supported these initiatives by exempting the interest earned on such bonds from income tax and prescribing guidelines for tax free municipal bonds. However, smaller local bodies are unable to access the capital market on their own. In 2006, the Government of India proposed development of a Pooled Finance Development Fund to institutionalize the support to smaller urban local bodies in this process. This improved the Public Finance Management and Accountability environment in the smaller urban local bodies through introducing the processes of updated accounts, improved financial planning, and sound reporting practices.

A task force was appointed in 2001 under chairmanship of the Deputy C&AG to develop an accounting system and process to be followed by the urban local bodies for better financial recording and reporting. Based on the recommendations of the Task Force, the Government of India initiated development of a National Municipal Accounting Manual for conversion of ULB accounting to double entry accrual based accounting in 2005. Some states, including Karnataka, Andhra Pradesh, Gujarat and West Bengal have already adopted the double entry accounting system.

Interestingly, in order to accelerate the process of urban reforms, the Government of India decided to provide reform linked financial assistance to states. In 2002, the Government set up an Urban Reform Incentive Fund (URIF) with an initial outlay of Rs. 500 crores per year. The URIF was designed to provide incentives for reforms in state and local government, including repeal of the Urban Land Ceiling Act, rationalization of stamp duty reform of rent control laws, introduction of computerized registration, reform of property tax, levy of user charges and adoption of double entry accounting system. JNNURM is also designed for integrated and planned development of 63 selected cities with focus on asset creation and management, efficiency in urban infrastructure and services delivery, community participation, and accountability. JNNURM has a central outlay of Rs. 50,000 crore for a seven year period. The programme requires a tri party Memorandum of Agreement between ULB's the State Government and the Central Government that charley identifies Public Finance Management and Accountability Reforms, among others, and a timeline for achieving the same at all levels. The reforms include modern and transparent budgeting system, shift to double entry accounting system, improved asset management, e-governance, updated financial management systems, enhanced property tax collection efficiency, enactment of Public Disclosure Law and Community Participation Law, levy of reasonable user charges, process reengineering for monitoring, financial operating plan under city development plans and credit rating (Chart 9).

Chart 9
Urban Reforms in India

Year	*Policy Intervention*	*Link with PFMA Context*
1985	7th Five Year Plan	Policy recommendations for revitalization of civic bodies; reform of municipal administration; constitution of State Finance Commission's; and constitutional status for local government.
1988	National Commission on Urbanization	Link between urbanization and economic growth explicitly acknowledge Reiteration of the need for decentralized urban growth and emphasis on the role of local governments.
1991-92	New Economic Policy	Autonomy of local governments seen necessary for deregulation and privatization of provision and maintenance of urban infrastructure and basis services.
1992	74th Constitutional Amendment Act	Devolution of powers (political, administrative and fiscal) to urban local bodies for functioning as 'independent institutions of self government'
1992-97	Formation of State Finance Commissions	To correct fiscal disabilities imbalances of local bodies and improve their financial situation and review financial position of urban local bodies and make

Contd...

Year	*Policy Intervention*	*Link with PFMA Context*
		recommendations regarding distribution of taxes, revenue-sharing arrangements, grant-in-aid system, etc.
1998	First Municipal Bond (Ahmedabad Municipal Corporation)	Landmark initiative followed by issue of guidelines for issuing tax free municipal bonds in February 2001 and increase in the limit from Rs. 2,000 million in 2001-02 in Rs. 5,000 million in 2002-03.
2000	11th Central Finance Commission	Recommend measures for augmentation of resources of states so that they can supplement resources of local bodies. Also recommended C&AG involvement in providing technical guidance and supervision to local bodies.
2000	The Transparency in Public Procurement Act	Karnataka was the first state to pass this legislation followed by Tamil Nadu
2002	Urban Reforms Incentive Fund	Policy initiative aimed to encourage reforms in urban local bodies (covered some PEMA areas like accounting, budgets, etc.)
	Supreme Court Judgment on Solid Waste Management	Highlight the issue of accountability of executives in urban local bodies for service delivery. Instituted reforms in accounts for greater transparency and better management of service costs.
	C&AG Task Force	Took the initiative to formulate policy guidelines on municipal accounting reforms through Double Entry Accrual-based accounting
	Pooled Finance	Precedence set by Tamil Nadu for smaller urban local bodies to raise funds from capital markets.
2003	Model Municipal Law	Template for states to revise their municipal legal framework. Key focus on improving state oversight of municipal finances through SFC recommendations
2005	Right to Information Act	Government of India initiative towards transparency and accountability. Adopted by most of the states.
	National Municipal Accounting Manual	Guidelines to the states/urban local bodies for accounting reforms on Double Entry Accrual System
	Launch of JNNURM and UIDSSMT	Reforms-driven, fast track mission for planned development of identified cities with focus on efficiency in urban

Contd...

Year	*Policy Intervention*	*Link with PFMA Context*
		infrastructure and services delivery, community participation, and accountability of local governments towards citizens.
2005-2010	12th Central Finance Commission	Recommends enactment of fiscal responsibility legislation at state level, which is likely to improve budget preparation, execution and monitoring situation in urban local bodies
2006	ULG Disclosure Act	Provide for transparency and accountability in the functioning of urban local bodies

Source: World Bank, 2007

A study of World Bank (2007) has highlighted that the main constraints to strong public finance arrangement and accountability in urban local bodies are the weak legal framework, low demand for accountability, lack of incentive for complaints or penalty for non compliance with existing rules, and limited use of available guidelines. The strengthened ULB budgeting process needs to include realistic and participatory framework for budget estimation and establishment of appropriate linkages with parastatal organizations and metropolitan plans.Similarly, effecting implementation of National Municipal Accounting Manual for accrual accounting and auditing of accounts of ULBs through technical guidance and supervision is called for.

CONCLUSION

India has a long tradition of urban local bodies dating back to 1688 when the Madras Corporation was constituted as the first Corporation in South Asia. This was followed by the Calcutta and Bombay Municipal Corporation in 1726. It provided the powers of governance to the local elite. These groups were set in place by virtue of their social standing, rather than via democratic elections. This was important to ensure political control and transfer of resources. Secondly decentralization enacted participation of community and control of functions pertaining to municipal governance. The elected representatives replaced managers. This brought opportunities for greater democracy and enhanced the role of local representatives. The institutional changes were made to effect comprehensive planning, however most large scale funding for infrastructure and other capital intensive works are routed through parastatal agencies. The burden of repayment of both capital and interest falls onto ULBs. A regime of parastatal organizations also reduces possibilities for public authorities especially ULB's to use economic sources. A regime of parastatal not only road blocks livelihood creation efforts but increases the dependence of local bodies on higher levels of government. Thus, ULB's need to regain the developmental terrain that has been encroached by higher level institutions. UNDP has been an active partner of national governments of the world over in promoting decentralized governance. In India, the UN System has adopted the United Nations Development Assistance Framework (UNDAF) with strengthening decentralization as one of the two key priorities, with the other being promotion of gender equality. Decentralization is thus the underlying strategy for all UN agencies in India.

There are at least three important reasons why a focus on decentralization in India can provide only a partial account of local governance. This is because, decentralization is minimalist in its conception and deign. Second, the achievement of an adequately robust form of decentralization remains a project beset with many difficulties, both institutional as well as social and political. Finally, there are enormous regional variations in the way in which decentralization has been designed and implemented and a comparison of states show variations. Theoretically, the normative appeal of arguments for local democracy has resided in the belief that the quality of political participation will be substantially transformed only when people together to collectively debate and deliberate on issues of common concerns and are provided with decision making powers to give effect to their shared concerns. Local democracy thus, become a way of enabling both participation and deliberations. In India the imperative for decentralization was political rather than administrative, which may suggest why the administrative aspects have received less than attention.

The list of any programme of decentralization is arguably the actual powers and functions that are devolved to the institutions of local government and the authority they enjoy in the exercise of these. The function at and financial devolution to local bodies show a mis-match. The limited fiscal autonomy of local bodies renders them excessively dependent on the central and state governments.The planning process is similarly encumbered. The constitutional amendment had envisaged a multi tiered and participatory planning process. A District Planning Committee was supposed to be constituted in every district to draft the development plans for the district as a whole, but there are only seven states in which it has been constituted in all districts.

The purpose and design of decentralization in India was driven by two objectives, first, democratization through representation and voice for disadvantaged groups; and second effective, because of more participatory, development. There remain serious constraints on the realization and institutionalization of both these goals. Insufficient devolution of functions, excessive dependence on state and central governments, and the dominance of mainstream administrative departments and functions are among the factors contributing to the poor performance of the local self governments. Resource constraints exacerbate the dependence on state agencies and administrative structures. Elected members often behave like contractors, while the poor are excluded from political participation. There is pressure to distribute the funds equally between all members, who decide which schemes to implement and to which contractor the work shall be awarded.

Lack of transparency and accountability is among the many interrelated problems in the local bodies. There are multiple challenges to accountability in local government. Despite political decentralization, there is limited administrative decentralization often leading to an overwhelming presence in local governance. The role of the bureaucracy and elected members is an integrated one involving planning and implementation. The bureaucracy plays an advisory role in planning and has a major role in the implementation of development works. The representatives have a critical role in planning, but only a supervisory role in implementation. The lack of experience of the representatives has led to an excessive dependence of the representatives on the officials.

The devolution of administrative and financial powers from the state to the civic bodies and further down to ward committees has been widely considered as axiomatic to the promotion of good urban governance. The importance of participation and transparency has assured added significance in the light of a visible change in popular perception about how governance should be re-engineered. There is now growing belief that all administrative action should be people centered rather than rule centered outward looking rather than inward looking, inclusive rather than exclusive. One of the encouraging features of urban life is the rise of civil societies and NGO's and their urge to increasingly participate in affairs of their cities. NGO's can play a healthy role in cities by leading strength to the voice and demands of the less privileged. They are likely to participate in implementation of urban development projects and promoting participation of poor and serving their interests. Transparency in municipal governance requires fundamental change in access of information and e-governance. The development of an appropriate, transparence code of conduct for elected representation and management has also been recommend as a bench mark for public behaviour. Such code would set the guidelines on how city managers need to conduct themselves and what standards should expect of their city representatives and managers.

SUGGESTIONS

- Development of a common knowledge base and data inventory for decentralization which would pave the way for joint programming and convergence of various initiatives is imperative.
- Inter-linkage of gender and decentralization initiatives.
- Training programmes for women representatives in ULB's should be organized.

- Support for networks of woman in ULB's and community organizations is essential.
- Support to district planning through development of manuals, modules and workshops is called for.
- Linkage with State Finance Commission in effecting financial devolution is suggested.
- Linkage with NGO's and civil societies as development agents for effective decentralized governance is imperative.
- Development of data base and information system for decentralized planning and implementation is essential.
- Creating a legal institutional framework aimed at enabling the municipalities to function as institutions of self government and implement plans for economic development and social empowerment is imperative.
- Reforming budgeting accounting and auditing procedures is essential in order to promote accountability on the part of municipal officials and to decentralize budget management to operational levels.
- A transparent system of municipal accountability and disclose to the public and the higher levels of government through laws and regulations should be ensured.
- Thrust of urban development policy under the decentralized regime should be towards promoting balanced regional development. The states must ensure that the autonomy of the local bodies and their capacity to take up routine activities is achieved.
- Financial institutions like HUDCO must pursue their schemes to provide concessional funds for infrastructural investment in backward regions, particularly in small and medium towns and arrange substantial funds for infrastructure development.

- Efforts should be taken to constitute and function District Planning Committees and Metropolitan Planning Committees and coordinate their functioning with the existing parastatals.
- Our approach for devolution of funds to local bodies should comprise five cardinal principles or Panchtatva, abbreviated as PEACE. It stands for (i) political feasibility; (ii) equity; (iii) adequacy, (iv) computational transparency, and (v) efficiency.

REFERENCES

Agrawal, Amba, (2005), Fiscal Decentralization in India: An Inter-State Analysis of Panchayat Finances, Serials Publications, New Delhi.

Aziz, A. *et. al.*, (2002), Decentralized Governance and Planning: A Comparative Study in Three South Indian States, Macmillan Pub., New Delhi.

Bardhan, P., (2003), Decentralization of Governance and Development, *Journal of Economic Perspective*, Vol. 16 (4).

Bardhan, P., (1997), Decentralized Development, V.K. Ramaswami Memorial Lecture, Delhi School of Economics, New Delhi.

Basu, Amitava, Road Map for Municipal Reforms, in Good Urban Government Campaign India Launch Learning from one another, VNCHSC habitat, September 4-6, 2001, New Delhi.

Benett, R.J. (ed), (1990), Decentralization, Local Government and Markets: Towards a Post-Welfare Agenda, Clarendon Press, Oxford.

Benett, R.J.(ed), (1994), Local Government and Market Decentralization: Experiences in Industrial Developing and Former East Block Countries, United Nations University Press, Tokyo.

Bird, Richard and Vaillan Court, F., (1998), Fiscal Decentralization in Developing Countries, Cambridge University, Press, Cambridge.

Blair, Harry, (1995), Assessing Democratic Decentralization: A Centre for Development Information and Evaluation, Concept Paper, USIAD,Washington D.C.

Bohra, O.P., (1998), State Level Fiscal Relations in India, National Book Shop and Dolphin Publications, New Delhi.

Carvajal, E.P., (1995), Decentralization Democracy: The New Latin American Municipality, CEPAL, Review, Vol. Number, April.

Cheema, G.S. and Rondinelli (ed) (1983), Decentralization and Development: Policy Implementation in Developing Countries, Sage, Pub., CA.

Crook R. and James (1994), Manor Enhancing Participation and Institutional Performance: Democratic Decentralization in South Asia and West Africa, Overseas Development Administration, London.

Dekeshbury, J.M., (1991), Decentralization and Democratic Pluralism: The Role of Foreign Aid, USAID Washington D.C .

Dellinger, William, (1994), Decentralization and Its Implications for Urban Service Delivery, Urban Management Programme Discussion Paper 16, World Bank, Washington D.C..

Gibson, J. and P. Hamson, (1996), Decentralization and Change in Post Communist Systems in J. Gibson and P. Hawson (ed) Transformation from Below: Local Power and the Political Economy of Post Communist Transitions, Edward Edgar, Cheltenham.

Government of India, Report of the Eleventh Finance Commission, Government of India, June 2000.

Huntington, S.P., (1992), The Third Wave: Decentralization in the Late Twentieth Century, University of Oklahoma Press, London.

Jayal, Nirza Gopal et. al., (2007), Local Governance in India, Oxford University Press, New Delhi.

Jenkin, Rober, (1997), Democratic Adjustment: Explaining the Political Sustainability of Economic Reform in India, University of Sussex.

Jha, R.N. (2007), The Salience of Poverty, Participation, Transparency, and Security in Good Urban Governance in Local Governance in India by Jayal, N.G., et. al., OUP, New Delhi.

Jha, S.N. and Mathur, P.C., (1999), Decentralization and Local Politics, Sage Pub., New Delhi.

Karnik, A. et. al., (2007), Developing Quantitative Framework for Determining Devolution of Funds from the State Government to Local Bodies in Local Governance in India by (ed) Jayal, N.G. et. al., OUP, New Delhi .

Das, A.K. and Benjamen S., (1999), Implications of 74th C.A. on Urban Management and Planning in Three South India States: Karnataka, Kerala and Andhra Pradesh, September.

Manor, J., (1979), The Failure of Political Integration in Sri Lanka, *Journal of Commonwealth and Comparative Politics*, 17(1).

Manor, James, (ed), (1991), Rethinking Third World Politics, Longmans, London.

Manor, James, (1995), Capacity Development and the Ability to Change, SIDA, Stockholm, .

Manor, James, (1981), Party Decay and Political Crisis in India, The Washington Quarterly, Summer .

Mathur, M.P., (2006), Finances and Functioning of Urban Local Bodies: A Situation Report, India Infrastructure Report, OUP, New Delhi.

Mathur, O.P., (1999), Decentralization in India: A Report Card NIPFP, New Delhi.

Mathur, O.P., Decentralization in India: A Report Card, NIPEP, New Delhi, 1999.

Mawhood, P. (ed), (1993), Local Government in the Third World Experience of Decentralization in Tropical Africa, Africa Institute of South Africa.

Mehta, A., (1978), Report of Committee on Panchayati Raj Institutions, Government of India, New Delhi,

Meriss A. and Lowder S. (ed) (1992), Decentralization in Latin America, Praeger, New York.

Mishra, K., Issues in Devolution of Functions and Fiscal Powers to Municipalities, Paper Prepared for the Second National Meet of the State Finance Commission, March 6-7, 1995, NIPFP, New Delhi.

NIUA, (1998), A Compendium of Municipal Legislation in Conformity With Constitution (74th) Amendment Act, 1992, NIUA, New Delhi.

Parker, Andrew, (1995), Decentralization: The Way Forward for Rural Development, Policy and Research Working Paper, Washington D.C., World Bank.

Pinto, M.R., (2007), People-Centered Development and Participatory Urban Governance: The Mumbai Experience, in Local Governance in India by (ed) Jayal N.G. et. al., OUP, New Delhi.

Prud Homme, Retry, (1995), The Dangers of Decentralization, The World Bank Research Observer, 10 (August).

Pulnam, R. et. al., (1993), Making Democracy Work, Princeton University Press, Princeton.

Riggs, F.W. (1963), Bureaucrats and Political Development: A Paradoxical View, in La Palombara (ed), Bureaucracy and Political Development, Princeton University Press, Princeton .

Robinson, M., (1988), Local Politics: The Law of the Fishes, Oxford University Press, Oxford .

Rondinelli, D., (1981), Government Decentralization in Comparative Perspective: Theory and Practice in Developing Countries, International Review of Administrative Science, .

Singh, Amita, (2007), Accountability in Local Governance: Infrastructure Development in the Industrial Townships of Faridabad and Gurgaon in Local Governance in India by (ed) Jayal, N.G., *et. al.*, OUP, New Delhi.

Singh, K., (2000), Trends in Decentralization and Urban Governance, Paper Presented at the Seminar on Emerging Perspectives on Urban Governance, Institute for Human Development, New Delhi.

Singh, Kulwant, (2001), Urban Governance in India: Trends and Issues in Decentralization, in Good Urban Governance Compaign-India Launch Learning from one another, UNCHS (Habitat), New Delhi, September 4-6 .

Smith, B., (1985), Decentralization: The Theoretical Dimension of the State, George Allen and Unwind, London.

Vijayalakshmi, V., (2007), Transparency, Accountability, and Governance: Local Governance in Kerala and Karnataka in Local Governance in India by Jayal, N.G. *et. al.*, OUP, New Delhi.

World Bank, Devolution of Resources to Local Bodies, its Occasional Paper Series, 21, World Bank, New Delhi, 1998.

World Bank, Fiscal Decentralization to Rural Governments in India, World Bank, OUP, New Delhi, 2004.

World Bank, India Urban Sector Strategy, Urban and Infrastructure Unit, South Asia, Regional Office, World Bank, New Delhi, 2002.

World Bank, India Synthesis Study of Public Financial Management and Accountability in Urban Local Bodies, Financial Management Unit, World Bank, New Delhi, March, 2007.

Zhand, Y., China: (1995), Democratization or Recentralization, The Pacific Review.

Zieton, G.K., (1996), Development, Devolution and Democracy: Village Discourse in West Bengal, Sage Pub., New Delhi .

3

INFRASTRUCTURE DEVELOPMENT

Infrastructure development has a key role in economic growth and development of the region. Progress in creating new infrastructure has been slow while demand for infrastructure services is burgeoning. As society changes the demand for infrastructure also changes. As society progress, the process of economic development and resulting urbanization get momentum which in turn creates demand for urban services and infrastructure facilities. The gap between demand and supply of essential urban services and infrastructure deteriorates the physical environment and quality of life in urban areas. The process of urbanization has created a huge gap between demand and supply of urban services and infrastructure. The pressure on infrastructure due to the existing demand is directly linked with the consumption pattern of the people. The escalating demand for basic services in urban centres is resulting in a serious deterioration of service quality across housing, transport, health care, power, water supply, sanitation and education. The benign neglect of urban sprawls by civic authorities has led cities to be vulnerable to natural disasters.

The Ninth Plan Working Group on Housing has estimated the investment requirement for housing in urban areas at Rs. 52,600 crores. The India Infrastructure Report estimated the annual investment need for urban water supply, sanitation and roads at about Rs. 28035 crores for the next ten years. The

Central Public Health Engineering has estimated the requirement of funds for 100 per cent coverage of urban population under safe water supply and sanitation services by the year 2021 at Rs. 172.905 crores. Estimates by Rail India Technical and Economic Services indicates that the amount required for urban transport infrastructure investment in cities with population 100,000 or more during the next 20 years would be of the order of Rs. 207000 crore. Such a big quantum of highest investment for supply of urban infrastructure cannot be allocated within the budgetary resources of the Central and State Government. Therefore, private sector participation is being envisaged. The government of India has merged all its urban improvement schemes into three schemes viz. (i) Jawaharlal Nehru National Urban Renewal Mission (JNNURM); (ii) Urban Infrastructure Development Scheme for Small and Medium Towns (UIDSSMT), (iii) Integrated Housing and Slum Development Programme (IHSDP). While JNNURM deals with 63 selected cities, the other two schemes cover the remaining urban local bodies.

The Jawaharlal Nehru National Urban Renewal Mission - a centrally sponsored scheme - covering seven mega cities, 28 million plus cities and 28 other identified important urban centres, was launched by the government in December, 2005. The JNNURM has two submissions namely (i) Urban Infrastructure and Governance under the Ministry of Urban Development, (ii) Basic services for urban poor, implemented by Ministry of Urban Employment and Poverty Alleviation.

A key assumption in designing the scheme is that urban infrastructure should be financially self sustaining. The JNNURM has the following features:

- Ensure that cities generate outcome oriented pro-poor plans through participatory processes.
- Pool all relevant programmes/schemes into a centralized Mission Fund.
- Secure effective linkages between asset creation and asset management so that the infrastructure services created in the cities are not only maintained efficiently but also become self sustaining over the time.

- Development of the cities is well planned including peri-urban areas, outgrowths, urban corridors, so that urbanization takes place in a dispersed manner.
- Water supply, sanitation, sewerage, solid waste management, hospital waste management, etc. are priority areas of development.
- Construction of working women hostels, marriage halls, old age and destitute children's home, night shelters with community toilets.
- Reforms oriented vision based implementation of infrastructure projects.
- Strengthening urban local bodies through reforms and resource mobilization.

In order to be eligible for assistance, respective ULB's and state governments have to undertake a set of mandatory reforms. In case of ULBs such reforms include full (O&M) cost recovery over 5 years, accrual accounting, e-governance, pro-poor budgeting. Similarly, mandatory reforms for states include repeal of Urban Land Ceiling and Regulation Act, reform of Land Control Laws, independent regulators for urban services etc. In addition, status and ULB's are required to implement any five optional reforms, such as VRS, by laws for rain water harvesting and computerization of land title system, in the first year. Each assistance seeking ULB would also be required to prepare a City Development Plan, based on a Rapid City Assessment. The Assessment is expected to help the ULB to (a) develop a vision for its city; (b) ascertain gap between infrastructure and investments and (e) set out priorities, sequencing and time lines for undertaking various reforms and investments. While preparing its CDP, the ULB is expected to pay particular attention to three key aspects, namely, delivery of services, governance, and financing, and identify investment projects for assistance under the Mission.

In view of the problems faced by urban local government bodies, the Rural-Urban Relationship Committee was set up by Government of India in 1963, which pointed out that local governments should not merely remain instruments of political education and civic conscience but should play a role in the promotion of social and economic development of local communities as well as be an integral part of the national government Committee also made significant recommendations on the criteria's for constitution of municipal bodies with clear delineation of powers, functions, and resources. However, until recently, urban local governments were weak and powerless. The 74th Constitution Amendment Act, 1992 proposed to form a uniform structure of Municipal Corporations, Municipal Councils, and Nagar Panchayats. The Constitutional Amendment Act seeks to introduce fundamental changes in urban local bodies. Its salient features are:

(1) Introduction of the Twelfth Schedule which lists the functions of the urban local bodies, covering planning, regulation and developmental aspects.

(2) Establishment of District and Metropolitan Planning responsible for the election of representatives for the preparation of development plans at district and metropolitan levels.

(3) Holding of periodic and timely elections in ULB's with specification by law of powers and responsibilities.

(4) Specifying by law the sources of municipal finance and their periodic review by a statutorily constituted SFC and by making it obligatory on the part of Central Finance Commission to recommend increases needed to augment state resources to assist the municipal governance.

(5) Restrictions or the power of state governments to do away with democratically elected municipal governments, and reservation of the third seats for woman and weaker sections in municipal bodies.

At the dawn of independence the government of India was faced with the challenge of rehabilitating the trans border migration due to partition. The first few plans had a strong housing focus and significant resources were allocated for the purpose. In the First Five Year Plan (1951-56), the emphasis was on construction of houses for government employees and weaker sections. The Ministry of Works and Housing was constituted and National Building Organization and Town and Country Planning Organization were set up at the central level. The scope for housing programme for the poor was expanded in the Second Plan (1956-61). Slum clearance and sweepers housing schemes were introduced. Town and Country Planning legislation was enacted in many states and necessary organizations were set up for preparation of Master Plans for important towns. Third Plan (1961-66) emphasized on coordination of efforts to concerned agencies and targeting of programmes to the needs of low income groups. The Fourth Plan (1969-74) stressed the need for decongestion or dispersal of population to prevent further crowding in large cities. This was to be achieved by creation of smaller towns and planning the spatial location of economic activity. The Fifth Plan (1974-79) reiterated the policies of proceeding plans to promote smaller towns as new urban centres in order to ease the pressure of increasing population migration. The thrust of the planning in the Sixth Plan (1980-85) was on integrated provision of services.

Along with shelter, particularly for the poor, centrally sponsored scheme called Integrated Development of Small and Medium Towns (IDSMT) was launched in towns with population below one lakh population for provision of roads, pavements, minor civic works, bus stands, markets, shopping complexes etc. The Seventh Plan (1985-90) stressed on the need to entrust the major responsibility of housing construction on the private sector. National Building Organization was reconstructed and a new organization called BMTPC was set-up for promoting commercial production of innovative building materials. The Plan recognized the problems of the urban poor and for the first time an urban poverty alleviation scheme was launched known as the Urban Basic Services for the Poor. The Eighth Plan (192-97) aimed at increased funding to existing urban services delivery institutions to meet the enormous backlog in terms of service delivery capacity. The Ninth Plan (1998-2002) identified the key urban concern of growing gap between demand and supply of basic services. The scheme-wise outlay of the Ministry is shown in Table - 1. The Tenth Five Year Plan made a provision of Rs. 7,000 crores for development in urban areas while under JNNURM Rs. 50,000 crores have been earmarked for the period of seven years.

The coverage of Central assistance in the past has been uneven and inadequate. The achievements of the infrastructure development schemes in the Ninth Plan were as follows:

AUWSP: Initiated in 1993-94, 575 schemes sanctioned with Central release of Rs. 265.57 crores.

Table 1
Scheme-wise Outlays of Ministry of Urban Development during 10th Plan (2002-07)

Scheme	*10th Plan Outlays*	*First 3 years of Plan Expenditure (2002-3 to 2004-05)*	
Urban Development		*Amount*	*Utilization*
IDSMT	1304.65	394.57	30.24
Mega City	1050.0	536.59	51.10
NCR Planning Board	350.0	162.0	46.29
Mission Mode on IT	0.0	5.00	–
Urban Mapping	20.0	–	–
Research in Urban & Regional Planning	15.0	1.93	12.87
Urban Transport	736.0	384.45	52.23
Water Supply & Sanitation			
Extension of AVWSP to Small Towns	900.0	408.24	45.36
Low Cost Sanitation	200.0	–	–
Solid Waste Management	99.4	40.99	41.26
Training in PHE	10.0	3.96	39.60
Equity to HUDCO for Water Supply	100.0	30.0	30.0
Public Works	595.0	30.0	30.0
New Schemes			
National Urban Information System	20.0	6.05	30.25
Pooled Finance Development Fund	400.0	10.0	2.50
City Challenge Fund	500.0	10.00	2.0
NE Lumpsum Provision	700.0	281.64	40.23
Grand Total	7000.00	6087.73	86.97

Source: Planning Commission, Government of India.

IDSMT: 1058 towns assisted since inception (1979-80) and Rs. 44.94 crores of central assistance released.

Mega City Scheme: The scheme initiated in 1993-94 is limited to the cities of Mumbai, Kolkata, Chennai, Hyderabad and Bangalore. Central assistance released was Rs. 578.01 crores

NCR Plan: Till March, 2001, Rs. 360.92 were released as central contribution.

Urban Infrastructure Development scheme for Small and Medium Towns (UIDSSMT) has been launched by central government which subsumes the existing schemes of IDSMT and AUWSP. The schemes aim at improving infrastructural facilities and helping to create durable public assets and quality oriented services in cities and towns. It also envisages enhancing public private partnership in infrastructure development. The duration of the scheme is for seven years from 2005-06. The schemes are applied in all the cities and towns except the cities covered under JNNURM. The scheme covers the following components:

(1) Urban renewal of inner city
(2) Water supply and sanitation
(3) Sewerage and solid waste management
(4) Communication improvement of drains/storm water drains
(5) Construction/upgradation of roads, high ways/express ways
(6) Parking lots/spaces on public private partnership basis
(7) Development of heritage areas
(8) Prevention and rehabilitation of soil erosion/landslides
(9) Preservation of water bodies.

The main thrust of the schemes to ensure improvement in urban governance so that ULBs and parastatal agencies become financially sound with enhanced credit rating and ability to access market capital for undertaking new programmes and expansion of services. The scheme equally emphasizes on implementing reforms in the local bodies and concerned states.

The scheme is expected to achieve the following outcomes:

(1) Modern and transparent budgeting, accounting, financial management systems designed and adopted for all the urban services and governance functions.
(2) City-wise framework for planning and governance.
(3) Energy access to basic urban services to all the residents
(4) Financially self sustaining agencies for urban governance and service delivery
(5) Transparence and accountable governance
(6) Introduction of e-governance in core-functions of ULBs.

Integrated Housing and Slum Development Programme aims at combining the existing schemes of VAMBAY and NSDP under the new IHSDP scheme for having an integrated approach in ameliorating the coordination of the urban slum dwellers that do not possess adequate shelter and reside in dilapidated conditions. The scheme is applicable to all the cities and towns expect the cities and towns covered under JNNURM. The scheme seeks to enhance public and private investments in housing and infrastructural development in urban areas. The components for assistance under the scheme include all slum improvement/up-gradation/relocation projects including up-gradation/new construction of houses and infrastructural facilities like water supply and sewerage, community toilets, community centres etc. The main thrust of the revised strategy is to ensure strengthening of local bodies to maintain and sustain the services and infrastructure created. Thus, the scheme is reforms oriented and highlights on augmenting the role of private sector and community based organizations in infrastructure development and improving the living standards of urban slum dwellers.

Privatization, partnership arrangements and community based projects have emerged as the major options for undertaking investments in infrastructure and amenities. The changed perspective and the decline in the pubiic investment likely to accentuate the disparity in the levels of basis amenities across the states and local bodies. Thus, efforts are being made to develop the capital market so that the parastatal and local agencies can mobilize resources by issuing bonds and credit instruments. Moreover, public-private partnership is viable option for development and management of infrastructural projects is being encouraged and promoted by urban local governments in different corners of the country.

PROFILE OF LUCKNOW CITY

Lucknow, being the capital of Uttar Pradesh, the most populous state of India, has several unique characteristics. The city is known as cultural heritage city. It is situated as the bank of river Gomti. The more densely populated areas of the city are on the southern bank of the river and several planned residential colonies have been developed to the north of the river.

The city is one of the oldest Indian cities with its unparalled composition of culture and historical buildings. The city was developed by the Shaikhs, Pathans, Nawabs and Mughals around the mosque and the shrine of Peer Mohammad Shah over a 'teela' located near the present CSM Medical University. The origin of the name Lucknow is not definitely traceable, and whatever traditions are available, are of extremely doubtful historical authencity. There were a number of stories regarding the historical development of the city. According to Ain-e-Akbari, a general of Mohammad Ghazanavi Syed Salar Masud came with his followers between 1031-1033 AD and his forces also settled at Bijnor Pargana about 10 km. south of Lucknow. The new comers were called Shaikhzadas and they built a stronghold which was called Quila Khana or the site of Teela Kothi Maszid and shrine where only a village of Ahirs had existed. The Quila and the town was named after an Ahir called Lakhna and with passage of time, the town came to be associated with its present name. The other story is related to the well known Hindu Scripture - Ramayan. According to which the town had been named after

Lord Ram's brother Lakshman. Traditions assert that it was originally allied Lakshmanpur after Lakshman. The Lakshman teela an artificial mound within the Macchi Bhawan area is said to be the site of the fort. Lakshman built for the defence of his capital. This teela later on became a place of reputed sanctity around which those existed a regular habitation. Some European authorities date the fort to about 5000 BC, thus claiming Lucknow to be of greater antiquity than Indraprastha. Till 1850 was the golden period when apart from unparallel construction and gardens, the city was recognized for its inherent cultural richness. After 1857, the traditional culture and glory of the city was shattered by the British rulers. Yet Lucknow remained an important seat for administration.

Former capital of United Province of Oudh and present seat of State Government of Uttar Pradesh, the Lucknow city is situated in between 26°52' North and 80°56' East on the banks of river Gomti. It is junction of Northern and North Eastern Railways. It was the largest city in the United Province of Oudh and the fourth largest in the British India. Lucknow is almost on a level plain with a few distinguished features. The climate of city is a mean between that of the cooler sub monstrance districts and the dry hot tracts south and west of it. The city has a humid subtropical climate with a cool dry winter from December to February and a hot summer from April to June. The city receives about 100 cm of annual rainfall mostly from the south west monsoons between July and September.

The city has expanded gradually. The geographical area of the city in 1951 was reported just 48 sq. km. which has increased to 310 sq. km. in 2001. However, it is expected that city will be further expanded upto 500 km^2 in the coming years, if the increasing population is to be accommodated (Table 2).

Table 2
Expansion of Urban Areas in Lucknow

Year	*Area (km^2)*	*Population (lakh)*
1951	48	4.4
1981	118	9.2
1991	310	16.69
2001	310	22.07

Source: Census Reports

Table 3
Expansion of Municipal Corporation Area in Lucknow

(Sq. km)

Particular	1961	1971	1981	1991	2001
Urban Agglomeration	135.43	127.66	145.94	337.50	-
Municipal Corporation	103.60	95.83	114.11	310.10	310.0

Source: Census Report.

Expansion of Municipal Corporation area in Lucknow is shown in Table 3. Most of the geographical areas fall within the boundary of corporation area. The geographical area has increased about 3 fold during 1961 and 2001.

Lucknow Urban Agglomeration became a million plus city in 1981. Besides the Lucknow cantonment, Census, 2001 reported the population of the Lucknow Agglomeration to be 22.67 lakh. This is included an estimated population of about 60,000 of Lucknow cantonment and 22.07 lakh population of Lucknow city (Table 4).

Table 4
Population of Urban Agglomeration in Lucknow

Decade	*Population of Municipal Corporation*	*Population of Urban Agglomeration*	*Rate of Growth*
1901	256239	256239	-
1991	252114	252114	-1.60
1922	240566	240566	-4.80
1931	251097	274659	14,17
1941	354560	381777	39.00
1951	444711	496861	30.14
1961	595640	655673	31.96
1971	749239	813982	24.14
1981	916254	1007604	23.78
1991	1619000	1669204	65.66
2001	2207340	2266933	135.80

Source: Census Reports, Government of India

The urban population growth during 1991-2001 was reported 35.80 per cent while it was recorded as high as 65.66 per cent in 1981-1991 decade. The Master Plan: 2021 of Lucknow city has projected urban population to be 3.23 million in 2011 and 4.50 million in 2021. The estimated population of the Lucknow Municipal Corporation would be 3.17 million and 4.44 million in 2011 and 2021, respectively. The decadal growth of population is liekly to be about 40 per cent (Table 5).

Table 5
Projected Population of Lucknow City

Particulars	*1981*	*1991*	*2001*	*2011**	*2021**
Lucknow Urban Agglomeration					
Population	1007604	1669204	2245509	3226000	4500000
Decadal Growth	23.79	65.66	34.53	43.66	39.49
Lucknow Municipal Corporation					
Population	947990	1619116	2185927	3166000	4440000
Decadal Growth	22.38	70.79	35.00	44.84	40.24
Lucknow Cantonment					

Source: Master Plan 2021,
*Projected figures.

Migration into city accounts for 36 per cent increase in population over the last decade. Thus, natural increase in population accounted for 64 per cent. Of the total migrants, 56.6 per cent persons were from rural areas. The main reasons of migration are related with economic factors such as employment and business. The city comprises of people practicing various religions. Besides Hindu and Muslims, the city has Buddhists, Christians, Jains, Sikhs and others. About one third population in Municipal Corporation area belonged to the Muslim community. About 10 per cent population of the city comprises of scheduled castes and tribes. The sex ratio, as per 2001 census was reported to be adverse since 893 women against 1000 males were reported, though number of women against 1000 men has risen from 829 in 1971 to 862 in 1991 and to 893 in 2001. The population density of the city is gradually increasing while 67 per cent were found living in a hectare in the city in 2001.

Based on the definition, estimates of slum population vary. The Census, 2001 originally did not report any slums and then later revised its findings. DUDA follows the dfinition as stated in U.P. Slum Areas Act, 1962. SUDA/UNCHS do not follow this definition but define poverty in terms of vulnerability as does OXFAM. Thus, the estimates of slum population of Lucknow city vary significantly. (Table 6)

Table 6
Slum Population of Lucknow City

(lakhs)

Particular	*1971*	*1981*		*1991*	*2001*		
	Slum Population	*Total Population*	*Slum Population*	*Total Population*	*Slum Population*	*Total Population*	*Slum Population*
Census	2.33	9.47	2.85	16.19	6.97	21.85	1.79
Master Plan 2021	–	9.47	2.85	16.19	6.97	21.85	1.79
DUDA (2005)						21.85	6.70
OXFAM (2005)						21.85	10.18
SUDA						21.85	11.00
UNCHS (2000)							

Source: Feedback Ventures, 2006

SUDA/UNCHS reported slum population to be 1.1 million while census reported just 0.18 million in 2001. DUDA (2005) in its survey found that 0.67 million people are slum dwellers in the city. It is estimated that more than one fourth of urban population is living in slums. The slum population of the city has increased from 1.86 lakh in 1979 to 6.53 lakhs in 2001-02 while it further increased to 6.70 lakh in 2005. (Table 7).

Table 7
Growth of Slum Population in Lucknow

(Lakh)

Year	*Total Urban Population*	*Slum Population*	*Percentage of Slum Population*
1979	–	1.86	–
1981	10.07	2.85	28.30
1990	13.2	3.94	29.84
1994	–	2.76	–
1997-98	–	6.53	–
2001-02	22.67	6.18	27.26

Source: District Urban Development Authority, Lucknow.

Zone wise slum population of Lucknow is shown in Table 8. There were 531 slum pockets scattered in 98 wards of the city.

Table 8
Zone-wise Slum Population of Lucknow

Zone	*No. of Slum Pockets*	*No. of Wards*	*Total Population*
I	144	26	129658
II	177	38	275560
III	210	34	212873
Total	531	98	618091

Source: District of Urban Development Authority, Lucknow.

There are a number of educational institutions in the city. Since 1991, there has been massive growth of professional institutions. Some of these include Jaipuria Institute of Management, Institute of Integral Technology (now University), Sherwood Institute of Management and Technology, CSM Medical University, K.G. Dental University, Babu Banarsi Das Institute of Engineering and Technology, Amity University, etc. Even the number of degree colleges has increased from 20 in 1991 to about 35 in 2006 (Table 9).

Table 9
Educational Institutes of Lucknow City

Particular	*1981*		*1991*		*2001 (District)*
	IA	*MC*	*UA*	*MC*	
Primary School	806	792	966	960	–
Jr. Basic Schools	101	99	169	165	1329
Senior Basic Schools					242
Higher Secondary	107	105	200	190	321
Polytechnic	5	5	5	5	–
Management and Engineering College	–	–	1	1	32
Degree Colleges	20	20	20	20	35
Universities	1	1	1	1	6

Source: Municipal Corporation, Lucknow.

The district is also well covered by the network of health and medical institutions. Recently, Trauma Centre has been established in CSM Medical University to provide trauma health and medical care to the road accidents victims. Moreover, Sahara, Mayo and other private sector managed health centres are providing health and medical care services. This has attracted migration of rural people as well. (Table 10).

Table 10
Health Centres in Lucknow

Health Centre	*Number*
Medical Institutions (Allopathic Medical)	144
Community Health Centers/PHC'S	54
Ayurvedic/Unani Hospitals	3
Homeopathic Hospitals	42

Source: Uttaranchal and U.P. At a Glance, 2005 Jagaran Research Centre, Kanpur

Literacy is an important social indicator of human development. As per 2001 census, 68.6 per cent population of the city is literate. The literacy rate has increased significantly from 50.90 per cent in 1971 to 68.62 in 2001 (Table 11).

Table 11
Literacy Rates in Municipal Corporation of Lucknow

Year	*Total Population ('000)*		*Literacy Rate*		*Urban*
	U.A.	*M.C.*	*U.A.*	*M.C.*	
1971	813.98 (368.71)	749.24 (339.64)	51.04	50.90	N.A.
1981	1007.60 (457.50)	916.95 (421.05)	57.04 (49.28)	56.81 (49.10)	45.88 (35.43)
1991	1669.20 (776.90)	1619.12 (751.71)	60.27 (53.42)	60.35 (53.41)	48.68 (40.72)
2001	2266.93	2207.34	68.78	68.62 (62.82)	70.61

Source: Census, 2001

The major industries in the Lucknow include aeronautics machine tools, distillery, chemicals furniture and chikan embroidery. Lucknow has traditionally been associated with chikan embroidery work on readymade garments, sarees etc. with most units being small scale and household based and located in old city and adjoining villages/towns of the district.

The market size of the chikan craft is estimated to be about Rs. 250 crores annually with the annual growth of 15-20 per cent. More than 6 lakh woman, children and others are engaged in this craft for their sustenance. Lucknow is also a major centre for research and development. The prominent institutions including CDRI, NBRI, CIMAP, ITRC, NHDC, RDSO, Birbal Shahni Institute of Palaeo Botany, IIM, SGPGIMS, Central BR Ambedkar Central University, CSM Medical University, etc.

The work participation ratio has been reported to be significantly high in Lucknow since more than one fourth population is working (27.51 per cent). This includes only main workers while marginal workers also account a large number. The working population is likely to increase in the coming decade (Table 12). Again, majority of the main workers are engaged in tertiary sector i.e. services sector for employment (79.93 per cent). Only 18 per cent workers were found engaged in industry sector. The contribution of agriculture sector in employment is likely to decrease in the coming years (Table 13). About 27 per cent workers were found graduates and above while one fourth workers were matriculation but below graduation.

Table 12
Working and Non-working Population of Lucknow City

Categories	*1981*	*1991*	*2001*	*2011*	*2021*
Working	279295	442450	617664	919410	1350000
	(27.71)	(26.51)	(27.51)	(28.5)	(30.00)
Non-Working	728705	1336754	1627845	2306590	3150000
	(72.29)	(73.49)	(72.49)	(71.5)	(70.00)
Population	1008000	1669204	2245509	3226000	4500000
	(100.00)	(100.00)	(100.00)	(100.00)	(100.00)

Source: Master Plan: 2021

Table 13
Working Population by Major Occupation Categories

Particular	*1981*	*1991*	*2001*	*2011*	*2021*
Primary	8706	32208	12783	9194	6750
	(3.12)	(7.28)	(2.07)	(1.0)	(0.50
Secondary	54474	93632	111180	174687	270000
	(19.50)	(21.16)	(18.00)	(19.0)	(20.0)

Contd...

Particular	*1981*	*1991*	*2001*	*2011*	*2021*
Tertiary	216115 (77.38)	316610 (71.56)	493701 (79.93)	735524 (80.0)	1073250 (79.5)
Total	279295 (100.00)	442450 (100.00)	617664 (100.00)	919410 (100.00)	1350000 (100.00)

Source: Master Plan: 2021

The current land use is shown in Table 14. About 67.2 per cent land is under residential purposes. The residential land use has grown dramatically in comparison to all other issues, although there has also been notable growth in commercial, industrial and public service land use. With the radial growth of the city, the cantonment has gradually been engulfed and is today more centrally located while the illegal land-use in the city has caused problems in development and maintenance of urban services (Table 15).

Table 14
Land Use Plan in Lucknow

Type of Activities	*Land Proposed in 1970 Master Plan (Hectares)*	*Percentage*	*Proposed Land Plan in 2001 (Hectares)*	*Percentage*
Residential	7105.7	48.73	159238	67.2
Commercial	377.4	2.58	936.2	3.9
Residential-cum-Commercial	–	–	47.0	0.2
Govt. or Semi Govt. Officers	160.6	1.10	378.5	1.7
Industrial	1514.5	10.39	731.0	3.1
Recreational (Parks, Play grounds, gardens)	1630,00	11,17	1868,5	7,9
Community Facilities	901.1	6.19	1537.0	6.5
Traffic and Transportation	2891.4	19.04	2260.0	9.5
Total	14580.7	100.00	23682	100.00

Source: Town & Country Planning Organization, Lucknow.

In absence of adequate measures taken to protect the environment, urban development and expansion has resulted in steady deterioration of the city's environment and ecology.

Even the dumping of untreated sewerage and uncollected wastes in - to river and water bodies has caused concern vehicular emissions are also causing air pollution in the city. The vehicular density has rapidly risen and has caused traffic congestion and road fatalities.

Table 15
Illegal Land use in Lucknow City

Land Use	*Hectare Land*
Residential	34.66
Commercial	54.89
Transportation	148.06
Parks-open space	192.58
Agriculture	642.09

Source: Dainik Jagaran, Lucknow April 8, 2003

The declining of ground water has also caused concern since surface water quality has already deteriorated. It is difficult to provide water supply though deep tube wells in the near future since the water table is gradually declining. There is already a huge deficit of water during summer. Importantly, the cultural city is losing its glamour since proper maintenance and conservation of heritage sites are not ensured. The water bodies (tanks, ponds, kunds, talab, jheels etc.) are in very poor shape. Some of these have already deserted. Thus, sustainable development of city is called for.

The above analysis simply demonstrates that urbanization has led the growth of business and employment opportunities in the city. This has caused growth of slums and deterioration of the quality of life in the city as there is stress on physical and social infrastructure. The unchecked migration of people from rural areas has increased the problems of municipal governance. Thus, the city needs huge investment for developing infrastructure and delivering services to urban dwellers.

Urban settlement is a part of the settlement fabric. It is treated as an organic whole with a distinction in build and structure etc. The urban activities are expressed in physical forms. Thus, the study of form or morphology of urban settlement is very important. The physical structure of the urban settlement is represented by the mode of arrangement of buildings and streets. Towns vary widely in their forms. They reflect the physical and cultural factors of the site and situation. Physical factors are not so important in determining the forms of town, as all towns are located along the rivers, sea or water bodies. Consequently, the cultural factors, such as forts, old market place, roads, railway stations and administrative offices are more important in determining the form of the towns. Lucknow is situated at the bank of river Gomati. The main markets are located in old city - Aminabad, Chowk, Kaiserbagh, while modern market centres have evolved in new areas such as Hazratganj, Kapoorthala, Gomati Nagar, Alambagh, Aliganj, Indira Nagar etc. The food grain markets are located in Mohillapur and Gosainganj while fruits and vegible markets are centred at Balaganj, Kaisherbagh, and Jankipuram.

Lucknow, the capital of state is second highly populated city of the state after Kanpur. Till the advant of railways, the Gomati river served as an important Channel of transportation. The city of Lucknow is favourably located in the heart of Gangetic Plain thus connecting the city by various trade routs from all directions. Lucknow has been a flourishing city of the state since 1775, when Asaf-Udaulla made it the capital of Oudh. From 1775 till 1856 it remained the capital city. Again, in 1922 it became the capital of United Provinces of Agra and Oudh. Even now it is the seat of state of Uttar Pradesh. The landscape of city is well marked with huge paratial buildings and parks. The architcture of the old city buildings is typically Muslim. Other structures in the various parts of the city are of the representatives of different parties. The Imambaras, Bhool Bhulaiya, Chhattar Manzil, Kaiserbagh, Baradari, Shah Najaf etc. represent the Muslim architecture. The Council House, Raj Bhawan, Secretariat, Charbagh Railway Station, General Post Office, etc are the products of the British period. Although, Lucknow is called the city of Gardens, it also carries the burden of dirt, congested areas, ill planned residences, narrow streets and blink álleys in its western part. The increasing population of the city has changed the urban morphology of the city. Even the non-regulation of housing construction and non-engineered buildings have increased the housing density in vulnerable areas.

Urban local bodies have a crucial role to play in urban development and managing the local affairs. The over increasing urban population and rapid growth of urbanization have put tremendous pressure on urban local bodies for the provision of urban civic services. They have to provide and maintain basic infrastructure for civic services like sanitation, health, drainage, drinking water, sewerage, lighting etc. and the related supplementary services. The present state of urban services is over stretched and there are very large gaps between the demand for the services and the supply situation.

The Uttar Pradesh Municipalities Act, 1916 and the U.P. Municipal Corporation Act, 1959 has already assigned the function of water supply to the local bodies as a prime function. The 74th Constitutional Amendment Act in addition, makes provision for water supply for domestic, industrial and commercial purposes as legitimate duty of the local bodies. Out of 628 local bodies in U.P., 610 urban local bodies have been provided with piped water supply in their municipal limits. The situation of water supply in many of the towns is erratic. The water supply scenario is quite grim so far as the provision of adequate infrastructure for water supply is concerned.

Piped water supply was first commissioned in Lucknow Town in 1895 with the construction of one in take works at Gaughat on river Gomati. Raw water from Gomati was pumped and supplied through Aishbagh water works in CIS Gomati area. Presently city has been divided into various zones for water supply. With the support from World Bank, state government improved water supply infrastructure in the city. Water supply network extends over most of the core city and perpherial areas but it does not meet the consumer demand. The U.P. Jal Nigam estimated that about half of the produced water is lost due to leakages and pilferage. As there is no watering of water supply, it is difficult to estimate the wastage of water. Surface water is the main source of water supply to the city. However, available discharge in the river Gomati is around 500 mld in lean period. The city has around 407 tube wells which produce about 190 mld of water. The average depth of tube wells installed is about 350-400 meters, but since the strata is over exploited, the yield is likely to decrease. The hand pumps are in use for water supply in slums, however, in almost all the parks, such pumps are installed to facilitate dwellers in access to drinking water. The demand of drinking water is estimated to be 468 mld which is likely to increase upto 546 mld in 2011 and 766 mld in 2021 (Table 16).

Table 16
Water Production in Lucknow City

Particular	*No./Capacity*
River Water	
200 mld from Aishbagh water works	240 mld capacity
70 mld from 2nd water works	90 mld capacity
Total 270 mld	330 mld capacity
Ground Water	
190 mld from 407 tube wells	15 mld from 6150 hand pumps
Total 205 mld	
Water Demand in mld	
2006	468
2011	546
2021	766

Source: Lucknow Jal Sansthan

The present status of sewerage and sanitation in urban areas of the state are grossly inadequate. As a matter of fact no town in the state at present has been able to ensure sewerage facilities for all the houses. Even the largest Municipal Corporations have a huge backlog both in terms of percentage and absolute figures. Status of sewerage presents a very dismal picture of the population covered by the sewerage in U.P. More than half of the population in Nagar Panchayats is not covered under proper municipal sewerage system. There are only 55 towns in the state which have partial sewer system and this is also crippling down under tremendous population pressure.

Out of 55 towns/cities which have some form of sewer system, only 5 towns/cities situated on the bank of river Ganga have sewerage treatment plants commenced under Ganga Action Plan. Under the Yamuna Action Plan, sewerage treatment plants in 6 towns have been completed.

The sewerage system in Lucknow was first provided in 1918. In 1948-49 a comprehensive drainage scheme for the city was prepared to cater the demand. The works under the scheme were completed in 1955. The flood of 1960-61 damaged the sewerage systems of the city. In 1987-88 another sewerage Master Plan was prepared. The present installed sewerage capacity is about 303 mld only (Table 17).

Table 17
Installed Capacity of Sewerage Pumping Stations in Lucknow City

Pumping Station	*Capacity (mld)*
CIS-Gomati Sewerage	250
Pumping Station	4
Trans Gomati Sewerage Station	40
Mahanagar Intermediate Pumping Station	7
Daliganj Intermediate Pumping Station	40
Paper Mill Sub-Pumping Station	3
Total	303

Source: U.P. Jal Nigam

The existing network of sewerage is categorised into (1) CIS-Gomati Trunk Sewer, (II) Trans Gomati Trunk Sewer; (III) the Eastern Inter-Capacity Sewer. The sewer network extends across the main city areas on the CIS-Gomati side as well as newly developed colonies on the CIS-Gomati and trans Gomati sides. However, only 45 per cent of house-holds in the core areas of tne city and 35 per cent of households in the peripheral areas were connected to the network. There are a large number of service latrines in the city area. These service latrines discharge into nearby open drains. About 82 thousand households are connected to the sewer network. While a significant number of septic tanks with overflowing leach-pits usually discharge into roadside drains. The city has about 135 operational community toilet complexes, mainly in the slums.

The city dis charge about 356 mld waste water while only 42 mld waste water is treated and rest is being directly discharged into river without treatment.

Most of the urban areas in the state are without sewer system and also have houses without any toilet facility. About one-third houses in urban areas in the state do not have toilet facility. The number of public toilets in various towns and cities is highly inadequate. In the smaller towns and cities, the manual scavenging is still prevalent, though any new construction of dry latrine has been made a cognizable offence under the law.

One of the most important civic convenience and a basic civic service, which unfortunately is quite neglected, is the street and the storm water drainage. Surprisingly, no municipal body in the state has 100 per cent area covered with the drains, which is a very sad state of affairs. The reason behind this is probably the lack of foresight and shortage of funds at the level of urban local bodies. But the recent floods have clearly demonstrated the crucial importance of the drainage system to the city life. The total city life came to a grinding half due to heavy rains in the catchments areas resulting in unprecedented floods.

Like other towns located along rivers storm run off drains into the river. The Lucknow main city has over 20 nallahs (drains) with a combined length of around 70 km. On the eastern side of the city, there is a canal that was build during the rule of Nawabs. The canal runs from the southeastern side of the city towards the northeast and drains into the river downstream. The canal now carries most of the storm water run off during the rains. There are 25 major drains. Most of the drains are made of bricks. The discharge of waste water by these drains is shown in table 4.3. It is expected that discharge quantity will increase over the period with the increase in population. The discharge of sewerage in Lucknow was reported 230 mld in 1993. It is expected that it will reach to 529 mld in 2021 and 596.20 mld in 2031. (Table 18)

The responsibility of draining rainwater into Gomati lies with 42 Flood Pumping Stations. However, the condition of these pumping stations is very poor. The installed capacity of these stations is about 3500 Quebec. It needs to add 1200 Quebec as per standards. Thus in absence of adequate facility of drainage, the problem of water logging in the city during rainy season is very common.

Table 18
Drains and Their Discharge in Lucknow City

(in mld)

Drain	*1996*	*1998*	*2001*	*2008*	*2011*	*2021*	*2031*
Gaughat	1.0	1.30	1.36	1.50	1.54	1.78	1.99
Sarkata	35.18	24.00	24.87	26.90	27.86	30.88	33.89
Pata	21.28	17.50	18.15	19.70	20.43	22.72	25.00
NER upstream	-	0.60	0.66	0.80	0.88	1.10	1.32
NER down stream	-	0.60	0.66	0.80	0.88	1.10	1.32
Wazirganj	64.11	58.00	60.10	65.00	67.35	74.61	81.86
Ghasyari Mandi	14.76	13.50	13.95	15.00	15.50	17.05	18.60
China Bazar	6.68	2.70	2.79	3.00	3.26	3.41	3.72
La Place	1.56	1.30	1.36	1.50	1.57	1.78	1.99
Jopling Road	1.27	1.30	1.36	1.50	1.57	1.78	1.99
G.H. Canal	69.14	98.00	101.60	110.0	120.23	126.44	138.86
Jiamau	3.00	0.60	0.66	0.80	0.99	1.10	1.32
La-Martinier	3.00	0.50	0.52	0.80	0.84	0.94	1.15
Maheshganj	4.57	0.50	0.52	0.80	0.73	0.94	1.15
Rooppur Khadra	0.65	0.60	0.66	0.80	0.88	1.10	1.32
Mohan Meakin	8.45	4.00	4.15	4.50	4.67	5.19	5.71
Daliganj No.1	9.93	8.80	9.82	12.20	13.61	17.41	21.2
Daliganj No. 2	0.65	1.30	1.36	1.50	1.57	1.78	1.99
Arts College	0.50	0.60	0.66	0.80	0.88	1.10	1.32
Hanuman Setu	5.24	0.60	0.66	0.80	0.88	1.10	1.32
TGPS	5.40	1.30	1.36	1.50	1.57	1.78	1.99
Kedarnath	4.18	2.80	2.72	3.00	3.14	3.56	3.98
Nishatganj	2.21	1.30	1.36	1.50	1.57	1.78	1.99
Kukrail	47.68	39.90	40.44	43.80	45.37	50.40	55.37
Babu ka Purwa	0.05	0.50	0.52	0.80	0.73	0.94	1.15

Source: Lucknow Nagar Nigam

The Municipalities Act 1916, and Municipal Corporation Act of 1959 of Uttar Pradesh entrust the urban local bodies with the obligatory functions of conservancy, cleaning and scavenging work. Solid waste management is a holistic term incorporating the total system but in place to cover all the processes from the collection of solid waste at the point of refuse to its safe disposal practices. It is estimated that 400 gms. per capita solid waste is generated in urban areas. It is assumed that local bodies of the state produce about 13.91 million tonnes garbage daily.

Table 19
Discharge of Sewerage in Lucknow

Drainage system	*Discharge in 1993 (MLD)*	*Discharge Adopted in PER (MLD)*		*Anticipated Discharge (MLD)*				
		1998	*2008*	*2001*	*2021*	*2016*	*2021*	*2031*
CIS Gomati Drains	163.50	219.90	257.30	239.24	282.22	284.69	284.69	325.21
Trans-Gomati Drains	46.50	61.10	72.00	64.23	75.60	81.37	87.08	98.49
Sewerage Flow from Sewers	20.00	30.00	45.00	34.50	51.75	60.38	69.00	130.50
Gomati Nagar	–	–	–	25.00	44.00	52.00	60.00	69.00
Total	230.00	311.00	374.30	362.97	439.24	475.97	529.00	596.20

Source: U.P. Jan Nigam

Lucknow city generates about 1500 mt. of solid wastes daily. It is estimated that there are around 2000 Kabariwallas in city who pick up waste from the households and sell to retail traders. In addition to this, there are about 8000 rag pickers who collect recyclable paper, plastic and metal wires from the garbage. The recycling industry is worth of Rs. 25 crores per annum handling about 200 tonnes daily. Around 60-70 per cent of waste generated comprises of biodegradable matters. Lucknow Nagar Nigam has the prime responsibility of solid waste management. There are about 3800 Safai Karmacharies working in the Corporation. The Municipality has a solid waste transport fleet of 75 vehicles. The fleet collects an estimated 850 to 1000 tonnes of waste per days from about 500 depots. Some NGO's have ventured upon the task of vermin composting in some wards and charge households a nominal amount per month for delivering services. Besides, about 2000 cleaners who charge individual households for service and clean service latrines in the city. The only plant of waste to energy established in the city earlier, is defunct presently, however efforts are being made to revive it.

A scientifically designed and well laid down road net work is a basis civic necessity for today's cities, where vehicular traffic has already grown out of proportion and there is widespread congestion and traffic jams. In fact, it is assured that in the coming years, it would be faster to walk than drive, if the traffic continues to grow at the same pace and no concrete efforts are made to develop new roads, bridges and flyovers in big cities. It is the responsibility of the urban local bodies to plan for the movement, regulation and flow of traffic. The traffic bottlenecks and jams have become a great hindrance for the smooth flow of traffic in metropolitan cities.

Lucknow has grown all around in a radius of 25 km. The growth of the city has resulted in vastly increased demand for transport and a dramatic rise in the number of vehicles. During 1994 and 2005, there has been 16.88 per cent growth in the registration of vehicles in Lucknow. The highest growth has been reported in the registration of car/jeep/vans (23.14 per cent). During 2005, 0.75 million vehicles were registered in Lucknow alone (Table 20). Out of total vehicles, more than 80 per cent vehicles were two wheelers. U.P. Transport Corporation operates a fleet of 98 buses with the estimated load of 47000 persons daily on ten different routes of the district. In absence of a proper public transport system, many inefficient modes of transport have emerged in the city. However, CNG based three wheelers are running on important routes which provide cost effective and clean transport facility to dwellers.

Street lighting has traditionally been an important function of the municipal administration and has become all the more important in the present scenario. The tremendous increase in the number and movement of the vehicular traffic, significant changes in life styles with an increased emphasis on high life, and a good network of internal roads have significantly increased the movement of citizen in nights as well. Therefore, street illumination has acquired the character of an estimated service for comfort, safety and feeling of security in addition to facilitating swift movement of the traffic among the night hours. The present status of street lighting in most of the towns and cities is not up-to the mark and therefore needs to be improved.

Table 20
Registration of Vehicles in Lucknow

Type of Vehicles	*1994*	*1998*	*2005*	*Annual Growth (1994-255)*
Two Wheelers	212774	285511	601745 (80.30)	16.62
Car/Jeep/Vans	27608	42855	98978 (13.06)	23.14
Bus	1126	1340	3553 (0.49)	19.59
Truck/HCV's	4219	5264	7742 (1.03)	7.59
Tractor and LCV's	10077	11014	19985 (2.67)	8.94
Three Wheelers	6487	8579	9567 (1.28)	4.32
Others				
Total	262291	354579	749395 (100.00)	16.88

Source: U.P. State Transport Department, 2006

There are multiple agencies responsible for urban governance and provision and management of infrastructure and services. Lucknow Nagar Nigam, Lucknow Jal Sansthan, Lucknow Development Authority and U.P. Jal Nigam are the key institutions of urban service delivery. Other prominent Departments/Institute includes Central and State Public Works Departments, Transport Department, Department of Environment etc. These departments lack coordination and institutional arrangements in urban infrastructure development and services delivery. The roles and responsibilities of officials and non officials of various agencies, on the basis of accountability, transparency and efficiency required for sustainable development, are also not defined.

The City Development Plan of Lucknow, has proposed Rs. 11855.9 crores for investment on urban infrastructure and services under Jawahar Lal Nehru Urban Renewal Missions scheme (Table 21). A large sum of investment has been earmarked on water supply, sewerage, drainage and roads.

Table 21
City Investment Plan

(Rs. Crores)

Sector	*Phase I (2006-12)*	*Phase II (2012-31)*	*Total*
Sub-Mission I			
(Urban Infrastructure and Governance)			
Water supply	675.6	602.0	1277.64
Sewerage	630.0	1429.0	2058.63
Drainage	444.3	111.0	1555.01
Construction of Roads			
Lohiya Path	69.0	–	69.0
Internal Roads	421.2	1053.0	1474.17
Road and Urban Transport	160.8	401.9	562.7
Parking Through PPP	21.79	109.6	153.36
Haider Canal Roads & Electrical Roadways		796.4	796.4
Solid Waste Management	46.14	43.2	89.34
City Beautification	11.11	27.77	38.88
River Front Development	16.21	–	16.21
Conservation of Ponds	–	170.0	170.0
Street Lighting	56.64	100.0	156.64
Conservation of Heritage Sites	15.97	144.03	160.0
Community Halls	3.47	–	3.47
Infrastructure Projects	845.0	507.0	1352.0
Water Supply, Sewerage, SWM, RWH	30.6	60.5	91.1
Sub-Total	3453.0	6555.0	10007.4
Sub-Mission II			
Basic Services for Urban Poor	1051.0	456.0	1506.5
Grand Total	4845.0	7011.0	11855.9

Source: City Development Plan Lucknow, Feedback Ventures, Delhi, 2006

The above analysis simply demonstrates that the urban infrastructure in Lucknow city is under stress due to increasing population pressure. The development and management of Urban Infrastructure and Services in the city requires a huge investment and thus resource mobilization is a main task of the government.

STRATEGIC ISSUES

Urban India is in the midst of transformation. In an era of economic reforms, liberalization, and globalization, cities and towns are fast emerging as centres of growth. It is estimated that by 2025, more than 50 per cent of the country's population will live in cities and towns. This is indicative of the likely increase in the demand of infrastructural facilities and services that could rise due to urbanization. This poses a serious challenge to urban planners, policy makers, and managers. This is high time to mobilise resources for financing urban infrastructure and services. We need to expand physical infrastructure - roads, airports, ports, railways, drinking water and water networks and above all electrical power - to satisfy the aspirations and rising expectations of our citizens. Much of the existing infrastructure is old, worn, and over exploited. It needs to be rebuilt, refurnished and maintained. Though there are vast improvements in basic amenities such as access to telecom services, electricity, water supply and sanitation, however the quality of basic services is declining. Increasing coverage of infrastructure is not matched by improvement in the service levels. Despite low growth of urbanization, urban population is likely to expand and decline in urban services be more glaring in the coming years.

Thus urban sector suffers from the tremendous infrastructure deficiencies, despite significant emphasis has given in the successive five year plans for the orderly development of core infrastructure services. The problems are not only associated with the accessibility of basic services to all the urban population of the country, but also of their inequitable distribution among the different sections of population.

There has been considerable debate in India about the quality of public service delivery. Service delivery in India remains poor on a whole, however, a national survey of major public services by Public Affairs (2002) Centre conducted that

India did well in terms of providing basic access to such services, but far less well in terms of ensuring their quality, reliability and effectiveness. Thus, concept of good governance has got momentum in order to improve service delivery. The instruments for improving service delivery include (i) promoting competition, (ii) simplifying transactions, (iii) restructuring agency process; (iv) decentralization; (v) building political support for programme delivery; (vi) strengthening accountability mechanisms etc. It is the general assumption that competition improves services delivery out comes. Simplifying transactions through greater use of e-governance is made easier for citizens to interact with the state governments. Similarly, restructuring agency processes involved change on several dimensions. Decentralization and strengthening of local governments have improved the functioning of public services in effective and efficient manner. Again, reducing premature transfers, fostering access to information, checking corruption through generating public pressure and public interest litigation may ensure accountability.

Public private partnership provides an opportunity for private sector participation in financing designs, construction and operations and maintenance of public sector programmes and projects. This is high time to forge a greater interface between the public and private sector in a wider range of activities in the country. The partnership falls into five main categories, viz. (i) contract services; (ii) privatization of services; (iii) designing, construction and operation of facilities; (iv) project financing, and (v) merchant facilities. The partnership in municipal services is expected to reduce cost of maintenance, increase efficiency and timely completion of new projects while community participation in operation and maintenance of services is expected to be of great importance. Government of India is committed to remove the roadblocks in delivery of services and creating infrastructure in collaboration with private sector under JNNURM. The Mission has two main submissions, focusing on infrastructure and governance and services to the urban poor respectively.

Report Card system is an effective tool and is useful in evaluating various aspects like people's participation, rule of raw, transparency, responsiveness, equity, effectiveness and efficiency, accountability and strategic vision etc. which may be utilized in general to promote good urban governance. Report Card System provides a mechanism to measure public opinion on quality of public services. The methodology of Report Card includes random sample surveys of households, focus group discussions, brief case studies of selected respondents, documentation of information provided to the public by service providers and interview with a sample of staff of the agencies. The Cards attempt to access, rank and benchmark the following parametres: (i) overall satisfaction with service delivery (levels of services), (ii) the extent and coverage of services; (iii) patterns of emerging problems, (iv) the response of agencies to reported problems and grievances; (v) the effectiveness of bribes in rectifying reported problems.

In order to remove road blocks in delivery of urban services, three types of triggers offer the potential for inducing reform in urban governance and services delivery. The first trigger could be fiscal flows. Second, decentralization has potential to spark change and create incentives for ensuring accountability in delivery of services. A third set of triggers would come from the demand side, essentially by making service providers directly accountable. The following issues of urban infrastructure development and management in Lucknow city are expected to help in understanding the dynamics of urban infrastructure development of the city:

- Population growth in Lucknow city is likely to higher due to high rate of migration from rural and smaller districts.
- The demographic profile of city has shown an increase in the number of women and therefore, social and economic implications would need to be taken into consideration while planning and preparation of development projects.
- The city has witnessed the rise of economic base, being the capital of largest state of India. There has been

remarkable increase in retail trade, professional services-health, education, tourism, real state etc. Thus, there will be enormous need of infrastructure both physical and social to cater the emerging needs.

- The city is well connected with rail network; however, existing levels of connectivity are inadequate for economic development. The city needs better connectivity of rail, roads, air and tele- communications etc.
- The private sector is coming forward due to existing institutional environment, quality of infrastructure, and regulatory arrangements. Therefore, conducive environment, deregulations, and institutional reforms are to be ensured.
- The city is growing rapidly in all directions but higher rate of growth along Faizabad road, in trans Gomati area, and south city has been reported. The new development areas will need additional infrastructure.
- There has been significant increase in slum dwellers across the city. The encroachment on public places, roads and streets is also gradually increasing. Thus, alternative land would be required for relocation of urban poor.
- The strict regulation of environmental laws would be required to reduce the air and water pollution.

  The well known monuments are relatively better maintained, however, heritage sites need proper maintenance with required public toilets.
- The city has grossly inadequate infrastructure for water supply, sewerage, drainage, solid waste management, and waste treatment. Thus the expansion of such infrastructure would be needed.
- There are several water bodies within the city limits which have been encroached, polluted and defunct. Thus, these water bodies are to be revived for maintaining ground water recharging and supply of drinking water.

- The city has intermediate and inadequate service delivery and management of water supply. The exploitation of ground water is expensive and unsustainable. The dumping of sewage into river Gomati through drains has caused concern and it would be difficult for managing water resources.
- Sewerage and sanitation challenges are daunting. The existing capacity of drainage and coverage of sewer line is grossly inadequate. The mechanical and electrical equipments are poor, old and defunct in some cases. The damaged manholes, sewer line, nallahs and connections cause over flowing of waste water and sewerage on streets and roads. The frequent sewer blockage and leakages also cause contamination of drinking water and water borne diseases.
- Despite the legal ban on dry latrines, there are about 4000 dry latrines who are managed by about 150 scavengers. Thus, the inhuman practice of manuals scavenging is still prevailing in the city. These dry latrines discharge sewerage into open nallahs, drains or water bodies and cause water borne diseases.
- There is no proper system of sewage treatment. The untreated sewage is being dumped into the water bodies, causing serious concern for environment and ecology of the city.
- The present arrangements for maintenance of drains are inadequate. Thus, planning and management issues are to be addressed. The water logging pockets are needed more attention for proper drainage so that during rains, there will be no problem of water logging. The encroachment and blockages of nallahs, drains, and water bodies are to be cleared.
- There is short fall of infrastructure for solid waste management. The sustainable availability of quality raw materials - wastes to project plant is difficult task and therefore, it is quite impossible to run mega power plant, based on wastes. The shortcomings in vehicles,

equipments, tools and depots pose serious challenges in management of solid wastes. The institutional inefficiencies exist. There is also no proper coordination between the various departments, agencies and stakeholders for managing the urban wastes.

- Rapid development of the peripheral areas of the city has increased demand for new connections, networks and transport facilities to deal the emerging challenge.
- The condition of roads requires attention for its widening, removing encroachments, constructing flyovers, developing parking places, and improving smooth movement of traffic.
- With the expansion of the city, there will be a rise in private vehicles which will increase traffic congestion. It will require construction and expansion of by pass high ways and express ways.
- There are many agencies and institutions responsible for service delivery in urban areas. Functional overlapping and lack of coordination among them create hindrance in development and management of infrastructural services in the city.
- The revenue base of the institutions and agencies involved in development and management of urban infrastructure and services delivery is weak resulting in high dependence on government for grants.
- The improvement of financial status of key institutions involved in urban development and governance is imperative. This may be ensured through increased level of public private partnership and introducing reforms - accounting, property tax, e-governance etc.
- The strategy for achieving the goals and objectives of city development stands on three pillars-infrastructure and service delivery, improvements, basic services for urban poor and institutional reforms for strengthening local governments.

POLICY RECOMMENDATIONS

The process of urbanization has gathered considerable momentum over the last decades. The growth of population has put urban infrastructure and services under severe strain. Urban areas in India present a grim scenario with regard to availability of basic infrastructure. The democratic decentralization of local bodies as envisaged in 74th Constitution Amendment Act, 1992 is still to be accomplished. Functional and financial autonomy of urban local bodies remains a distant dream. The Tenth Plan acknowledged that there is a pressing need for capacity building of municipalities through training of elected and appointed officials and representatives and by restructuring of ULB's for efficient management of civic services. This is also well reflected in the newly launched urban infrastructure development schemes of Government which are reforms oriented and emphasize on public private partnership building. It is daunting challenge for municipal governments to mobilize resource for financing urban infrastructure development projects.

RECOMMENDATIONS

- In face of mounting fiscal pressures on the local bodies and the rapid demand for urban services and infrastructure, the present institutional arrangements for provision of services and development of infrastructure are unlikely to sustain. The policy regime, oriented towards market based economy led growth objectives, would entail significant contribution of the urban sector and efforts would be needed to reduce infrastructure bottlenecks and increase urban productivity and employment.
- Privatization of municipal services is an option to improve service levels in urban areas and attract private capital and management skills in provision and maintenance of urban services. However, the local government staff and officials will need to be trained properly for institutional arrangement for delivery of services with private sector.

- Innovative strategies are required to be developed by the local bodies to finance urban infrastructure and services. The existing funds available from plan allocation, institutional finance and other sources could be supplemented by private sector as also through accessing the capital market.
- Public Private Partnerships should be promoted specially in projects with e-governance, water, sanitation, solid waste management etc.
- Government should conduct functional review of service providing agencies in order to examine road blocks in delivery of services and improving the coverage and quality of services.
- Better coordination mechanism should be created to foster inter agency collaboration for effective implementation of reforms and delivery of services as well as implementing of urban infrastructure projects.
- Report Card System should be introduced by private independent agencies to assess the performance and quality of services as well as governance. The feedback of citizens regarding quality and coverage of services provided by agencies may increase accountability and efficiency in service delivery.
- Municipalities should limit its role to regulation of services, however private sector participation may be taken for monitoring, direction, auditing and performance evolution of services by municipalities.
- Public utilities need to reinvent rather than just reform. A new governance structure for services sector needs to be evolved.
- Community participation in delivery of urban services may be augmented through strengthening NGO's, local bodies, public associations and SHG's. However, orientation and training will be required for creating awareness and sensitizing representatives of these associations and organizations.

- Experiences of best practices in the field of water supply, rainwater harvesting, water resources management, solid waste management, sewerage, drainage etc. should be documented and also used in planning and implementation of urban infrastructure projects.
- Ground water depletion can be checked by under taking rain water harvesting in all the urban centres. Specific programmes, schemes should be initiated for aquifer recharge. These schemes and programmes should be based on decentralized approaches of water resources management and water harvesting.
- All the urban local bodies should be made compulsory to impose user charges for urban basic services such as water supply, drainage, solid waste management, parking, street sweeping, sewerage etc. However, the quality of service has to be improved in order to augment financial resources though imposing user charges.
- Improving cost recovery should be linked with grants or fiscal transfers. Financial incentives may also be given to urban local bodies showing improved cost recovery.
- Private sector participation should be encouraged. Unbundling of services may improve efficiency of urban local bodies. The regulatory role of urban local bodies should be given to them while other functions may be given to private sector. Private sector may also be encouraged for participation in urban infrastructure projects.
- Rationalization of tariff structure would require necessary legislative changes and developing a system of incentives and sanctions at state level to encourage reforms.
- Reforms are also needed for restructuring water bodies - Jal Nigam and Jan Sansthan by disaggregating them by function seperating service provision from regulatory and policy responsibilities, commercializing

the service provision entities and evolving the private sector in management of new commercialized entities.

- The urban local bodies are also supported to develop best practices and procedures in areas of accounting, auditing, procurement, tariff rationalization, customer consultation, and integrating service to disadvantaged groups with maintenance of service delivery.
- The state government should facilitate urban local bodies for preparation of City Development Plan, Detailed Project Reports as well as their timely approval in order to avail the benefits of JNNURM, UIDSSMT and IHSDP schemes.
- All the properties and holdings should be brought into the tax net of local bodies. This may be ensured through application of GIS in larger cities and towns while timely and regular enumeration of houses may be ensured by local bodies. This will improve the financial health of local bodies.
- The local bodies need help and assistance for having access to capital market and mobilization of resources for meeting out the desired expenses in terms of share in centrally sponsored urban infrastructure development projects-JNNURM, UIDSSMT and IHSDP.
- The Master Plan of cities should also contain the details of urban infrastructure services, urban transport system, development of new townships and other public utilities. Detailed Plans for power, water supply, sewerage, drainage, roads, street lights transportation system, communication, environment, parks, parking zones and other basic needs of civic life must be integral part of the Master Plan.
- People should be made to realize that unless they make timely payment of all the taxes and charges, the civic services and their maintenance cannot be kept as per their expectations.

- Wastage of drinking water, pilferage and theft of power, misuse of public land and roads cost very heavily on the already inadequate resources of the city. The people should be made to understand that those resources belong to them and they have to act as custodians.
- It is imperative to create an enabling legal institutional framework for the planning, financing, management and regulation of urban development with the objectives of sustainable augmentation of housing, infrastructure and civic services to the people without deteriorating to the living environment.
- Suitable financing systems with a view to building the basic foundation for city productivity and economic growth be adopted for undertaking sustainable expansion of urban infrastructural facilities.
- In order to meet out the travel demand and manage urban traffic, Mass Rapid Transport System should be developed and a Cell of Urban Transport Management be established in the Department of Urban Development.
- Urban Infrastructure Development Fund be created for the resource pool and development of urban infrastructure. Urban Development Company/ Corporation may also be established for the development and management of urban infrastructure.
- In order to ensure effective and efficient functioning of urban infrastructure development schemes, a unit of project management be established at the Department of Urban Development. The specialists, consultants, engineers should be associated with the unit for managing the urban infrastructure projects and facilitating urban managers including development functionaries.
- River Conservation and River Front development should be ensured in order to mitigate water pollution and sustaining the rivers.

REFERENCES

Ansari, A.S., (2000), Urban Renewal and Development: A Case of Hyderabad, Rawat Pub. Jaipur .

Bhargav, G., (1981), Urban Problems and Policy Perspectives, Abhinav, New Delhi.

Feedback Bencher,(2006), City Development Plan: Lucknow City, Feedback Bencher, Delhi.

Govt. of India, Urban Infrastructure (Chapter II), Tenth Five Year Plan, Planning Commission, Government of India, Delhi.

Hall, Peter, (1996), Cities of Tomorrow - Blackwell, Massa Chursetts.

Kundu, Amitabh, (2006), Trends and Patterns of Urbanization and their Economic Implications, India Infrastructure Report, 2006, OUP, Delhi.

Kundu, Amitabh, (2001), Urban Development, Infrastructure Financing and Emerging System of Governance in India: A Perspective, Management of Social Transformations, UNESCO, Delhi, April.

Mathur, Mukesh, (2006), Norms and Standards for Basic Urban Infrastructure and Services in Urban Governance and Management by (ed) Rao, P.S.N., Kanishka Pub., Delhi.

Misra, J.S., (2002), A Quest for Dream Cities, Har Anand Pub. Delhi.

Mohan, Rakesh and Das Gupta S., (2004), Urban Development in India in the 21st Century: Policies for Accelerating Urban Growth, Standford University, October.

Mohanty, P.K., (2005), Urban Sector Reform Agenda: Financing Civic Services and Development, Centre for Good Governance, Hyderabad, April.

Planning Commission Report of the Working Group on Urban Water Supply and Sanitation Sector for Ninth Plan, Planning Commission, Government of India, Delhi., 1996.

Rai, Nishith and Singh, A.K., (2007), Urban Water Supply and Water Tariffs in Uttar Pradesh, Regional Centre for Urban and Environmental Studies, Lucknow.

Rao, P.S.N., (ed), (2006), Urban Governance and Management: Indian Initiatives, Kanishka Pub., Delhi.

Savage D. and Das Gupta, S., (2006), Governance Framework for Delivery of Urban Services, India Infrastructure Report, 2006, OUP, Delhi.

Sharma, Chetan, (2006), City Development Plan: Lucknow City, Datamation Consultants Pvt. Ltd., Bombay.

Shivramakrishnan, K.C., (1992), Urban Governance in India, Centre for Policy Research, New Delhi.

Singh, A.K., (2006), Restructuring of Municipal Services in India, *Indian Journal of Public Administration,* Vol. L11 No.3, July-September.

World Bank - Urban Infrastructure Services Review, World Bank, Delhi., 1997.

World Bank - Urban Water Supply and Sanitation, World Bank, Delhi, 1999.

4

URBAN ENVIRONMENT

India is a large, diverse and poor country that faces severe environmental problems. The range of environmental problems confronting India is vast. The natural resource base of the economy provides support to three fourth of its population. Though, agriculture is the backbone of economy, however, the quality of agriculture land is poor and gradually declining due to several factors. India has also a very large and rapidly growing urban population. Basic amenities such as sanitation, water supply, electricity, housing and transport have not kept pace with rapid urbanization. As a consequence, the quality of urban environment has deteriorated significantly.

The range of environmental problems confronting India is vast and mitigation measures are expensive. The problems may be classified under two heads: (1) those arising from industrialization and urbanizations such as pollution, solid waste etc., and (ii) natural resource based problems such as deforestation, and degradation, biodiversity loss etc. Importantly, many of the industrial urban environmental problems have their genesis in the growth strategies adopted in post independence era. In India, air pollution is a primarily an urban phenomenon, with main sources being motor vehicles, industries, thermal power plants, and use of coal and firewood in domestic sector. It is to be noted that 6 of the 10 largest cities in India - Mumbai, Kolkata, Delhi, Ahmadabad, Kanpur, and Nagpur - have annual average levels of particulate matter (P.M.) at least three times as high as the Word Health organization (WHO) standard. While only a few cities have high concentration of nitrous oxion (NOX) and sulphar dioxide (SO), this picture is likely to worsen with growing industrialization and motorization. Almost all surface water in India is unfit for human consumption. There are three major sources of pollution viz. domestic sewage, industrial effluents, and agricultural run off. Of these the first two are most important. Total sewage generated by urban centre increased from 5 billion liters/day in 1997 to 30 billion liters/day in 1997. Treatment capacity, however, is only about 3 billion liters/day. Even this capacity does not function properly and remains closed for long period due to various reasons. Industrial effluents are generated by a few sub sectors mainly in the forms of toxic wastes and organic pollutants.

As mentioned earlier that green environmental problems are mainly deforestation, biodiversity loss, and soil degradation. Forests in India have been shrinking for several decades owing to pressure of population on land for competing uses, such as agriculture, irrigation and power projects, industry, roads etc. During 1995-97, alone, about 5,48,200 hectares of forest land was lost, mainly in the states of Andhra Pradesh and Maharashtra. During the period, 1.95 million hectare of dense forest degraded to open forest, 39,200 hectare become scrub and 312100 hectare were converted to non-forests areas. One of the main causes of deforestation has been the diversion of prime forest land for agricultural purposes. Large scale development projects have also contributed substantially to deforestation. Indiscriminate and unscientific mining is also another significant cause of deforestation. Again, habitat destruction, hunting and over exploitation, pollution and poisoning and displacement by exotics over the last few decades have led to the decline in India's wild bio-diversity.

Urbanization in India is characterized by unplanned and uncontrolled growth which leads to urban sprawl. Land use planning and pattern of development have considerable impact on the environment. Due to lack of resources, inadequate resource mobilization capability to adopt proper city planning and inadequate monitoring and regulation, most municipal governments fail delivery services effectively; People in urban India face severe problems related to water, waste water and wastes disposal, and pollution. A survey (2000) of 241 Class 2 towns in 17 states of India under taken by the Central Pollution Control Board, Delhi indicated that 90 per cent of water supplied is polluted. This is because of the fact that our rivers are highly polluted due to non-regulation of waste dumping and discharging waste water into them while ground water is polluted due to silting of solid wastes, waste water and industrial effluents. About 30.5 million Disability Adjusted Life Years (ALY) are lost annually owing to poor quality of drinking water and the absence of sanitation facilities. The financial loss in terms of productivity has been quantified at Rs. 360 billion annually. Most of the urban local bodies do not have adequate infrastructure facilities such as required capacities for treatment of raw water, adequate testing facilities and technical man power for operations and management. Only 72 of 4400 towns in the country have partial sewerage facilities and 17 have some form of primary treatment facilities before disposal. Of the 229 class 1 cities, 160 have sewerage systems for more than 75 per cent of the population and 92 cities for more than 50 per cent of the population while waste generation in class I cities has more than doubled from 1978 to 1995, the treatment capacity has decreased during the same period. Of the total waste water generated in the metropolitan cities, barely 30 per cent is treated before disposal. Untreated water is thrown into water bodies such as rivers, lakes, Oceans and seas. In 118 cities, it is discharged indirectly into rivers, lakes, ponds, or creeks, while in 63 cities it is used for agriculture. Most of the urban local bodies do not have sewerage line for disposal of waste water, and sewerage. This leads to degradation of the environment and effect the quality of life of inhabitants. It is estimated that 75-80 per cent of water pollution is caused by domestic sewerage.

It is estimated that urban India generates about 40 million tonnes of solid wastes every day. Of this only 72 per cent is collected daily and remaining wastes is allowed to create problems of urban environment. This also creates health problems. More than 70 per cent Indian cities have inadequate waste transportation facilities. They mainly choose land filling for disposal of wastes. However, the land fill sites are poorly managed and are prone to ground water contamination because of lea chats. The land fill workers have also higher incidence of diseases such as diarrhea, as well as fungal and skin infections due to working in unhygienic conditions. Moreover, the compliance of Bio-Medical Waste Management Rules is still low. About 25 per cent of the waste generated is called hazardous. A survey (2001) of 120 health care centres in West Bengal, Gujarat, Punjab, Tamil Nadu, Haryana, Delhi and Uttar Pradesh found that 42 per cent of health care workers did not have knowledge about classification and segregation of biomedical waste. The survey revealed gross inadequacy of equipments and tools. Open dumping or burning of bio-medical waste was reported as common practice. This enhances the emissions of gases and air pollution.

The increasing levels of air pollution in urban areas have caused alarming situation since most of towns and cities have crossed danger limit. There are about 2.5 million premature deaths due to increased air pollution. The air quality was rated dangerous or bad in 34 cities out of 62 cities in 1994. However, this proportion has come down in 2000 due to introduction of CNG gas in public vehicles in the metropolitan cities.

Industrial effluents also cause serious air pollution and occupational health hazards. The rapid industrialization in India has resulted in the increased need for proper disposal of industrial wastes. The industries such as pesticides, drugs, pharmaceuticals, textiles, dyes, fertilizers, tanneries, paint, etc. generate hazardous wastes. About 50 per cent of total hazardous waste in the country is generated from Maharastra, Gujarat, Tamil Nadu, U.P., Rajasthan, Andhra Pradesh and Karnataka. Improper storage, handling, transportation, treatment and disposal of industrial waste may adversely impact the environment. The improper industrial waste disposal has caused land contamination.

WASTE GENERATION

Waste management in urban areas is one of the priority areas of service delivery; however, it is becoming most challenging task before the urban local bodies. Urban India produces about 50 million tons of waste annually and a significant proportion of it remained uncollected which causes severe problems to the city dwellers. The basic principles for the solid waste management including collection, segregation, handling, transporting, disposal and treatment are not being ensured by the local bodies due to their own problems. The Government of India has already introduced Municipal Solid Waste Rules in 2000 with the intervention of Supreme Court. However, the most of the local bodies failed to comply these rules.

Table 1
50 Years of Waste Generation

Particulars	*1947*	*1997*
Urban Population (Millions)	56.9	247
Daily Per Capita Waste Generation (Grams)	295	490
Total Waste Generated (Million Tons)	6	48
Area Under Land Fills ('000' Hectares)	0.12	20.2
Annual Methane Emissions (Tons) from Landfill Sites	0.87	7.1

Source: Management of Municipal Solid Waste, Central Pollution Control Board, Ministry of Environment & Forests.

There has been significant increase in waste generation in urban India during last 50 years. The daily per capital waste generation was reported 295 grams in 1947 which increased by 490 grams in 1997. Similarly, the area of landfills has increased tremendously (Table 1).

The percentage of solid waste disposal in India is shown in Table 3. There has been significant improvement in the proportion of waste water treated and solid waste disposal during 1993 and 1998. However during 1998 in most of the cities, the solid waste was reported to be dumped in open dump yards. In Jaipur city, about 15 per cent of solid waste was reported to be burned while this has been banned by the Supreme Court.

Table 2
Selected City-Wise Percentage of Solid Waste Disposal In India

City	Percentage of Waste Treated		Percentage of Solid Waste Disposal: Open Dumping		Recycled		Burned (Openly)		Sanitary		Incinerated		Others	
	1993	1998	1993	1998	1993	1998	1993	1998	1993	1998	1993	1998	1993	1998
Bangalore	78.80	82.90	75.90	60.80	11.90	14.50	0.00	0.00	0.0	0.0	0.0	0.0	12.2	24.7
Chennai	60.00	70.00	70.00	100.00	100.00	0.00	0.00	0.00	0.0	0.0	0.0	0.0	0.0	0.0
Guwahati	0.00	0.00	58.00	60.00	12.00	12.00	5.00	5.00	0.0	0.0	0.0	0.0	25.0	23.0
Indore	16.50	0.00	65.00	71.70	15.00	18.00	0.00	0.00	0.0	0.0	0.0	0.0	20.0	10.3
Jaipur	11.13	7.91	65.00	65.00	15.00	15.00	15.00	15.00	0.0	0.0	0.0	0.0	5.0	5.0
Ludhiana	0.00	0.00	61.20	76.50	0.00	0.00	0.00	0.00	0.0	0.0	0.0	0.0	38.8	23.5
Mumbai	10.30	37.80	0.00	0.00	0.00	3.40	0.00	0.00	93.9	95.0	0.0	0.1	6.1	1.5
Mysore	37.60	13.00	100.00	100.00	0.00	0.00	0.00	0.00	0.00	0.0	0.0	0.0	0.0	0.0
Patna	12.40	42.10	33.60	43.10	0.000	0.00	0.00	0.00	66.4	56.9	0.0	0.0	0.0	0.0
Vjayawada	27.00	22.00	80.00	65.00	0.00	33.00	0.00	0.00	20.0	0.0	0.0	2.0	0.0	0.0

Source: Handbook of Housing Statistics 2003, Ministry of Urban Development & Poverty Alleviation, Govt. of India.

Table 3
Status of Municipal Solid Waste Treatment and Disposal in Metro Cities

Metro City	*Solid Waste Collection (Tons/day)*	*Treatment (Tons/day)*	*Mode of Disposal (%)* Dumping	Composting	Others
Ahmedabad	1683	84	95.00	5	–
Bangalore	2000	200	90.00	10	–
Bhopal	546	100	82.00	18.0	–
Bombay	55355	500	91.00	9.0	–
Calcutta	3692	Nil	100.00	–	–
Coimbatore	350	Nil	100.00	–	–
Delhi	4000	300	93.00	7.5	–
Hyderabad	1566	100	94.00	6.0	–
Indore	350	50	86.00	14.0	–
Jaipur	580	Nil	100.00	–	–
Kanpur	1200	300	75.00	25.0	–
Kochi	347	Nil	100.00	–	–
Lucknow	1010	Nil	100.00	–	–
Ludhiana	400	Nil	100.00	–	–
Madras	3124	Nil	100.00	–	–
Madurai	370	Nil	100.00	–	–
Nagpur	443	Nil	100.00	–	–
Patna	330	Nil	100.00	–	–
Pune	700	50	93.00	–	7.0
Surat	900	225	25.00	25.0	–
Vadodara	400	100	75.00	–	5.0
Varanasi	412	Nil	100.00	–	–
Visakhapatnam	300	–	100.00	–	–

Source: Status of Solid Waste Generation, Collection, Treatment and Disposal in Metro Cities, Central Pollution Control Board, Ministry of Environment and Forest.

Most of the cities have the mode of dumping for the solid waste disposal. In the cities like Bhopal, Indore, Kanpur, Surat and Bangalore, a significant proportion of the solid waste was reported to be composted (Table 4).

The collection efficiency of solid waste is shown in Table 5. The cities like Bombay, Chennai, Ahmedabad, Bhopal, Lucknow, Hugli-Dharwad and Gulbarga were reported to be good collection efficiency while the cities like Calicut, Triruchi and Salem were the poor collection efficiency.

Table 4
Total Amount of Solid Waste Collected and the Collection Efficiency in Some Towns/Cities

Towns	*Population*	*Solid Waste (Tons)* Generated	Collected	*Collection Efficiency %age*
Bombay	8227332	3200	3100	96.9
Chennai	4276635	1819	1637	90.0
Bangalore	2913537	1800	1225	68.1
Ahmedabad	2515195	1200	1080	90.0
Kanpur	1688424	2142	1500	70.0
Pune	1685300	1000	700	70.0
Lucknow	1006538	600	500	83.3
Total		*11761*	*9742*	*82.8*
Coimbatore	917155	175	113	64.6
Madurai	904362	310	160	51.6
Indore	827071	120	100	83.3
Baroda	744043	321	193	60.1
Cochine	685686	230	120	52.2
Bhopal	672329	321	300	93.5
Tiruchi	607815	130	60	46.2
Calicut	546060	200	75	37.5
Meerut	538461	120	70	58.3
Hubli-Dharwad	526493	75	60	80.0
Trivendrum	519766	120	75	62.5
Salem	515021	130	25	19.2
Mysore	476446	204	122	59.8
Thane	388577	350	200	57.1
Jamnagar	317037	149	89	59.7
Gulbarga	218621	10	8	80.0
Sambalpur	162190	60	36	60.0
Total		3025	1806	59.7

Source: Ministry of Agriculture.

Table 5
Garbage Management in Some Cities

City	*Garbage Generated (ton per day)*	*Garbage Cleared (ton per day)*	*Clearing Efficiency (%)*
Delhi	3880	2420	62.37
Calcutta	3500	3150	90.00
Bombay	5800	5000	86.20
Bangalore	2130	1800	84.50
Madras	2675	2140	80.00
Lucknow	1500	1000	66.66
Patna	1000	300	30.00
Ahmedabad	1500	1200	80.00
Surat	1250	1000	80.00

Source: Urban Statistics, Hand Book 2000, National Institute of Urban Affairs.

The garbage clearing efficiency in some of the cities is shown in Table 6. Calcutta, Bombay, Bangalore and Chennai were reported to have good clearing efficiency while the cities like Patna had only 30 per cent clearing efficiency of garbage during 2000.

Table 6
Solid Waste Generation in Million Plus Cities

(April 2000)

Urban Agglomeration/City	*Quantity of Solid Waste Generated Per Day (in MT)*
Greater Mumbai	6000
Kolkata	2500
Delhi	6000
Chennai	2500
Bangalore	2500
Hyderabad	2100
Ahmedabad	1273
Pune	1200
Surat	1035
Kanpur	1300
Jaipur	1000
Lucknow	1150
Nagpur	600
Patna	330
Indore	600
Vadodara	560
Bhopal	480
Coimbatore	670
Ludhiana	1200
Kochi	250
Visakhapatnam	600
Agra	575
Varanasi	576
Madurai	480
Meerut	625
Nashik	280
Jabalpur	300
Jamshedpur	140
Asabsol	78
Dhanbad	285
Faridabad	550
Allahabad	305
Amritsar	600
Vijayawada	475
Rajkot	450

Source: Lok Sabha Unstarred Question No. 621, dated 10.05.2005.

Solid waste generation in million plus cities is shown in Table 7. A large quantity of solid waste is being generated in the metropolitan cities including Greater Mumbai, Kolkata, Delhi, Chennai, Bangalore, Ahmedabad and Kanpur.

Table 7
State-Wise Status of Municipal Solid Waste Treatment and Disposal in Class-I Cities

States/ UTs	*No. of Cities*	*Solid Waste Collection MT/day*	*Treatment MT/day*	*Mode of Disposal (%)*		
				Dumping	*Composting*	*Others*
Andhra Pradesh	32	3943	2985	94	5	1
Assam	4	196	–	100	–	–
Bihar	17	1479	–	100	–	–
Gujarat	21	3805	439	80	20	–
Haryana	12	623	–	100	–	–
Himachal Pradesh	1	35	–	100	–	–
Karnataka	21	3118	258	99	1	–
Kerala	14	1220	60	86	14	–
Madhya Pradesh	23	2286	150	96	4	–
Maharashtra	27	8589	769	90	4	6
Manipur	1	40	–	100	–	–
Meghalaya	1	35	–	–	100	–
Mizoram	1	46	–	100	–	–
Orissa	7	646	–	100	–	–
Punjab	10	1001	–	100	–	–
Rajasthan	14	1768	71	90	10	–
Tamil Nadu	25	5021	54	95	4	1
Tripura	14	33	–	100	–	–
Uttar Pradesh	41	5515	300	98	11	1
West Bengal	23	4475	–	100	–	–
Chandigarh	1	200	–	100	–	–
Delhi	1	4000	400	90	10	–
Pondicherry	1	60	–	100	–	–
India		48134	2786	94	5	1

Source: Status of Municipal Solid Waste Generation Collection, Treatment and Disposal in Class-I Cities, Central Pollution Control Board, April, 2000. Ministry of Environment & Forests, Govt. of India.

Municipal solid waste treatment and disposal in class-I cities is shown in Table 8. Most of the generated solid waste in million plus cities is being dumped in the open yard. However, in the cities in Meghalaya, Gujarat, Rajasthan, Uttar Pradesh, Delhi and Andhra Pradesh, significant proportion of solid waste is also being composted.

Table 8
Basin-wise Solid Waste Generation In Class-I Cities

Major River Basin	*No. of Cities*	*Municipal Population*	*Municipal Solid Waste MT/day*	*Basin-wise Per Capita Generated Kg/day*
Brahmani	1	398864	119	0.298
Brahmaputra	7	1415601	280	0.218
Cauvery	16	8212863	3333	0.252
Ganga	103	49478976	1798	0.259
Godavari	25	6919320	2263	0.316
Indus	15	4192909	1659	0.281
Krishna	27	12659457	4190	0.278
Mahanadi	9	2476450	872	0.305
Mahi	3	1311534	457	0.252
Narmada	4	1183593	345	0.258
Pennar	6	974371	307	0.301
Sabarmati	7	3678921	1816	0.231
Subamarekha	2	1059883	335	0.315
Tapi	8	3444041	1562	0.373
Coastal	29	23275720	10689	0.313
No Major Basin	37	7434362	2216	0.244
Total	299	128113865	48134	0.376

Source: Status of Municipal Solid Waste Generation Collection Treatment and Disposal in Class-I Cities, Central Pollution Control Board, April 2000, Ministry of Environment & Forests.

Basin-wise solid waste generation in class-I cities is shown in Table 9. Cauvery, Krishna, Sabarmati, Ganga, Godavari are some of the major river basins which generate a large quantity of solid waste. Moreover, class-I cities of coastal areas generate about 11000 metric tons of solid waste daily. The per capita generation of solid waste has been reported high in the river basin of Godavari, Mahanadi, Pennar, Tapti and coastal areas.

Basin-wise solid waste generation in metro cities is shown in Table 10. The metro cities located in the river basin of Ganga, Cauvery, Krishna, and the coastal areas generate a large quantity of solid waste daily. The per capita solid waste generation has been reported high in the river basin as compared to the non-basin/coastal areas.

Table 9
Basin-wise Solid Waste Generation In Metro Cities

Major River Basin	*No. Cities*	*Metro City*	*Municipal Population*	*Municipal Solid Waste Tons/day*	*Basin-wise Per Capita Generated Kg/day*
Cauvery	2	Bangalore	4130288	2000	0.484
		Coimbatore	816321	350	0.429
Sub Total	*2*		*4946609*	*2350*	*0.475*
Ganga	9	Bhopal	1062771	546	0.515
		Calcutta	10643211	3692	0.347
		Delhi	8419084	4000	0.475
		Indore	1091674	350	0.321
		Jaipur	1458483	580	0.398
		Kanpur	1874409	1200	0.64
		Lucknow	1619115	1010	0.624
		Patna	917243	330	0.36
		Varanati	1030863	412	0.4
Sub Total	*9*		*28116853*	*12120*	*0.431*
Godavari	1	Nagpur	1624752	443	0.273
Indus	1	Ludhiana	1042740	400	0.384
Krishna	2	Hyderabad	4098734	1566	0.382
		Pune	2244196	700	0.312
Sub Total	*2*		*6342930*	*2266*	*0.357*
Mahi	1	Vadodara	1031346	400	0.388
Sabarmati	1	Ahmedabad	2876710	1683	0.585
Tapi	1	Surat	1498817	900	0.6
Coastal	4	Bombay	12288519	5355	0.436
		Kochi	670009	347	0.518
		Madras	4752976	3000	0.657
		Visakha-patnam	752337	9126	0.399
Sub Total	*4*		*18463541*	*9126*	*0.488*
No Major Basin		Madurai	940989	370	0.393
Grand Total/ Average	*23*		*66885287*	*30058*	*0.449*

Source: Status of Municipal Solid Waste Generation Collection Treatment and Disposal in Metro Cities, Central Pollution Control Board, Ministry of Environment & Forests.

Table 10
Basin-Wise Status of Municipal Solid Waste Treatment and Disposal in Class-I Cities

Basin	*No. of Cities*	*Solid Waste Collection MT/day*	*Treatment MT/day*	*Mode of Disposal (%)*		
				Dumping	Composting	Others
Brahmani	1	119	–	100	–	–
Brahmaputra	7	280	–	86	14	–
Cauvery	16	3333	210	99	0.6	0.4
Ganga	103	17982	850	98	1	1
Godavari	25	2263	85	98	1	1
Indus	15	1359	–	100	–	–
Krishna	27	4190	427	94	3	3
Mahanadi	9	872	–	100	–	–
Mahi	3	457	104	75	2	2
Narmada	4	354	–	75	–	–
Pennar	6	307	–	100	–	–
Sabarmati	7	1816	84	99	–	–
Subamarekha	2	335	–	100	–	–
Tapi	8	1562	305	78	9	9
Coastal	29	10689	560	85	1	1
No Major Basin	37	2216	161	90.5	0.5	0.5
Total	299	48134	2786	94	1	1

Source: Status of Municipal Solid Waste Generation Collection Treatment and Disposal in Class-I Cities, Central Pollution Control Board, April 2000, Ministry of Environment & Forests.

Basin-wise status of solid waste treatment and disposal in class-I cities is shown in Table 11. In most of the class-I cities the standard mode of disposal of waste is reported to be dumping. However, the class-I cities located in Brahmaputra and Tapti river basin, a significant proportion of solid waste is also being composted.

Table 11
State-Wise Quantities of Hazardous Waste Generation

State/ UTs	*No. of Districts*	*Hazardous Waste Units*	*Quantity of Waste Generated (Waste Type) (TPA)*			
			Recyclable	*Incinerable*	*Disposable*	*Total*
Andhra Pradesh	23	22	42634	4931	34986	82551
Assam	23	8	–	–	166008	166008

Contd..

State/ UTs	No. of Districts	Hazardous Waste Units	Quantity of Waste Generated (Waste Type) (TPA) Recyclable	Incinerable	Disposable	Total
Bihar	55	10	NA	NA	NA	31400
Chandi-garh	1	1	–	–	30	30
Delhi	9	9	NA	NA	NA	59423
Goa	2	2	NA	NA	326	8742
Gujarat	24	24	259000	19963	159000	439000
Haryana	17	15	–	–	31046	31046
Himachal Pradesh	12	6	NA	NA	NA	NA
Karnataka	27	25	13330	3328	16641	3382
Kerala	14	8	17582	5069	780014	870015
Maha-rashtra	33	33	800000	44000	1145600	1950000
Madhya Pradesh	61	NA	NA	NA	NA	1319779
Orissa	30	17	NA	NA	NA	1483824
Jammu & Kashmir	14	NA	NA	NA	NA	9768
Pondi-cherry	1	1	8010	171	754	8935
Punjab	17	15	NA	NA	NA	11025
Rajasthan	32	26	7994	18985	2239730	2266709
Tamil Nadu	29	29	193507	4699	196002	394210
Uttar Pradesh	83	75	3150	10650	32500	47000
West Bengal	17	9	7240	650	121767	129657
Total	524	335	1352447	112446	4924404	9342404

Source: Air Quality Status and Trends in India.

The quantity of hazardous waste generated is shown in Table 13. There were 335 hazardous waste units located in 524 districts of the country. These units generate about 9.3 million tons of hazardous waste and most of the hazardous waste is found to be disposable.

The estimated quantity of infectious bio-medical waste is shown in Table 14. During 1993, the infectious bio-medical waste generation was reported to be about 1500 tons per day. Most of such infectious bio-medical waste generation was reported in Karnataka, Maharashtra, Gujarat, Andhra Pradesh, Uttar Pradesh, West Bengal and Tamil Nadu. It is expected that by this time, the quantity of infectious bio-medical waste generation has increased tremendously.

Table 13
Number of Beds and Estimated Quantity of Infectious Bio-Medical Waste

(As on 01.01.1993)

States/UTs	*Total No. of Beds*	*# Estimated Quantity of Infectious Bio-Medical Waste Generation(kg/day)*
Andhra Pradesh	26791	6698
Arunachal Pradesh	2476	619
Assam	12661	3164
Bihar	29030	7273
Goa	3644	911
Gujarat	58984	14746
Haryana	7028	1757
Himachal Pradesh	3852	963
Jammu & Kashmir '89	8202	2051
Karnataka	37929	94811
Kerala	77199	19300
Madhya Pradesh	18141	4534
Maharashtra	78920	19730
Manipur	1561	299
Meghalaya	1867	467
Mizoram	1304	326
Nagaland	1050	263
Orissa	14494	3624
Punjab	14671	3668
Rajasthan	20465	5115
Sikkim '92	575	144
Tamil Nadu '86	48780	12195
Tripura	1730	433
Uttar Pradesh '86	47278	11820
West Bengal	54767	13692
Andaman & Nicobar Islands	576	144
Chandigarh	500	125
Dadra & Nagar Haveli	70	18
Daman & Diu '92	150	38
Delhi	18770	4693
Lakshadweep	70	18
Pondicherry '92	2608	652
India	596203	149051

Source: Manual on Hospital Waste Management, Central Pollution Control Board, Ministry of Environment & Forests, Govt. of India.

In India, municipal governments are responsible for the provision and maintenance of a number of civic amenities such as water supply, sanitation, refuse collection and disposal, drainage, sewerage, conservancy, primary education, public health, street lighting, roads and public works within their jurisdiction. Various studies and reports indicate that the municipal authorities in India have not been able to provide basic services at a satisfactory level. Rapid population growth, urbanization and industrial growth have led to severe problems of waste management in cities. The problems of solid waste disposal and sanitation appear almost intractable as urban India today is a site of rotting garbage (Hindu, 1995).

Reliable estimates of solid waste generation are not-readily available. Most estimates are based on per capita norms. It is estimated that each urban resident generates 350 to 1000 grams of solid waste every day. If wastes from commercial and industrial establishments are added, then the total waste generation every day will add up to an enormous quantity (Hindu, 1995). Studies have shown that it varies from a low of 294 grams to a high of 484 grams per capita per day (NIUA, 1989); the variation being explained by a variety of reasons including the size of cities, their functions, households income and the level of economic development. A large quantity of waste requires proper systems of collection, transportation and disposal. It also requires knowledge of what the wastes are made-up of, how they need to be collected and disposed. Recycling of waste and energy generation from waste has great potential. Proper solid waste management requires commitment and resources to deal with. Municipal authorities do not have adequate resources and technical capacity to deal with the gigantic problem. Successful waste management requires involvement of the community and private entrepreneurs to work with local governments. Therefore, the collection efficiency of municipal solid waste has been reported low. On an average, roughly 30-40 per cent of total waste generated remains uncollected, which is one of the biggest sources of environmental degradation.

The options for the treatment and disposal of household and commercial waste have largely been confined to landfill, which constitutes a major share while incineration of household waste is much under-utilized option. Recycling and reuse of household and commercial waste are similarly under-utilized options, with only small proportion falling into these categories. Thus, landfill is chosen at the most suitable option in most cases because of its low cost, ready availability and applicability for a wide range of wastes. Landfill can also be regarded as an environmentally acceptable method of waste disposal.

In most cities, solid waste is collected from and around bins of inadequate capacity and transported to dump sites at the periphery. The indiscriminate dumping of waste in the nearest available low-lying area often causes damage to the soil. Very few cities practice scientific method of sanitary landfill or convert the waste into compost or energy. Almost no city has arrangements to separate garbage before collection. In large cities, the landfill sites and bins therefore attract a large number of poor people who scavenge for bits of metal, paper and plastic to feed the recycling trade (Mathur, 2001). Interestingly, conservancy activity is usually entrusted to the health department in a municipality in almost all cities and towns in India. This is mainly because of the association of sanitation and public hygiene with public health. The transport of waste is done by mechanised and non-mechanised modes from collection point to the disposal sites. The transport vehicles are maintained by the Engineering Wing headed by an Engineer. For street sweeping, collection of refuse and for loading and unloading, the municipal bodies employ a large number of conservancy staff. They also provide dustbins depots or places for temporary deposit of rubbish at convenient locations, and require the occupant of premises to deposit the rubbish in those deposits and dust bins (Mathur, 1994). The sanitary workers are being provided wheelbarrow to collect rubbish from such locations and dump at outskirts of street. From such locations mechanised vehicle collect the rubbish and is being dumped at landfilling sites. In actual practice, in smaller and medium sized urban centres households and commercial establishments throw the refuse and offensive matters on the streets, from where it is collected by the municipal bodies. In larger local bodies, where door to door collection by municipal agencies is not practised, the households enter into private arrangement with the sweepers to get the refuse and offensive matter collected from the houses and disposited in the dust bins. The refuse collected from various points is disposed off by different methods in different urban centres viz. dumping, sanitary landfill and composting. Majority of the municipal bodies adopt dumping due to non-availability of mechanized forms of transport. Generally, the low-lying areas and the outskirts of the towns are used for this purpose. However, they constitute a health hazard and become breeding grounds for flies, mosquitoes, bacteria's and viruses.

With the liberalization of economy, the active participation of private sector including NGO's in provision of services has been well recognized. Municipal field is no exception of it. Though management of municipal waste is wholesale responsibility of municipal bodies, however, private partnership has enhanced the efficiency and improved the sanitary conditions. Public-private partnerships have resulted in cost savings for most public agencies that have used such arrangements.

An enormous variety of technologies are either available or potentially available for the management of municipal wastes. These technologies are mainly landfill, composting, pulverization, baling, pyrolysis and thermal processing, incineration, biological processing etc.

Our experience reveals that in most of the cities, methods adopted for collection, segregation, disposal and treatment of waste are not proper and adequate. Most of the cities and towns lack proper and adequate infrastructure for collection, segregation and disposal of waste. Moreover, in most of the cities and towns landfill sites have been absorbed and require proper space for creation of new landfill sites. However, there is no provision for allocating land for landfill sites in master plan and generally housing authorities allow to dump urban waste where such authorities are planning to develop land for housing purpose in near future.

Waste generated in India has less fuel efficiency since the content of waste is not suitable for energy generation like gasification, brequetting, composting, etc., however, some part of waste generated may be used for composting and production of bio-fertilizers. Vermi-compost units may be established at nearby temples and markets of fruits and vegetables since degradable waste from fruits and vegetables and flowers is best suited as raw materials for vermi-composting.

Community participation is lacking in sustainable solid waste management in most of the cities and towns in India. However, some NGOs and other community-based organizations have shown credentials in this field. Thus, community is supposed to be educated, mobilized and motivated for adopting safe practices of collection, segregation, recycling and disposal of waste at household level.

The planning for solid waste management is required to be promoted on sound management practices such as identification of alternatives, content analysis, evaluation of alternatives, selecting course of action, formulating derivative plans, control process, monitoring, auditing and performance evaluation of adopted practices and intervention, etc.

In India, domestic and industrial wastewaters have to meet the standards setout in the Environmental (Protection), and Water (Prevention & Control of Pollution) Act, 1974. In order to meet the general discharge standards, adequate treatment has to be given for discharge either to surface waters, coastal waters, public waters, public sewers or land. However, the pathetic situation is that in most of the cities and towns, the coverage of sewerage line is grossly inadequate and even the sewer lines are choked for a long time, causing health hazardous. Even in some cases, water supply lines are parallel with sewer lines, causing the risk of water silting from sewer lines resulting in water-borne diseases. Thus, the coverage of sewer lines and effective system of sewerage designs is required for sage disposal of human excreta and wastewater. The lost cost sanitation programme is also to be strengthened for construction of low cost sanitary latrines, conversion of dry latrines into sanitary latrines and rehabilitation of manual scavengers.

Only 70 per cent of India's urban population has adequate excreta disposal facilities. It has long been government policy not to built sewerage systems in towns of less than 10 million people. Even, there is widespread ignorance among officials for the existing levels of access to excreta disposal facilities. Due to inadequate sewerage and lack of wastewater treatment facilities, river water and other sources for drinking water supply are accessibly polluted, putting further demands on water treatment process and contributing to the increase of water-borne diseases.

The institutional deficiencies related to urban water supply and sanitation may be summarized as:

(1) management, autonomy and accountability,

(2) consumer orientation

(3) management structures and continuity

(4) organizational resource management, and

(5) accounting and financial management.

Lack of autonomy and accountability results in unnecessarily risk averse, rule bound behaviour and ignorance of the problems. General lack of consumer orientation is reflected in a lack of consumer consultation, participation and re-enforcement of urban water supply and sanitation programme. In proper management structures and continuity prevent development of specific skills and a longer-term outlook among managers. Poor procurement of materials, poor construction practices and inadequate maintenance has reduced the operating deficiencies of water supply and sanitation in urban areas. Lack of institutional and managerial autonomy and accountability in urban water supply and sanitation programme may also lead to institutional deficiencies. Thus, appropriate institutional arrangements, regulations and municipal reforms are required for improving the efficiency of urban water supply and sanitation.

Waste generated at residents needs proper collection. Separation or segregation of waste in degradable and non biodegradable form at household level will enhance the efficiency of collection and disposal system. Research studies should be encouraged, sponsored to analyse the generation, collection and the efficiency and effectiveness of the municipal services. Moreover, the studies should be aimed at analysing the physical composition of waste and potentials of energy recovery, assessing potential technologies for safe disposal of waste and effective utilization of waste. Studies should be also aimed at examining existing system of municipal solid waste management and possibilities of private-public partnerships, ensuring community participation. Proper installation of community bins of appropriate sizes, frequency of their cleaning is necessary to have clean environment. The sites of dumping and landfill are required to be well planned in terms of perspective planning and scientifically designed. Environment education programmes should be formulated and implemented, involving community organizations and private partnerships. Privatization of solid waste operations is a possible solution, which needs to be explored. This possibility should be properly assessed and local NGO's should be entrusted the task of mobilising residents for safe disposal of domestic waste, construction of sanitary latrines, vermiculture, effective participation in sanitation programmes and collection and disposal of municipal solid waste. Improving the morale of the conservancy staff through proper incentives and support. Effective supervision of scavengers, sweepers and other sanitary workers to increase their productivity. Proper maintenance of vehicles and equipment is required. More addition of mechanised vehicles and equipments will improve the efficiency of solid waste collection and disposal. Training for sanitary workers, officials and local NGO's and also private organizations should be ensured to impart technical education for construction and designing of dumping and landfill sites, planning and education of waste management and disposal technologies, etc. Empowerment of sanitary workers, particularly scavengers is the need of hour. It can be achieved through imparting skill development programmes and training. Moreover, construction of individual latrines in urban localities should be ensured through monitoring provisions and community mobilization. Effective check on hazardous waste disposal in water bodies should be ensured along with effective and efficient system for maintenance of community toilets. Moreover, open burial and dumping of dead animals in water bodies should be checked effectively. For the purpose, electric burials at river ghats should be revived.

AIR POLLUTION

In India, air pollution is primarily an urban phenomenon, with main sources being motor vehicles, industries, thermal power plants, and the use of coal and firewood in the domestic sector. Air pollution is the release of particles into the air from burning fuel for energy. There are large quantities of gases in the atmosphere which are creating air pollution and causing global warming. The release of noxious gases such as sulpher dioxide, carbon-mono-oxide, nitrogen-oxide and chemical vapours is causing green house effect. Green house effect is also referred as global warming.

Table 14
Contribution of Green House Gases to Atmosphere in India (2001)

Green Houses Gases	*Contribution to Atmosphere (%)*
Carbon-dioxide	55
Methane	15
CFCs 11 & 12	17
Nitrous-oxide	6
Others	7

Source: Compendium of Environment Statistics, 2001, Ministry of Statistics and Programme Implementation, Govt. of India.

Air pollution in urban areas is mainly contributed by vehicle emissions. Even in the vehicle emissions, the major contribution is reported to be two-wheelers emissions. Carbon-mono-oxide, nitrogen-oxide and hydro-carbons contribute in the vehicle emissions (Table 16).

Contribution of green house gases to atmosphere in India is shown in Table 14. Carbon-dioxide is the only major green house gas that effects atmosphere adversely.

Table 15
Urban Air Pollution from Vehicular Emissions

Pollutant	*Sources of Emission*	*Contribution (Percent) of the source to Total Emissions*	*Remarks*
Carbon Mono-oxide	Petrol-driven vehicles	85.0	Contribution of two-wheelers is expected to rise
Unburnt Hydrocarbons	Two and Three-wheelers	35 to 65	–
Nitrogen Oxides	Diesel-driven vehicles	90 or more	–
Particulates	Diesel-driven vehicles	–	–

Source: Urban Statistics, Hand Book 2000, National Institute of Urban Affairs.

Category-wise pollution load of vehicles is shown in Table 3.57. The major contribution in the vehicle emissions has been reported to be from two-wheelers, private carrier goods, three-wheelers and trucks. The use of CNG in automotive sector has reduced drastically the emissions from vehicles. Therefore, in most of the cities and towns, CNG is widely used in three-wheelers, buses and other commercial goods carriers (Table 18).

Table 18
Reduction in Emission in Automotive Sector Due to Use of CNG

Emissions	CNG gm/Km	Diesel gm/km	% Reduction
Particulate	0.04	0.44	90
Carbon Monoxide	0.68	2.40	71
Nitrogen Oxide	6.26	22.50	72
Non-Methane Hydrocarbon	1.25	1.50	17
Total	8.23	26.84	69

Source: Air Quality Status and Trends in India.

The industrial and commercial activities in the urban areas are increasing the noise levels which is causing detrimental to

Table 17

Category-Wise Pollution Load Of Vehicles (2005)

(In Thousand Tons)

Vehicles	*CO*	*HC*	*NO_x*	*PM*	*Benzene*	*BUTDN*	*Ozone Potential*
Buses	24.7472	5.527692	76.4352	6.3844	0.026171	0.0048	19.1597
Taxis	2.204345	0.421481	1.020249	0.510331	0.024397	0.007556	1.4609
PCG	595.1925	102.9881	114.5861	5.37958	6.357509	0.93816	357.0164
PCD	2.8754	0.50072	1.431865	0.571527	0.028627	0.008752	1.7357
MUV-G	16.00954	2.242921	3.108215	0.168137	0.167631	0.024967	7.7751
MUV-D	30.15951	1.804338	16.11801	7.291563	0.175473	0.058491	6.25488
3W	63.41416	44.8064	0.968903	1.129543	1.575929	0.069132	155.3234
4S/2W	40.24123	11.3397	4.773367	0.926914	0.669075	0.088262	39.3099
2S/2W	391.206	281.8195	4.46923	6.65697	4.013949	0.435521	1028.249
Trucks	55.25224	11.58194	74.72162	11.86569	0.05888	0.011176	40.1496
LCV	104.6087	3.303424	30.03871	7.829501	0.165171	0.047691	11.4513
Total	1325.911	466.3362	327.6715	48.71416	13.26281	1.694508	1667.886

Source: Transport Fuel Quality For Year 2005. Central Pollution Control Board, Ministry of Environment and Forests, Government of India.

the human health. The noise level has been reported high in the industrial and commercial areas as compared to residential areas. Even noise level has been reported high during festive seasons such as Diwali and Dusshera. The average noise level in various metropolitan cities of India is shown in Table 19.

Table 19
Average Noise Levels in Various Metropolitan Cities of India (2001)

(DB [A])

Metropolitan Cities	*Day/Night*	*Industrial Area*	*Commercial Area*	*Residential Area*	*Silence Area*
Calcutta	Day	78	82	79	79
	Night	67	75	65	65
Mumbai	Day	76	75	70	66
	Night	65	66	62	52
Chennai	Day	71	78	66	63
	Night	66	71	48	49
Bangalore	Day	78	76	67	67
	Night	53	57	50	NA

Source: Compendium of Environment Statistics, 2001, Ministry of Statistics and Programme Implementation, Govt. of India.

The atmosphere that surrounds the Earth contains many types of gases, including those known as "greenhouse gases". Greenhouse gases (GHG) absorb and retain heat from the sun. They regulate the Earth's climate by holding warmth in an atmospheric blanket around the planet's surface. Scientists call this phenomenon the "greenhouse effect". Without greenhouse gases, the average temperature on Earth would be –2 degrees Fahrenheit instead of the current 57 degrees Fahrenheit. Excess greenhouse gases in the atmosphere, however, can raise global temperatures. In the past 100 years, scientists have detected an increase of 1 degree Fahrenheit in the Earth's average surface temperature. Solid waste disposal contributes to greenhouse gas (GHG) emissions in a variety of ways. The disposal of solid waste produces GHGs in a number of ways. Solid waste disposal and recycling increases emission of gases as it involves lot of energy consumption. The anaerobic decomposition of waste in landfills produces methane, a GHG 21 times more potent than carbon dioxide. The incineration of waste produces carbon dioxide as a by-product. In addition, the transportation of waste to disposal sites produces GHGs from the combustion of the fuel used in the equipment. Falling of green cover and increasing solid waste is contributing to increased amount of carbon dioxide in the atmosphere. Rising levels of greenhouse gases in the Earth's atmosphere are causing changes in our climate, and some of these changes can be traced to solid waste. The manufacture, distribution, and use of products all result in greenhouse gas emissions. Waste prevention and recycling are real ways to help mitigate climate change.

Climate change is one of the most important global environmental challenges facing humanity with implications for food production, nature, eco-systems, fresh water supply, health, etc. The Earth's climate system has changed on both global and regional scales. The global warming is attributable to human activities. The Inter-governmental Panel on Climate Change (IPCC) has projected that the global mean temperature may increase between 1.4 and 5.8 degree Celsius by 2100. This unprecedented increase is expected to have served adverse impacts on environment and ecology. The impact would be particularly severe in the tropical areas, which mainly consist of developing countries, including India.

The UN Conference on Environment and Development (UNCED) in 1992 at Rio-de Janeiro led to Framework Convention on Climate Change (FCCE), which led to the framework for the eventual stabilization of green house gases in the atmosphere. The Convention came into force in 1994. Subsequently, the 1997 Kyoto protocol, which came into force in 2005, reasserted the importance of stabilizing green house gas concentrations in the atmosphere and adhering to sustainable development principles. The combustion of fossil fuels and other human activities are the primary reasons for increased concentrations of CO_2 and other green house gases. Between 199 and 1999, an estimated 6.3 GTC/year was released due to the combustion of fossil fuels and another 1.6 GTC/ year was released due to burning of forest vegetation. Thus, controlling the release of green house gases from fossil fuels, change in land use and burning of vegetation affects temperature. Reducing green house gas emissions can lesser the increasing rate of global warming. Among the green house gases emissions, CO_2 accounted for 63 per cent, methane 24 per cent, nitrous oxide 10 per cent and other gases the remaining 3 per cent of the carbon equivalent emissions in 2000.

The industrialized countries have been the primary contribution to emissions of CO_2 and they are responsible for about 83 per cent of the rise in cumulative fossil fuel related CO_2 emissions. Developing countries account for only 37 per cent of cumulative CO_2 emissions from industrial sources and land use change in 1999. India is a developing country with a large population directly depending on climate sensitive sectors and natural resources for their subsistence and livelihoods. India's contribution to the cumulative global CO_2 emissions from 1980 to 2003 is only 3.11 per cent. Thus, India's share in the carbon stock in the atmosphere is relatively very small as compared to its population size. India's carbon emissions per capita are far less than most Western Europe and Japan. However, India has already adopted Clean Development Mechanism (CDM) which focuses on environmentally sustainable technologies to promote energy efficiency renewable energy and foresting activities that contribute to sustainable development.

The United Nations supported Inter-Government Panel on Climate Change (IPCC) has submitted its fourth assessment of global warming in early 2007. The Report produced incontrovertible evidence that the atmospheric concentration of green house gases like carbon dioxide methane and nitrous oxide has by far exceeded the usual range of last years. The CO_2 concentration has touched the highest levels in recorded history. The gases cause a giant greenhouse effect by forming them around the Earth, trapping infra-red rays could send temperatures soaring to dangerously high levels and trigger catastrophic changes in the climate. India is among the countries that will suffer the most serious consequences as a result of such global warming. The global warming in India will result in drop in per capita water availability, as drought would become frequent. There will rise in sea levels in coastal areas, as Himalayan glaciers will melt. The Himalayan glaciers will disappear, causing catastrophic disruptions. In the plains, winter precipitation would decline, causing water shortage, shrinking grass lands and triggering a fodder crisis. There will be a fall in wheat yields in India with the increasing temperature. Thus, food grain production in India is likely to drop. Since the Gangentic plain warned turn infertile. Vector-borne diseases, like dengue and malaria, are expected to rise sharply across India as changes in temperature make it conducive for mosquitoes to thrive. The bio-diversity in India will be at risk because of climate change. The country's grasslands are expected to decline precipitously. The forest resources will deplete rapidly and country mangroves are likely to be wiped out due to rising of sea levels. It would also lead to salt dissolution, severely impacting marine life and fisheries. Thus, strategies to cope up with the emerging challenges of global warming must be developed and enforced effectively and efficiently.

The global consumption of resources is increasingly resulting in climate change, damage to bio-diversity and depletion of water supplies. Thus, urgent action is required to both reduce our climate impacts and improve resource efficiency. The waste management and climate change have direct co-relations. In order to ensure resource efficiency and climate change, we must phase out the residual waste, which is currently land filled or incinerated. The following waste policies to maximize resource efficiency may be adopted to show the way: (i) waste prevention or mitigation – the best environmental option and avoiding resource use; (ii) re-use – reducing need for resources and manufacturing; (iii) recycling – reducing need for extraction and processing of new resources; (iv) composting – return nutrients and structure to soils while anaerobic digestion produces methane which may be used as renewable energy source. The land filling bio-degradable wastes lead to methane production and contribute negatively to climate change. The land filling of materials that could be recycled have to be replaced. Thus, diversion of bio-degradable wastes through composting and recycling is imperative. It is also necessary to ban land filling of renewable, recyclable and compostable materials. Thus, efforts are needed to reduce the volume of residual wastes and methane production in landfill. Mechanical biological treatment to residual waste prior to land filling is also important. Incineration creates a demand for residual waste and generates energy inefficiency while emitting fossil fuel derived CO_2. Moreover, phasing out of residual waste will also require other changes, such as re-designing of goods to be reusable, recyclable or compostable.

In view of the above, effective waste prevention programmes need to be developed. Importantly, segregation, proper collection, transportation, treatment and disposal of wastes are to be ensured by local bodies in order to reduce the adverse impact of wastes on climate change.

Summing up, global climate change has emerged as a threat to sustainability. In the absence of adaptation and mitigation strategies climate change can seriously damage agriculture, water resources, forests, coastal areas and health, etc. in the Indian economy. Thus, adequate focus on institutional arrangements to devise suitable strategies is needed. Moreover, Clean Development Mechanism for mitigating the emissions of green house gases has to be promoted to provide energy intensive industries and using renewable resources in production and operations of projects

REFERENCES

ADB (2000), India: Mainstreaming Environment for Sustainable Development, Asian Development Bank, Manila, .

Akolkar, A.B. (2005), Status of Solid Waste Management in India: Implementation Status of Municipal Solid Wastes, Management and Handling Rules, 2000, Central Pollution Control Board, New Delhi.

Bhattacharya S. et. al. (2004), Soil Degradation in India: An Environmental and Socio-economic Hazard, in integrating the Rural Poor into Markets by (ed), Bibek Debroy and Amir Ullah Khan, Academic Foundation, Delhi.

Bose, R.K.G.et. al.(1998), India's Environmental Pollution and Control, Tata Energy Research Institution, New Delhi.

CPCB (1998), Status of Water Supply and Waste Water Collection, Treatment and Disposal in Class I and Class II Cities, Central Pollution Control Board, New Delhi.

CPCK (2000), Status of Municipal Solid Waste, Waste Generation, Collection, Treatment and Disposal in Class I Cities, Central Pollution Control Board, Delhi.

Girand, P.N. et. al. (2004), Lessons for the Policy Makers: Elements for Sustainable Water Policy for Indian Cities, CERNA and MEEDSA Research Report, Paris.

Kothari, Ashish (1997), Understanding Biodiversity: Life Sustainability and Equity, Orient, Longman, New Delhi .

Mahapatra, R. (2001), Drought of Relief, *Down to Earth,* June, 15 .

MOA (1996), Status of Land Degradation in India, Ministry of Agriculture, Government of India, Delhi.

MOEF (2000), Status of Implementation of the Hazardous Waste Rules, 1989, Ministry of Environment and Forests, Delhi.

MOUD (2005), Management of Solid Waste in Indian Cities, Ministry of Urban Development, Government of India, Delhi.

NIUA (2000), Status of Water Supply, Sanitation and Solid Waste Management in Urban India, National Institute of Urban Affairs, Delhi .

Pandey, S. et. al. (2006), Urban Environment in India, Infrastructure Report, 2006, OUP, Delhi .

Paul, S. and S. Sekhar (2000), Benchmarking Urban Services, Public Affairs Centre, Bangalore.

Ruet, J. and Zerah, M.H. (2002), The Water & Sanitation Scenario in Indian Metropolitan Cities, Centre de Sciences, Humaines, New Delhi.

Sainath, P. (2000), Everybody Loves A Good Drought, In India Disasters Report, OUP, Delhi.

Sehgal, J.L. et. al. (1989), Soil Degradation in India: Status and Impact, OUP, New Delhi .

Sengupta, S. (2000), Droughts: Reaping Scarcity in India Disasters Report, OUP, Delhi,

Singh, A.K. and S. Khanna (2005), Solid Waste Management in India, *Indian Journal of Development Research & Social Action,* Vol. 1(1), January-June.

Singh, K. and Steinberg, F. (ed) (1996), Urban India in Crisis, New AgeInternational Ltd., New Delhi.

Singh, U.B. and Singh A.K. (2004), Socio-economic Dimensions of Natural Disasters in India: Suggested Strategies for Mitigations, paper presented in World Congress on Natural Disaster Mitigation, organized by World Federation of Engineering Organizations, Delhi, 19-22, February.

TERI (1998), Green India 2047: Looking Back to Think Ahead: Growth with Resource Enhancement of Environment and Nature, Tata Energy Research Institute, Delhi.

UNDP (1993), Land Degradation in South Asia: Its Severity, Causes and Effects Upon the People, UNDP, FAO,UNEP.

UNEP (2001), State of the Environment India, 2001, UNEP, Thailand.

Usnani, P.U. (2006), Solid Waste Management, In India Infrastructure Report, 2006, OUP, Delhi.

World Bank - India's Environment (1996), Taking Stock of Plans, Programmes and Priorities: An Assessment of the Environment Action programme - India, South Asia Regional Office, Washington DC.

Zerah, M.H. (2006), Urban Water and Waste Water, In India, Infrastructure Report, 2006 OUP, Delhi .

5

URBAN SANITATION AND HYGIENE PROMOTION

INTRODUCTION

Urbanization in India is characterized by unplanned and uncontrolled growth which leads to urban sprawl. It has generated a series of negative environmental and social effects. The urban local bodies do not have adequate resources and infrastructure facilities for delivery of civic services effectively. As growth of urbanization continues, the environmental problems are escalating. While environmental problems such as air pollution, water pollution and degradation of natural resources are occasionally addressed by local governments, the insanitary conditions of large population are ignored. The environmental conditions in Indian cities are worse and urbanization caused by migration escalates the housing problems, resulting in growth of slums. The sanitation and water supply systems are causing serious concern for environmental pollution. A large section of urban population is being ignored for providing proper sanitation and water supply services. The sanitation movement had a very limited impact on the population in India due to poor attention paid on public health, sanitation and hygiene. On the one hand, a large population in urban areas still lacks proper sanitation facilities, while on the other, manual scavenging still prevails in large parts of the country due to ineffective enforcement of Employment of Manual Scavengers and Construction of Dry Toilets (Prohibition) Act, 1993. The outbreak of plague in Surat City in 1994 forced the various levels of government to intervene in the sector.

TRENDS OF URBANIZATION

In 2000, the world's urban population had increased to almost 2.9 billion, about 47 per cent of the total population. Today Asian countries have emerged as most populous countries. According to United Nations Study (1995), by the year 2015 ten of the world's fifteen largest cities will be in Asia, three of these will be in India. Of the 10 most populous countries, 6 are in Asia.

The demographic and economic growth in India is likely to be concentrated in and around fifty to sixty large cities with population of about a million or more. There is migration from villages to town and cities which results in growth of metropolitan cities since they provide multiple avenues, services and amenities viz. education, health care, employment, business and entertainment options etc. People also migrate for economic opportunities and urban life styles. Though urbanization brings about development in the social, economic and cultural spheres of life, but sometimes it disturbs the ecological system. Rapid and unplanned growth of urban agglomeration generates a series of negative environmental and social effects. Today urban India presents a very pathetic scene. Cities have become a site of rotting garbage, degrading drainage system and shocking night soil removal system. Besides, poor have practically no access to covered toilets and in many towns and cities, the majority have to defecate in the open. Moreover, the untreated sewage being dumped into the nearest water body leads to health hazards.

India is one of the least urbanized countries in the world because between 1951 and 2001, the level of urbanization increased by 13 percentage points only. However, it has the second largest urban population in the world and more than two-third of it lives in the 423 cities that have population of over one lakh. The four mega cities of viz., Mumbai, Kolkata, Delhi and Chennai with a population of more than 6 millions each in 2001 account for almost one fourth of population living in cities. As per the 2001 Census, 285 million population i.e. 27.8 per cent of 1027 million total population of India is residing in 4,368 cities and towns in the country, whereas in 1991, 25.7 per cent population lived in urban areas. The decadal growth in urban population during 1991-2001 has been 31.2 per cent, whereas at the beginning of the 20th century, only 10.8 per cent of total 218 million population of the country resided in cities and towns. The number of million plus cities has increased to 35 in 2001 from 12 in 1981 and 23 in 1991. These 35 million-plus cities account for 107.9 million urban population of the country. As per projections of Government of India, the urban population of the country in 2011 will be 405.26 million and 553.04 million in 2021. Thus, around one third population is expected to live in urban areas.

There has been phenomenon growth in the number of towns and urban agglomerations over the period of 1981 to 2001, however, annual exponential growth rate of urban population is low. There has been just 2.06 percentage points increase in proportion of urban population to total population during 1991 to 2001.

An analysis of the distribution of urban population by size categories reveals that the process of urbanization in India has been oriented towards large cities, since a high proportion proved that a high proportion of urban population is concentrated in Class I cities, which has gone up systematically over the decades in the last century. The massive increase in proportion of Class I cities from 26 per cent in 1901 to 85.20 per cent in 1991 while it decline to 68.67 per cent in 2001, has been attributed to faster growth of large cities.

The startling fact is that the proportion of population living in smaller towns has shown declining trend over the period, while there has been a marked growth in population of larger towns. Importantly, growth of population in smaller towns has been reported negative while the growth of population in large cities and towns has been found massive. During 2001, a high percentage of urban population had been reported in Delhi, Pondicherry, Goa, Chandigarh, Maharashtra, Mizoram, Lakshadweep, Tamil Nadu, Karnataka, Gujarat etc.

Uttar Pradesh occupies the central position in the northern India. It is the most populous state in the country. The state witnessed a tremendous growth in its urban population during the last three decades. Between 1971-81 the decadal growth was about 60.62 per cent, the highest in the country. In 1981-91 this growth was about 38.97 per cent, second after Orissa. As per the 2001 Census, every fifth person in the state is residing in urban centres. The total urban population of the State has increased to 347 million showing an increase of about 33 per cent during the decade 1991-2001. However, the pace of urbanization and level of urbanization has been reported lower than most of the other States. In 2001, 20.78 per cent population of Uttar Pradesh was found to be living in urban areas. It may be mentioned that during 1991-2001, urban population grew by 2.84 per cent per annum.

As per census, there are 670 towns and cities in the state. Most of the towns and cities are categorized as class IV and Class III having population in between 10,000 to 50,000. However, urban population is concentrated in large towns and cities. As per information available from SUDA, Uttar Pradesh, 4.3 million population is living in more than seven thousand slum pockets in the State. About 28 per cent slum dwellers do not have proper drainage facility and adequate sanitation coverage.

The task of improving urban services is constantly more challenging due to the large increase in population. This has put a strain on the present management and delivery systems. In many cases delivery mechanisms would need to be redesigned to meet the large demand. If urban population growth is to be accelerated, it will need even greater acceleration in urban infrastructure investment. With the rapid urbanization that is now expected in ensuing decades in India, it would be better to decentralize the instruments of infrastructure provision so that the agencies providing such infrastructure services are able to finance themselves and can respond flexibly to the changing demand of growing city. It would be better if private agencies are given more opportunities to perform the functions of financing, planning and management of urban infrastructural services and amenities. There is a strong demand for wider coverage of urban infrastructure services, which is a daunting task given the expected huge growth in urban population and secondly, for improvement in the quality of urban infrastructure services especially in large cities.

The Tenth Plan had, in the context of urban development, laid stress on improving the functional and financial autonomy of urban local bodies, strengthening of their finances through smooth implementation of State Finance Commissions' awards, rationalization of property taxation system and levy of user charges. The Plan advocated broad-based measures for urban sector reforms and emphasized that public-private-partnership should be brought on the urban agenda in order to improve the efficiency and delivery of services.

The responsibility for urban water supply and sanitation lies with local governments. However, other stake-holding agencies extend support to urban local bodies in the delivery of sanitation and water supply services in urban areas. The Government of India and several State Governments have also lauched programmes for improving coverage, strengthening infrastructure and delivery mechanism. However, gaps still persist between access to water supply and sanitation infrastructure and access to services as far as the following four main criteria are concerned, reliability, financial sustainability, environmental sustainability and affordability.

STATUS OF URBAN SANITATION

In most developing countries, the three most important environmental health problems that affect a large majority of population are contaminated water supply, inadequate sanitation and untreated solid wastes. The Global Water Supply and Sanitation Assessment Report by WHO and UNICEF, 2000 states that at the beginning of that year, one-sixth of the world's population was without access to improved water supply and two-fifths lacked access to improved sanitation. In absence of proper sanitation, people suffered from high levels of infections diseases leading to high incidences of morbidity and mortality. About 2.4 billion people lacked access to adequate sanitation facilities and four out of five of these un-served people lived in Asia alone. Inadequate sanitation like unsafe disposal of human excreta, open defection, lack of infrastructure (sewerage, drainage, (sullage), and absence of hygiene management constitute a major threat to the health of the people. However, improving urban environmental health can prevent upto 44 per cent of the burden of the disease in cities of the developing world.

In recent years, there has been increasing recognition of the importance of sanitation not only due to its direct impact upon health, but also for its contribution to improved living environment, dignity, improved education outcomes and poverty reduction. In response, in 2002 at the World Summit or Sustainable Development in Johannesburg, international delegates acknowledged that it was not possible to reduce poverty without improved access to basic sanitation. This led to sanitation being included into the Millennium Development Goals (MDG's) and world leaders pledged their commitment to halve the proportion of people without access to basic sanitation by 2015.

It may be mentioned that poor sanitation and unsafe water have a high health risk but improvement in sanitation has greater impact on vector - related diseases. Due to lack of proper sanitation, water is contaminated, environment is polluted, vectors are increased, resulting in major health hazards. According to WHO Report of 2001, every year more than 5 million people die from illness linked to excreta disposal and improper hygiene practices. The World Bank, 1999 reported that by providing access to adequate sanitation and safe water to all who currently lack these facilities would result in a million fever deaths each year from diarrhoea among children of less than 5 years of age and 200 million fewer episodes of diarrhoea annually.

Sanitation (sewage, seepage, night soil, grey water and other forms of waste water and their sludges) can contain faecal matter responsible for a broad range of diseases that include diarrhoea, dysentery, gastroenteritis, cholera and intestinal worms like hook worm and ascariasis, tapeworm, threadworm and whipworm, hepatitis, typhoid, polio and range of fevers due to blood parasites. In addition, filarial and schist-psoriasis are spread to humans indirectly by mosquitoes and snails respectively which depend on excreta for their life cycles. Many diseases like diarrhoea and some worm infections can be transmitted in several ways. Invariably, faecal infective material enters the human body in or through some medium, like drinking water, the hands, soil, food, utensils and toys. Many possibilities for transmission can be attributed - faecal material may drain into a water source, hands may not have been washed after defecation or before handling food, flies or other insects may transmit infective organisms from faeces to food, etc.

Table 1 provides a comparative situation of availability of toilets for households in 1991 and 2001 for major States. At the national level, 76 per cent of the households were not having toilet facilities in 1991. This figure came down marginally to 64 per cent in 2001. During 1991, availability of toilets for households in urban areas was recorded high in Assam, followed by West Bengal, Punjab Madhya Pradesh and least in Orissa. During 2001, availability of toilets in urban households was reported high in Assam, Madhya Pradesh, Punjab, Uttaranchal, West Bengal, Haryana and Gujarat.

Table 1
Availability of Toilets for Households in Urban India

(Percentage)

	1991		*2001*		*No Toilet*	
State	*Total*	*Urban*	*Total*	*Urban*	*1991*	*2001*
Andhra Pradesh	18.40	54.60	32.99	78.07	81.60	67.01
Assam	37.43	86.06	64.64	94.60	62.57	35.36
Bihar	11.75	56.54	19.19	69.69	88.25	80.81
Chhatisgarh	–	–	14.2	52.59	NE	85.80
Delhi	63.38	66.64	77.96	79.03	36.62	22.02
Gujarat	30.60	65.71	44.60	80.55	69.31	55.40

Contd..

State	1991 Total	1991 Urban	2001 Total	2001 Urban	No Toilet 1991	No Toilet 2001
Haryana	22.45	64,25	44,50	80.66	37.55	55.50
Jharkhand	–	–	19.67	66.68	NE	80.33
Karnataka	24.13	62.52	37.50	75.23	75.87	62.50
Kerala	51.28	72.66	84.01	92.02	48.72	15.99
Madhya Pradesh	15.07	53.00	23.99	67.74	84.93	76.01
Maharastra	29.56	64.45	35.09	58.08	70.44	64.91
Orissa	9.81	49.27	14.89	59.69	90.19	85.11
Punjab	33.18	73.23	56.84	86.52	66.82	43.16
Rajasthan	19.57	62.24	29.00	76.11	80.43	71.00
Tamil Nadu	23.13	57.47	35.76	64.33	76.87	64.84
Uttar Pradesh	18.02	66.54	31.43	80.01	81.98	68.57
Uttaranchal	–	–	45.20	86.88	NE	54.80
West Bengal	31.51	78.75	43.71	84.85	68.49	56.29
India	23.70	63.85	21.92	73.72	76.30	63.59

Source: Census of India, 1991 and 2001.

The percentage of households without toilet facility has been reported to be 53.6 per cent in 2001. It was recorded much higher in rural areas i.e. 65.8 per cent as compared to urban areas (22.1 per cent). In urban areas, the proportion of households without toilet facility was reported to be higher in Kerala, Assam, Jharkhand, Mizoram, Chhatisgarh and Arunachal Pradesh as can be seen in the following Table.

Table 2
Percentage of Households having no Toilet in India

State	Total	Rural	Urban
India	53.6	65.8	22.1
Jammu & Kashmir	59.4	73.2	18.2
Himachal pradesh	62.8	69.2	13.9
Punjab	17.8	21.9	10.2
Uttaranchal	51.9	65.0	11.8
Haryana	23.2	28.3	11.6
Delhi	10.1	25.5	9.0
Rajasthan	63.5	76.8	19.8
Uttar Pradesh	29.5	35.0	7.6
Bihar	62.0	65.1	31.4
Sikkim	60.6	68.4	5.8
Arunachal Pradesh	65.5	73.9	36.7
Nagaland	54.7	61.4	27.8
Manipur	61.0	67.2	42.9

Contd..

State	*Total*	*Rural*	*Urban*
Mizoram	55.8	75.2	37.0
Tripura	70.9	76.3	46.9
Meghalaya	62.8	73.7	23.3
Assam	79.6	85.0	47.4
West Bengal	69.2	84.1	32.9
Jharkhand	70.	82.3	27.6
Orissa	79.3	85.1	42.5
Chhatisgarh	78.9	88.7	37.0
Madhya Pradesh	65.8	80.2	24.1
Gujarat	61.2	86.3	21.7
Maharastra	39.2	58.9	12.4
Andhra Pradesh	48.4	58.6	17.7
Karnataka	48.8	64.6	19.0
Kerala	80.3	84.0	69.1
Tamil Nadu	54.9	72.6	30.0

Source: Census 2001, Government of India

Table 3
Types of Toilet at Household Level (2001)

(Percerntage)

				Urban			
State	*Pit Toilet*	*Water Closet*	*Other Toilet*	*Pit Toilet*	*Water Closet*	*Other Toilet*	*Total*
Andhra Pradesh	8.55	98.20	6.32	15.10	46.97	16.0	78.07
Assam	43.94	15.90	4.81	26.39	58.88	9.33	94.60
Bihar	6.48	7.87	2.92	5.15	38.82	8.62	52.59
Chhatisgarh	2.42	8.87	2.92	5.15	38.82	8.62	52.59
Delhi	16.36	45.47	16.13	15.18	47.36	16.49	79.03
Gujarat	8.73	31.09	4.78	9.75	62.11	8.69	80.55
Haryana	22.29	10.91	11.30	26.48	30.99	23.19	80.66
Jharkhand	3.27	10.73	5.67	27.41	41.24	18.03	66.68
Karnataka	13.38	18.64	5.48	20.70	44.86	9.67	75.23
Kerala	12.36	65.19	6.46	11.11	74.76	6.16	92.02
Madhya Pradesh	5.93	12.47	5.58	11.89	41.10	14.74	67.74
Maharastra	8.89	21.85	4.34	7.08	44.37	6.63	58.08
Orissa	3.97	8/79	2.14	9.48	43.05	7.15	59.08
Punjab	24.33	20.40	12.11	20.53	46.52	19.48	86.52
Rajasthan	10.47	11.93	6.60	18.21	40.58	17.33	76.11
Tamil Nadu	7.30	23.22	4.63	11.16	45.47	7.71	64.33
Uttar Pradesh	10.29	7.98	13.16	11.07	31.98	29.96	80.01
Uuaranchal	18.71	15.45	11.04	26.72	40.82	19.35	86.08
West Bengal	17.53	20.95	5.23	22.89	55.20	6.76	84.95
India	11.50	18.02	6.88	14.60	46.12	13.00	73.72

Source: Census, 2001

The Census of 2001 also provides information regarding the type of toilets used in both rural and urban areas. Basically, there are three categories: pit toilets, water-closet toilet and other type of toilets mainly including service toilets. Service toilets are dry types of toilets from where human excreta are removed by scavengers. Out of 36 per cent of the households having toilet facilities at the national level, half of them had water closet toilets, wherein the faecal matter is removed without the need for scavenging and about 12 per cent of the households had pit toilets. In urban India, 40 per cent of the households used water closet toilet and around 15 per cent pit toilets. The trend is, however, reverse in rural areas where 10 per cent have pit toilet and only 7 per cent use water closet toilets (Table 3). In Uttar Pradesh, more people continue to use service toilets than pit and water closet toilets. In States such as Delhi, Haryana, Punjab and Uttaranchal, the usage of service toilets is quite high, even at present.

The National Sample Survey also provides information regarding the usage of toilets by households. Among those who had access to toilets, 74 per cent of the rural and 62 per cent of the urban households used them exclusively. About 29 per cent of the surveyed households had to share the toilets with other households. The proportion of households having sole access to the toilet used by them is steadily increasing over the years both in rural as well as urban areas. Most of the urban households had toilet within their home promises (89.2 per cent), while about 8.8 per cent households had toilet facility outside their home premises (Table 4).

The State-wise status of sanitation in urban India is shown in Table 5. During 1997-98, 0.83 million scavengers engaged in manual scavenging were identified. The largest number of scavengers was recorded in Uttar Pradesh, Maharastra, Gujarat, Bihar, Madhya Pradesh, Rajasthan and West Bengal. During 2001, 0.11 million scavengers were liberated while 3.5 million dry toilets were converted into pour-flush toilets. In 2002-03, the Union Ministry for Social Justice and Empowerment admitted the existence of 6.76 lakh people who lift human excreta for a living and the presence of 92 lakh dry

Table 4
Usage of Toilet by Urban Households in India (1998)

(Percerntage)

State	Type of Usage			Availability of Toilet		
	For Exclusive use of HH	Shared by Restricted set of HH	For Community use	Within Premises	Less than 0.5 km. distance	Beyond 0.5 km. distance
Andhra Pradesh	62.6	34.5	1.6	90.5	4.1	1.6
Assam	68.6	23.5	2.4	91.4	7.4	–
Bihar	66.74	28.9	1.8	96.7	1.6	–
Gujarat	73.7	20.2	5.7	89.6	10.4	–
Haryana	76.8	22.4	0.8	98.6	1.2	–
Karnataka	64.1	32.4	3.4	92.6	7.3	–
Kerala	85.81	14.0	0.1	98.5	1.0	0.5
Madhya Pradesh	69.4	16.9	1.8	86.8	3.7	0.1
Maharastra	46.4	28.5	24.3	75.3	23.6	0.3
Orissa	71.4	25.5	–	81.1	0.1	12.8
Punjab	61.5	37.1	0.3	98.1	1.5	0.2
Rajasthan	65.4	32.2	0.8	98.5	2.1	1.4
Tamil Nadu	59.7	37.3	2.4	91.1	7.0	0.1
U. P.	65.6	25.3	8.0	97.4	2.1	–
West Bengal	54.2	41.9	2.9	86.1	7.5	0.1
India	61.9	29.2	7.4	89.2	8.3	0.5

Source: NSSO 54th Round, Department of Statistics, NSSO, Government of India, 1999

toilets spread across 21 States and Union Territories. However, the National Convener of Safai Karmachari Andolan (SKA) remarked that the problem is not about identifying, educating or providing alternatives, but is one of attitude. The estimated number of manual scavengers is more than 1.3 million. This figure is far in excess than the number of scavengers identified and liberated during 1997-98 to 2001 in India.

Table 5
State-Wise Status of Sanitation in Urban India

State	*Percentage of Population Covered by Sewerage (1989)*	*No. of Scavengers (1997-98)*	*No. of Scavengers Liberated (2001)*	*No. of Conversion and Construction of Toilets (2001)*
Andhra Pradesh	11	7453	3136	604448
Assam	16	16873	1881	90340
Bihar	23	40249	–	9465
Gujarat	38	62842	–	–
Goa	13	–	–	45500
Haryana	28	25279	7982	200224
Himachal Pradesh	14	4760	–	–
Jammu & Kashmir	8	4150	1900	61845
Karnataka	38	14555	3227	177689
Kerala	28	1339	726	1450
Madhya Pradesh	8	80072	3361	113216
Maharastra	40	126691	2990	199466
Meghalaya	NA	607	30	5290
Nagaland	NA	1800	–	–
Orissa	10	19103	856	51597
Punjab	49	31290	15353	223777
Rajasthan	10	57736	11506	423947
Tamil Nadu	48	35561	4393	155561
Tripura	13	–	-	18788
Uttar Pradesh	14	246916	43404	775113
Uttaranchal	-	-	2415	4092
West Bengal	20	30000	8996	299820
Chhatisgarh	–	–	210	6194
Delhi	–	17420	–	–
Jharkhand	–	–	–	1771
Sikkim	-	400	-	–
India	28	825572	112460	3492955

Source: India Infrastructure Report, 2001

According to the 2001 Census, 54 per cent of the households in India had no drainage facilities (66 per cent in rural and 22 per cent in urban areas). The proportion of households with no drainage facility was relatively lower in Delhi, Punjab and Haryana. There are two categories of connectivity of waste water outlet, namely, closed drainage and open drainage. Accordingly, 4 per cent of the households in rural and 35 per cent in urban areas had connectivity to closed drainage to carry away the waste water generated by the people living in it. The coverage of open drainage facility was 30 per cent and 43 per cent in rural and urban areas respectively. The proportion of urban households having the facilities of closed drainage was reported high in Gujarat followed by Delhi, Karnataka, Maharastra, Punjab and Andhra Pradesh while it was reported to be least in Assam (9.84 per cent). The proportion of urban households without drainage facilities was reported high in Kerala, Assam, Orissa, Chhatisgarh, West Bengal and Bihar (Table 6).

Table 6
Drainage Facility in Urban India (2001)

(Percentage)

	Total			Urban		
State	Closed Drainage	Open Drainage	No. Drainage	Closed Drainage	Open Drainage	No. Drainage
Andhra Pradesh	13.65	37.90	48.44	36.02	46.27	17.71
Assam	2.18	18.27	79.55	9.84	42.78	47.38
Bihar	4.46	33.59	61.95	22.15	46.46	31.39
Chhatisgarh	4.41	16.73	78.86	17.12	45.85	37.04
Delhi	49.16	40.78	10.06	51.68	39.35	8.96
Gujarat	27.24	11.60	61.16	59.26	19.03	21.71
Haryana	12.86	63.94	23.2	35.01	53.39	11.59
Jharkhand	6.36	23.26	70.37	23.79	48.57	27.64
Karnataka	17.26	23.97	48.77	41.64	39.33	19.03
Kerala	8.04	11.68	80.28	14.85	16.04	69.11
Madhya Pradesh	7.71	26.48	65.81	24.50	51.92	24.07
Maharastra	22.02	38.75	39.20	95.07	42.51	12.92
Orissa	4.91	15.84	79.26	19.61	37.88	42.51
Punjab	18.46	63.70	17.84	44.97	44.80	10.23
Rajasthan	7.93	28.58	63.49	24.12	56.07	19.81
Tamil Nadu	16.89	28.23	54.89	34.56	35.46	29.98

Contd..

State	Total			Urban		
	Closed Drainage	Open Drainage	No. Drainage	Closed Drainage	Open Drainage	No. Drainage
Uttar Pradesh	9.54	60.95	29.51	26.46	64.91	7.62
Uttaranchal	10.37	37.69	51.94	28.36	59.88	11.76
West Bengal	7.31	23.45	69.24	21.85	46.30	32.86
India	12.46	33.93	53.40	34.50	43.37	22.13

Source: Census, 2001.

NEED FOR SANITATION AND HYGIENE PROMOTION

Presently, access to sanitation services is markedly less than access to water supply in both rural and urban areas. Thus, there is an imperative need to focus attention on provision of sanitation. The provision of adequate sanitation facilities in urban areas is an important investment which safeguards people's health and well-being. It also protects the environment and ensures reduction in the spread of diseases. For healthy cities, adequate sanitation is essential as the chances for transmission of excreta related diseases are higher in densely populated areas. People also value the privacy and convenience of being able to use toilets within their home premises. Women, in particular, value a sense of security by using toilet within the home premises. In urban areas, there is hardly any open space for defecating. However, in the absence of adequate toilet facility, the poor and slum dwellers are forced to defecate in open or near rivers, lakes, ponds, railway tracks, roads, etc. People also prefer to live in clean and healthy environment. However, adequate sanitation requires political commitment and huge investment. A common problem with many of the efforts of urban governments to improve sanitation is reported to be largely supply-driven rather than demand-driven. The sanitation facilities should be affordable and households should be consulted regarding their willingness to pay for use and maintenance of alternative sanitation systems and technologies. Thus, Water Supply and Sanitation Collaborative Council, 2004 has suggested the following steps in urban sanitation planning viz. (i) request for assistance; (ii) launch of the planning and consultative process; (iii) assessment of current status, (iv) assessment of user priorities; (v) identification; (vi) evaluation of feasible service combinations; (vii) consolidated sanitation plans; (viii) finalizing consolidated plans; and (ix) monitoring.

The common elements of sanitation promotion initiatives include the following approaches:

- identifying key target groups to be reached
- identifying core messages to be communicated
- awareness of the prevailing socio-culutural framework
- consideration of sanitation as a consumer good, not just as a potential health benefit; and
- using a mix of communication methods in vernacular language with clear messages.

In recent years there has been increasing recognition of the importance of sanitation, not only due to its impact on health directly, but also for its effect on improved living environment, human dignity and poverty reduction. Effective sanitation ensures a transformation of the living environment, especially in urban areas, and includes waste water treatment and disposal and solid waste management. Sanitation promotion is imperative because our past experience demonstrates that a supply driven strategy to simply build more toilets with household's subsidies may result in unused facilities. For instance, in Maharastra, 1.7 million rural toilets were constructed with subsidies from the State Government over a four year period, but only 57 per cent were actually used. Similarly, a three country study in East Asia suggests that dispite high average, only about 12 per cent of the poor households in Vietnam and Cambodia had effective access to toilets in 2001. Many cities in developing countries have similar problems with urban sewerage systems and this has led to a growing consensus on the importance of sanitation promotion in order to ensure that facilities are actually used and the intended health benefits become a reality.

There are three methods used for promotion of sanitation, viz. increased health and hygiene awareness; social marketing; incentives for sanitation projects. The increased health and hygiene awareness approach is based on three practices i.e. (i) participatory hygiene and sanitation transformation which was first developed in Africa and implemented through trained community faciiities; (ii) health education and school sanitation which focuses on health education through schools or special health clubs; and (iii) community led promotion, which emerged mainly in South Asia and is implemented through rural communities and Panchayati Raj Institutions. Social marketing is broadly recognized as the use of marketing strategies and techniques to achieve a social goal. It is being widely used in the health sector.

It may be mentioned that the marketing concept is focused on 4 P's i.e. product, price, place and promotion. *Promotion* is the integrated use of tools such as advertising, public relations, media message, positioning, communications channels, selling strategies and media advocacy. For sanitation promotion, social marketing covers both demand and supply sides. It aims to stimulate a desire for toilets and then meet the client's needs by tailoring the design and range of the toilets to what the client wants and he can afford. For incentives and sanctions, governments and NGO's have used indirect methods to promote sanitation, including both incentives and sanctions. Incentives often take the form of subsidies at the household level or awards for achieving total sanction at community level. Sanctions have been mainly through national or state level legislations such as bye-laws, rules, regulations, acts etc.

There are three models for implementation of sanitation promotion. The first model is called NGO programme which is being promoted by NGOs and civil societies. Another emerging model is to use the competitive advantages, resources and skills of both public and private sector. This is called as public-private-partnership model, since, private sector participation has the potential to improve efficiency and quality of service delivery. The third model is government projects/programme. There may be programmes both externally funded government projects and government funded projects.

The Ministry of Urban Development, Government of India, in December 2005 announced the Jawaharlal Nehru National

Urban Renewal Mission (JNNURM) to provide support to renewal and development of city development plans, including plans for water and sanitation. The Ministry has also constituted a national taskforce on universal sanitation in urban areas. Two sub-committees under the task force have been set up - one on a National Urban Sanitation Policy and another to formulate a campaign for open defecation free slums. Toilet complexes in urban slums offer hope for improvement in living conditions for slum dwellers. There are two types of urban toilet complexes - firstly, the public toilets in commercial areas like markets, trade centres and bus stations, etc. These public toilets are characterized by very high incomes and are like any other economic activity in a market place. The work done by Sulabh International, Infosys and other NGOs', operated public toilets come under this category. The second type of urban toilets complexes are the community managed toilets which are usually in low density slum locations. There have been successful examples of community managed toilet in Trichy, Mumbai, and Pune. With the collaboration of the Municipalities and local NGOs working in these cities, the poor quality public toilets were transformed into a model that is managed by local woman groups.

The process of change which advocacy aims to bring about may occur at different levels, from the community level to the state and national levels. The change may occur at different stages in the decision making process. Thus, an important aspect of advocacy is the involvement of communities themselves in advocating for change. It also seeks to build alliances in order to change the process of decision making at all levels and involvement of communities in those decisions. Thus effective advocacy in sanitation sector include not only the promotion of positive water supply, sanitation and hygiene initiatives, but also the dimensions of decision making process.

Water and sanitation are key areas of concern for sustainable development. A large section of population does not have access to safe and affordable water supply and adequate sanitation. Most of them who do not have access to sanitation facilities belong to the poorest sections of the society. In absence of adequate sanitation facilities, people suffer from burden of communicable and non-communicable diseases. Proper sanitation and hygiene may reduce the morbidity and mortality caused by water and air borne diseases. In view of the above fact, concerted efforts were undertaken by water and sanitation activists from around the globe, including Water, Sanitation and Hygiene (WASH) Campaign, a target for sanitation was finally agreed at the World Summit on Sustainable Development in Johannesburg in September, 2002.

The year 2008 has been declared as the International Sanitation Year by the United Nations. Moreover, India will be organising the World Toilet Summit in 2008 at New Delhi, in order to facilitate the thread bare discussions and deliberations for sanitation and hygiene promotion.

The Water, Sanitation and Hygiene (WASH) Campaign focused *inter alia* on promoting the adoption of a sanitation target at the World Summit on Sustainable Development in 2002. Its activities centred on obtaining high level political support internationally and also focused on national activities to raise awareness about the importance of sanitation, hygiene and water supply. On the whole, WASH aims to raise the commitment of political and social leaders to achieving the goals of drinking water, sanitation and hygiene a reality for all and effecting the necessary behavioural changes through various information and communication channels, using traditional and mass media, hygiene promotion in schools, training and building local capacity in communication and improving networking and research.

SOLID WASTE MANAGEMENT

Rapid population growth, urbanization and industrial growth have led to severe problems of waste management in cities. The problem of solid waste disposal and sanitation appears almost intractable as urban India today is a site of rotting garbage. It is estimated that Indian cities generate 48 million metric tonnes of solid waste annually. TERI has estimated that the waste generation will exceed 260 million tonnes per year by 2047, i.e. more than 5 times the present level.

A survey of 241 Class II towns in 17 States of India was undertaken by the Central Pollution Control Board, Delhi in 2000 which indicated that 90 per cent of water supplied is polluted. This is because of the fact that our rivers are highly polluted due to non-regulation of waste dumping and discharging waste into them, while ground - water is polluted due to silting of solid wastes, waste water and industrial effluents. About 30.5 million Disability Adjusted Life Year (ACY) are lost annually owing to poor quality of drinking water and the absence of sanitation facilities. The financial loss in terms of productivity has been quantified as Rs. 360 billion annually. Most of the urban local bodies do not have adequate infrastructure facilities such as required capacities for treatment of raw water, adequate testing facilities and technical man power for operations and management. Only 72 of 4400 towns in the country have partial sewerage facilities and 17 have some form of primary treatment facilities before disposal. Of the 229 class 1 cities, 160 have sewerage systems for more than 75 per cent of the population and 92 cities for more than 50 per cent of the population. While waste generation in Class I cities has more than doubled from 1978 to 1995, the treatment capacity has decreased during the same period. Of the total waste water generated in the metropolitan cities, barely 30 per cent is treated before disposal. Untreated water is thrown into water bodies such as rivers, lakes, oceans and seas. In 118 cities, it is discharged indirectly into rivers, lakes, ponds, or creaks, while in 63 cities it is used for agriculture. It may be mentioned that most of the urban local bodies do not have sewerage line for disposal of waste water, and sewerage. This leads to degradation of the environment and affects the quality of life of inhabitants. It is estimated that about 75 to 80 per cent of water pollution is caused by domestic sewerage. Of the generated solid wastes in urban areas, only 72 per cent is collected daily and the remaining wastes are allowed to create problems of urban environment. This also creates health problems. More than 70 per cent Indian cities have inadequate waste transformation facilities. They mainly choose land filling or dumping for disposal of wastes.

However, the landfill or dumping sites are poorly managed and lead to ground water contamination because of leachates. The land fill workers have also higher incidence of diseases such as diarrhoea, as well as fungal and skin infections due to working in unhygienic conditions. About 25 per cent of the waste generated is classified as hazardous.

A survey of 120 health care centres in West Bengal, Gujarat, Punjab, Tamil Nadu, Haryana, Delhi, and Uttar Pradesh in 2001 found that 42 per cent of health workers did not have knowledge about classification and segregation of bio-medical wastes. The survey revealed gross inadequacy of equipments and tools. Open dumping or burning of bio-medical waste was reported as a common practice. The risks and problems associated with solid wastes include blockage of drains, resulting in flooding, water logging and insanitary conditions; breeding of flies, bacteria and virus that spread diseases; breeding of mosquitoes, spreading malaria and dengue; providing shelter to rats that spoil food, and spread diseases; combusting of wastes causing air pollution; occupational health hazards who are engaged in waste collection and disposal; water pollution from leachates at dumping or landfill sites; emission of landfill gases dealing to climate change; and fires on disposal sites, thus causing major air pollution.

Environmental sanitation and human health are closely linked. Poor management of human wastes can lead to direct or indirect disease transmission. The main organisms that pose a threat to health are pathogenic bacteria, viruses, parasitic protozoa and helminthes that are excreted in large number. The sources of pollution affecting the occurrence and abundance of pathogens in a water shed and receiving coastal regions are primarily due to the direct or indirect load of excreta. Thus, proper sanitation is imperative to reduce the burden of diseases as well as improving efficiency of human population. Well planned water and sanitation interventions have been shown to be effective in reducing a number of diseases. Interventions to promote personal and domestic hygiene are also effective in reducing diseases. In particular, hand-washing with soap; after defecation; after handling babies faeces; before feeding and eating; and before preparing food have significant impacts on diarrhoea related morbidity.

DISPOSAL OF HOUSEHOLD GARBAGE

Waste management is also an important aspect of sanitation and includes collection, handling, transport and disposal of wastes generated. Due to the effective collection and disposal of waste material, rodents and flies breed, resulting in the spread of diseases. The untreated wastes components may pollute the surface water and ground water, resulting in adverse health and environmental consequences. Thus, effective waste management can result in the improvement of health and reduction of morbidity and mortality, improvement of water and air quality and economic development.

The proportions of households reporting removal of their household waste by different modes have been estimated by NSSO. There are four categories of disposal methods, namely by local authorities, private arrangements, household members, and other arrangements. Most of the households reported that their own members are responsible for the removal of garbage from their houses. In urban areas, local authorities and private arrangements also play a major role in the removal of garbage (Table 7).

Table 7
Disposal of Household Garbage in Urban India (1999)

	Percentage of Households by removal of garbage by			
State	*Local Authorities*	*Private Arrangement Among Residents*	*Household Members*	*Other Arrangements*
Andhra Pradesh	14.5	8.1	75.3	2.2
Assam	4.0	9.3	78.1	8.7
Bihar	2.0	7.6	82.6	7.6
Gujarat	28.8	9.1	60.9	1.3
Haryana	8.4	14.6	76.9	0.1
Karnataka	20.4	4.8	70.3	4.5
Kerala	2.4	1.9	93.4	2.3
Madhya Pradesh	5.7	6.7	84.9	2.6
Maharastra	6.9	22.6	65.2	5.3
Orissa	3.0	0.4	96.4	0.2

Contd..

State	Percentage of Households by removal of garbage by			
	Local Authorities	Private Arrangement Among Residents	Household Members	Other Arrangements
Punjab	3.4	13.6	78.7	4.3
Rajasthan	15.1	8.8	74.6	1.5
Tamil Nadu	17.9	3.0	76.4	2.7
Uttar Pradesh	14.4	14.5	69.0	2.1
West Bengal	28.7	8.8	59.7	2.8
India	13.7	11.9	71.2	3.2

Source: NSSO 54 Round, 1999.

However, there are efforts by various agencies in cities and towns to address the challenges of waste management. In urban India solid waste management comes under the purview of local municipal authorities who are responsible for the collection, segregation, transportation, storage, handling and CBO's also assist municipal authorities in managing solid wastes. The disposal method for solid wastes is mainly confined to dumping (Table 8).

Table 8
Arrangement for Shifting Garbage after Removal from House (1998)

	Percentage of Households Reporting Garbage Shifted to			
	Biogasplant for Manual pit	Community Dumping Spot	Households Individual Spots	Others
Andhra Pradesh	1.1	55.9	29.8	13.1
Assam	0.1	20.4	55.9	23.6
Bihar	1.6	14.3	47.9	35.9
Gujarat	2.8	57.2	22.0	17.9
Haryana	5.6	20.0	6.7	8.8
Karnataka	1.0	52.9	26.1	20.0
Kerala	2.2	7.6	75.2	15.0
Madhya Pradesh	1.5	35.0	33.7	29.6
Maharastra	1.9	70.4	11.5	16.0
Orissa	–	26.3	61.5	12.2
Punjab	0.2	45.4	15.2	39.2
Rajasthan	0.1	32.7	27.7	39.5
Tamil Nadu	3.1	49.1	32.8	14.9
Uttar Pradesh	0.4	35.0	32.2	32.4
West Bengal	0.3	49.8	36.6	13.1
India	1.4	47.2	29.6	21.7

Source: NSSO 54th Round, 1999

The projected municipal waste generation in urban India is 48 million tonnes per year. It is likely to increase to 220.7 million tonnes by 2030 and 160.1 million tonnes by 2025. (Table 9)

Table 9
Projected Municipal Waste Generation in Urban India

Year	*Projected Urban Population (Millions)*	*Waste Generation (gms/capita/day)*	*Total MSW Generation (Million tonnes)*
2000	281.25	327	33.7
2005	315.53	391	45.0
2010	355.21	471	61.0
2015	401.90	571	83.0
2020	455.82	696	115.8
2025	517.18	848	160.1
2030	586.05	1032	220.7

Source: World Bank, 2006.

The World Bank Study (2006) has estimated that cost of municipal solid waste management varies from city to city. Composting technology is the most suited and cost effective technology for disposal of solid waste. The cost of solid waste management per capita per annum is variable, depending upon the size of city. However, in the mountain cities, the cost may be higher side.

Table 10
Status of Compliance of Municipal Solid Wastes Rules 2000 by Class I Cities

Particulars	*Percentage*
Storage at Source	41.77
Segregation of Recycles	36.47
Primary Collection	38.36
Street Sweeping	76.10
Storage Depot	28.40
Transportation	53.10
Processing of Waste	9.18
Disposal (Sanitary Landfill)	1.73

Source: USAID, 2005

The compliance of Municipal Solid Wastes Rules, 2000 by Class I cities has been reported to be poor. Except in case of street sweeping (76.10 per cent), most of the parameters for handling and arranging solid wastes by municipal authorities are reported to be poor. (Table 10).

Keeping the present status in view, the Government of India is providing adequate funds under provision of infrastructure development schemes and also through devolution by the Finance Commission for ensuring proper system of collecting, storage, segregation, transportation, handling and disposal of solid wastes. Ever since the scheme of Liberation and Rehabilitation of Scavengers and their Dependents was launched in 1991-92 with a total outlay of Rs. 50.50 crores as central assistance, there has been steady increase in fund allocation. The accumulative assistance of Central Government under the scheme during 1991-92 to 1999-2000 has been reported to be Rs. 531.07 crores.

The Government of India has established the National Scavenging Employees Finance and Development Corporation for the purpose and Rs. 2164.97 lakh had been released to the States from 1997-98 to 1999-2000. The Corporation has sanctioned 6149 units which were expected to benefit 6344 persons.

MANUAL SCAVENGING

Scavengers and sweepers still carry out the basic sanitary services in cities and towns. While many are employed by urban local authorities to clean the sewers and sweep the streets, a significant number still work in their traditional occupations. This means that scavengers are still cleaning toilets by hand and carrying night soil in baskets/buckets on their heads or waists. As their occupation renders them permanently polluted, scavengers are treated as 'untouchables', even by other Scheduled Castes. Again, scavengers are not limited to urban areas only. In rural areas also they are engaged in cleaning of service (dry) toilets as well as safe disposal of wastes including lifting and flaying of fallen carcass (dead animals) and also processing, tanning and manufacturing of leather goods. These activities are performed by a specific caste or community in the rural areas. In Uttar Pradesh 'Chamar' and 'Jatav' (Scheduled Castes) are engaged in this job while in some parts of the State a sizeable number of lower castes of both Muslims and Hindus are engaged in this job. This means that scavengers have extremely limited job opportunities compared to those engaged in other sanitary work such that they have to live in acute poverty and in segregated communities and have extremely low level of literacy and job mobility. Such socio-economic conditions for scavengers still persist, despite various provisions in the Indian Constitution which stipulate that the State should promote the economic and educational interests of Scheduled Castes and protect them from discrimination and exploitation.

Interestingly, in 1993 the Employment of Manual Scavengers and Construction of Dry Toilets (Prohibition) Act 1993 was implemented in the country to abolish scavenging and rehabilitate scavengers. It was estimated that the dehumanizing practice of scavenging was continued in 2587 towns, involving 7,00,000 scavengers during 1995. Although accurate figures of scavengers, including sweepers is not available, yet it is estimated that in India more than 150 million untouchable's are engaged in lower jobs, like cleaning toilets, streets, sewers and handling municipal solid wastes including industrial wastes; lifting and flaying fallen carcass; handling hides and colleting trash. Obviously, they are marginalized and living in sub- human conditions.

In generalized terms, the reality of scavengers could be described as under: (i) Scavengers constitute an underprivileged social group treated as 'impure' and consequently socially ostracized and ritually avoided; (ii) Like "Pariah" groups, they are treated as inferior and often regarded as less than human. They live on the fringe of society, often excluded from social contact, even though their services are accepted as highly valuable; (iii) They are socially ostracized because of practicing a polluting profession, as also for certain peculiar and objectionable habits; (iv) They are backward, and often oppressed, not because they are racially, socially and culturally inferior than others, but simply because they have been assigned the lowest of the low status in social hierarchy; having suffered condemnable human indignities throughout the ages; (vi) They have been treated like dreaded contagious disease calling for a disdainful distance and the most minimal social contact; (vii) Because of their degradation, scavengers have been compelled to live their life as socially disadvantaged persons reluctantly resigned to accepting their social degradation and discrimination as part of their fate; (viii) Besides social backwardness, scavengers are economically backward too. Most families of scavengers therefore live in poverty because of both structural and personal factors - Structural factors being the low family income on account of engagement in low paying occupations, and personal factors being their large family size and male members' indulgence in smoking, drinking and gambling; (ix) Most scavengers are illiterate and thus educationally backward. In spite of the facilities for their free education, children are not sent to schools in an overwhelming number of cases, and female education is not considered to be at all important; (x) The economic and educational backwardness has deprived many scavenger families from the advantage of the Constitutionally concerned privileges meant for the welfare of the dispossessed; (xi) Politically too, scavengers are least organized as compared to people of other low-born sub-castes.

The objective of the above - mentioned Act was to liberate them from their existing hereditary, obnoxious and inhuman occupation of manually removing night-soil and filth and to provide for alternative and dignified occupations within a period of five years.

On the whole, the Scheme had the following components:

(a) Time-bound programme for identification of scavengers and their dependents and their aptitude for alternative trade.

(b) Training in identified trades for scavengers and their dependents in the nearest local training institutions/ centres of various departments of State Governments, Central Government and other semi-government and non-government organizations.

(c) Rehabilitation of scavengers in various trades and occupations by providing subsidy, margin money, loan and bank loan also.

The responsibility of rehabilitation of municipal scavengers in the service of local bodies has been entrusted to the local bodies themselves.The scheme proposes to provide rehabilitation training to private scavengers and their dependents, including the dependents of scavengers employed by local bodies. The scheme arranges for training of all the scavengers, whether they are partially or wholly engaged in the said occupation.

The rehabilitation of scavengers thus freed from the traditional work of disposing night soil as head load, is the responsibility of the Ministry of Social Justice and Empowerment. This is the 'soft core' work of the entire scheme of liberation and rehabilitation. To meet this objective, the scheme evolved three time-bound programmes of identification of scavengers and their dependents at the national level in different States/Union Territories and up to the level of village, besides surveying of aptitudes of scavengers for alternative jobs or trades and a comprehensive training programme for identified trade or job.

In India even today, there are a large number of manual scavengers. According to official estimates of the Ministry of Social Justice and Empowerment, Government of India, the number of manual scavengers in the country during the year 2002-03 was 676009. The highest number was in Uttar Pradesh (1,49,202), followed by Madhya Pradesh (80,072) and Maharastra (64,785). Delhi alone had a population of 17,420 manual scavengers. The actual figures would be more than 1.3 million manual scavengers. It is likely that the private manual scavengers have not been taken into account in the official estimates.

According to an estimate in the year 1989, there were 7.20 million dry toilets in the country and by 31st March, 2000 this number increased to 9.6 million. These are still being cleaned manually by scavengers. Under Low Cost Sanitation Project, implemented by the Ministry of Housing and Poverty

Alleviation, between 1980 to and 2005, 2.08 million toilets were constructed and only 45,447 manual scavengers were liberated. The Ministry of Social Justice and Empowerment, claimed that 1.56 lakh people were trained and 4.08 lakh were rehabilitated until 2002 and that Rs. 712.14 crores had been released to different States.

A press release of the Union Ministry of Social Justice and Empowerment on July 22, 2005, estimated the total number of manual scavengers in the country as 6.76 lakh. According to estimates, the largest number of scavengers is in Uttar Pradesh (1.49 lakh), followed by Madhya Pradesh (80,000) and Gujarat (64,000). Despite the sheer admission by the Central Government, almost all the State Governments have denied the existence of manual scavengers and dry toilets in their States before Supreme Court. The Petitioners advocated effective implementation of the Employment of Manual Scavenging and Construction of Dry Toilet (Prohibition) Act, 1993, which has banned manual scavenging. They held that 12 lakh people in the country were still engaged in the degrading practice and 95 per cent of them are Dalits, who were compelled to undertake this traditional occupation.

COMMUNITY TOILETS

The scheme of Low Cost Sanitation for liberation of the scavengers started from 1980-81, also included community toilets. In urban areas, urban local bodies have constructed community toilets. Community toilets not only provide sanitation facility, but at the same time have a demonstrative effect as well. The people using these become habitual users of toilets, and in turn realize the need for individual household toilets. Thus, community toilets may be important tools for bringing about behavioural changes among the communities and particularly in the slum pockets. HUDCO has reported that 3,966 number of units were sanctioned, 2982 completed and 193 were in progress during 2005. Most of the sanctioned units were reported in the State of Maharastra (2,809) followed, by West Bengal (400) and Tamil Nadu (372). Similarly, the largest number of completed units were reported in

Maharastra. HUDCO is also involved in the implementation of the 'pay and use' toilets programme under the Night Shelters Scheme, and has reported sanctioning of 69 schemes for 'pay and use' toilets, under which a subsidy per seat is provided. This scheme had been merged with the scheme of Valmiki Ambedkar Awas Yojana (VAMBAY), as part of the sanitation component of the scheme for which 20 per cent of the funds were earmarked.

Community toilets are needed for slum and pavement dwellers, rickshaw pullers and the floating population. However, the experience of maintenance and upkeep of these units by municipal authorities has been dismal. The construction and maintenance of 'pay and use' toilets for the floating population should be ensured by NGOs working in the field. Community Managed Toilets (CMT's) are very successful in Trichy, Mumbai and Pune. These are being managed by NGOs like SPARC and Gramalaya. The community toilets in municipal areas are maintained by the urban local bodies through their health departments.

It has been generally observed that the proper maintenance of community toilets could not be ensured to a greater extent. Many community toilets have also become non-functional on account of a variety of reasons ranging from non availability of water, faulty construction, lack of safety and security for women, absence of operation and maintenance, lack of special provision for children and disabled and insufficient funds for running the system etc.

A study conducted by Directorate of Urban Administration and Development, Government Madhya Pradesh during 2005, regarding community toilets in Bhopal, Indore, Gwalior and Jabalpur, under Water and Asian Cities Programme - UN Habitat, demonstrated that the use of community toilets depends on the availability of infrastructure facilities such as water, bathing facility, effluent disposal in sewer line or in septic tank. The status of infrastructure in community toilets has been reported to be poor. The facilities for bathing and water availability were reported very low. Even, the toilets are not been properly maintained. One of the important factors determining the proper operation and maintenance of community toilets is the availability of funds for operatio and maintenance. However, majority of the community toilets do not charge for delivery of services. It appears that for ensuring functional and structural sustainability of community toilets, a participatory demand-driven approach is required.

PUBLIC-PRIVATE-PARTNERSHIP

Public-Private Partnership is the newly emerging instrument for resource mobilization, sharing responsibilities, tasks and resources. In the context of sanitation and water supply, ULB's, CBO's, NGO's and private organizations may be the stakeholders. The effective implementation of sanitation and water supply projects depends upon the partners or stakeholders. Thus, sharing responsibilities, tasks and resources among the stakeholders is imperative. The World Economic Forum's Financing for Development Initiatives emerged from the UN Conference on Financing for Development in 2002 which called for greater coherence between public and private sectors to achieve development goals. The Round Table Conference on Development Driven Public-Private-Partnerships in Water and Sanitation look place in London, in May, 2005. The discussions revolved around eight major dimensions viz. availability of information; effectiveness of the public-private partnership process; risk transfer to the private sector; social versus commercial objectives; role of multilateral agencies; partner commitment; scope of partnerships; and regulation.

Conventional public finance in sanitation has largely been concentrated on subsidies for household and public toilets and grant for urban sewerage and solid waste systems. However, the focus of public finance must be shifted to sanitation promotion and to covering additional resources. Public expenditure on sanitation programme is justified as it enhances sustainability and helps to leverage additional resources. Sanitation promotion for various sub sectors has different implications for demand, supply and for leveraging resources.

The financial arrangements in sanitation may include community resources, market based resources, and civil societies based resources. However, successful financing for scaling up sanitation access will require support from a range of stakeholders, including various sectors of government and non-government departments/organizations.

EXPERIENCES IN SANITATION PROMOTION

Sulabh International

Sulabh International Social Service Organisation (SISSO), a NGO, founded by Dr. Bindeshwar Pathak has demonstrated the success of low cost, pour flush, water-seal toilets with twin leach pits for on-sit sanitation technology throughout the country. This technology is affordable even by the economically weaker sections of the society and is designed to suit different levels of income groups. SISSO had constructed over 8,00,000 twin pit flush toilets by 1997. It has made nearly 240 towns scavenging free where about 40 thousand scavengers have been relieved of the degrading human practice of manual removal and transport of human excreta. In the towns which have become scavenging free, all dry or bucket toilets have been converted into the twin pit pour-flush toilets. It has built and maintained about 3,200 community toilets which are run on pay-and-use basis. Over 10 million people use the sanitation facilities provided by SISSO daily. A key to the success of SISSO lies in creating public awareness and seeking community participation in implementing and maintaining the infrastructure. It is also involved in research and development activities to promote low cost sanitation technology and the method to reach the people for its successful implementation.

PARIVARTAN

Parivartan Project, Ahmedabad, India: Households in Ahmedabad's slums were mobilized to invest in one third of the development costs of community infrastructure. Despite initial success, expansion has been slow. Effort is being directed at formalizing a public-private-NGO arrangement for funding and implementation.

USER CHARGES FOR PUBLIC TOILETS

In Kenya, an association of business owners contracted private operators to rehabilitate and operate the local authority toilets, which were in disrepair. Currently between 500 and 1,000 people, each paying between $0.06 and $0.12 per use to the private operator, use each facility every day. In India, Sulabh piloted a concept of user fee backed management of public toilets, which has been very successful. It has subsequently spread the concept throughout the country. In Pune, India, an NGO, SPARC, together with two people's organizations, had built 114 toilet blocks through a contract with local government. The toilet block includes a room for the caretaker to reduce maintenance costs and families using the toilet blocks buy a monthly pass for Rs.20 (US$0.44). In Bamako, Mali an annual fee of US$600 is levied and besides operational costs, covers capital cost recovery.

SOLID WASTE DISPOSAL CONCESSIONS IN INDIA

Over 50 municipal authorities in India have been awarded such concessions. As an example, Kolhapur Municipal Corporation has entered into a 30-year concession to develop a waste treatment facility (270 tons per day capacity). The private operator is responsible to raise the project finance based on returns from sale of compost generated from the operation.

POOLED FINANCING FOR WATER AND SEWERAGE PROJECTS IN INDIA

Using the framework of US Bond Banks, a Water and Sanitation Pooled Fund (WSPF) was created in the state of Tamil Nadu to enable small urban areas to borrow funds for Water Supply and Sanitation Scheme. Pooling allowed better risk sharing and lower market rates for capital market borrowing. Credit enhancement mechanisms such as debt service reserve fund and partial guarantees through USAID's Development Credit Authority also helped to lower the cost of funds. Based on this experience, Government of India program has been developed to support creation of state level pooled funds.

COMMUNITY-LED INFRASTRUCTURE FINANCE FACILITY (CLIFF)

CLIFF developed out of partnership by the UK-based Homeless International and its Indian partners, the National Slum Dwellers Federation (NSDF), Mahila Milan (a community-based finance system), and SPARC, a Mumbai-based NGO. DFID primarily funds the CLIFF initiative, which is focused on providing for three critical elements of community infrastructure financing: (a) development of pilot and demonstration projects; (b) bridging finance for initial scaling up; and (c) partial support for risk management and mitigation. CLIFF's operations require that the basic mobilization work has already been done and a strong institutional base of reputable stakeholders exists. CLIFF is managed globally by Homeless International, and in the first phase is being implemented by a special company (Nirman) set up by the Indian partners. Plans to expand this to countries in Africa are under-way. This initiative combines the basic features of project development support, partial guarantees for risk mitigation, and accessing market-based investment funds.

"CLEAN SURAT"

Plague hit the city of Surat (Gujarat) in September 1994, known for its filthiest slums swollen with migrant workers. However, In 1997, Surat (population 3.4 million) was ranked by India's heritage trust as the country's "second cleanest city". Municipal administrators have been streaming in to learn from the mobilisation campaign by the City Commissioner Mr. S. R. Rao. He attributes the success "to the people of Surat, their representatives, the 15, 000 employees of the Surat Municipal Corporation, the press and the judiciary". He encouraged the authorities and leaders and citizen groups to get involved in the making of new Surat. He also demonstrated that his Corporation could 'deliver'.

Sanitation has been a key focus in the "My Surat - Clean Surat" campaign which also targets 18 other action areas. Daily fieldwork is organised by city zones, each of them networked with a central control system through computer and radio links. Everyone, from Commissioners to cleaners, is expected to be out on the job each day between 7:30 am and 12:30 pm. A micro plan for sanitation divides the city zones into sectors of 3500 square meter, each with its own supervisory and task forces. Public toilets and urinals are cleaned each day, while every afternoon another group of cleaners moves out to follow up on the morning's activity. Special ward maps help these teams pinpoint critical locations. Defaulting citizens have to pay administrative charges for cleaning them up ranging from Rs. 50 to Rs. 5,000, depending on the mess. At 3:00 p.m. each afternoon, Surat's 15 commissioners meet, armed with 9-page computerized reports for a "free and fair discussion and joint decision-making". Sharing of experiences and random cross-checks are especially encouraged.

Over 50 "Pay and Use" toilets for men, women, and children operate through private initiative, and include the participation of the well-known Sulabh Corporation and Akhil Bharatiya Paryavaran Sansthan. 1600 public "pay" toilets were constructed and more than 90 per cent were located inside the slums. They can be used free of charge by women and children, and males over 12 years pay Rs. 0. 50, a very small sum. People demonstrated their willingness and ability to pay and this small payment has kept all of these units operating. The feedback system operating out of each ward office includes deadlines for responding to categorised complaints. This is 48 hours for cleanliness of public toilets and cesspool overflow, and 24 hours for solid waste disposal. City media have been mobilised to keep a close tab on the progress and help educate the public regarding new patterns of behaviour. Eighty per cent of Surat's slums have now been provided with sanitation and other basic facilities.

Public support has made sanitation a political issue for the first time. Surat demonstrates what people and the political system can do together if there is will on both sides. "The Surat Miracle" has been achieved within the constraints of existing administrative and financial procedures. All the money required for this change came from funds available in the normal budget, supplemented by funds raised by the citizen's groups brought together by the Commissioner. No State or Central funds were divested for sanitation. In other words, the new sanitation effort is sustainable for the long term. Naturally, one may ask–"if Surat can do it, what excuse does that leave other cities for not following suit?"

THE COMMUNITY-MANAGED SANITATION PROGRAMME IN KERALA

The Socio-Economic Units (SEUs) of the State of Kerala initiated a programme in 1988 with support from the governments of the Netherlands and Denmark to assist the Kerala Water Authority (KWA) to promote community approaches for effective implementation and management of sanitation facilities. The programme emphasised the promotion of toilet constructions, handwashing with soap, construction of drainage at public taps, chlorination of traditional wells and improvement of school sanitation. The goal was to provide poor households with permanent toilets of good quality, in such a way that they appreciated the facility and would used it properly. The programme has given priority to the mobilisation and motivation of the users, and promotion and monitoring for good practices that includes flexibility in planning, negotiation with local elected bodies, decentralised and local management, partnership (involving personnel affiliated to all major local institutions - schools, nursery schools, clinics, women's or youth groups), education and capacity-building, financial contributions from local governments and households, reliance on local materials, local masons, and competitive tenders. The local committee undertook a wide range of activities related to education and sanitation. These activities include mapping, site selection, organising education programmes, home visits, and managing household selection, purchase, transport, etc. The committee monitors the use and cleanliness of the toilets and the indicators for other good hygiene.

The physical achievement of the programme was 35,500 toilets construction. These toilets facilitated about 2,00,000 low income (below poverty line) people with hygiene education programme. The SEU succeeded to cover a total 60 per cent of poor population in the programme areas. This achievement was more than double as compared to the achievement of other programmes which were implemented before the SEU. Each SEU serves an average 20 panchayats (a population between 400, 000 to 1,000,000). About 85 to 98 per cent of the toilets in each area are found to be very clean, more than 80 per cent have water stored within or very near the toilet and about 20 to 70 per cent of the families have soap available in the toilet. A total of 274 school health clubs had been formed and was operating under this programme. The school health club is usually composed of all children in the fifth standard (about 10 to 11 years of age). The school health clubs are involved in a wide range of activities, such as ensuring the school grounds clean and waste containers (which are used) in each class, monitoring the use of toilets and helping to clean them, monitoring washing of hands and cleaning of containers for food, monitoring the school water point and ensuring correct use, and holding campaigns for special health issues in the school and community. The parent-teacher associations pay 25 to 50 percent of the cost of toilet facilities in the school. The project considers the school health clubs, a majority of which are very active, to be a good investment in safe hygiene behaviours of the future generation.

The success of this experimental project lies in its involvement of people of all political and cultural affiliations. The focus has been on developing a decentralised strategy managed by local governments and voluntary community groups.

WATER AID INDIA SANITATION IN TAMIL NADU

Water Aid India, with its NGO partners, creates an enabling environment for the successful sanitation programme. Community groups are facilitated to provide fundamental sanitation and hygiene information. Technology is made available at an affordable price to accommodate the growing demand for sanitation facilities. Both production and promotion are decentralized so as to allow for competitive pricing and innovations. Credit and other financial opportunities are also provided for those in need. These are not disbursed as a form of reward, but rather as an enabling factor for those who might otherwise not be able to afford a toilet. The individual subsidy that comes from the Government is redirected to a village development fund based on community consensus and decision. The community for common village development activities manages the fund. Banks and local financial institutions recognise sanitation as a priority investment and credit is available to community groups at market interest rate. No household is excluded and both the burden and benefits are shared through cooperation.

REFERENCES

ADB, India (2000), Mainstreaming Environment for Sustainable Development, Asian Development Bank, Manila .

Akolkar, A.B., Status of Solid Waste Management in India (2005), Implementation Status of Municipal Solid Wastes, Management and Handling Rules, 2000, Central Pollution Control Board, New Delhi.

Bose, R.K.G. et. al.(1998), India's Environmental Pollution and Control, Tata Energy Resource Institute, Delhi.

Cairncross, S., (1992), Sanitation and Water Supply, Practical Lessons form the Decade, Water and Sanitation Discussion Paper Series No. 9, World Bank, Washington D.C.

Cairncross, Sandy, Sanitation in the Developing World (2003), Current Status and Future Solution, International Journal of Environmental Health Research 13, June.

Chandra, Ramesh, (1999), Rehabilitation of Scavengers, Economic and Political Weekly, September 11.

Chaplin S.E., Scavengers (1997) , Still Marginalized, the Administrator, Vol. XIII, January-March.

Chaplin, S.E. (1999), Cities, Sewers and Poverty: India's Politics of Sanitation, Environment and Urbanization Vol. II (1) April .

Cooper, K. J., (1997), Human Waste Overwhelms India's Water or Disease, Foreign Service, February, Washington Post.

CPCB (2000), Status of Municipal Solid Waste: Generation, Collection, Treatment and Disposal in Class I Cities, Central Pollution Control Board, New Delhi.

CPCB, (2000), Status of Municipal Solid Waste, Waste Generation, Collection, Treatment and Disposal in Class I Cities, Central Pollution Control Board, New Delhi.

CPCB, (1998), Status of Water Supply and Waste Water Collection, Treatment and Disposal in Class I and Class II Cities, Central Pollution Control Board, New Delhi.

Government of India (2000), Manual on Municipal Solid Waste Management, MOUD, New Delhi.

Government of India, Towards Total Sanitation and Hygiene: A Challenge for India, www.ddwsnic.in.

Hasan, Arif (1998), Low Cost Sanitation for a Squatter Community, World Health Forum, 9(3) .

IRC - International Water and Sanitation Centre, www.irc.org

Krishna Kumar A., A (2003), Sanitation Emergeny, Frontline, 20(24).

Kundu, A.(1991), Micro Environment in Urban Planning: Access to Poor to Water Supply and Sanitation, Economic and Political Weekly, Vol. xxiv(37).

Kurup, B.K., (1996), The Community Managed Sanitation Progrmme in Kerala, Learning from Experiences, IRC, Hague .

Lesotho, (2002), How Political Leadership Achieved Long Term Results, WSP-AF.

Mc Kenzic, D. and Isha Raj, (2004), Household Water Delivery Options in Urban and Rural India, Paper Presented in 5th Stanford Conference on Indian Economic Development, June, 3-5.

MOUD, (2005), Management of Solid Wastes in Indian Cities, Ministry of Urban Development, Government of India, Delhi.

NIUA, (2000), Status of Water Supply, Sanitation and Solid Waste Management in Urban India, National Institute of Urban Affairs, Delhi .

NSSO, (1999), 54th Round Drinking Water, Sanitation and Hygiene in India, National Sample Survey Organization, Government of India.

Pasha, H. et. al., (1989), Rural Water Supply and Sanitation in Pakistan: Lessons from Experience, World Bank, Washington D.C.

Pathak, B., (1997), Cost Effective and Appropriate Sanitation System, Nagarlok, Vol. XXXIX(4).

Planning Commission, (1995), Report of the High Power Committee on Urban Solid Waste Management in India, Planning Commission, Government of India, Delhi.

Rai, N. and Singh A.K., (2007), Urban Water Supply and Water Tariffs in Uttar Pradesh, RCUES, Lucknow .

Rai, N. and Singh A.K., (2007), Sustainable Waste Management Contribution a Climate Protection, Theme Paper, RCUES, Lucknow, June.

Rout, J. and Zerah, M.H., (2002), The Water and Sanitation Scenario in Indian Metropolitan Cities, Centre for de Sciences, Humana's, New Delhi .

Roy, M.N., (1996), An Alternative Approach for Sustainable Development of Rural Sanitation: West Bengal Experience, Journal of Rural Development, 15(1).

Sekher, T.V., (2007), Environmental Health and Sanitation Facilities: Challenges for India, Working Paper, Institute for Social and Economic Change, Bangalore .

Seragddin, I., (1994), Water Supply Sanitation and Environmental Sustainability, World Bank, Washington DC .

Shi, A., How Access to Urban Potable Water and Sewerage Conventions sAffects Child Mortality, Policy Research Working Paper, World Bank, Washington, D.C., 2000.

Singh A.K., Empowerment of Female Scavengers(2006), Liberation From Social and Occupational Bondage, in Empowerment of Women in Urban Administration edited by U.B. Singh, Serials Publications, New Delhi .

Singh S.K. and Singh A.K., Management of Sanitation in Urban India (2002), Challenges for Urban Environment, Urban Panorama, RCUES, Lucknow, Vol. (2) .

Singh, A.K., (2006), Sustainable Waste Management and Its Implications on Climate Protection, Urban Panorama, RCUES, Lucknow Vol. V(2), July-December.

Singh, A.K., (2007), Urban Waste Management in India, in Sustainable Urban Management (ed) by Nishith Rai, and Anjuli Mishra, New Royal Book Co., Lucknow.

Singh, S.K., Dalit Women: Socio (2000), Economic Status and Issues, New Royal Book, Company, Lucknow.

Singh, U.P. and Singh A.K., (1999), Human Ecology and Development in India, APH, Pub. Corp. Delhi.

UN Habitat, Water and Sanitation in the World's Cities: Local Action for Global Goals, Earth Scan Publications Ltd., 2003.

UNDP, (2004), Reforms in Drinking Water and Sanitation, UNDP-TERI, Delhi.

Usmani, P.V., (2006), Solid Waste Management in India Infrastructure Report, OUP, Delhi.

Vistorti, J. *et. al.* Environmental Health, Bridging the Gaps, World Bank, Washington D.C.

WACP - Rejuvenation of Community Toilets, Water for Asian Cities Programmes - U.N. Habitat, Nairobi,

Water Aid - Advocacy Source book(2003), A Guide to Advocacy for WSSCC Campaign, Water Aid, Switzerland.

WEF (2005), Development Driven Public Private Partnership in Water, World Economic Forum Financing for Development Initiative, Switzerland.

WHO, Water Related Diseases, www.who.ch

WHO/UNICEF, (2000), Global Water Supply and Sanitation Assessment 2000 Report WHO/UNICEF, New York.

World Bank, Improving Management of Municipal Solid Waste in India (2006), Overview and Challenges, World Bank, Delhi .

World Bank, India (2006), Water Supply and Sanitation Bridging the Gap Between Infrastructure and Service, World Bank, New Delhi, January.

World Bank, (1998), Urban Water Supply and Sanitation Report Vol. 1, India, Water Resources Sector Review, World Bank, Delhi.

World Bank, (1999), Urban Water Supply and Sanitation, IBRD, World Bank, DFID, Allied Pub. Ltd., Delhi.

World Bank, (1999), Urban Water Supply and Sanitation, World Bank, New Delhi.

WSP (2004), The Challenge of Financing Sanitation for Meeting the Millennium Development Goals, WSP, World Bank, April.

WSSCC - A Guide to Advocacy for WSSCC Coordinators Working on theWASH Campaign, www.wsscc.org.

Zaidi, Annie, (2006), India's Same, Frontline, September 22.

Zerah, M.H., (2006), Urban Waster and Waste Water in India Infrastructure Report, OUP, Delhi.

6

WATER SUPPLY AND WATER TARIFFS

The growing population of urban areas and exerting considerable pressure on urban services, Indian cities are not able to supply water services adequately and efficiently. Most urban areas have depleted, polluted and destroyed their local sources of water. Most urban water supply authorities face problems of water deficit. The cost of water production is gradually increasing while the cost recovery is becoming a daunting task. The revenue deficit is gradually increasing and local bodies are facing problem in cost recovery since water is a merit good. They find themselves in different situation for sustaining and maintaining water resources and water supply to consumers. Most of the local bodies in the state of Uttar Pradesh face acute problem of resourcelessness and in absence of rationalized water pricing their problem becomes more chronic. Against this view point, present study purports to review the status of urban water supply and tariff in Uttar Pradesh and suggesting measures for augmenting resources and improving water supply in the state. The report is based on secondary data and pertinent literature collected from internet, published and documented sources. It is hoped that the study will be useful in understanding the dynamics of urban water supply and improving the resource recovery.

WATER RESOURCES

Historically, civilization in India have largely evolved and developed around water bodies. During the last decades since

Independence, India has witnessed phencmenon development of water resources and has largely successfully met the demand of water for many of the diverse uses in the country. Consequently, the country has achieved self sufficiency in food grains. Investments in water related infrastructure in the country have resulted in rapid expansion in the urban energy and industrial sectors. Infrastructure for safe drinking water has been provided to about 85 per cent of India's urban and rural population. However, these remain significant challenges in providing sustainable services, especially for the poor. India's fragile water resources are stressed and depleting, while sectoral demands (including drinking water, industry, agriculture and others) are growing rapidly accordance to urbanization, population increase, rising incomes and industrial growth. In the era of liberalization and globalization, cities and towns are emerging as the centre of growth. Thus, water supply and sanitation could arise due to urbanization. Intersectoral allocations, planning and management of increasingly fragile water resources have emerged as a major challenge due to declining per capita water availability and deteriorating quality of water.

India receives an annual rainfall equivalent of about 4000 billion cubic meters (BCM). This source of water is unevenly distributed both spatially as well as temporarily. Most of the rainfall is confined to monsoon season, from June to September and levels of precipitation vary from 100 mm a year in western Rajasthan to over 9000 mm a year in northeastern state of Meghalaya. India's rivers carry 90 per cent of water during the period from June-November. Thus, only 10 per cent of the river flow is available during the other six months. The utilizable water resource availability in the country varies from 18417 cubic meters in Brahmaputra valley to as low as 180 cubic meters in the Sabarmati basin. Rajasthan has only one per cent of the country's water resources while Bihar has just five per cent of the water resources. At the Independence India's population was less than 400 million and per capita water availability over 5000 cubic meters per year. Today, the population has grown to over a billion and per capita water availability has fallen to hardly 2000 cubic meters per annum and actual usable quantity is around 1122 cubic meters per annum.

Environmental problems including water quality degradation from agro-chemicals, industrial and domestic pollution, ground water depletion, water logging, soil salinization, siltation, degradation of wastelands, eco system impacts and various health related problems have caused concern to policy makers and administrators. Thus, management of water resources is imperative rather than development of the resources.

WATER AND SANITATION PROGRAMMES

Water supply and sanitation were added to the national agenda during the first five year planning period (1951-56). In 1954, the first national water supply programme was launched as part of the government's health plan. Central and state administration provided equal funding mainly for rural piped water supply schemes, with limited provision for point sources such as wells and boreholes. The Ministry of Water Resources drafted a National Water Policy in 1987 to guide the planning and development of water resources through out the country. The policy included several recommendations which were subsequently adopted by the states. The recommendations focussed on the need for introducing (i) water resource management and accorded domestic water supply the highest priority; (ii) design standards for ground water structures to protect ground water sources, (iii) water quality monitoring and mapping and (iv) data management and valuation. The policy has been recently revised in 2002 and has accorded primacy to drinking water. The features of the National Policy as under:

(1) Drinking water should be a priority in the providing and operation of water supply systems including irrigation systems.

(2) Maintenance of existing water resources schemes should be given special attention under these institutional arrangements.

(3) A participatory approach should be adopted, and water user associations and local bodies should be involved in related operations. There should also be maintenance training leading to the eventual transfer of management to local bodies and user groups.

(4) Private sector participation should be encouraged in planning, development and management to introduce corporate management practices and improve service efficiency.

(5) A standardized national information system with a network of data banks and databases, which integrate and strengthen the existing central and state level agencies should be established.

(6) Exploitation of ground water resources should be so regulated as not to exceed the recharging possibilities as also to ensure social equity. While states have been asked to formulate state water policies based on National Water Policy, 2002 within the next two years, some states such as Karnataka, Madhya Pradesh, Orissa, Rajasthan and Tamil Nadu have already drafted state policies based on the new national policy.

Water supply and sanitation were added to the national agenda during the first five year planning (1951-56). Since then successive plan periods have made provisions for strengthening the water supply and sanitation sectors in different ways. From the 8th Plan period (1992-97) onwards, greater efforts were made through reform and restructuring agendas to deal with the problems that had been identified in the sector. The 9th Plan (1997-2002) took this agenda forward by advocating the decentralization of distribution system to local bodies and the private sector including management of capital works. The focus on private sector participation in construction, financing and maintenance of water supply in urban and rural areas was strengthened. The emphasis was given on demand driven participatory efforts to set up and manage the water supply systems. The 10th Plan (2002-07) envisages 100 per cent coverage of rural and urban areas through institutional reforms, efficient operation, management, and equitable distribution. The plan recognizes the challenge of providing water supply and sanitation to a rapidly providing urban population and lays emphasis on urban water supply and sanitation by highlighting the problems and suggesting measures for alleviating them. Some of the measures advocated are restructuring of the water bodies and other local institutions in water supply and achieving sustainability through effective operation and maintenance (Table 1).

Table 1
Milestones in Water Supply and Sanitation in India

Years	*Focus*
1951-56 (First Five year Plan)	Water Supply and Sanitation adopted to national agenda
1954	First National Water Supply and Sanitation Programme was launched as part of Health Plan
1956-61 (Second Five Year Plan)	Funds were provided to develop and strengthen State Public Health Engineering Department
1961-66 (Third Five Year Plan)	Problem villages were identified as those without drinking water source within distance of 1.6 km.
1968	Priority given to villages with acute scarcity of drinking water
1972-73	Accelerated Rural Water Supply Programme (ARWSP) was launched.
1975	ARWSP was replaced by 20 Points Minimum Needs Programme aimed at full rural coverage
1977-78	ARWSP reintroduced
1980-85 (Sixth Five Year Plan)	Importance given to WSS sector increased
1980-81	Low Cost Sanitation Scheme initiated for urban areas
1985	Rural Water Supply and Sanitation was handed over to Department of Rural Development under Ministry of Agriculture
1986	Central Rural Sanitation Programme and National Technology Mission launched
1987	National Water Policy drafted by the Ministry of Water Resources with emphasis on domestic water supply, protection of ground water sources and water quality monitoring and mapping

Contd...

Years	*Focus*
1991	National Technology Mission was renamed as Rajeev Gandhi National Drinking Water Mission aimed at covering rural areas cost effectively before the end of the 8th Five Year Plan
1992-97 (Eighth Five Year Plan)	Problems with sector identified and reform agenda put forward. Emphasis on treating water as commodity, privatization, local bodies for operation and maintenance, proper linkages between water supply and sanitation.
1993-94	Mega city scheme for five metro cities
1997-2002 (Ninth Five Year Plan)	Provisions were made for 100 per cent water supply coverage in urban and rural areas, 60 per cent sanitation in urban areas and 30 per cent in rural areas, emphasis on decentralization and privatization.
2002	National Water Policy priority was given for providing drinking water to humans and animals, regular monitoring of surface and ground water quality, regulating to use of groundwater.
2002-07 (Tenth Five Year Plan)	Provisions were made for 100 per cent coverage of urban and rural population, managing water as commodity, change in the role of government from direct service provider to facilitator leading to privatization. Focus was given not only on investment requirements, but on institutional re-structuring, better services, people's participation, and managerial improvement also.

Source: Ganesh Pangare *et. al.* Springs of Life, Academic Foundation, Delhi, 2006

The First Five Year Plan periods were characterized by relatively negligible investments in water supply and sanitation. Since the beginning of the Sixth Five Year Plan (1980-85) and the launch of the International Drinking Water Supply and Sanitation Decade, India has substantially increased its commitment to the water supply and sanitation sector. The Ninth Plan provided for Rs. 395 billion as outlay from the water supply and sanitation sector, which works out to about 4.6 per cent of the plan outlay. Over the various plan periods, there has however been a shift in the ratio of UWSS to RWSS. Up-to the Fifth Plan (1974-1979), investments in UWSS were relatively higher. This changed since Annual Plan of 1979-90, and the RWSS sector was the focus of increasing investments. However, during the Ninth Plan, the gap has narrowed. (Table 2).

Table 2
Plan Investment in Water Supply and Sanitation in India

Plan Period	Outlays (Rs. million)	Percentage of Total Plan outlay	UWSS Plan Outlays (Rs. million)	Percentage of Urban Outlay
I (1951-56)	490	1.46	430	1.28
II (1956-61)	720	1.07	440	0.65
III (1961-66)	1057	1.23	897.7	1.04
Annual Plan (1966-69)	1064	1.60	430	0.18
IV (1969-74)	4370	2.75	2820	1.77
V (1974-79)	10306	2.62	5494.4	1.40
Annual Plan (1979-80)	4302	3.43	1979.3	1.58
VI (1980-85)	40470	4.15	17666.8	1.81
VII (1985-90)	65224	3.62	29657.5	1.65
Annual Plan (1990-92)	44272	3.23	17213.7	1.26
VIII (1992-97)	167110	3.85	59822.8	1.38
IX (1997-2002)	395380	4.60	186240	2.17

Source: Planning Commission, Government of India, Delhi, 2002

The projections made by the Ministry of Urban Development for the Tenth Plan period for urban water supply and sanitation are Rs. 283 billion and Rs. 494 billion, respectively. Investments necessary for urban water supply by 2015 and 2025 will be Rs. 96 billion and Rs. 258 billion, respectively and for urban sanitation, the figures will be Rs. 208 billion and Rs. 539 billion by 2015 and 2025, respectively.

The institutional responsibility for supplying water in urban areas is divided between centre and the states. The Central Government's role is to formulate policies, frame guidelines, monitor and finance the services, while the state governments plan, design, and execute water supply projects through local bodies such as municipal boards and water agencies. The Ministry of Urban Development is the main central level Department responsible for India's urban infrastructure. The CPHEEO, created in 1953 is the technical wing of the Ministry. The state Government allocates water resources, generates funds and frames policies. The urban local body is responsible for distribution and supply through piped networks, augmentation of water supplies, purification, operation and maintenance and collection of water charges. The urban local bodies are classified into Municipal Corporations, Nagar Palika Parishads and Nagar Panchayats, depending on the population size.

Government of Uttar Pradesh constituted a Corporation by the name of Uttar Pradesh Jal Nigam in the year 1975 which came into existence with effect from 18 June, 1975. Its area of operation extends to whole of Uttar Pradesh excluding cantonment areas under an Act called as Uttar Pradesh Water Supply & Sewerage Act, 1975. The basic objective of creating this Corporation is development and regulation of water supply and sewerage services and for matters connected therewith. Piped water supply facility has been provided in 623 towns and in 28923 habitations through 1037 schemes. Interestingly, till the time of independence piped water supply was provided in 28 towns of the state, but now all the towns are covered under piped water supply networks.

The Accelerated Urban Water Supply Programme was initiated in 1993-94 to provide safe and adequate water supply facilities for towns having population less than 20,000 as per 1991 census. Under the scheme, the Centre matches the funds provided by the state government which includes a 5 per cent town contribution. In special cases, 100 percent finance is available as the central share. The AUWSP is being administered through the CPHEEO at the Centre. Until March, 2002, 223 projects for 654 towns were approved at an estimated cost of Rs. 817.70 crores. An amount of Rs. 337.37 crores has been released by the centre to the states for the implementation of these projects. About 240 schemes have been completed with 98 being in the state of Uttar Pradesh.

The Mega city scheme was initiated in 1994-95 and is applicable to Mumbai, Kolkata, Chennai, Bangalore and Hyderabad. The sharing of grants between central and the state governments is th ratio of 25:25 and the balance 50 per cent is expected to be met by financing institutions and the capital markets. Borrowing could be by the implementing agencies. The implementing agency provides project related finance for urban infrastructure including water supply, sewerage, drainage, sanitation, city transport networks, land development, slum improvement and solid waste management.

Revolving funds for water supply and sewerage schemes in Uttar Pradesh is shown in Table 3.

Table 3
Revolving Funds for Water Supply and Sewerage Schemes in U.P.

Year	*Funds Released (Rs. in Lakh)*	*Funds Received by U.P. Jal Nigam (Rs. in lakh)*	*Expenditure (Rs. in lakh)*
2000-01	6327.15	6174.91	2566.18
2001-02	2623.26	2938.94	1444.48
2002-03	3448.43	3290.00	1944.68
2004-05	2515.47	2515.17	4762.46
2005-06	3508.17	3508.17	667.64

Source: U.P. Jal Nigam, Lucknow

After discontinuance of grant-in-aid to urban local bodies as a consequence of 74th Constitutional Amendment Act, state government started giving interest free loan from revolving fund to various urban local bodies on their request for implementation of water supply and sewerage schemes in urban areas. Importantly, Accelerated Urban Water Supply Programme was started in 1994-95 and is being implemented in phases in 425 towns having population less than 20,000 as per 1991 census. Out of these 425 towns, Government of India has sanctioned schemes for 390 towns costing Rs. 308.30 crore and remaining 35 towns are already having adequate water supply system. Out of 390 schemes 202 schemes have been commissioned till date and remaining 188 are under construction which are scheduled to be completed by March 2007 (Table 4).

The state government included urban water supply under district plan for the first time in 2003-04 and a budget of Rs. 1119.65 lakh was sanctioned which was subsequently increased to Rs. 2000.00 lakhs and Rs. 5966.68 lakh in 2004-05 and 2005-

06. For the year 2006-07, the proposed outlay is Rs. 5967 lakh. After 74th Constitutional Amendment Act, the practice of giving aid to urban local bodies for implementing water supply schemes was discontinued. However, from the year 2005-06 the programme of urban water supply has been revised and budget provision of Rs. 2680 lakh has been made for water supply in various towns of the state. For the year 2006-07, the proposed outlay is Rs. 1000.00 lakh. Government of India has launched National Urban Renewal Mission in December 2005 for providing infrastructure facilities in towns having population of more than one million. Under this programme, 7 towns viz., Kanpur, Agra, Varanasi, Allahabad, Lucknow, Meerut, and Mathura have been included. The City Development Plans of a few cities have already been approved while Detailed Projects Reports are being prepared for availing financial support from Central Government. Integrated Infrastructure Development for Small and Medium Towns has also been implemented in the state in order to improve the urban infrastructure, including water supply and sanitation.

Table 4

Accelerated Urban Water Supply Programme in U.P.

(As on April 2005)

Phase	*Number of Towns included*	*Estimated Cost of the Phase (Rs. in lakh)*	*Expenditure (Rs. in lakh)*	*Towns where Projects have been Commissioned*
1.	41	2833.20	3129.21	41
2.	26	2213.33	2208.49	26
3.	25	1949.23	2069.38	25
4.	41	3483.93	3390.16	41
5.	57	4505.01	3804.94	54
6.	65	5150.14	2941.68	14
7.	126	9807.95	2782.54	1
8.	2	84.01	17.00	–
9.	7	802.95	–	–
Total	390	30829.75	20423.40	202

Source: U.P. Jal Nigam, Lucknow

WATER SUPPLY

In 1991 census data claimed that nearly two thirds of the households in India had access to safe drinking water. The current figures indicate that around 92 per cent of the urban population is taking water from a protected source. However, there are states like Assam, Kerala, Mizoram, Orissa and Sikkim who get inadequate water supply coverage (Table 5).

Table 5
Water Supply in Urban Areas of India

Level of Water Supply Population Provided with water supply (%)	*States*
High (more than 85%)	Andhra Pradesh, Arunachal Pradesh, Delhi, Gujarat, Haryana, Himachal Pradesh, Jammu & Kashmir, Karnataka, M.P., Maharashtra, Meghalaya, Nagaland, Rajasthan, U.P., West Bengal
Medium (75-85%)	Bihar, Goa, Manipur, Punjab, Tamil Nadu, Tripura
Low (less than 75%)	Assam, Kerala, Mizoram, Orissa, Sikkim
Per capita water availability	
High (over 160 lpcd)	Delhi, Jammu & Kashmir, Maharashtra, Orissa, U.P., Chandigarh, Pondicherry
Medium (Between 120-160 lpcd)	Andhra Pradesh, Bihar, Gujarat, West Bengal
Low (less than 120 lpcd)	Haryana, Karnataka, Punjab, Rajasthan, Tamil Nadu, Kerala, M.P., Manipur, Tripura

In terms of per capita availability of drinking water in class I cities across the states, water shortage was reported to be more acute in eastern coastal states, while the larger states were fairly able to meet the 125 litres per capita per day requirement. In terms of per capita availability across the metropolitan cities, availability of water varied from 75.8 lpcd in Chennai to 307 lpcd in Kanpur during 1995. An assessment of the water supply status in class I cities indicate that about 37 per cent of them received less than 100 lpcd water supply followed by 31 per cent between 100-145 lpcd and rest 32 per cent more than 145 lpcd in 1995. The water shortage appears to be more acute in the class I cities of Haryana, Andhra Pradesh, Rajasthan and

Tamil Nadu, whereas 55.6 to 68.4 per cent of these cities received less than 100 lpcd of water. The situation is much more grim in case of the increasing class II towns. The analysis indicates that 21 to 30 per cent of the class II towns in the states of Tamil Nadu, Rajasthan and Gujarat received less than 40 lpcd of water during 1995. Out of 3931 cities in the country about 77 cities have 100 per cent water supply coverage. The per capita water supply ranges from as low as 9 lpcd in Tuticorin to as high as 584 lpcd in Triuvannamalai. Similarly around 203 of the class II towns have low per capita supplies of less than 100 lpcd. About 40 per cent of households living in slums are without access to safe drinking water. Water is generally available for only two to eight house a day in most cities. Even, in many towns and cities like Bhavnagar in Gujarat, Agartala in Tripura, Chennai in Tamil Nadu, water is supplied for a few hours every 2 to 3 days in a week. The availability of safe drinking water in metropolitan cities vary from 58 lpcd in Visakhapattanam to 264 lpcd in Lucknow (Table 6).

Table 6
Availability of Safe Drinking Water in Metropolitan Cities of India

City	*Per capita Water Supply (lpcd)*
Greater Mumbai	170
Kolkata	100
Delhi	155
Chennai	65
Bangalore	100
Hyderabad	90
Ahmadabad	116
Pune	220
Surat	180
Kanpur	118
Jaipur	97
Lucknow	264
Nagpur	130
Patna	107
Patna	107
Indore	80
Vadodara	135
Bhopal	130
Coimbatore	109

Contd...

City	*Per capita Water Supply (lpcd)*
Ludhiana	140
Kochi	129
Visakhapattanam	58
Agra	134
Varanasi	103
Madurai	72
Meerut	185
Nashik	140
Jabalpur	95
Allahabad	111

Source: Rajya Sabha Unstarred Question, dated 12-7-2004.

A Study of NIUA (2005) indicated that coverage by water supply is higher in metropolitan cities (98 per cent) than in Class I cities (91 per cent) and class II towns (89 per cent). Importantly, supply for non-domestic uses exceeded one fourth of the total sample. The average per capita supply in the sampled urban centres was reported to be 150 litres per capita per day with a range of 20 lpcd to 308 lpcd. The metropolitan cities have almost one and a half times the average supply available in class I cities and over the times the average per capita domestic supply in the sampled urban centres was reported to be 128 lpcd with a range of 14 to 258 lpcd. Interestingly, water supply situation in urban India is distressing with almost 46 per cent the sampled urban centres are not getting adequate water supply as per CPHEEO norms. An estimation of the demand supply gap in water supply indicates that an additional 1466 mld of water would be required to bridge the gap between demand and supply in the 137 urban centres that do not get adequate water.

As it has been already mentioned that 623 towns of the Uttar Pradesh have been covered with piped water supply but still a very large number of towns either do not have water supply as per the prescribed standards or they lack in terms of storage capacity or distribution system. Mega cities (3) receive 150 lpcd, towns with population more than one lakh (34) were sewerage system exists 135 lpcd, and other towns (586) get 70 lpcd water supply. The status of availability of water supply against the norms is shown in Table 7.

Table 7
Demand and Supply Position of Water in Metro Cities (2001)

City	*Demand (million ltr./day)*	*Supply (million ltr./day*	*Supply against demand (%)*
Delhi	3830	880	22.97
Lucknow	560	120	21.42
Kokata	2258	690	30.55
Jaipur	349	313	89.68
Bhopal	335	70	20.89
Indore	318	134	42.13
Vishakhapattanam	305	146	47.87
Mumbai	4000	1030	25.75
Hyderabad	956	186	19.45
Chennai	1894	105	5.54
Bangalore	840	135	16.07

Source: NIUA, 2001, Delhi.

Water supply in municipal Corporations in U.P. is shown in Table 8.

Table 8
Water Supply in Municipal Corporations of U.P.
(As on April 2005)

City/ Local Body	*Population (2001 census)*	*Standard Rate of Water Supply as per norms (lpcd)*	*Water Available (mld)*	*No. of Tube-wells*	*Distribution Network (km.)*	*No. of Hand pumps*
Agra	1275134	135	270	55	690	4094
Aligarh	669087	135	75.08	58	502	1970
Allahabad	135	217.00	147	1090	2505	1018092
Bareilly	718092	135	119.81	40	50350	1250
Kanpur	2532138	150	367.0	127	13150	8470
Lucknow	2207340	150	440.0	349	1800	4500
Ghaziabad	968521	135	240	202	980	2915
Meerut	1074229	135	163.70	74	960	3551
Varanasi	1400000	150	125.0	113	544	2140
Gorakhpur	622701	135	70.0	55	550	1866
Moradabad	641240	135	85.0	34	285.0	1275
Jhansi	383644	135	100.50	12	320	1882

Source: U.P. Jal Nigam, Lucknow, 2006

The largest distribution network has been reported in Lucknow, Kanpur, Meerut and Allahabad where as the availability of water has been reported higher in Lucknow, Kanpur, Agra, and Allahabad.

The status of water supply in India is shown in Table 9.

Table 9
Status of Water Supply in India

Indicator	*Metropolitan cities*	*Class I cities*	*Class II cities*	*Total*
Population '000	71429	59123	10473	141025
Coverage of Pop.(%)	98	91	89	94
Per capita Supply (lpcd)	182	124	83	150
Per Capita domestic supply (lpcd)	148	106	69	128
% of Urban Centres	50	40	52	46
Water PC Supply below city norms	68	76	79	77
% of Supply required to be added to reach city norms	5	25	42	13
Out of water required to each city norms (mld)	1397	2209	439	4045
Unaccounted for water (%)	24	16	11	21
% of Connection (metered)	60	52	39	55
Staff per 1000 connections	14.5	7.9	6.8	10.9
Cost Recovery (%)	70	55	44	65
Revenue Receipts (Rs. per kl.)	2.16	1.02	1.21	1.73
Revenue Exp. (Rs. per kl)	3.09	1.88	2.44	2.66
Deficit per kl (Rs.)	-0.93	-0.86	-1.23	-0.93
Revenue Receipt./ per capita	149.43	48.65	39.41	100.55
Revenue Exp. per Capita	214.12	89.40	77.86	153.89
Per capita Deficit (Rs.)	-64.69	-40.75	-38.45	-53.34

Source: NIUA, June, 2005

The per capita water supply ranges in between 83 lpcd in class II towns to 182 lpcd in metropolitan cities while per capita domestic supply ranges in between 69 lpcd in class II towns to 148 lpcd in metropolitan cities. The cost recovery of water supply is in between 44 per cent in class II towns to 70 per cent in metro cities. Thus, there is revenue deficit of Rs. -0.93 per kl. It has been reported higher in class II towns as compared to other urban centres.

Per capita water supply in the cities of Uttar Pradesh is shown in Table 10. The per capita water supply ranges in

Table 10
Water Supply in Cities of U.P.

City/Town	Quantity of water supplied by uses (mld)						
	Total Quantity of Water Supplied (mld)	Domestic	Non Domestic	Per Capita Supply (lpcd) Capacity	Installed Production capacity (mld) per day	% of utilization	Average hours of supply
Kanpur	310	225	85.0	124	350	89	5
Lucknow	410	349	61.5	164	455	90	6
Varanasi	220	198	22.0	191	360	61	8
Agra	250	201	49	217	376	66	8
Aligarh	47	35	12	78	48	97	6
Allahabad	210	181	29	207	230	91	9
Bareilly	80	72	8	107	110	73	8
Etawah	20	18	1	139	24	81	10
Faizabad	22	–	–	127	29	74	6
Ghaziabad	110	–	–	124	120	92	6
Gorakhpur	74	58	16	123	82	90	6
Hapur	14	–	–	70	14	100	4
Jhansi	77	76	1	152	70	110	2
Mathura	27	–	–	67	33	80	3
Meerut	132	–	–	106	150	88	5
Mirzapur	25	24	0.5	119	28	89	5
Moradabad	48	–	–	72	55	87	8
Muzaffarnagar	46	36	10	142	48	96	8
Rae Bareilly	13	11	2	74	15	90	6
Rampur	20	–	–	62	20	89	12
Saharanpur	49	36	13	91	50	98	9
Sitapur	17	–	–	114	22	78	6
Unnao	21	21	–	174	24	88	6

Source: NIUA Survey, 1999.

between 48 lpcd in Firozabad to 217 lpcd in Agra. The larger cities like Agra, Lucknow, Kanpur, Varanasi, and Allahabad have larger quantity of water supply while smaller towns get low quantity of water supply. Importantly, installed production capacity (mld) has been reported to be high in Lucknow followed by Agra, Varanasi, Kanpur and Allahabad, however, utilization capacity in these cities for a larger duration of water supply however, actual duration of water supply is observed to be low. Even, the pressure of water supply is found to be low in most of the cities and towns.

The provision of safe drinking water as per stipulated norms and standard in urban areas for towns with piped water supply but without sewerage system is 70 litres per capita daily (lpcd), for cities with piped water supply and existing or planned sewerage system, it is 135 lpcd, for metropolitan and mega cities with piped water supply and sewerage, it is 150 lpcd and for public stand posts it is 40 lpcd. According to the guidelines of Central Public Health and Environmental Engineering Organization (CPHEED)per capita water supply in class I cities should be in the range of 150 to 200 lpcd, while in reality in all class I cities, it ranges from 50 to 140 lpcd, for below the guidelines. The gap in demand is taken care of by private vendors, who run as unregulated and unorganized water markets. Even, in certain urban centres, people collect rain water for domestic use. They have also installed their endegenous hand pumps and tube-wells for drawing water for different uses. In most cities and towns, the existing systems are not operated and maintained to their full capacity. The capacity utilization has been less than 50 per cent in 40 per cent towns. Even, physical losses are typically high due to leakages. Most of the towns lack treatment facilities and thus, effluents entering the water sources are highly hazardous. Sources of drinking water is shown in Table 11.

Water supply through tap is found to be low i.e. 36.7 per cent as per 2001 census. This is found more pronouncing in Assam, Bihar, and Kerala while water supply through tap is found significantly high in Mahrashtra, Karnataka, Gujarat, Tamil Nadu, and Andhra Pradesh. Water supply through

Table 11
Source of Drinking Water in Selected States

State	Tap			Hand Pumps/Tube Wells			Well		
	Census 2001	NSSO 1998	NFHS 1998-99	Census 2001	NSSO 1998	NFHS 1998-99	Census 2001	NSSO 1998	NFHS 1998-99
India	36.7	24.4	38.7	41.2	46.2	39.2	18.2	23.7	18.7
Punjab	33.6	27.6	36.7	64.0	70.6	62.2	0.8	1.7	1.0
Haryana	48.1	37.9	47.1	37.9	45.6	40.1	11.7	16.4	11.8
Rajasthan	35.3	24.8	24.8	32.9	45.6	40.1	11.7	16.4	11.8
Uttar Pradesh	23.7	10.9	13.5	64.1	62.9	72.1	11.6	21.0	12.7
Bihar	3.7	1.5	7.8	82.9	69.7	67.6	12.6	27.7	22.5
Assam	9.2	7.8	11.0	49.6	49.4	49.1	26.7	27.6	29.1
West Bengal	21.4	9.9	25.3	67.1	71.5	64.0	10.0	16.7	9.1
Gujarat	62.3	52.9	70.3	21.8	28.2	14.2	11.7	13.9	10.3
Maharashtra	64.0	55.1	68.0	15.8	19.2	13.8	17.8	22.3	15.8
Andhra Pradesh	48.1	32.1	51.7	32.0	42.8	26.8	16.5	18.9	18.0
Karnataka	58.9	33.3	68.0	25.7	48.6	19.0	12.4	14.5	11.7
Kerala	20.4	13.3	17.7	3.0	1.6	2.2	71.982.4	2.4	77.9
Tamil Nadu	62.5	55.8	67.6	23.0	28.1	17.4	10.6	11.6	11.2

Source: Census 2001, NSSO 1999, NFHS 1998-99

handpumps and tubewells has been found to be significantly higher in West Bengal, Punjab, Bihar, and Assam. Even, a larger propotion of households fetch drinking water from surface sources i.e. wells. Urban centres depend on both surface and ground water sources for supplying water. However, the dependence on any source would be based on the availability and the cost factors. While some urban centres may depend entirely on surface sources, such as rivers, lakes, and reservoirs, others may use a combination of surface and ground water sources. The survey of NIUA, 1999 indicate that almost two-thirds of the urban centres depend on surface water and one-third on ground water. Metropolitan cities mainly depend on surface water sources with partial dependence on ground water sources. In Uttar Pradesh, Kanpur, Varanasi, Agra, Moradabad and Jhansi, are mainly depend on surface water sources. However, smaller towns and cities are mainly depend on ground water sources, through ground water sources are depleting gradually and demand for rainwater harvesting (Table 12).

Table 12
Source of Water Supply

City/Towns	*Present Source of Water Supply (mld)*			*% of water*	
	Surface source	*Groundsource*	*Total*	*Surface*	*Ground*
Kanpur	310	–	310	100	–
Lucknow	240	170	410	59	41
Varanasi	220	–	220	100	–
Agra	250	–	250	100	–
Aligarh	–	47	47	–	100
Allahabad	90	120	210	43	57
Bareilly	–	80	80	–	100
Etawah	–	20	20	–	100
Faizabad	–	22	22	–	100
Firozabad	–	12	12	–	100
Ghaziabad	–	110	110	–	100
Gorakhpur	–	74	74	–	100
Hapur	–	14	14	–	100
Jhansi	68	9.2	77	88	12
Mathura	–	27	27	–	100
Meerut	–	132	132	–	100
Mirzapur	8.0	17	25	32	68

Contd...

City/Towns	Present Source of Water Supply (mld)			% of water	
	Surface source	Groundsource	Total	Surface	Ground
Moradabad	48	–	48	100	–
Muzaffarnagar	–	46	46	–	100
Rai Bareilly	–	13	13	–	100
Kanpur	–	20	20	–	100
Saharanpur	–	49	49	–	100
Sitapur	–	17	17	–	100
Unnao	–	21	21	–	100

Source: NIUA, Survey 1999

Table 13
Water Supply, Demand and Supply Deficit as per CPHEEO Norm and City Norm, 1999

	Water Supplied		CPHEEO Norm		Demand for Water		Supply Deficit (mld)	
City/Town	mld.	lpcd.	Norm lpcd	Adopted by city (lpcd)	CPHEEO Norm	City Norm	CPHEEO Norm	City Norm
Kanpur	310	124	150	200	375	500	65	190
Lucknow	410	164	150	250	375	625	0	215
Varanasi	220	191	150	270	173	311	0	91
Agra	250	217	70	150	81	173	0	0
Aligarh	47	78	135	97	81	58	35	12
Allahabad	210	207	135	250	137	254	0	44
Bareilly	80	107	135	225	101	169	21	89
Etawah	20	139	70	175	10	25	0	5
Faizabad	22	127	70	130	12	22	0	0.50
Ghaziabad	110	124	135	200	120	177	10	67
Gorakhpur	74	123	135	150	81	90	7	16
Hapur	14	70	135	200	27	40	13	26
Jhansi	77	152	70	160	35	81	0	4
Mathura	27	67	135	200	54	80	27	53
Meerut	132	106	135	200	169	250	37	118
Mirzapur	25	119	135	200	28	42	3	17
Moradabad	48	72	70	120	47	80	0	32
Muzaffarnagar	16	142	70	200	23	65	0	19
Rae Bareilly	19	74	70	160	12	28	0	15
Rampur	20	62	70	200	22	63	2	44
Saharanpur	49	91	70	225	38	122	0	73
Sitapur	17	114	70	200	11	30	0	13
Unnao	21	174	135	180	16	22	0	0.78

Source: NIUA, Survey 1999.

Deficit of water supply is shown in Table 13. The larger cities have more supply deficit while smaller towns and cities have less water supply deficit. The water supply has been reported worst in Lucknow, Kanpur, Bareilly, Faizabad, Mathura and Gaziabad. The problem becomes acute when the quality of drinking water deteriorates due to hydrological and pollution factors.

Options for water supply to urban areas could be explored through in-situ water harvesting, repairing, renovating and properly maintaining existing water storage structures, huge scope of demand side management measures including proper pricing, saving from wastage and conservation, and recycling waste water. In Delhi, and Tamil Nadu, some efforts are already underway to harvest local water sources for the augmenting water supply in the respective cities. Having exhausted, destroyed and polluted the nearby sources and neglected using the potential of local sources, cities are reaching out to far away sources for their water supply needs. Bangalore (K.R. Sagar), Ahmadabad (Dharoi), Hyderabad (Nagarjuna Sagar), Delhi (Tehri and Renuka dam) Chennai (Telugu Ganga) are planning to exploit new sources of drinking water from 100 to 480 km. distance.

It is often recommended that all connections should be metered so as to improve revenues from water supply as also to improve supplies. Metering will allow charging by the quantity of water consumed and well also allow for leakages detection. Unmetered connections will generally encourage wastage of water, through the amount of water that can be drawn will be determined by the duration of supply. The survey undertaken by NIUA, 1999 indicates that less than one third of the sampled urban centres do not have any metered connections. The proportion of metered connections ranges from 9 to 100 per cent. The situation is grim in Meerut, Mirzapur, Allahabad and Gorakhpur where most of the water connections were found non-metered (Table 14).

Table 14
Water Supply Connections and Percentage of Connections Metered in U.P.

	No. of Water Supply Connections			*% of Connections Metered*		
City/Town	*Domestic*	*Non-Domestic*	*Total*	*Domestic*	*Non-Domestic*	*Total*
Kanpur	115073	3250	118323	43	100	93
Lucknow	180000	11023	191023	61	68	62
Varanasi	70567	2190	72757	62	64	62
Agra	108800	2900	111700	97	100	97
Aligarh	30750	3300	34050	100	100	100
Allahabad	87000	1215	88215	45	100	46
Bareilly	46625	2172	48797	100	99	100
Etawah	14430	884	15314	100	34	96
Faizabad	11965	1410	13375	100	100	100
Firozabad	17300	2125	19425	100	100	100
Ghaziabad	8482	0	8482	65	–	65
Gorakhpur	15825	344	16200	95	80	94
Hapur	8014	5141	13155	57	53	55
Jhansi	27487	552	28040	99	100	100
Mathura	15302	1000	16302	62	–	58
Meerut	70314	4598	84912	3	100	9
Mirzapur	16100	365	16465	40	96	42
Moradabad	31000	1000	32000	–	–	–
Muzaffarnagar	26860	650	27510	–	–	–
Rae Bareilly	4131	542	4773	100	100	100
Rampur	13995	302	14297	86	100	86
Saharanpur	28200	2530	30730	100	100	100
Sitapur	7000	400	7400	91	100	91
Unnao	4700	350	5050	100	100	100

Source: NIUA Survey 1999.

WATER PRICING

Water pricing is a complex issue because water is merit good. Water pricing policy is intended to save many objectives such as equity, efficiency, financial sustainability, and full cost recovery. Urban water is under priced in relation to the cost incurred on the provision of water resulted in serious concerns about the financial viability and sustainability of urban water utilities. Under pricing has resulted in poor and un-reliable water services. Water is provided at subsidized rate because poor could not afford it. However, in practice, it is the rich, not the poor who always benefit disproportionately from subsidized water services. Unreserved people in urban areas pay much higher price for the water. Thus, water pricing is important for water demand management to achieve efficient and sustainable use of water.

Several types of water tariffs are used in water sector. They include (i) increasing block tariffs, (ii) uniform volumetric charge, (iii) linear water charges. The increasing block tariff is an alternative to marginal cost. It is based on volumetric component. In the price structure, water use per billing is divided into a number of discrete blocks for which separate prices can be set. A water user in particular category, such as domestic water consumption, is charged a relatively low per unit price for consumption up to a specified amount. This amount defines the end of the initial or first block. A user who consumes more water faces a higher per unit price for this additional consumption until reaching the end of the second block, and then a still higher price until reaching the end of the top block structure. Increasing block tariffs are popular tariff structure in many developing countries. Water utilities in Bangalore, Delhi, and Hyderabad use block tariff for domestic and non-domestic supplies in combination with other price structures. Bangalore uses five water blocks with each block of 25 kls, the price per unit in the fifth block is set 9.4 times the price in the first block. In Delhi, there are four blocks of 10 kls each, with the unit price in the terminal block being 8.6 times that in the initial block Hyderabad uses four blocks of unequal sizes, and the price per unit of water in the fourth block is set 3.7 times higher than the price in the first block. Increasing block tariff is commonly used in non-domestic metered supplies. Compared with domestic supplies, the price structure for non domestic supplies is several times higher. A uniform volumetric charge may differ according to the category of users. Although simple to use, a uniform rate does not provide any incentive to consumers to affect savings on water use. Single tariff rate is in use in Kanpur, Indore, Surat, Madurai and other cities. The differentiation of rate ranges in between Rs. 2 per kl to Rs. 5 per kl for domestic use and Rs. 8 per kl to Rs. 22 per kl for industrial use in these cities.

A linear water charge rises with consumption. It prevails in Kerala where a monthly water charge is specified for discrete quantities of water. Thus, a consumer in Kerala is required to pay a monthly charge of Rs. 22 or a consumption not exceeding 10 kls, the charge increases to Rs. 25 for a consumption level of 11 kls, and rises to Rs. 550 for a consumption of 100 kls per month.

These pricing structures show sharp variations and complex nature. Where the water charges are levied by the Municipal Corporations, little change have been made in their format and structure, however, mere statutory board has been set up for the provision of water, attempts have been made for revision in water pricing in order to meet the rising cost of water provision. In the state of Uttar Pradesh, Municipal Corporation Act has mode provision for imposing tax in order to maintain water structures and sustain water supply. Water tax in Municipal Corporations is levied in between 7.5 per cent to 12.5 per cent of Annual Rental Value of house while 22 per cent to 32 per cent of ARV is being levied for property tax. Thus, Municipal Corporations cannot impose higher rate of water tax unless the Act is amended. The other local bodies have no such binding however they have to pass the water tax rates from their respective Boards for imposing the tax and its recovery. Generally, water tax is levied in between 7 per cent to 12 per cent of ARV. In most of the cities and towns, there is no water tax, however, water charges are being imposed which range in between Rs. 120 to Rs. 360 per annum. Some local bodies also charge connection charges for water supply. Interestingly, most of the local bodies in U.P. provide water supply only for domestic purposes; however, users generally convert it for non-domestic, commercial and institutional purposes.

REVENUE RECEIPTS AND EXPENDITURE

It is found that prices charged for urban water utilities donot covers the costs incurred on its provision. A recent study conducted by NIUA, 2005 showed that (i) the cost of water provision were in excess of recoveries in nearly 76 per cent of cities and towns, and (ii) the operation and maintenance costs of water supply systems were approximately 22 per cent higher than the receipts from water charges and water tax levied in lieu of water charges. The deficit i.e. costs in excess of revenue receipts are estimated at Rs. 524 mld. The annual deficits on account of water were Rs. 20 per capita in metropolitan cities, Rs. 40 per capita in cities in the population range of 100,000 and one million, and Rs. 30 per capita in towns which have a population of over 50,000 but less than 100,000 persons. The survey has shown that the annual losses on operation and maintenance of the urban water supply systems would be in between Rs. 9000 to Rs. 10000 million.

Thus, nominal pricing of water by the local bodies and poor recovery of dues has made the urban local bodies bankrupt. They have little or no funds to maintain the water supply networks and upgrades the treatment plants. Revenue generations is poor due to lack of proper tariff and failure in the recovery of dues. Overtime, demand increased, while the infrastructure continued to deteriorate and costs escalated. Due to a paucity of funds, many water service providers are not financially viable and are unable to maintain services without subsidies. The percentage of revenue generation to operation and maintenance costs in Kolkata, Nagpur, Pune, Ludhiana and Lucknow was found less than 50 per cent. The recovery revenue against cost of water production in a few cities of Uttar Pradesh shows variations. The least recovery was reported in Moradabad (16.57 per cent followed by Aligarh (25.5 per cent), and Gorakhpur (49.76 per cent) while recovery has been found satisfactory in Ghaziabad (91.67 per cent), and Allahabad (75.44 per cent). Thus, cost of production of water is much higher as compared to recovery of revenue (Table 15).

Table 15

Cost of Production of Water and Recovery in Selected Cities of U.P.

City	*Cost of Production*	*Recovery*	*Percentage of Recovery*
Lucknow	2.53	1.59	62.84
Moradabad	1.75	0.29	16.57
Jhansi	0.04	0.03	75.0

Contd...

City	*Cost of Production*	*Recovery*	*Percentage of Recovery*
Allahabad	4.56	3.44	75.44
Gorakhpur	2.11	1.05	49.76
Kanpur	0.16	0.08	50.0
Aligarh	2.00	0.51	25.5
Gaziabad	0.12	0.11	91.67
Agra	4.47	2.99	66.89

Source: Rastriya Sahara, 15 January 2007

Per capita revenue receipts and revenue expenditure is shown in Table 16. Per capita revenue receipts has been found higher in Bangalore, Chennai, Mumbai and Hyderabad, while in most of the cities of Uttar Pradesh, it ranges in between Rs. 3 to Rs. 83. Similarly, per capita revenue expenditure is found low in most of the cities in the state. However, per capita revenue expenditure is reported higher than per capita revenue receipts in most of the cities and towns. Thus, annual revenue gap has been found higher in Delhi, Kolkata, Ahmadabad, Faizabad, and Chennai. Cost recovery and revenue expenditure gap in U.P. as shown in Table 17 also show dismal picture. Saharanpur, Muzaffar Nagar, Allahabad and Agra have managed some how to recover the cost of water supply to the greater extent while cost recovery is found dismal in Unnao, Sitapur, Rai Bareilly, Moradabad, Mirzapur, Jhansi, Faizabad and Bareilly. Revenue expenditure gap (Rs. per kl) is reported significantly high in Bareilly, Faizabad, Lucknow and Kanpur.

Table 16

Per Capita Revenue Receipts and Revenue Expenditure in U.P.

City/ Town	*Revenue Receipts (Rs. lakhs)*	*Revenue Expenditure (Rs. lakhs)*	*Annual Revenue Receipts per Capital (Rs.)*	*Annual Revenue Expenditure per Capita (Rs.)*	*Annual Revenue Gap per Capita (Rs.)*
Ahmadabad	270	3947	7.9	116	-108
Bangalore	15384	14909	333	323	10
Kolkata	947	7534	16	131	-114
Chennai	16258	11858	379	276	102
Delhi	7547	46829	67	416	-349

Contd...

City/ Town	*Revenue Receipts (Rs. lakhs)*	*Revenue Expenditure (Rs. lakhs)*	*Annual Revenue Receipts per Capital (Rs.)*	*Annual Revenue Expenditure per Capita (Rs.)*	*Annual Revenue Gap per Capita (Rs.)*
Hyderabad	10623	10052	266	252	14
Kanpur	1090	926	45	38	7
Lucknow	1159	2118	49	89	-40
Varanasi	540	779	48	69	-21
Mumbai	35513	26275	324	240	84
Agra	920	1008	83	91	-8
Aligarh	122	108	20	18	2
Allahabad	565	645	57	65	-8
Bareilly	123	485	17	67	-50
Etawah	17	52	13	38	-25
Faizabad	49	228	30	139	-110
Firozabad	14	26	6	11	-5
Ghaziabad	251	287	31	35	-4
Gorakhpur	106	178	18	30	-12
Hapur	22	29	11	15	-4
Jhansi	95	197	20	41	-21
Mathura	46	97	12	26	-14
Meerut	113	201	10	17	-7
Mirzapur	17	46	8.5	22	-14
Moradabad	21	50	3	8	-5
Muzaffarnagar	87	87	27.88	27.87	0.01
Sitapur	8	25	5.7	17	-12

Source: NIUA Survey 1999.

In the state of Uttar Pradesh, most of the cities and towns do not collect user charges for water supply. The revenue collection is more or less confined to water tax which is a crucial part of holding tax (property). However, water charges are collected in Meerut, Moradabad, Aligarh and Allahabad to the greater extent. Connection charges are also being imposed in most of the cities and towns, however, its contribution in revenue receipts is found to be nominal (Table 18).

Revenue expenditure on water supply is mainly confined to salary and wages of staff, consumables including electricity. There is no fund for maintenance of water structures. During

Table 17
Cost Recovery and Revenue Expenditure Gap in U.P.

City/Town	Water Supplied(mld)	Revenue Receipts (Rs. lakh)	Revenue Expenditure (Rs. lakhs)	Cost Recovery (% Receipts to Expenditure)	Receipts Expenditure Gap (Rs. lakhs)	Revenue Expenditure Gap/kl (in Rs.)
Kanpur	310	1090	926	118	164	0.1
Lucknow	410	1159	2118	55	-959	-0.6
Varanasi	220	540	779	69	-239	-0.3
Agra	250	920	1008	91	-80	-0.1
Aligarh	47	122	108	113	14	0.1
Allahabad	210	565	645	88	-79	-0.1
Bareilly	80	123	485	25	-362	-1.2
Etawah	20	17	52	34	-35	-0.5
Faizabad	22	49	228	21	-179	-2.3
Firozabad	12	14	26	52	-13	-0.3
Ghaziabad	110	251	287	87	-36	-0.1
Gorakhpur	74	106	178	60	-72	-0.3
Hapur	14	22.5	29.3	77	-16.9	-0.1
Jhansi	77	95	197	48	-101	-0.4
Mathura	27	46	97	48	-50	-0.5
Meerut	132	113	201	56	-88	-0.2
Mirzapur	25	17	46	38	-29	-0.3
Moradabad	48	21	50	41	-24	-0.2
Muzaffarnagar	46	87.28	87.25	100	0.03	0
Rai Bareilly	13	17	45	39	-27	-0.5
Rampur	20	15.8	22.9	69	-7.1	-0.1
Saharanpur	49	79.7	78.3	102	1.4	0.01
Sitapur	17	8	25	33	-17	-0.3
Unnao	21	9	29	30	-20	-0.3

Source: NIUA, Survey 1999.

Table 18
Revenue Receipts from Water Supply (%)

City	*Water Tax*	*Water Cess*	*Water Charges*	*Connection Charges*	*Supply charges*	*Others*
Kanpur	44	–	–	–	55	1
Lucknow	77	–	23	–	–	–
Varanasi	78	–	14	92	–	7
Agra	17	79	–	–	–	4
Aligarh	34	–	66	–	–	–
Allahabad	16	–	84	–	–	–
Bareilly	80	–	17	3	–	–
Etawah	96	–	2	–	–	2
Faizabad	38	–	12	–	–	50
Firozabad	93	–	-5	0.05	–	1.2
Ghaziabad	89	–	8	–	–	8
Gorakhpur	99.8	–	–	–	0.2	–
Hapur	85	–	12	2	–	0.7
Jhansi	9	85	–	–	0.9	5
Mathura	98	–	0.8	0.9	–	–
Meerut	–	–	91	9	–	–
Mirzapur	80	10	–	0.03	–	10
Moradabad	–	–	88	12	–	–
Muzaffarnagar	62	–	26	1.6	–	11
Rai Bareilly	97	–	-	–	0.3	1.7
Rampur	65	–	35	–	–	0.1
Saharanpur	96	0.1	2	2	–	–
Sitapur	95	5	–	–	–	0.5
Unnao	97	–	–	–	–	5

Source: NIUA, Survey 1999.

1997-98, revenue expenditure on water supply was reported significantly high in larger cities i.e. class one cities and municipal corporations (Table 19).

Table 19
Revenue Expenditure on Water Supply in U.P.

City	*Salary and Wages*	*Electricity*	*Consumables*	*Repairs and Replacements*	*Others*	*Interest*	*Total (Rs. lakhs)*
Kanpur	71	15	6	7	1	–	926
Lucknow	54	38	5	4	–	–	2118
Varanasi	54	34	9	3	–	–	779
Agra	53	10	20	4	14	–	1008
Aligarh	67	5	27.4	–	0.6	–	107.8

Contd...

City	Salary and Wages	Electricity	Consumables	Repairs and Replacements	Others	Interest	Total (Rs. lakhs)
Allahabad	71	11	5	13	–	–	645
Bareilly	25	31	14.4	–	–	–	485
Etawah	–	100	–	–	–	–	52
Faizabad	12	88	-0.4	–	–	–	228
Firozabad	–	100	–	–	–	–	26
Ghaziabad	45	–	54.6	–	–	–	287
Gorakhpur	46	3	26	11	14	–	178
Hapur	96	–	3.7	–	–	–	29
Jhansi	40	22	1	24	3	–	197
Mathura	74	–	24.9	–	1	–	97
Meerut	–	–	100	–	–	–	201
Mirzapur	–	–	100	–	–	–	46
Moradabad	91	–	9.8	–	–	–	50
Muzaffar nagar	49	1	–	5	45	–	87
Rai Bareilly	92	–	7	–	–	0.4	44.5
Saharanpur	76	–	13.7	–	–	–	78
Sitapur	–	–	100	–	–	–	25
Unnao	–	–	100	–	–	–	29

Source: NIUA Survey, 1999.

Volumetric rates (Rs. kl/m) are imposed in cities and towns. Water charges for industrial and commercial purposes are found to be significantly higher as compared to the water rates for domestic and institutional purposes. However, the present rates are very low in most of the cities and towns as against the increasing cost of water production (Table 20).

Table 20
Water Tariffs in U.P.

City/ Town	Cost of Production of water (1997-98)Rs./kl	Consumption Based Rates		Volumetric Rates (Rs/kl/m on total)		
		Domestic	Non Domestic	Industrial	Commercial	Institutional
Kanpur	3.48	2.00	–	10	6.0	4.0
Lucknow	4.00	2.00	–	–	6.00	4.0
Meerut	–	2.20	10.0	–	–	–
Agra	1.10	3.00	–	22.80	22.80	–

Contd...

City/ Town	*Cost of Production of water (1997-98)Rs./kl*	*Consumption Based Rates*		*Volumetric Rates (Rs/kl/m on total)*		
		Domestic	*Non Domestic*	*Industrial*	*Commercial*	*Institutional*
Allahabad	3.00	2.50	–	12.50	7.50	5.0
Ghaziabad	–	0.60	–	1.50	1.10	0.60
Bareilly	1.70	0.75	–	2.50	2.00	0.75
Moradabad	–	–	–	–	–	–
Gorakhpur	1.70	0.75	–	2.00	2.00	2.00
Aligarh	4.95	0.75	-	3.00	3.00	3.00
Saharanpur	–	0.60	1.10	–	–	–
Jhansi	9.00	2.00	4.00	–	–	–
Mathura	–	1.00	–	2.00	2.00	1.00
Muzaffarnagar	–	0.60	1.10	–	–	–
Rampur	–	0.80	1.50	–	–	–

Source: NIUA Survey, 1999.

The water tax ranges in between 7 per cent of ARV to 17.50 per cent of ARV depending upon the size of the town / city or water need.The local bodies also charge one third water connection charges which range in between Rs. 120 to 5000 for domestic purposes; Rs. 120 to Rs. 1560 for industrial, commercial and institutional purposes (Table 21).

Table 21
Water Tax and Connection Charges in U.P.

City/ Town	*One time water connection charges (Rs.)*				*Year of last Revision*	*Water Tax*
	Domestic	*Industrial*	*Commercial*	*Institutional*		
Kanpur	1000	1000	1000	–	1994	–
Lucknow	–	–	–	–	1996	12.5 ARV
Varanasi	1560	1560	1560	–	1994	14% of ARV
Meerut	500	500	500	–	1998	–
Agra	275	275	275	275	1994	14% of ARV
Allahabad	5000	–	–	–	1999	14% of ARV
Ghaziabad	–	–	–	–	–	10% of ARV

Contd...

City/ Town	One time water connection charges (Rs.)				Year of last Revision	Water Tax
	Domestic	Industrial	Commercial	Institutional		
Bareilly	120	120	120	120	1986	10% of ARV
Moradabad	300	–	450	–	1990	14% of ARV
Gorakhpur	500	1000	1000	1000	1990	14% of ARV
Aligarh	–	–	–	–	1997	7% of ARV
Saharanpur	500	–	1250	500	1987	12% of ARV
Jhansi	650	650	650	650	1994	12.5% of ARV
Mathura	250	250	250	250	1999	17.5% of ARV
Muzaffarnagar	500	1000	1000	1000	1998	12% of ARV
Rampur	250	250	250	250	1999	10% of ARV

Source: NIUA Survey, 1999

The one time water connection charges are found to be very nominal in most of the cities and towns. The local bodies mainly impose and collect water tax which is also insignificant as against increasing cost of water production and water supply (Table 22).

Table 22

Existing Structure of Water Tax and Charges in U.P.

Name of Town/City	Water Tax	Connection Charges (Rs.)	Water Charges (per year)	Year of last Revision	Water Tax/ Charges	
					Domestic	Non Domestic
Firozabad	10% of ARV	180	–	–	–	–
Khandla	10% of ARV	22	–	1996	–	–
Shahjahanpur	10% of ARV	–	–	2003	–	–

Contd...

Name of Town/City	*Water Tax*	*Connection Charges (Rs.)*	*Water Charges (per year)*	*Year of last Revision*	*Water Tax/ Charges*	
					Domestic	Non Domestic
Faizabad	10% of ARV	50	–	2004	–	–
Farrukhabad	12% of ARV	53	120	1978	–	–
Mirzapur	10% of ARV	700	–	1995	–	–
Bahraich	7% of ARV	–	120	2003	–	–
Aligarh	12% of ARV	–	240	–	–	–
Badaun	10% of ARV	600	300	2001	–	–

Source: Discussions held with Tax Superintendents, RCUES, Lucknow, 20th January, 2007.

PRIVATIZATION OF WATER

The poor performance of water supply agencies has been used for encouragement of private sector participation in urban water supply. The World Bank claims that the private sector participation can yield improvement in water supply, provide additional management skills and improve management incentives, having government agencies on policy decisions. In certain cities, public private partnership models have been introduced in order to improve urban water supply and reduction in water production cost.

Water markets or trading of water for commercial and non commercial proposes have arisen mainly out of scarcity and because public utility systems are unable to meet the demands of the population. The sale of water through tankers is one of the most lucrative small scale business today. Besides tankers, small scale vendors sell water in tins and cans, transporting them from the source to the consumers in a variety of vehicles. In many places, suppliers install bore-wells and lay pipelines to supply water directly to households and commercial establishments. Aside, from these small scale vendors, the bottled water industry has become one of the fasted growing industries in the country. Today, the bottled water sector is one of the fastest growing industries in the country. Globalization, an increase in income levels among people and greater awareness about safe drinking water, rise in water crisis and declining water quality has triggered off the trade of bottled water in India. The market for packaged water is in between Rs. 8 billion to Rs. 10 billion which is increasing at the rate of 40 per cent per annum.

NEED FOR REFORMS

The growing emphasis on fiscal discipline in the post liberalization era has made it difficult for governments to continue to provide financial support to loss making infrastructure services, particularly water supply and sanitation. There is now a growing consensus for augmentation and management of environmental infrastructure services through public-private partnership and restructuring service delivery mechanism.Augmentation of water supply, sanitation, and solid waste services and improvement in service, quality call for significant investment. However, the state cannot finance all such infrastructure projects on its own. Thus, private investment would be required to augment the efforts of the state in these critical sector of development.

The constitutional Amendments in 1992 have led to decentralization of responsibility to the local bodies, thereby increasing the latter's functional areas and giving them more powers. However, these institutions are still in the process of building their financial capabilities and institutional capabilities to address issues in service delivery. For instance, service departments within the municipal authorities charged with water supply and sanitation functions, often work with limited resources and without any commitments towards resource mobilization. Due to lack of coordination among the organizations, a situation has emerged when the responsibilities and powers of various authorities in delivering a single service are ambiguous and unclear. Moreover, inefficient revenue collection by the local bodies coupled with inadequate and highly subsidized user charges for provision of services and high administration costs is a major problem. This has deteriorated the financial health of urban local bodies and thus increaing dependence on state governments and other external agencies for loans and grants. Enforcement of rational tariffs and cost recovery would be pre-requisites for expanding institutional financial flows. However, these reforms cannot take place unless proper legal and regulatory frameworks for such investments are created and developed to ensure full cost recovery.

It is imperative to upgrade existing urban infrastructure to enable it to deliver effectively urban services. The role and responsibilities of urban local bodies have been redefined in the context of decentralized governance. Thus, urban service providers are to be well equipped with a broad spectrum of skills, and expertise to undertake a wider variety of taxes pertaining to different developmental activities. Thus, training needs for municipal employees is imperative. In the changed context, role of government at state and local levels should only be as a facilitator and not as a provider of services. Various studies of regulatory mechanisms for infrastructure sector in country show that strengthening of regulatory agencies would be required in order to separating regulatory and operational services and also increasing the role of private sector. Moreover, for real decentralization, alongwith the devolution of functions and powers to local bodies to raise financial resources and enhancing technical capabilities would also be required. The need for effective regulation of ground water extraction is also well realized. Similarly, water sources and promoting water treatment, privatized or funds could be tapped to generate resources to augment service coverage. In the post liberalization era, it would be difficult for the state government to perpetually finance losses in public sector enterprises. Private capital and initiative may help accomplish operational efficiency and investment. The local bodies may contract services of billing metering, maintenance of water sources, treatment of water collection of user charges, tax water cess etc. while regulatory role may be strengthened through community participation. The six components in the water and sanitation delivery system viz. (i) capturing water at its sources; (ii) transmitting water to a place; (iii) treating water; (iv) delivery water to the users; (v) collecting waste water from users, and (vi) treating the waste water. Similarly, water tariffs are to be rationalized through regular revision and using appropriate models of water pricing.

Options for water supply to urban areas could be explored through water harvesting. It could be one of the promising options in order to meet the growing water requirement. Water harvesting is not a new technology, though such practices are prevalent to overcome the vagaries and inadequacy in water supply. There are two practices of rain water harvesting viz. (i) roof top harvesting, recharge ground water and storage it in underground tanks; (ii) recycling waste water. These practices may improve water level in ground aquifer and water quality and quantity in the residential areas. Restoring the existing water harvesting structures such as lakes, ponds, open well, Bavalies and other water bodies is also imperative. We have to utilize the full potential of existing infrastructure and local water harvesting systems. Institutional approach is required the understanding the role of community, environment and the governance system in solving the resource crisis. Adequate awareness building measures are imperative to facilitate innovative methods of water supply option. Decentralization may also ensure the sustainability of the water supply programme. The decentralized system with participation of residents of rain water harvesting may be introduced in order to improve the recharge of groundwater and water supply. Urban water supply agencies need to decentralize planning, regulation and monitoring functions for evolving efficient water supply options. Participation by water users well ensures the use of appropriate design choices, and management practices of diverse water supply options in accordance with local requirements.

RECOMMENDATIONS

- Experiences of best practices in the field of water supply, rainwater harvesting, water resources management, water pricing, privatization of water, water supply options waste water treatment, decentralization of water supply, and management options etc. should be documented and also used in planning and implementation of water supply in the state and also to promote cross sectoral learning in this sector.

- Measures should be taken to initiate capacity building in urban centres for estimation of unaccounted for water. Metering of connections, both for bulk supply and rational distribution must be encouraged. Standard meters should be made available at reasonable cost to all urban local bodies for the purpose.
- Tariff should be rationalized with the introduction of increasing block tariff structure in local bodies. The water pricing should be based on categories of water users such as domestic, non-domestic, institutional, industrial and commercial while domestic consumers should charged less for water supply and industrial users should be charged comparatively high. The increasing rate of water tariff should also be imposed on the bodies of categories of domestic and non-domestic users, depending on size of water consumption.
- Tariff should be increased at certain given intervals depending on inflation, power tariff, increasing cost of water production and maintenance of water utilities.
- Ground water depletion can be checked by under taking rainwater harvesting in all the urban centres. Specific programmes/schemes should be initiated for aquifer recharge. These schemes and programmes should be based on decentralized approaches of water resources management and water harvesting.
- The local bodies should be strengthened through providing them capacity building and autonomy to decide on increase in water tariff required to cover at least operation and maintenance costs.
- All the urban local bodies should be made compulsory to impose user charges for water supply to be various categories of consumers. Besides imposing water tax, local

bodies should also impose water price depending upon the size of water consumption. The water price should vary depending on the categories of users and size of water consumption.

- Improving cost recovery should be linked with grants or fiscal transfers. Financial incentives may also be given to urban local bodies showing improved cost recovery.
- Private sector participation should be encouraged. Unbundling of services such as billing, metering, collection, recovery etc. may improve efficiency of urban local bodies. The regulatory role of urban local bodies should be given to them while other functions may be given to private sector. Private sector may also be encouraged for participation in water production and supply to different users.
- Public private partnership must be couraged for financing water supply projects to cover the entire urban population. The best practices of public private partnership should be learnt and be adopted for managing the water supply based on it.
- The existing pricing structure is unsustainable and lacks incentives. It calls for reforms urgently and essentially. Tariff should be designed to cover costs incurred on supplying water. The water charges based on property tax need reforms to bring changes in property tax and Rent Control Act.
- The differentiation in the water charges, water tax and water pricing is needed to achieve revenue targets while promoting at the same time efficiency and equity objectives in service provision.
- The revenue base of water utilities is grossly unbalanced. Hence, water utilities must rationalize price structure depending on the size of water consumption and uses of water.
- Rationalization of tariff structures would require necessary legislative changes, and developing a system of incentives and sanctions at state level to encourage reforms. Large governing water and municipal government in the state

need reforms in order to implement the 74th Amendment for devolving urban water supply and sanitation responsibility to municipalities and discharging these responsibilities.

- Reforms are also needed for restructuring water Boards - Jal Nigam and Jal Sansthan by disaggregating them by function, separating service provision from regulatory and policy responsibilities, commercializing the service provision entities, and evolving the private sector in management of new commercialized entities.
- The urban local bodies are also supposed to develop best practices and producedures in areas of accounting, auditing, procurement, tariff rationalization, customer consultation and integrating service to disadvantaged groups with the maintenance of service delivery.
- Consumer and citizens groups used to be involved in the development of customer consultation mechanisms and in the development of reforms at the local body level. Civil societies need to contribute to the development of new mechanism and pilot projects to involve and serve disadvantaged groups.

REFERENCES

Boland J. and Whittington D. (2000), The Political Economy of Water Tariff in Developing Countries: Increasing Block Tariff Verses Uniform Price with Rebate, in Political Economy of Water Pricing Reforms (ed) by Ariel Diner, Oxford University Press, Oxford .

Dinar, Ariel and Subramaniam (ed) (1997), Water Pricing Experiences: An International Perspectives, World Bank Technical Paper, No. 386, World Bank, Washington.

Government of India (1987), National Water Policy, Ministry of Water Resources, New Delhi, .

Government of India (2002), National Water Policy, Ministry of Water Resources, New Delhi .

Marie, W. and Zeran et. Marie Llorente (1999), Institutional Innovation in the Indian Water Supply Sector, Centre de Sciences Humanities, New Delhi.

MIDS (1995), Policies of Urban Water Supply: A Strategy Paper, Madras Institute of Development Studies, Chennai.

MUAE (1996), Report of the Working Group on Urban Water Supply and Sanitation Sector for the Ninth Five Year Plan (1997-2002); Ministry of Urban Affairs and Employment, Government of India, New Delhi.

NIUA (2005), Status of Water Supply, Sanitation and Solid Waste Management in Urban Areas, National Institute of Urban Affairs, New Delhi, June .

NIUA (2005), Water Supply and Water Tariff, Statistical Volume I, National Institute of Urban Affairs, New Delhi, June .

ORG (1996), Financing, Pricing and Cost Recovery of Water Supply and Sanitation Services, Operations, Research Group, New Delhi.

Padwal, Rajan, Issues of Pricing Urban Water Department of Economics, University of Mumbai, Working Report, No. 13

Pangare, Ganesh et. al., (2006), Springs of Life: India's Water Resources, Academic Foundation, Delhi.

Planning Commission (2002), Report of the Steering Committee on Drinking Water Supply and Sanitation for the Tenth Five Year Plan, Planning Commission, New Delhi, February.

PSI (1998), Future Domestic Water Requirements Working Paper, People's Science Institution, Dehradun, .

Rent, Joel, V.S. Saravaran, The Water Sanitation and Marie Helene Zerrah Scenario in Indian Metropolitan Cities: Resources and Management Occasional Paper, Centre de Sciences Humanities, New Delhi.

SANDRP (1999), Assessment of Water Supply Options for Urban India, South Asia Network on Dams, Rivers and People, New Delhi, November .

Thakkar (1997), Urban Water Sector: Some Important Issues, Centre for Science and Environment, New Delhi.

UN (2004), Guidelines on Strategic Planning and Management of Water Resources, United Nations, New York, .

UNDP (2004), Reforms in Drinking Water and Sanitation, UNDEP - teri, Delhi.

World Bank(1998), Urban Water Supply and Sanitation Report, Vol. I, India Water Resources Sector Review, World Bank, Delhi.

World Bank (1999), Urban Water Supply and Sanitation, IBRD, World Bank, and DFID, Allied Publishers Ltd., Delhi .

World Bank (1997), Water Pricing Experiences: An International Perspective, World Bank, Washington.

7

RESTRUCTURING OF MUNICIPAL SERVICES

Millennium Development Goals commit the international community to a comprehensive vision of development and governance of public services. These goals have become the most widely accepted yardstick of development efforts by government and non-government organizations. The Millennium Development Goals (MDG's) are a set of numerical and time bound targets to key achievements in human development. The findings of a World Bank study (2005) suggested that the attainment of the MDG's will remain challenging in poor states of India. There are large interstate and intra-state variations in terms of performance on millennium development indicators. Many of the millennium development indicators have high level of geographical concentration in India. Bihar, Uttar Pradesh, Madhya Pradesh, Orissa and Rajasthan are at critical junction in terms of attaining Millennium Development Goals. Though, decentralization initiative has brought about the improvement in municipal services in India, however, urbanization, unplanned urban development and inadequate infrastructure and resources have stressed urban services. The urban services have not been able to keep pace with the fast growing population. Against this backdrop present paper purports to review the status of municipal services and efforts for its restructuring in the changed environment and new policy regime.

There has been considerable debate in India about the quality of public services delivery. Services delivery in India remains poor on a whole, however, a national survey of major public services by Public Affairs Centre conducted that India did well in terms of providing basic access to such services, but far less well in terms of ensuring their quality, reliability and effectiveness (Public Affairs Centre, 2002). A recent study by Transparency International found high levels of corruption in services as diverse as health care, education, power, land administration and the Police (Transparency International India, 2005). Again, progress towards achieving the Millennium Development Goal's has been slow (World Bank, 2004). The civil service is burdened by expanding expenditure. Short tenures caused by premature transfers of officials responsible for delivering public services have undermined continuity (World Bank, 2006). The weakness of accountability mechanisms is a barrier to improving services while bureaucratic complexity and procedures make it difficult for a ordinary citizen to navigate the system for his/her own benefit (World Bank, 2006). Civic pressure by Civil Societies for change is not robust. Lack of accountability provides opportunities for corruption. The unregulated cost of elections and lack of legitimate funding sources have created incentives to extract rents from administrative functions (World Bank, 2006). Thus, concept of good governance has got momentum in order to improve service delivery. The instrument for improving service delivery include (1) promoting competition, (ii) simplifying transactions, (iii) restructuring agency process, (iv) decentralization; (v) building political support for programme delivery; (vi) strengthening accountability mechanisms, etc. It is the general assumptions that competition improves service delivery outcomes. Simplifying transactions through greater use of e-governance made easier for citizens to interact with the state governments. Similarly, restructuring agency processes involved change on several dimensions. Decentralization and strengthening of local governments have improved the functioning of public services in effective and efficient manner. Again, reducing premature transfers, fostering access to information, checking corruption through generating public pressure and public interest litigation may ensure accountability.

Urban India is in the midst of transformation. In an era of economic reforms, liberalization, and globalization, cities and towns are fast emerging as centres of growth. It is estimated that by 2025, more than 50 per cent of the country's population will live in cities and towns. This is indicative of the likely increase in the demand of infrastructural facilities and services that could rise due to urbanization This poses a serious challenge to urban planners, policy makers, and managers. This is high time to mobilize resources for financing urban infrastructure and services on the basis of public private partnership while community participation in delivery of public services may be increased through adoptions of Report Card System to measure public opinion on governance.

STATUS OF MUNICIPAL SERVICES

According to 2001 census, 27.78 per cent of the India's population resides in cities, compared to 17.3 per cent in 1951. But, in terms of population size, India's urban population is vast. Moreover, population in large cities has grown rapidly and this has led to serious infrastructural deficiencies in urban India (Kundu, 2006). The massive increase in the percentage share of urban populations in Class I cities from 26.0 per cent in 1901 to 68.7 in 2001 has often been attributed to faster growth of large cities, without taking into consideration the increase in the number of these cities (Kundu, 2006). Small cities and towns in most of the states are either stagnating or decaying, despite the efforts of governments. The small and medium towns are likely to experience serious problems due to infrastructural deficiencies. Interestingly, urban local bodies are supposed to function as democratic institutions based on principles of decentralization, participatory development and governance. Due to massive urban growth, quality of urban life has deteriorated, creating an urgent need for strengthening urban local bodies that can deliver adequate services and improve living conditions of citizens. The 74th Constitutional Amendment Act has made provisions for introducing Twelfth Schedule of the Constitution which lists the functions of urban local bodies, covering planning regulation and developmental aspects.

In view of increasing demand of urban services and infrastructure, National Commission on urbanization recognized the role and importance of the urban sector for the national economy. The estimates of the Expert Group on Commercialization of Infrastructure Projects (ECGIP, 1996) for annual investment need for urban infrastructure are most recent. The annual investment need urban water supply, sanitation, and roads, stood at Rs. 280 billion for the period of 1995-2005. Another estimate made for the Ninth Five Year Plan had estimated the investment requirement for urban housing at Rs. 526 billion. The Central Public Health Engineering has estimated the requirements of funds for 100 per cent coverage of the urban population with safe water supply and sanitation services by the year 2021 at Rs. 1729 billion. Estimates by RITES indicate that the investment required for urban transport infrastructure in one lakh plus cities during the next 20 years would be of the order of Rs. 2070 billion (Savage and Dasgupta, 2006). Traditionally, the provision of urban infrastructure and services has been the primary functions of government, however, most of municipalities face problems of resources and these are effectively dependent on their respective state governments for allocating or transfer resources to them. In absence of resources, fragmentation of schemes, and increasing stress on services, the quality of basic services is declining. Even the increasing coverage of infrastructure is not matched by improvement in the service levels. The failures in urban service delivery are caused by overlapping of policy, regulation and operational roles; fragmentation and duplication; limited autonomy to ULBs; weak links with citizens; lack of capacity; lack of incentives; etc.

Solid waste management is one of the important essential urban services provided by municipalities. Urban India produces about 48 million towns solid waste annually. It is estimated that by year 2047, waste generation will increase to 200 million tonnes, five times to present level (TERI). Cities with 1,00,000 plus population contribute 72.5 per cent waste generated in the country as compared to 3955 urban centres that produce only 17.5 per cent of the total waste (MOUD, 2005). The collection, segregation, storage, transportation, treatment, and disposal arrangements of waste are not proper and scientific. It leads to health hazards, and inefficiency in solid waste management. The bio-medical waste is also not properly managed in most of towns and cities. A study was conducted to ascertain the status of compliance of MSW Rules, 2000 by class one cities in India. The study shows that there is insignificant progress in the matter of processing of waste and construction of sanitary land fills (Asnani 2004).

Water supply and sanitation hold very important place in urban services. India's urban water supply and sanitation (UWSS) sector focus many problems and require a huge investment for revamping. Many service providers are not financially viable and are unable to maintain services without extensive subsidies. The services fall short of full coverage of the population and are often of low quality due to insufficient funding of operation and management. Environmental degradation has also deteriorated the quality of services. The latest data provided by the 58th round of the National Sample Survey (2002) specify the level of disparities in the modes of access for water supply across states. The states performing poorly in providing tap water to urban households are Bihar (35 per cent), Assam (35.5 per cent, Kerala (40 per cent), U.P. (50 per cent) and Orissa (50 per cent). In nine other states including large states such as Maharashtra, Andhra Pradesh and Gujarat, 90 per cent of the urban population receives tap water. Data on sanitation services, from the 54th round of NSS (1998) also indicate considerable state wise variations. Sanitary standards are abysmally low in the urban areas of Bihar and Madhya Pradesh where more than 45 per cent of the population has no access to any type of latrine. The septic tank is the most common mode of sanitation in use with more than one third of the urban population relying on them. Sewerage is virtually non-existence in Bihar, Madhya Pradesh, Orissa, and Assam. Punjab, Mahrashtra, Gujarat and Tamil Nadu are placed better. (Zerah, 2006).

The official statistics show that service coverage of water supply is quite high. However, low pressures and intermittent supplies allow back symphonage resulting in contamination of water in distribution network. The metering of domestic consumers in most of the cities is rarely taken seriously. Only 70 per cent of India's urban population has adequate excreta disposal facilities. There has been government policy not to build sewerage systems in towns of less than 10 million people. Thus due to inadequate sewerage and lack of waste water treatment facilities, river water and other sources for drinking water supply are excessively polluted. The uncollected solid waste creates hurdles in drainage system in most cities and causing flooding and water lagging in monsoon rains.

The increasing population in urban India has led to the gorwth of variety of economic activities which demand for a variety of transport modes and travel operators. A study carried out in 21 cities suggests that more than 75 per cent of the trips in a city are on account of either employment or education (RITES, 1998). However, the congestions in urban transport is gradually increasing due to increase in vehicles and inadequate expansion of road network. The increase in vehicles has caused air pollution and road accidents. Though India has developed an extensive public delivery system for the provision of health care and education, however, role of public sector in delivery of health and education services is gradually reducing. Only one third schools are managed by local bodies (35.6 per cent). The quality of infrastructure in schools run by local bodies is found to be poor. Though municipal hospitals exist in most Indian cities but generally public hospitals are quite inadequate for rapidly expanding urban population. Most of the health centres do not cover the slum populations. (Sahni and Kshivsagar, 1993). The access of poor to health care services managed by government is also declining.

CORRUPTION IN MUNICIPAL SERVICES

The Indian corruption study 2005 by Transparency International India is unique for its scope and sample size. It takes into account both perceptions and experience of actually paying a bribe to get attended to or serviced by public service providers. The study covered 11 public services viz. Police, Judiciary, Municipal Services, Government Hospitals, Electricity, Public Distribution System, Income Tax, Water Supply, Schools and Rural Financial Institutions. As high as 62 per cent of citizens think that the corruption is not a hear-say, but they have had first hand experience of paying a bribe or using a contact to get a job done in a public office. Three fourths of the citizens think that the level of corruption in public services has increased during 2004-05. According to study, police stands out high on the corruption score. Judiciary and land administration are rated next. Kerala stands out as the least corrupt state in India. Bihar is the most corrupt state. Jammu and Kashmir is the next to Bihar. The main factors of corruption in public services were reported to be (Transparency International 2005): lack of transparency and accountability in system; (ii) lack of an effective corruption reporting mechanism; (iii) lack of honesty among officials in government; (iv) acceptance of bribe us a way of life, custom and culture; (v) ineffective anti corruption institutions, (vi) poor economic policies; (vii) inadequate training and orientation of government officials.

The study highlighted the following facts in the context of municipal services (Transparency International India, 2005): (1) about 17 per cent households have interacted with municipalities to get one or the other service during 2004-05; (ii) nearly one-fourth of those interacted with the municipalities had actually paid bribes; (iii) more than one third had visited municipality more than four times in last one year; (iv) nearly three fourths opined that there was corruption in the municipality; (v) about three fifth believed that corruption had increased in last one year; (vi) two fifths had taken recourse to alternate methods like paying bribe or using influence to get their work done.

The service provides have their own view that due to shortage of staff, finances, inadequate training and orientation to staff, and lack of coordination between various departments of municipalities and also centralized decision making authority, the municipality is finding it difficult to deliver services effectively. Organizing training and orientation to staff and elected representatives, registration of complaints, computerization of departmental procedures, simplification of procedures and transparency in work, and also public private partnership initiatives have improved the efficiency in public service delivery system.

In order to improve the urban services, government now recognizes that greater accountability for service delivery performance is a pre-requisite for augmenting the coverage and quality of services. The urban governments are attempting to improve the urban services through public private partnership initiatives and introducing Report Card Systems.

PUBLIC PRIVATE PARTNERSHIP

Public Private Partnership provides an opportunity for private sector participation in financing, designing, construction and operations and maintenance of public sector programmes and projects. This is high time to forge a greater interface between the public and private sector in a wide range of activities in the country (planning Commission, 2004). The overwhelming response of private sector, including civil societies in the Tsunami earth quake in India was an outstanding example of public-private partnership.

Most of the public services have been traditionally provided through in house facilities of governments, financed, and managed directly by them. Public Private Partnersip is an approach under which services are delivered by the private sector while the responsibility for providing the services rests with the governments. This arrangement requires the government to either enter into a 'contract' with the private partner or pay for the services rendered by the private sector. Contracting prompts a new activity when neither the public sector nor the private sector existed to provide the service

(Planning Commission, 2004). Three things distinguished Public Private Partnership from direct provision of services by governments are (i) a partnership based on well articulated contact; (ii) a long term relationship between the public and private sector; and (iii) flexibility and responsiveness in decision making. The involvement of private sector participation for financing urban infrastructure and services, particularly water supply and environmental sanitation has not been very encouraging in India till recently. However, some private sector initiatives for financing long term capital investments in urban basic services, particularly water supply and solid waste management in recent years have indicated the potential of public-private partnership in delivery of services in urban sector. However, the basic hindrance towards the successful private sector participation in financing urban basic services is mainly, the failure of the governance system to create the conducive atmosphere in this regard rather than the failure of the initiative in itself. In order to derive the advantage inherent in public sector as well as private sector enterprises, the role of public-private partnership is considered to have great potential in some important areas in delivery of municipal services. The partnership fall into five main categories viz. - (i) contract services; (ii) privatization of services; (iii) designing, construction and operation of facilities; (iv) project financing and; (v) merchant facilities. The partnership in municipal services is expected to reduce cost of maintenance, increase efficiency and timely completion of new projects while community participation in operation and maintenance of services is expected to be of great importance. Government of India is committed to remove the roadblocks in delivery of services and creating infrastructure in collaboration with private sector under Jawahar Lal Nehru Urban Renewal Mission. The Mission will have two main components, focusing on infrastructure and governance and services to the urban poor respectively. The government now recognizes that greater accountability for service delivery performance is a pre-requisite for improvement in the coverage and quality of services.

REPORT CARD SYSTEM

Report Card System is an effective tool and is useful in evaluating various aspects like people's participation, rule of law, transparency, responsiveness, equity, effectiveness and efficiency, accountability and strategic vision etc. which may be utilized in general to promote good urban governance.

A number of studies have been undertaken by various bodies to establish and monitor public opinion with respect to the delivery of public services. Report Cards are a method of measuring public opinion in a structured way. The main problems related to public services are (i) citizens have no effective voice to influence service delivery; (ii) the quality of service delivery by public services is very poor; and (iii) public authorities have no effective way to assess public satisfaction. Thus, Report Card System provides a mechanism to measure public opinion on quality of public services. The methodology of Report Card include random sample surveys of households, focus group discussions, brief case studies of selected respondents, documentation of information provided to the public by service providers and interviews with a sample of lower level staff of the agencies. The cards attempt to assess, rank and benchmark the following parameters; (i) overall satisfaction with service delivery (levels of service), (ii) the extent and coverage of services; (iii) patterns of emerging problems; (iv) the response of agencies to reported problems and grievances; (v) the effectiveness of bribes in rectifying reported problems. (World Bank, 1999). The studies in Ahmedabad, Bangalore, Pune highlighted that (i) the administration of public services is uniformly low across the cities; (ii) supply shortages are in many cases 'manmade' and information is manipulated for personal gain; (iii) the popular belief that public services are cheap is a myth. Report Card system, under UNDP Project on "Capacity Development for Urban Governance" in Uttar Pradesh and Uttaranchal states was applied in selected urban local bodies viz. Dehradoon, and Nainital in Uttaranchal and Malihabad, Basti, Mirzapur and Moradabad in Uttar Pradesh during 2002-04. The analysis of research findings suggest that there has been marked improvement in governance of municipal services. The 7 broad categories were made by Regional Centre for Urban and Environmental Studies (RCUES), Lucknow to measure the public opinion on municipal services. These include community awareness, community participation, rule of law, transparency, responsiveness, effectiveness and efficiency, and accountability. The two subsequent surveys conducted in local bodies demonstrated that there has been positive impact of project intervention on municipal governance (Dwivedi and Narayan, 2004). RCUES, Lucknow has introduced the report card system in selected cities and towns of Uttar Pradesh, Bihar, Madhya Pradesh and Jharkhand states. The following implications of study findings are noteworthy: (i) improvements in service delivery and consumer satisfaction can be improved at very reasonable cost; (ii) consumers are willing to pay more for services; (iii) consumers have to play an active role in the planning and monitoring public services; and (iv) the non-responsiveness of public services is directly linked to their monopolistic status (World Bank, 1999).

REFORMS IN MUNICIPAL SERVICES

In order to remove road blocks in delivery of urban services, three types of triggers offer the potential for inducing reform in urban governance and service delivery. The first trigger could be fiscal flows. Second, decentralization has potential to spark change and create incentives for ensuring accountability in delivery of services. A third set of triggers would come from the demand side, essentially by making service providers directly accountable (Savage and Dasgupta, 2006).

The incentive based approach may be useful in revamping municipal services. The key elements in incentive based approach are (i) democratic decentralization, (ii) commercialization of service providers; (iii) market oriented financial systems. The provision of water and sanitation services should become the responsibility through a variety of arrangements. Devolution of responsibilities to municipal authorities will also lead to be accompanied by good practices.

The existing state owned service providers need to be radically reformed. This will include unbundling by functions, removing monopolies to encourage competition, and corporatization of disaggregated entities leading to privatization. These reforms may be supported by (i) enhancing private sector participation; (ii) developing appropriate comparative competition facilities; (iii) customer responses and feedback mechanisms. (World Bank, 1999). Tariff rationalization is also necessary for ensuring financial viability of services. The subsidy provided to poor should be explicit, transparent and target oriented.

CONCLUSION

Despite increasing financial support by the central government, the quality of services in cities is declining. In order to remove the roadblocks in improving service delivery, the central government has launched Jawahar Lal Nehru National Renewal Mission for large cities while Integrated Infrastructure Development Scheme for Small and Medium Towns is already targeted to improve the coverage and quality of basic urban services. However, state level response to the policy shifts is reported to be poor which creates hurdles in the efforts of central government. The main instruments for improving service delivery should include:

- Government should promote greater competition in service delivery across sectors. Regulation may be solution to the existing problem of predatory behaviour of service providers.
- Government may encourage the wider use of e-governance to simplify interaction between governments and citizens.
- Public Private Partnerships should be promoted specially in projects with e-governance, water, sanitation, solid waste management etc.
- Governments should conduct functional review of service providing agencies in order to examine road blocks in delivery of services and improving the coverage and quality of services.

- Better coordination mechanism should be created to foster inter agency collaboration for effective implementation of reforms and delivery of services.
- Report Card System should be introduced by private independent agencies to assess the performance and quality of services as well as governance. The feedback of citizens regarding quality and coverage of services provided by agencies may increase accountability and efficiency in service delivery.
- Citizen's charters are useful method for disseminating information to clients. These charters should be developed after consultation with staff, and citizens.
- Municipalities should limit its role to regulation of services, however private sector participation may be taken for monitoring, direction, auditing and performance evaluation of services by municipalities.
- Voluntary Tax Assessment, based on Unit Area Method depending on location, nature of usage, built up area, year/period of construction, and range of municipal services available, may be introduced in a large number of municipalities. This will reduce the corruption and enhance municipal revenues to urban local bodies.
- Transfer of certain funds to Ward Committees or Resident Welfare Associations to under take maintenance and repair work in their respective area may ensure decentralization and devolution of functions.
- Privatization of maintenance and operation works of certain civic amenities may be useful in improving the coverage and quality of urban services.
- Public utilities need to reinvent rather than just reform. A new governance structure for the services sector needs to evolve.
- Community participation in delivery of urban services may be augmented through strengthening NGO's

local bodies, public associations and SHG's. However, orientation and training will be required for creating awareness and sensitizing representatives of these associations and organizations.

REFERENCES

Agrawal, O.P. (2006), Urban Transport in India Infrastructure Report, 2006, OUP, Delhi.

Akolkar, A.B.(2005), Status of Solid Waste Management in India, Central Pollution Control Board, New Delhi.

Asnani, P.V., (2006), Solid Waste Management IN India Infrastructure Report, 2006, OUP, Delhi.

Bhandari, Laveesh (2006), Social Infrastructure: Urban Health and Education IN India, Infrastructure Report, 2006, OUP, Delhi.

Dwivedi, S.K. and Narayan, Rajeev (2004), Capacity Development for Urban Governance, Regional Centre for Urban and Environmental Studies, Lucknow.

Kundu, Amitabh (2006), Trends and Patterns of Urbanization and their Economic Implications IN India Infrastructure Report, 2006, OUP, Delhi.

Mathur, O.P. (ed) (1999), India the Challenge of Urban Governance, National Institute of Public Finance and Policy, New Delhi.

NIUA (1997), Financing Urban Infrastructure in India, National Institute of Urban Affairs, Delhi.

NSSO (2000), Drinking Water Sanitation and Hygiene in India, 54th Round, National Sample Survey Organization, Delhi.

Planning Commission (1996), Report of the Working Group on Urban Water Supply and Sanitation Sector for Ninth Plan (1997-2002), Planning Commission, Government of India.

Planning Commissioner (2004), Report of the PPP sub-Group on Social Sector - Public Private Partnership, Planning Commission, Government of India, Delhi.

Rastogi, Anupam (ed) (2006), India Infrastructure Report, 2007, OUP, Delhi.

RITES (1998), Traffic and Transportation Policies and Strategies in Urban Areas in India, Ministry of Urban Development, New Delhi.

Savage D. and Dasgupta, S.(2006), Governance Framework for Delivery of Urban Services in India Infrastructure Report, 2006, OUP Delhi.

Transparency International India (2005), Corruption Study to Improve Governance, Transparency International India, Delhi.

World Bank (2005), Attaining the Millennium Development Goals in India, World Bank, Delhi.

World Bank (1997) , Urban Infrastructure Services Review, World Bank, Washington.

World Bank (1999), Urban Water Supply and Sanitation, World Bank, New Delhi.

Zerah, M.H. (2006), Urban Water and Waste Water in India Infrastructure Report, 2006 OUP, Delhi.

8

URBAN POVERTY ALLEVIATION

Urban poverty is a major challenge before the urban managers and administrators of the present time. Though the anti-poverty strategy comprising of a wide range of poverty alleviation and employment generating programmes has been implemented but results show that the situation is grim. Importantly, poverty in urban India gets exacerbated by substantial rate of population growth, high rate of migration from the rural areas and mushrooming of slum pockets. Migration alone accounts for about 40 per cent of the growth in urban population, converting the rural poverty into urban one.

Moreover, poverty has become synonymous with slums. The relationship is bilateral i.e. slums also breed poverty. This vicious circle never ends. Most of the world's poor reside in India and majority of the poor live in rural areas and about one-fourth urban population in India lives below poverty line. If we count those who are deprived of safe drinking water, adequate clothing, or shelter, the number is considerably higher.

Further, the vulnerable groups such as Scheduled Castes, Scheduled Tribes, minorities, pavement dwellers etc., are living in acute poverty. Housing conditions in large cities and towns are depicting sub human lives of slum dwellers. With the reconstruction of poverty alleviation programmes in urban India, it is expected that social and economic benefits will percolate to the population below the poverty line. However, eradication of poverty and improving the quality of life of the poor remain one of the daunting tasks.

Against this view point present paper purports to analyze perspective of urban poverty, emerging trends, dimensions, poverty alleviation programmes and to suggest strategies for formulation of micro action plans.

CONCEPTUALIZATION

Poverty generally arises from lack of income or assets. The low income of the poor can be attributed to the following problems facing them (Venkateshwaraloo, 1998): (i) Low access to financial resources and production assets which are necessary to sustain the micro-enterprises beyond day today basis, (ii) Monopolistic control over micro-enterprises by larger entities which, through control over inputs and/or insecurity of wage employment, compel the poor to accept lowest wages and to work overtime without pay. The urban poor have low access to formal education, health services, shelter and safe living environments. Moreover, poverty is also perpetuated by division of labour and time, away from income earning uses and towards daily physical, environmental and energy management tasks, necessary to sustain life itself. This diversion further limits chances of investing household resources in skill attainment and enterprises.

Poverty has been measured on the basis of nutritional requirement, monthly per capita expenditure and housing conditions. Thus income-based poverty lines set for the whole country do not allow for high costs of living in cities. No single poverty line can take into account the large differences in the availability and cost of food, shelter, water sanitation and health care services. Housing poverty has been defined by UNCHS as lack of safe, secure and healthy shelter with basic infrastructure like piped water and adequate provision for sanitation, drainage and removal of household's wastes. The definition of poverty line in India was set for the first time in 1962 by a working group after taking into account the recommendations of the Nutrition Advisory Committee of the

Indian Council of Medical Research (1958) regarding balanced diet. The working group proposed the poverty norm in money terms in urban and rural areas. It was based on broad judgment of minimum caloric need. Importantly, the Planning Commission in 1977 constitutes a Task Force on projections of Minimum Needs and Effective Consumption Demand. It defined the poverty line as a per capita consumption expenditure level which meets the average per capita daily caloric requirement of 2400 calories in rural areas and 2100 calories in urban areas long with a minimum of non-food expenditure. The Planning Commission constituted the Expert Group on estimation and number of poor in 1989. It did not redefine the poverty line but estimated separate poverty line for each state by desegregating the national level poverty line. It used the state-wise consumer price index of industrial workers for updating urban poverty line (Singh and Mitra, 2000).

State-wise specific poverty lines are shown in Table 1. The urban poverty lines vary from Rs. 379 in Assam to Rs. 666 in Maharashtra. The poverty lines are lower in rural areas as compared to urban areas.

Table 1
State-Specific Poverty Lines 2004-2005

(Rs. Per Capita per month)

State	*Rural*	*Urban*
Andhra Pradesh	292.95	542.89
Assam	387.64	378.64
Bihar	354.36	435.00
Chhatisgarh	322.41	560.00
Delhi	410.38	612.91
Goa	362.25	665.90
Gujarat	353.93	541.16
Haryana	414.76	504.49
Himachal Pradesh	394.28	504.49
Jammu & Kashmir	391.26	553.77
Jharkhand	366.56	451.24
Karnataka	324.17	599.66
Kerala	430.12	559.39
Madhya Pradesh	327.78	570.15
Maharashtra	362.25	665.90

Contd...

State	Rural	Urban
Orissa	325.79	528.49
Punjab	410.38	466.16
Rajasthan	374.57	559.63
Tamil Nadu	351.86	547.42
Uttar Pradesh	365.84	483.26
Uttarakhand	478.02	637.67
West Bengal	382.82	449.32
Dadra & Nagar Haveli	362.25	665.90
All India	356.30	538.60

Source: CGG, Hyderabad, 2007.

The poverty is broadly defined in terms of material deprivation, human deprivation and a range of other deprivations such as lack of voice, vulnerability, violence, destitution, social and political exclusions, and lack of dignity and basic rights. In India, and indeed throughout the world, the conventional approach equates poverty with material deprivation and defines the poor in terms of incomes or levels of consumption. The Planning Commission has defined poverty in terms of the level of per capita consumer expenditure sufficient to provide an average daily intake of 2400 calories per person in rural areas and 2100 calories per person in urban areas, plus a minimal allocation for basic non-food items. There is no doubt that material deprivation is a key factor that underlines many other dimensions of poverty. Despite uncertain progress at reducing material deprivation, there has been greater progress in human development in the states throughout the 1990's. Human Development Indicators capture important dimensions of well-being and reflect not just the rate of growth in the economy but also levels and quality of public spending (World Bank, 2002). Effective public spending on basic services (education, health, water and sanitation) can compensate for limited capacity of the poor to purchase these services through the market. Education is a key indicator of human development. Many desirable social and economic outcomes are limited to rising levels of education, particularly education of women and of socially vulnerable groups. Health status is another key indicator of human development. Vulnerable, powerlessness, exclusion and social identity crises are some of the issues related with human poverty. Vulnerability is a fact of life for the poor. They are distressed not only by current low levels of resources and incomes, but also by the possibility of falling into deeper poverty and destitution. The poor are at risk because they lack the income, the assets and the social ties that protect the better off from the impact of unexpected setbacks. Illness requires expensive treatment; the temporary or permanent disability of a breadwinner, or a natural or man-made disaster can obliterate a poor household's small savings. Death, disability, disease, etc. are such factors, which are linked with vulnerability. Widowhood or desertion by a spouse, often led to destitution in poor and low caste women (Unni, 1998; Dreze, 1990). In urban areas, the following types of vulnerability of the poor are reported:

(i) *Housing Vulnerability:* Lack of tenure, poor quality shelter without ownership rights, and no access to individual water connection/toilets, unhealthy and unsanitary living conditions.

(ii) *Economic Vulnerability:* Irregular/casual employment, low paid work, lack of access to credit or reasonable terms, lack of access to formal safety net programmers, low ownership of productive assets, poor net worth and legal constraints to self employment.

(iii) *Social Vulnerability:* Low education, lack of skills, low social capital/caste status, and inadequate access to food security programmes, lack of access to health services and exclusion from local institutions.

(iv) *Personal Vulnerability:* Proneness to violence or intimidation, women, children and elderly, disabled and destitute, belonging to low castes and minority groups, lack of information, lack of access to justice.

The poor lack the leverage to ensure that state institutions serve them fairly and thus often lack access to public facilities or receive goods of inferior quality. Importantly, caste, status and gender is linked to poverty in a number of ways. Deep and continuing social inequalities mark many facets on the society. Individuals with low caste status are for more likely to be employed as low paid; low status labourers live in poorly constructed houses with limited access to water and sanitation. Importantly, poor are the truly destitute. Destitute households have fewer and often very weak ties of mutual assistance and support than their wealthier counterparts. They lack of formal and informal safety nets. Poor women face high risks of destitution. A significant number of women poor belong to female-headed households.

The majority of the urban poor tend to fall within the following generic occupational categories (Oxfam, 1997):

(i) Casual workers, unskilled, non-unionized wage workers;
(ii) Unskilled, non-unionized service industry workers;
(iii) Street vendors;
(iv) Construction workers;
(v) Rickshaw pullers;
(vi) Sweepers;
(vii) Domestic workers;
(viii) Rag pickers;
(ix) Sex workers;
(x) Beggars.

In the housing category of poverty based on physical conditions and environment, urban poor may include:

(i) Pavement dwellers;
(ii) Nomadic pavement dwellers;
(iii) Recognized slum dwellers;
(iv) Unrecognized slum dwellers; and
(v) Squatters.

Three groups tend to be most vulnerable in urban context- women, children and minorities. In general women and children fall at the bottom and of the sub-contracting chain, performing the lowest paid activities such as home based prices and domestic services. In urban settings, the family support chain often breaks down with women facing particular stresses as they attempt to balance their work and domestic tasks. The impact of media, alcohol, drugs etc. on conditions of worsening deprivation of women tend to face harassment and physical abuse form within the households, the community and from employers. The health status of women and children, is also particularly bad in relation to men. Women are forced into becoming sex workers as a result of their economic circumstances, in turn making their health extremely vulnerable (Oxfam, 1997).

SOCIAL ASPECT OF POVERTY

Poverty has been examined in mainly economic terms such as per capita income or calorie criterion. The social aspect of poverty, particularly the culture and value aspects, which poverty creates breeds and transmits and which have larger implications for the overall quality of life have not been seriously examined (Thakur, 1998). Cities and towns generally show the following characteristics (OSD):

(1) Very fast rate of population growth due to rural-urban migration for lack of adequate job opportunities in rural areas and small towns;

(2) Rapid increase in the scale of urban poverty and deprivation;

(3) Increasingly deficient infrastructure and services e.g. housing facility, water supply, sanitation, education, health etc.;

(4) Growing shortage of productive jobs;

(5) Chronic shortage of financial, managerial and technical resources and

(6) Growing gap between the rich and the poor, between the urban elite and poverty stricken rural and urban poor.

There is general consensus that greater part of India's poverty is rural but urban and rural poverty are intimately connected. The problem of rural poverty is flowing into the urban areas (Dandekar and Rath, 1971). The larger cities are growing in the number of poor people (Desai, 1968). The urban growth is a result of population shift from poverty stricken hinterland to the cities (Kopardekar, 1986). Importantly, the vast majority of urban workers come from villages and continues to have their roots there. The poorest among them come from the most helpless strata of rural population (Thakur, 1988). Thus, the vast majority of the urban poor are migrants, rural poor, landless labourers and petty farmers. Acute impoverishment of these farmers, near hunger situation of rural landless labourers led to their distress and migration to cities (Jha, 1986). Interestingly, cities provide a market for their cheap labour and they cling to the city, developing a culture of survival. The culture of poverty has the following characteristics (Lewis):

(1) Lack of effective participation and integration of the poor with the major situations of larger society;
(2) Low wages, chronic unemployment and under unemployment leading to low income, absence of savings, absence of food reserves and a chronic shortage of cash;
(3) Low level of literacy and education, no membership of labour union or any political party, no participation in the national welfare programme;
(4) Community spirit in the slums and the slum neighbourhood;
(5) The absence of childhood as a specially protected stage in the life cycle, early initiation into sex, a relatively high incidence of abandonment of wives and children;
(6) Strong feeling of marginality, helplessness, dependence and inferiority;
(7) High incidence of material deprivation, little ability to plan for the future, sense of resignation and fatalism.

Living in a state of perpetual poverty and deprivation, the poor generally develop and acquire habits, which may be characterized as their typical slum habits and which get transmitted to the children as well. These habits generally are (Thakur, 1988):

(i) Idle gossiping;

(ii) Backbiting, leg pulling and slandering;

(iii) Gossiping about the affair of the neighbour;

(iv) Quarrel over small matters;

(v) Bearing tales and spreading rumours;

(vi) Use of abusive language in minor incidents and quarrels among children or women;

(vii) Little regard for public property not much hesitation in breaking street-light, removing lid cover of pit holes etc.;

(viii) Mutual jealousy, suspicion;

(ix) Smoking;

(x) Tobacco, drug abuse, spitting in public places;

(xi) Gambling;

(xii) Playing cards; and

(xiii) Little respect for other's viewpoints, opinion, comforts and time.

POVERTY ESTIMATES

Poverty alleviation has been on the national policy agenda for more than 50 years. As early as 1938, the Indian National Congress constituted a National Planning Committee which had declared that social objective should be to ensure an adequate standard of living for the masses. The importance of reduction in poverty and provision of other basic needs has been emphasized in all the five year plans since Independence particularly since the 5th Five Year Plan. The estimates on poverty based on NSS data show that poverty in India in 1997 was around 37 per cent (rural poverty ratio was 38 per cent and urban poverty ratio was 34 per cent) (Dev, 2000). The concept of poverty is multi-dimensional viz. income poverty and non-income poverty. It covers not only levels of income and consumption but also health and education, vulnerability and risks and marginalization and exclusion of the poor from the mainstream of society (Dev, 2000). According to some researchers, reforms would benefit the poor in the medium and long run, although they may have adverse effect in the short-run (Bhagwati and Srinivasan, 1993, Tendulakar, 1998, Joshi and Little, 1996). Some others argue that reform package has internal contradictions and it might have adverse effect on the poor in both short and long run (Nayyar, 1993, Ghosh, 1995, Bhaduri, 1996). The pro-reformers argue that the reforms would increase efficiency and higher growth and in turn reduce poverty. It is also argued that one has to look at counter factional situation while analysing the impact of reforms.

The trends during 24 years of pre-reform period (1951 to 1973-74) show that the (a) rural poverty varied between 44 per cent and 64 per cent and (b) urban poverty varied between 36 per cent and 53 per cent. Both rural and urban poverty showed a decline in the late 1970's and in the 1980's. The estimates for the period 1960-61 to 2004-2005 are given in Table 2.

Table 2
Urban Poverty in India

Year	*Poverty Ratio (%)*	*Number of Poor (Millions)*	
		Urban	*Total*
1960-61	40.4	32 (18.50)	173
1961-62	39.4	32 (18.08)	177
1963-64	42.5	37 (17.79)	208
1964-65	45.7	42 (18.58)	226
1965-66	46.4	44 (18.80)	234
1966-67	48.4	47 (16.91)	278
1967-68	48.3	49 (17.19)	285
1968-69	45.5	47 (17.80)	264
1969-70	44.4	48 (18.32)	262
1970-71	41.5	46 (17.97)	256
1972-73	44.6	53 (18.93)	280
1973-74	49.6	60 (18.69)	321
1877-78	45.2	65 (19.76)	329
1982-83	40.8	71 (21.98)	323
1987-88	38.2	75 (24.43)	307
1993-94	32.4	76 (23.75)	320
1999-2000	23.6	67 (25.77)	260
2004-2005	25.7	81 (26.82)	302

Figures in parentheses denote percentage to total number of poor.
Source: Hand Book of Urban Poverty in India, OUP, Delhi, 2006.

The above table shows that rural poverty declined in the 1980's but it increased to above 40 per cent in 1992 and 1994-95. On the other hand, urban poverty declined significantly in the 1990's. The urban poverty in 2004-2005 was reported 25.7 per cent which is slightly higher than the poverty ratio reported during 1999-2000. The number of urban poor has increased from 67 million in 1999-2000 to about 81million in 2004-2005.

Again, about 81 million persons in urban areas were reported living below poverty line during 2004-2005. Importantly, Uttar Pradesh, Maharashtra, Madhya Pradesh, Andhra Pradesh and Bihar account for larger share in urban poor. The percentage of urban poor was recorded highest in Orissa (44.3 per cent), Madhya Pradesh (42.1 per cent), Uttar Pradesh (30.6 per cent), Bihar (34.6 per cent) and Maharashtra (32.2 per cent). Indian poverty is predominant in the rural areas where more than three quarters of all poor people reside, though there is wide variation in poverty across different states. Moreover, progress in reducing poverty is also very uneven across different states of the country. The state-wise numbers of urban poor are shown in Table 3. Largest numbers of urban poor were reported in Maharashtra followed by Uttar Pradesh, Madhya Pardesh, Tamil Nadu, Karnataka, Andhra Pradesh and Rajathan (Table 3).

Table 3
Population below Poverty Line by States

(2004-2005)

	Rural		*Urban*		*Combined*	
States/UT	*No. of persons (Lakh)*	*% of Persons*	*No. of persons (Lakh)*	*% of Persons*	*No. of persons (Lakh)*	*% of Persons*
Andhra Pradesh	64.70	11.2	61.40	28.0	126.10	15.8
Arunachal Pradesh	1.94	22.3	0.09	3.3	2.03	17.6
Assam	54.50	22.3	1.28	3.3	55.77	19.7
Bihar	336.72	42.1	32.42	34.6	369.15	41.4
Chhatisgarh	71.50	40.8	19.47	41.2	90.96	40.9
Delhi	0.63	6.9	22.30	15.2	22.93	14.7
Goa	0.36	5.4	1.64	21.3	2.01	13.8
Gujarat	63.49	19.1	27.19	13.0	90.69	16.8
Haryana	21.49	13.6	10.60	15.1	32.10	14.0
Himachal Pradesh	6.14	10.7	0.22	3.4	6.36	10.0

Contd...

States/UT	No. of persons (Lakh)	% of Persons	No. of persons (Lakh)	% of Persons	No. of persons (Lakh)	% of Persons
Jammu & Kashmir	3.66	4.6	2.19	7.9	5.85	5.4
Jharkhand	103.19	46.3	13.20	20.2	116.39	40.3
Karnataka	75.05	20.8	63.83	32.6	138.89	25.0
Kerala	32.43	13.2	17.17	20.2	49.60	15.0
Madhya Pradesh	175.65	36.9	74.03	42.1	249.68	38.3
Maharashtra	171.13	29.6	146.25	32.2	317.38	30.7
Manipur	3.76	22.3	0.20	3.3	3.95	17.3
Meghalaya	4.36	22.3	0.16	3.3	4.52	18.5
Mizoram	1.02	22.3	0.16	3.3	1.18	12.6
Nagaland	3.87	22.3	0.12	3.3	3.99	19.0
Orissa	151.75	46.8	26.74	44.3	178.49	46.4
Punjab	15.12	9.1	6.50	7.1	21.63	8.4
Rajasthan	87.38	18.7	47.51	32.9	134.89	22.1
Sikkim	1.12	22.3	0.02	3.3	1.14	20.1
Tamil Nadu	76.50	22.8	69.13	22.2	145.62	22.5
Tripura	6.18	22.3	0.20	3.3	6.38	18.9
Uttar Pradesh	473.00	33.4	117.03	30.6	590.03	32.8
Uttarakhand	27.11	40.8	8.85	36.5	35.96	39.6
West Bengal	173.22	28.6	35.14	14.8	208.36	24.7
A & N Islands	0.60	22.9	0.32	22.2	0.92	22.6
Chandigarh	0.08	7.1	0.67	7.1	0.74	7.1
D & Nagar Haveli	0.68	39.8	0.15	19.1	0.84	33.2
Daman & Diu	0.07	5.4	0.14	21.2	0.21	10.5
Lakshadweep	0.06	13.3	0.06	20.2	0.11	16.0
Pondicherry	0.78	22.9	1.59	22.2	2.37	22.4
All India	2209.24	28.3	807.96	25.7	3017.20	27.5

Source: Planning Commission, Govt. of India, 2007.

INCIDENCE OF POVERTY

Poverty is a complex, deep-seated pervasive reality. Virtually half of the world lives on less than US $2 a day. More than 1.2 billion people struggle on $1 a day or less. A further 1.6 billion people live on $1 to 2 a day and are thus also poor, insecure and at risk of falling to the level of bare subsistence (ILO, 2003). About half of the people living in poverty are of working age (between 15 and 64 years). Although most family members have to contribute in one way or another to the household's welfare, the earning power of adults is a critical determinant of the well being of the family. For individuals, poverty is a nightmare. It is vicious circle of poor health, reduced working capacity, low productivity and shortened life expectancy. For families, poverty is a trap. It leads to inadequate schooling, low skills, insecure income, early parenthood, ill health and an early death. For nations, poverty is a curse. It hinders growth, fuels instability and keeps poor countries from advancing on the path to sustainable development (ILO, 2003).

There is another face of poverty. People living in conditions of material deprivation draw on enormous reserves of courage, ingenuity, persistence and mutual support to keep on the thread mill of survival. After all, for most people living in poverty, there is no safety net and little state support. However, poor do not cause poverty. Poverty is the result of structural failures and ineffective economic and social systems. Thus, the poverty may be alleviated only through institutional support, political will and effective administrative machinery for social safety net and creation of employment opportunities.

India has made significant progress in reducing poverty at the national level during the period 1956-2000. Poverty has declined in all states, with substantial differences across states. The absolute number of rural poor, which accounted for about three-fourth of the country's poor rose from 182 million in 1956-67 to 261 million in 1973-74, accounting for nearly half of the additions to the rural population during the period. In the second phase, from the mid 1970s to the close of the year 2000, the country achieved substantial reduction in the incidence of poverty. However, 302 million poor were reported in 2004-2005 and most of them were from rural areas (221 million). The number of urban poor has increased from the previous surveys.

The proportion of the country's population living in poverty declined from half to one quarter. Due to methodological changes, in the collection of NSS data in the 55th Round (1999-2000), comparison of the pre and post-reform period growth rate is problematic. Undoubtedly, India has made substantial progress in the reduction of poverty. Yet, as many as 260 million persons are living below the poverty line. According to UNDP's Human Development Report, 2003, India has the target number of poor among the countries of the world and is home to one fourth of the World's poor.

A large number of hardcore poor are located in remote and inaccessible areas. The problem of poverty alleviation is going to be far more difficult than in the past. Since, those who were near the poverty line might have crossed it (Radha Krishnan and Rao, 2006). The regional differences in poverty reduction are substantial. The decline between 1973-74 and 1999-2000 in state's incidence of poverty in rural areas ranged between 12-50 percentage point during 1973-2000 and 20-40 percentage points in urban areas.

The inter-state variations in the rural poverty reduction during 1957-90 have been attributed to the variations in their agricultural productivity improvement (Datta and Ravallion, 1992). In addition, variations in initial endowments of physical infrastructure and human resources contributed to the inter-state variations in the performance of the states such as Andhra Pradesh, Kerala, and West Bengal, which had a higher rural poverty ratio in the first phase, had lower rural poverty ratios in the second phase. Importantly, urban poverty ratio has declined sharply in the states of Tamil Nadu, Gujarat, Karnataka, Haryana, West Bengal, Andhra Pradesh, Kerala, Uttar Pradesh, Assam and Bihar over the period of 1973-74 to 2004-2005. Surprisingly, poverty ratio in Assam has declined from 35.9 per cent in 1973-74 to just 3.3 per cent in 2004-2005. Similarly, poverty ratio has dropped up to 13 per cent in 2004-2005 from 52.57 per cent in 1973-74 in Gujarat (Table 4).

Table 4
Change in Poverty Ratio in Urban India

(Percentage distribution)

State	*1973-74*	*1983*	*1993-94*	*1999-2000*	*2004-2005*
Tamil Nadu	49.4	46.96	39.77	22.11	22.2
Maharashtra	43.87	40.26	35.15	26.81	32.2
Gujarat	52.57	39.14	27.89	15.59	13.0
Karnataka	52.53	42.82	40.14	25.25	32.6
Haryana	40.18	24.15	16.38	9.99	15.1
West Bengal	34.67	32.32	22.41	16.86	14.8
Andhra Pradesh	50.61	36.20	38.33	26.63	28.0
Madhya Pradesh	57.65	53.06	48.38	38.44	42.1
Kerala	62.74	45.68	24.55	20.27	20.2

Contd...

State	*1973-74*	*1983*	*1993-94*	*1999-2000*	*2004-2005*
Rajasthan	52.13	37.94	30.49	19.85	32.9
Uttar Pradesh	60.09	49.82	35.39	30.89	30.6
Orissa	55.62	49.15	41.64	42.83	44.3
Assam	35.92	21.73	7.73	7.47	3.3
Bihar	52.96	47.33	34.50	32.91	34.6
India	49.01	40.79	32.36	23.62	25.7

Source: Planning Commission, Govt. of India, New Delhi.

The composition of the poor has been changing. The rural poverty is getting concentrated in the agricultural labour and artisan households while urban poverty is concentrated the casual labour households. The share of agricultural labour households, which accounted for 41 per cent of rural poor in 1993-94 increased to 47 per cent in 1999-2000 (Radha Krishnan and Roy, 2004). In contrast, the share of self employed in agriculture in rural poor dropped from 33 to 28 per cent. Casual labour households accounted for 32 per cent of the urban population living in poverty in 1999-2000, increasing from 25 per cent in 1993-94. The increase in its share was due to both the increased dependence of urban households on urban casual labour market as well as higher incidence of poverty among casual labour households. It needs to be recognized that increased dependence of rural and urban households on casual labour market exposes the poor to market risks and tends to increase transient poverty, whereby households move in and out of poverty due to fluctuations in the labour market.

The urban poor have been increasingly concentrated in Uttar Pradesh, Maharashtra, West Bengal, Madhya Pradesh and Andhra Pradesh. Their share in all India urban poverty rose from 56 per cent in 1993-94 to 60 per cent in 1999-2000. Scheduled Castes, Scheduled Tribes and backward castes accounted for 81 per cent of the rural poor in 1999-2000, considerably more than their share in the rural population. The poor among the Scheduled Castes in rural areas were concentrated in Uttar Pradesh, Madhya Pradesh, Bihar and West Bengal. These states accounted for 58 per cent of the Scheduled Castes population living in poverty. In urban areas, Madhya Pradesh and Uttar Pradesh accounted for 41 per cent of the Scheduled Castes population living in poverty. The incidence of poverty among Scheduled Castes was higher in Bihar, Madhya Pradesh, and Uttar Pradesh in both rural and urban areas. The proportion of Scheduled Tribes among the rural population living in poverty has been increasing rapidly from 14.8 per cent in 1993-94 to 17.5 per cent in 1999-2000. The poverty levels of Scheduled Tribes in rural areas were high in Orissa, Bihar, Madhya Pradesh and West Bengal while in urban areas poverty ratio among Scheduled Tribes was reported high in Orissa, Karnataka, Andhra Pradesh and Bihar. In the terms of human deprivation or poverty, (education, health, etc.) the Scheduled Tribes are at the bottom.

The increasing concentration of poverty in tribals who suffer from multiple deprivations is a matter of concern. The incidence of poverty among females tended to be marginally higher in both rural and urban areas. The proportion of females living in poor households in rural areas was 37 per cent and 27 per cent in 1993-94 and 1999-2000, respectively with the corresponding percentage for urban areas being 34 and 25 per cent. In contrast, the percentage of males living in poverty in rural areas was 36 per cent and 26 per cent in 1993-94 and 1999-2000 respectively, while those in urban areas was 32 and 23 per cent, respectively. Females accounted for slightly less than half of the poor, about 49 per cent in both rural and urban areas in both the years. Importantly, child poverty is widespread in India both in rural and urban areas. The percentage of children aged below 15 years living in households below the poverty line in rural areas was 44 per cent and 33 per cent in 1993-94 and 1999-2000, respectively while the corresponding percentages for urban areas stood at 41 and 33 per cent.

Among poor people, the share of children in rural areas increased from 44 per cent in 1993-94 to 46 per cent in 1999-2000 and in urban areas from 41 per cent to 42 per cent during corresponding period. The high level of child poverty would result in a high incidence of child malnutrition (Radha Krishnan and Rao, 2006).

The states with high incidence of human poverty, such as Bihar, Orissa, Madhya Pradesh, Uttar Pradsh and Rajasthan are found at the bottom on the Human Development Index ranking. Kerala was the best performer in both rural and urban areas and Bihar the worst performer in rural areas and Uttar Pradesh in the urban areas. Bihar, Orissa, Madhya Pradesh, and Uttar Pradesh consistently showed poor performance on three indices and Kerala and Punjab showed consistently better performance. Rajasthan performed better on poverty rank than HDI and HPI ranks. Tamil Nadu and Maharashtra performed better on HDI rank than poverty and HPI ranks.

The factors contributing to human poverty are not a unique set for the entire country, and vary from state to state and even across regions. The poverty reduction measures are generally focus on livelihood development, employment generation, skill enhancement, rights advocacy, strengthening cooperatives and people's associations and accessibility of micro credit, etc.

Analysis shows that poverty reduction has been uneven between the states. There is no correlation with per capita income or other development indicators like per capita consumption, levels of industrial and infrastructural development etc. in urban areas during the 1990's (Planning Commission, 2001). Again, rapid economic growth has not led to a corresponding decline in poverty. Urban poverty thus, emerges as a more complex phenomenon than rural poverty.

The urban poor faces more problems related with housing amenities, urban infrastructure, size of town or city, and vulnerabilities—housing, economic, social and personal. The urban poor are characterized by deprivation and misery while they are classified as core poor, intermedial poor, and transitional poor. Another study classified them as declining poor, coping poor and improving poor, with different degrees of poverty for three basic needs of survival, security and quality of life.

GOVERNMENT INITIATIVES

The government policies on urban poverty have followed three paths:

(i) Those that seek to enhance productive employment and income for the poor;

(ii) Those that are directed towards improving the general health and welfare services;

(iii) Those that focus on infrastructure and built environment of poor neighbourhood.

Though several programmes of poverty alleviation have been initiated by government but effective dent on poverty could not be ensured. The schemes had certain limitations, which ultimately resulted in poor results or failure. Environment Improvement of Urban Slums (EIUS) launched in 1972 provided physical infrastructure and could not cover social services like health, education, community development, etc. The scheme could not help in preventing growth of new slums.

Similarly UBSP was designed to foster Neighbourhood Development Committees in slums for ensuring the effective participation of slum dwellers in developmental activities and for coordinating the convergent provisions of social services, environmental improvement and income generation activities of the specialist departments (Venketeshwaraloo, 1998). The low level of resource allocation for the scheme led to sub critical releases to the state governments, which consequently gave low priority to the scheme.

Importantly, NRY scheme was launched in 1989 to provide employment to the unemployed through setting up of micro-enterprises and wage employment through shelter upgradation works and creation of useful pubic assets in low income neighbourhoods. The scheme could not yield good results due to shortfall in employment generation on account of some states not taking up labour intensive schemes. Importantly, progress under Housing and Shelter Upgradation Scheme was recorded slow growth due to non-completion of the necessary documentation and procedural formalities. Interestingly, PMIUPEP was launched in 1994 and sought to improve the quality of life of the urban poor by creating a facilitating implementation (Venketeshwaraloo, 1998). The scheme provided for the creation of a National Urban Poverty Eradication Fund (NUPEF) with contribution from private sector.

The National Slum Development Programme (NSDP) was initiated in 1996 as a centrally sponsored scheme. The scheme highlighted on the creation of community structures as the basis for slum development and gives the maximum possible leeway to the states, ULB's and the community development societies at the slum level to plan and carry out development works as per the local assessed needs. The SJSRY was initiated in 1997 and was designed to replace the UBSP.

PLANNED INTERVENTIONS

The policies of urban development and housing in India have come a long way since 1950's. The pressure of urban population and lack of housing and basic services were very much evident in the early 1950's. The First Five Year Plan (1951-56) emphasized on institution building and on construction of houses for government employees and weaker sections. The scope of housing programme for the poor was extended in the Second Plan (1956-61). The Industrial Housing Scheme was widened to cover all workers. Three new schemes were also introduced viz., Rural Housing, Slum Clearance and Sweepers Housing. The general directions for housing programmes in the Third Plan (961-66) were coordination of efforts of all agencies and orienting the programmes to the needs of the Low Income Groups.

The balanced urban growth was accorded high priority in the Fourth Plan (1969-74). The plan stressed the need to prevent further growth of population in large cities and need for decongestion or dispersal of population. A scheme for Environmental Improvement for Slums was undertaken in the central sector from 1972-73 with a view to provide a minimum level of services, like water supply, sewerage, drainage, street pavements in 11 cities with a population of 8 lakh and above. The scheme was later extended to 9 more cities.

The Fifth Plan (1974-79) reiterated the policies of the preceding plans to promote smaller towns in new urban centres in order to ease the increasing pressure on urbanization. The Urban Land (Ceiling and Regulation) Act was enacted to prevent construction of land holding in urban areas and to make available urban land for construction of houses for the middle and low income groups.

The thrust of the planning in the Sixth Plan (198-85) was on integrated provision of services along with shelter, particularly for the poor. The Seventh Plan (1985-90) stressed on the need to entrust major responsibility of housing construction on the private sector. A three-fold role was assigned to the public sector, namely, mobilization for resources for housing, provision for subsidized housing for the poor and acquisition and development of land. The Plan explicitly recognized the problems of the urban poor and for the first time an Urban Poverty Alleviation Scheme known as Urban Basic Services for Poor (UBSP) was launched. As a follow up of the Global Shelter Strategy, National Housing Policy was announced in 1988. The policy envisaged to eradicate houselessnes, improve the housing conditions of inadequately housed and provide a minimum level of basic services and amenities to all.

During the Eighth Plan (1992-97) another Urban Poverty Alleviation Programme known as Nehru Rojgar Yojana was launched. In the Ninth Plan (1997-2002), a new convergence based scheme of urban poverty alleviation known as Swarn Jayanti Shahari Rojgar Yojana was initiated. It subsumed the erstwhile schemes of urban basic services for the poor and Nehru Rojgar Yojana.

The Tenth Plan (2002-2007) witnessed the launch of Valmiki Ambedkar Avas Yojana and the National Slum Development Progamme. A Draft Slum Policy (2001) was also prepared. The National Common Minimum Programme of the Government attached higher priority to social housing and urban renewal. The result has been the launch of JNNURM and IHSDP. The sub-mission on urban Basic Services to the Urban Poor (BSUP) and the Integrated Housing and Slum Development Programme address the consensus of urban poor people and urban slum dwellers. In order to provide informal sector employment a good initiative in the form of National Policy on Urban Street Vendors has also been started.

There is increasing recognition that the urban development policy framework be inclusive of the people residing the slums and informal settlements. This has led to be a more enabling approach to the delivery of basic services accessible to the poor, through a more effective mobilization of community resources and skills to complement public resource allocations. The implementation of various Central Government schemes provided a wide range of services to the urban poor including slum dwellers. However, implementation of these programmes suffered from narrowly sectoral and fragmented approach; low quality of inputs with marginal impacts; wider dispersal of limited resources over a large area, rather than focusing a concentration of integrated area intensive efforts, inadequate participation of community in the planning and designing of innovative solutions; and multiplicity of agencies after working at cross purposes leading to a dissipation of efforts.

The Million Summit established the goal of improving the lives of at least 100 million slum dwellers by 2015. UNDP supports policy interventions designed to tackle urban poverty through improved urban governance, while living attention to urban environment improvements. These interventions relate to participatory planning process to improve housing, water and sanitation, waste management, job generation and other aspects.

National Strategy for Urban Poor (NSUP) project is a joint initiative of the Union Ministry of Housing & Urban Poverty Alleviation and the UNDP aimed at addressing the key concerns in promoting urban poverty eradication and sustainable urban livelihoods. The project envisages institutional reforms for improving efficiency and accelerating progress towards human development.

In line with Approach People for 11th Five Year Plan, which adopts "Inclusive Growth" as the key them for the country, the Ministry of Housing and Urban Poverty Alleviation, Govt. of India is developing an agenda for developing "inclusive cities". The development of this agenda is being supported by the NSUP project. The project will provide technical support in this regard which will cover the areas of: (i) inclusive urban and regional planning systems; (ii) inclusive urban infrastructure; (iii) integration of informal sector into the formal urban economies; (iv) affordable land and housing to the poor; (v) inclusive city development process for developing infrastructure and services; (vi) inclusive social development and convergence of programmes; (vii) financial inclusion of urban poor through access to credit, microfinance, etc; and (viii) capacity building and skill development of urban poor to cater the needs of emerging markets.

Ministry of Housing & Urban Poverty Alleviation has set up a Task Force under the chairmanship of Secretary, with the objective to evolve formulations for a viable micro credit mechanism for urban poor/informal sectors. It is expected that about 10 million urban vendors would be benefited under National Policy on Urban Street Vendors. Urban vending is not only a source of employment but provide affordable services to the majority of urban population. The National Policy is aimed at providing a supportive environment for earning livelihoods to the street vendors, as well as ensures absence of congestion and maintenance of hygiene in public spaces and streets.

The Ministry has also set up a Task Force on Urban Poverty with the objective of in-depth systematic and comprehensive assessment and analysis of the issues relating to urban poverty and suggesting strategies in the national level to alleviate urban poverty in the country. The Ministry has also set up a Task Force on Land Tenure for in-depth systematic and comprehensive assessment and analysis of the issues relating t security of land tenure for the issues relating to security of land tenure for the urban poor specially with reference to provide them appropriate environment for facilitating micro credit to cater to their consumer and housing needs.

The JNNURM comprises two sub-missions – one for infrastructure and governance, and the other for basic services to urban poor. The programme is being implemented in 63 selected cities in the country. The sub-mission in Basic Services to Urban Poor (BSUP) is being implemented by Ministry of Housing & Urban Poverty Alleviation, Govt. of India. The following are the main objectives of the sub-mission:

(i) Focused attention to integrated development of basic services to the urban poor;

(ii) Security of tenure at affordable price, improved housing, water supply and sanitation;

(iii) Convergence of services in fields of education, health and social security;

(iv) Providing housing near the place occupation of the urban poor;

(v) Effecting linkages between and asset creation and asset management to ensure efficiency;

(vi) Scaling up delivery of civic amenities and provision of utilities with emphasis on universal access to urban poor;

(vii) Ensuring adequate investment of funds to fulfill deficiencies in the basic services to the urban poor.

The following are the admissible component under the Sub Mission:

(i) Integrated development of slums i.e. housing and infrastructure projects in slums;

(ii) Projects involving development/improvement/ maintenance of basic services to the urban poor;

(iii) Slum improvement and rehabilitation projects;

(iv) Projects on water supply/sewerage/drainage/ community toilets/ bath etc;

(v) Houses at affordable costs for slum dwellers/urban poor;

vi) Construction and improvement of drains/storm water drains;

vii) Environmental improvement of slums and solid waste management;

viii) Street lighting;

ix) Civic amenities like community halls, child care centres etc.;

x) Convergence of health, education and social security schemes for the urban poor.

For other than mission cities, IHSDP and UI DSSMT have been launched by Government of India. The erstwhile, VAMBAY and NSDP are subsumed in IHSDP. The IHSDP has been launched with the objective to strive for holistic slum development, with a healthy and enabling urban environment by providing adequate shelter and basic infrastructure facilities to the slum dwellers of the identified urban areas. The admissible components of the scheme are as follows:

- Provision of shelter including upgradation and construction of new houses;
- Provision of community toilets;
- Provision of physical amenities like water supply, storm water drains; community-bath, widening and paving of existing lanes, sewers, community latrines, street lights etc;
- Community infrastructure like provision of community centres to be used for pre-school education, non-formal education, adult education, recreational activities, etc;
- Community Primary Health Centre buildings can be provided;
- Social amenities like pre-school education, non-formal education, adult education, maternity, child health and primary health care including immunization, etc;
- Provision of Model Demonstration Projector;
- Sites and services/houses at affordable costs to EWS & LIG categories;
- Slum improvement and rehabilitation projects.

The JNNURM and IHSDP schemes are reforms oriented. Three municipal reforms under NURM schemes directly impact the urban poor viz.:

- internal earmarking of funds for services to urban poor;
- provision of basic services tu urban poor; and

- earmarking atleast 20-25 per cent of developed land in all housing projects for EWS/ LIG category with a system of cross subsidization.

Internal earmarking of funds for basic services to the urban poor is one of the mandatory reforms under JNNURM. Under this, the urban local bodies are expected to allocate a specific percentage of funds in their budget for services delivery to the urban poor. One of the mandatory reforms at ULB's level are expected to update their database, prepare a comprehensive policy with stakeholder involvement on basic services to all urban poor including tenure security and housing at affordable prices, rank and priorities the poor settlements in a participatory manner to facilitate investment decisions and benchmark the services and prepare a time frame to achieve them during the mission period. Earmarking of developed land for poor is an optional reform under JNNURM. Under this at least 20-25 per cent of developed land in all housing projects both public and private sectors should be earmarked to the EWS/LIG's in order to meet the housing needs.

The comparative matrix of UPA initiatives under JNNURM is shown in Chart 1. Most of the cities are trying their best to ensure the compliance of municipal reforms for empowering urban poor and improving the efficiency in governance as well as delivery of municipal services.

Chart 1

A Comparative Matrix of UPA Initiatives & JNNURM

City		*Emphasis on Urban Poor*
Ahmedabad	Whether the CDP has been Participatory with respect to the Urban Poor.	Indirectly represented by NGOs
	Emphasis	Separate chapter on Urban Poor and housing given
	Population/Households	Slum population-9 lakhs **No. of Slum Households**-1.76 lakh-1/4th population or AMC and 1/5 of AUDA
	Access to basic Services	Details given, deficient in terms of basic services. Zero Open defecation envisioned.

Contd...

City		Emphasis on Urban Poor
Surat	Whether the CDP has been Participatory with respect to the Urban Poor.	Indirectly represented by NGOs
	Emphasis	Separate chapter on Housing and Slums. Map provided.
	Population/Households	**Slum population**-5.69 lakhs **No. of Slums-312** **No. of Slum Households-** 9365519% of total population.
	Access to basic Services	Discussed, given in table, 72% of households have private water taps and 35% have private toilets. City without Slums envisioned.
Vadodara	Whether the CDP has been Participatory with respect to the Urban Poor.	Indirectly represented by NGOs who participated in an opinion poll ranking the basic services in order of priority. Special survey on the existing situation of the urban poor done by SEWA.
	Emphasis	Status well examined. Details provided. Separate section on 'Urban Poor' included in the CDP.
	Population/ Households	**No. of Slums** -336 **No. of Slum Households-** 5143920% of total population.
	Access to basic Services	80% have access to water 46% to drainage, 42% to toilets.190 slums identified for providing on site service.
Rajkot	Whether the CDP has been Participatory with respect to the Urban Poor.	Indirectly represented in 4 group meetings by RMC.
	Emphasis	Status well presented and provided.
	Population/Households	84 notified slums as per 2001 20% of RMC resides in slums
	Access to basic Services	10% has no access to water, 6% defecates in the open. Slum improvement dealt separately indicating projects to be undertaken with criteria of creating zero slum area and access to all.
Visakapatnam	Whether the CDP has been Participatory with respect to the Urban Poor.	Represented in stakeholder consultations.

Contd...

City		*Emphasis on Urban Poor*
	Emphasis	Status presented elaborately.
	Population/Households	**No. of Slums** -472 in GVMC41% of total population as per 2005 data, 24% as per 2001.
	Access to basic Services	60% of slum area has drinking water, 25% has sewerage. Strategies to attain achievable goals formulated. City without slums envisioned by 2021
Vijaywada	Whether the CDP has been Participatory with respect to the Urban Poor.	NA
	Emphasis	Well provided. Information of poverty reduction initiatives and schemes also discussed.
	Population/Households	30% of slum population in municipal areas52% in peripheral areas.
	Access to basic Services	20% of slums have water supply, 2% have sewerage and 75% have access to community toilets. Comprehensive plan for urban poor given.
Raipur	Whether the CDP has been Participatory with respect to the Urban Poor.	Stakeholder consultations not taken. The CDP completely misses the views and opinions of the people.
	Emphasis	The section on urban poor provides only a list of the slums, Details not provided.
	Population/Households	Not provided
	Access to basic Services	Not provided, Vision presented in a generalized manner. Specific details on strategies are not provided.
Hyderabad	Whether the CDP has been Participatory with respect to the Urban Poor.	Broad based stakeholder consultations held. Indirectly represented.
	Emphasis	Separate chapter on Basic Services to Urban poor provided.
	Population/Households	14% of population BPL, 39% lives in the slums.
	Access to basic Services	Details given. Basic infrastructure in slums-minimal and inadequate. Separate plan for urban poor envisioned.

Contd...

City		Emphasis on Urban Poor
Kohima	Whether the CDP has been Participatory with respect to the Urban Poor.	The Urban Poor are secondary stakeholders. Indirectly represented by NGOs.
	Emphasis	Chapter 6 of the CDP gives a profile of the Urban Poor.
	Population/Households	24% of the city identified as BPL, 26% lives in slums.
	Access to basic Services	9% benefited through anti-poverty programmes. 25% have individual toilets; access to PHED water supply is absent. Poor education levels.
Chandigarh	Whether the CDP has been Participatory with respect to the Urban Poor.	NA
	Emphasis	Pg 80 has been dedicated to the basic services for urban poor Details have not been provided.
	Population/Households	15% of population living in unauthorized or temporary
	Access to basic Services	100% access to water, sanitation, education, and health

Source: NIUA, New Delhi, November, 2006.

FINANCIAL ASSISTANCE UNDER URBAN POVERTY ALLEVIATION PROGRAMMES

With a view to provide gainful employment to the urban unemployed through encouraging the setting up of self employment ventures or provision of wage employment -- Swarn Jayanti Shahari Rojgar Yojana (SJSRY) was launched in 1997 after subsuming the earlier three schemes of UBSP, NRY and PMIUPEP. SJSRY is funded on a basis of 75:25 between the Centre and states. The scheme rests on a foundation of community empowerment towards this ends, community organizations like Neighbourhood Groups (NHG's), Neighbourhood Committees (NHC's) and Community Development Societies (CDS's) are to be set up in the target areas. These CDS's may also self themselves up as thrift and credit societies to encourage community savings and also other group activities. The scheme has two major components. One is related with urban self employment programme which envisages setting up micro enterprises and skill development, training and infrastructure support, and Development of Women and Children in Urban Areas (DWCUA). The second component is concerned with urban wage employment programme. Funds released under the different poverty alleviation programmes are shown in Table 5.

Table 5
Central Release under SJSRY, VAMBAY, NSDP, NSLRS

(Rs. Crores)

Year	*SJSRY*	*VAMBAY (Allocation)*	*NSDP*	*NSLRS*
1997-98	98.63	–	290.99	90.0
1998-99	158.47	–	351.63	5.90
1999-2000	118.77	–	384.96	70.0
2000-2001	85.13	–	247.34	60.92
2001-2002	38.31	69.0	282.40	9.20
2002-2003	100.92	256.85	333.44	40.95
2003-2004	100.74	238.50	335.08	21.41
2004-2005	122.01	280.58	613.77	13.56
2005-2006	155.88	249.00	–	–

Source: Ministry of Housing & Urban Poverty Alleviation, Govt. of India, New Delhi.

There has been increasing trend in funds release except in case of National Scheme for Liberation and Rehabilitation of Scavengers. Funds allocation under SJSRY in the selected states are shown in Table 6.

During 1997-98 to 2006-2007, largest fund were allocated in the states of Uttar Pradesh, Madhya Pradesh and Bihar. However, there are discrepancies in funds allocated and funds released to the states. In Uttar Pradesh higher funds were released as against also cited funds while Bihar received less amount of allocated funds (Table 7).

The financial progress of scheme is shown in Table 8. Expenditure as percentage of funds available was recorded highest in Uttar Pradesh (94.45 per cent) followed by Bihar (79.53 per cent), Orissa (78.15 per cent) and Madhya Pradesh (77.80 per cent).

Table 6
Budget Allocation under SJSRY in India

(Rs. Lakh)

Year	Bihar	Jharkhand	Chhatisgarh	MP	Orissa	UP	Uttarakhad
1997-98	506.09	—	—	927.18	223.11	1181.03	—
1998-99	779.22	—	—	1511.77	360.44	1988.42	—
1999-2000	872.36	—	—	1692.17	403.63	2202.09	—
2000-01	606.30	422.69	202.10	1143.05	375.11	1956.43	102.97
2001-02	606.30	422.69	202.10	1143.05	375.11	1956.43	102.97
2002-03	427.02	236.41	213.37	813.93	330.94	1450.29	76.18
2003-04	425.38	235.88	212.31	818.32	329.69	1453.55	76.49
2004-05	468.09	278.58	156.02	753.15	322.65	1422.61	74.82
2005-06	681.66	405.67	227.16	1096.76	469.86	2071.43	109.14
2006-07	1173.65	698.46	391.11	1888.35	808.97	3566.49	187.91
Total	6146.07	2700.38	1604.17	11787.73	3909.51	19248.77	730.48

Source: Ministry of Housing & Urban Poverty Alleviation, Govt. of India, New Delhi.

Table 7
Year-Wise Fund Released under SJSRY

Year	*Bihar*	*Jharkhand*	*Chhatisgarh*	*MP*	*Orissa*	*UttaraKhand*	*U.P.*
1997-98	350.84	155.25	–	927.18	223.11	–	1181.03
1998-99	540.18	239.04	–	1511.77	360.44	–	1988.42
1999-2000	283.29	125.34	–	1836.21	460.83	–	2344.02
2000-01	–	202.10	422.69	888.59	69.24	102.97	1340.78
2001-02	–	66.64	128.44	304.02	300.00	27.88	733.07
2002-03	–	–	236.41	683.93	381.48	16.33	1671.76
2003-04	425.38	–	229.65	818.32	–	46.27	1571.74
2004-05	468.09	–	119.31	931.49	48.91	160.31	2622.61
2005-06	681.66	–	405.67	1596.76	469.86	309.14	3071.43
2006-07	586.83	–	698.46	2388.35	808.97	93.96	4566.49
Total	3436.27	788.37	2240.63	11886.62	3122.84	756.86	21091.35

Source: Ministry of Housing & Urban Poverty Alleviation, Govt. of India, New Delhi.

Table 8
Financial Progress under SJSRY (From 1997-98 till Now)

(Rs. Lak h)

State	Funds Released	Funds Available	Expenditure
Bihar	4260.58	7346.31	5842.77 (79.53)
Chhatisgarh	3356.00	3356.00	2012.09 (59.96)
Jharkhand	886.71	2311.18	0.00
Madhya Pradesh	18968.99	22022.94	17134.46 (77.80)
Orissa	4592.30	5708.64	4461.57 (78.15)
Uttarakhand	1184.43	1184.43	623.40 (52.63)
Uttar Pradesh	29871.01	37634.44	35547.50 (94.45)
Total	59285.72	25763.94	61606.79

Source: Ministry of Housing & Urban Poverty Alleviation, Govt. of India, New Delhi.

PHYSICAL PERCENTAGE OF UPA PROGRAMMES

Physical progress under SJSRY is shown in Table 9. Number of beneficiaries assisted under USEP was recorded high in Uttar Pradesh and Madhya Pradesh while number of women beneficiaries under DWCUA groups were reported high in Bihar as compared to other states. A large number of persons were given training under USEP in Madhya Pradesh and Orissa while employment was created high in Uttar Pradesh as compared to other states.

Table 9
Physical Progress under SJSRY

Particulars/ States	*Bihar*	*Jhar-khand*	*Chhatis-garh*	*MP*	*Orissa*	*Uttara-khad*	*U.P.*
No. of beneficiaries assisted under USEP	15429	NA	13166	10777	27997	812	149394
No. of DWCUA groups formed	2250	NA	421	4037	1855	2	3434
No. of women beneficiaries under DWCUA groups	19245	NA	1362	11614	13317	20	10148

Contd...

Particulars/ States	*Bihar*	*Jhar-khand*	*Chhatis-garh*	*MP*	*Orissa*	*Uttara-khad*	*U.P.*
No. of persons trained under USEP	4860	NA	16094	148232	22408	1414	150562
No. of thrift and credit societies formed	0	NA	4907	15867	2297	23	8472
No. of mandays of work generated under UWEP (in lakh)	56.30	NA	5.32	32.10	24.11	0.07	79.96
No. of beneficiaries covered under community structure (in lakh)	12.02	NA	5.61	30.30	9.40	56.23	

Source: Ministry of Housing & Urban Poverty Alleviation, Govt. of India, New Delhi.

Similarly, a large number of beneficiaries were covered under community structure in UP as against other states. Physical targets for 2007-2008 under SJSRY are shown in Table 10. The physical targets to set up micro enterprises have been at the higher level in Bihar and Orissa while targets for providing training are higher in Uttar Pradesh.

Table 10
Physical targets for 2007-2008 under SJSRY

State	*No. of beneficiaries assisted for setting up of micro enterprises*	*No. of beneficiaries provided skill training*
Bihar	4767	5958
Jharkhand	2884	3605
Chhatisgarh	1870	2338
Madhya Pradesh	12136	15170
Orissa	4276	5345
Uttarakhand	1364	1705
Uttar Pradesh	17679	22098
Total	44976	56219

Source: Ministry of Housing & Urban Poverty Alleviation, Govt. of India, New Delhi.

Under the VAMBAY Scheme targeted to construct 411478 dwelling units and 64247 community toilets during 2001-02 to 2005-2006. Similarly, under the NSDP, Rs. 3089.62 crores was released for development of urban slums. The scheme aimed at upgradation of urban slums by providing physical amenities like water supply, storm water drains, community bath, widening and paving of existing lanes, sewers, community latrines, street lights etc. Besides, the funds under the scheme and be used for provision of community infrastructure and social amenities like pre-school education, non-formal education, adult education, maternity, child health and primary health care including immunization. Besides, DFID assisted projects in Andhra Pradesh and West Bengal aimed at development of physical infrastructure and provision of civic amenities as well as community development and provision of social, economic and education inputs which assisted in raising the standard of living of slum dwellers. Andhra Pradesh Urban Services for poor project intended to bring about more effective urban poverty reduction through the convergence and developing existing poverty alleviation schemes in three programme areas viz. economic, environmental and social. Kolkata Urban Services for the poor proogramme aims at improving urban planning and governance, access to basic services for the poor and providing economic growth in Kolkata Metropolitan Areas. APUSP and KUSP are in implementation stage and likely to be completed in 2008 and 2001, respectively.

LIMITATIONS IN UPA PROGRAMMES

Viewed from the conceptual framework, one finds that the thrust of the programmes in India has been to reach the urban poor through strategies that are related to employment, urban services and shelter. The impact of these programmes and strategies on the incidence of urban poverty has not been encouraging. The limitations of programmes are (Sen, 2000):

(i) Inadequate financial resources to ULB's for poverty alleviation in proportion to the magnitude of the problem;

(ii) Lack of guarantee to get institutional finance;

(iii) Lack effective coordination among implementing agencies;

(iv) Lack of a coherent policy framework;

(v) Failure to build partnership with ill-equipped municipal bodies;

(vi) Political interference;

(vii) Poor loan recovery.

BOTTLENECKS ENCOUNTERED IN THE IMPLEMENTATION OF SJSRY

During the course of implementation of the Scheme of Swarna Jayanti Shahari Rozgar Yojana (SJSRY), several bottlenecks were observed for effective implementation of the Scheme. Some of the major hindrances, as manifested by the implementing agencies are as under:

- Project ceiling of Rs. 50000/- for individual projects is too less.
- There are educational qualification limit criteria for beneficiaries under Urban Self Employment Progamme (USEP).
- The minimum number of women for the DWCUA Groups is not justified.
- The funding pattern of 75:25 is difficult to provide the matching State share.
- There is no scope for the innovative/special projects under the Scheme guidelines.
- There is no provision for financial support for Self-Help Group formation activities.
- There is no regular dedicated cadre of functionaries for the implementation of the Scheme. Most of the officials are on contract basis or on deputation from other departments and therefore there is no motivation/incentive for better performance.
- The ceiling on per capita skill training cost is too low to cover the modern and efficient training in modern upcoming trades like computers etc.

- The budget allocation for the Scheme is too low. Keeping in view the ceilings fixed for the A&OE/IEC expenditure as percentage of allocation, the situation becomes more alarming.
- Authentic data regarding BPL population is not available. Updated BPL survey has not been done in many States/UT.
- Lack of cooperation from banks is a major impediment in the Self-employment programme.
- The awareness about the Scheme in masses is lacking.
- Sensitization of functionaries, bankers, NGOs towards the problems of urban poor is lacking.
- Lack of clarity in the Guidelines regarding expenditure on community empowerment activities is awesome.
- There is lack of proper marketing support for the products of the enterprises set up under the Scheme.

FUTURE STRATEGIES FOR POVERTY REDUCTION

Global and national structures for poverty reduction should provide a framework for local strategies to escape cycles of low incomes from work and social exclusion International Labour Organization (2003) has developed policy instruments in the following areas:

(i) Training and skill development;
(ii) Investing in jobs and the community;
(iii) Micro and small enterprises;
(iv) Micro-finance;
(v) Cooperatives;
(vi) Social security;
(vii) Hazards at work;
(viii) Eliminating child labour;
(ix) Overcoming discrimination.

Skills are essential to improve productivity, incomes, and access to employment opportunities. Thus, poverty reduction strategy should focus on vocational education and training since vast majority people living in poverty cannot afford and have access to training opportunities, which are commercially managed. International Labour Organization has invested in the field of employment intensive infrastructure programmes. It has now widely recognized that these programmes are effective in bringing much needed income to poor families and their communities.

Thus, financial investment in jobs and employment may create addition opportunities to poor youth. The labour intensive projects should respect standards, promote gender equality and encourage enterprise development through contracting systems. The entrepreneurship development may promote income generating enterprises and livelihood development. This will also promote self-employment among educated unemployed youth. Interestingly, it is impossible to build an enterprise without access to credit. Micro-finance activities should be promoted, strengthened and encouraged along with entrepreneurship for enabling poor to borrow for productive purposes.

Moreover, participation and inclusion are central to new approach to poverty reduction. Cooperatives and people's associations including Self Help Groups are ideal instruments in such a strategy. Cooperatives have proved to be a key organized form in building new models to combat social exclusion and poverty. Similarly, SHG's are proving crucial instrument for availability of micro-finance and social empowerment of poor. Significantly, discrimination is a basis for social exclusion and poverty. Promoting gender equality and eliminating all forms of discrimination at work are essential to defeating poverty. Child labour is both a cause and a system of poverty.

The importance of universal access to basic health care and primary and secondary education is well recognized by many countries. For a poor family, securing a basic income, basic health care and school places for the children is a foundation for participating productivity in society and the economy (ILO, 2003). The poor workers need protection from occupational health hazards, accidents, diseases etc.

Thus, by focusing directly on creating the conditions for people living in poverty to work for a better future, the decent work approach mobilizes the broad spectrum of support across society is needed to maintain progress and harmony and should reach to all poor communities. Eradicating poverty calls for the coordination of policies that focus on different dimensions of the life of people living in poverty.

REFERENCES

Bhaduri, Amit (1996), Employment, Labour Market Flexibility an Economic Liberalization in India, Indian Journal of Labour Economics, Vol. 39 (1).

Bhagawati, J. and Srinivasan, T.N. (1993), India's Economic Reforms, Ministry of Finance, Govt. of India, New Delhi.

CGG (2007), Reading material for RTP under JNNURM, Centre for God Governance, Hyderabad.

Dandekar, N.M. and Rath, N. (1971), Poverty in India, Indian School of Political Economy, Bombay.

Datta, G. and M. Rovallion (1997), Micro-Economic Crises and Poverty Monitoring: A Case Study for India, Review of Development Economics, Vol. 1 (2).

Desai, P.B. (1968), Economy of Indian Cities', Indian Journal of Public Administration, Vol., XIV (3), July-Sept.

Dev, S.M. (2000), Economic Reforms, Poverty, Income Distribution And Employment, Economic & Political Weekly, March.

Dreze, J. (1990), Widows in Rural India, London Schools of Economics, London, STICERD DEP No. 26.

Ghosh, Jayati (1995), Employment and Labour Under Structured Adjustment: India Since 1991, Indian Journal of Labour Economics, Vol. 38 (4).

Gurumukhi, K.T. (2000), Slum Related Policies and Programmes, Shelter, Vol. 3 (2), April.

ILO (2003), Working Out of Poverty, International Labour Organization, Geneva.

India Development Report, 1999-2000, IGIDR, Oxford University Press.

Jha, S.S. (1986), Structure of Urban Poverty, Popular Prakashan, Bombay.

Joshi, Vijai, and Little (1946), India's Economic Reforms: 1991:2001, Oxford University Press, New Delhi.

Kopardekar, H.D. (1986), Social Aspects of Urban Development, Popular Prakashan, Bombay.

MOHUPA, (2007), Annual Report, 2006-07, Ministry of Housing & Urban Poverty Alleviation, Govt. of Inida.

Nayar, Deepak (1993), Economic Reforms in India A Critical Assessment, ILO-ARTEP, New Delhi.

ODSG, Overseas Development Paper No. 19, Urban Poverty, Overseas Development Study Group, London.

Oxfam (India) Trust, (1997), Urban Poverty in India: Strategy for Research and Action Report, Feb.

Planning Commission (2001), Report of the Steering Committee on Urban Development for Tenth Plan, Planning Commission, Govt. of India, Delhi.

Radha Krishnan and Rao H. K. (2006), Poverty, Unemployment and Public Intervention, IN India Social Development Report, OUP, Delhi .

Radha Krishnan and S. Roy (2004), Poverty in India: Dimensions and Character IN India Development Report, OUP, Delhi, 2004-05.

Sen, A.K. (2000), Role of Urban Local Bodies in Poverty Alleviation Programmes, Shelter, Vol. 3 (2), April.

Singh Kulwant & Maitra, S. (2000), Urban Poverty in India: Approaches and Initiatives, Shelter Vol. 3 (2), April.

Takru, Rajiv (1997), Issues of Slum Development in India, Paper Presented At National Seminar on Future Cities – Urban Vision 2021, Delhi, Oct.

Tendulkar, S.D. (1998), Indian Economic Policy Reforms and Poverty: An Assessment in I.J. Ahluwalia and IMD Little (ed.) 'India's Economic Reforms and Development: Essays for Mohan Singh', Oxford University Press, New Delhi.

Thakur, R.N. & Dhadave, M.S. (1989), Slum & Social System, Archives Publishers, New Delhi.

Thakur, R.N. (1988), Social Aspect by Urban Povertyu, Nagarlok, Vol. XX (4), Oct.-Dec.

Unni, J. (1998), Gender Dimensions of Poverty, SEWA Gujarat Institute of Development Research, Ahmedabad.

Venkateshwarlu, U. (1998), Urbanization in India: Problems and Prospects, New Age International Publishers, Delhi.

World Bank (2002), Poverty in India: Challenge of Uttar Pradesh, World Bank, Delhi.

9

GEOGRAPHIC INFORMATION SYSTEM APPLICATIONS IN URBAN MANAGEMENT

Geographic Information System (GIS) is the emerging field with diversified applications in civil engineering, geosciences, forestry, disaster mitigation, environment and ecology, infrastructure planning, utility mapping etc. Nowadays GIS is a billion dollar industry with applications in varied discipline, and it is being used by professionals from various disciplines. GIS was pioneered in the 1960's by Canadian forestry mapping initiative and continued to develop as Canadian, U.S., and other government and university researchers sought to represent the earth's geography using a computer data base, display on a computer terminal, and plot it on paper. They also developed computer programmes for quick search and analysis of data. Several corporations were supported in 1970's to develop and sell systems for computer mapping and analysis.

Two leading GIS software developers trace their roots to early days and emphasize on two different aspects of technology. Intergraph Composition of Huntsville, Alabama, focused on efficient input and storage of GIS data as well as preparation of computer generated maps that rivaled traditional maps for their cartographic quality. The Environmental Systems Research Institute of Redlands, California, focused on providing a tool kit of computer commands for the analysis of GIS data. Today there are over hundreds of web sites that publish GIS data on the World Wide Web. As a result, the worldwide market for all GIS products and services was about $7 billion in 1999. Significantly, developed countries are using GIS widely in many areas but developing countries are moving towards the development of GIS database for their resources. Remote Sensing, aerial photography, cartography, surveying and other field instruments for attribute data collections contributes to the data acquisition. Cartography, surveying, geography, geology contributes for the mapping process, while disciplines like Computer Science and Statistics, Mathematics are involved in processing and analyzing data. Computer Science and Mathematics are involved in storage of data structure. GIS mapping has several advantages over paper map in the digital age. However, GIS data base creation is a time - consuming and tough job. Therefore it is dealt as a separate discipline in the name of Geometrics, Geoinformatics, and Spatial Information Technology.

CONCEPTUALIZATION

Commonly accepted definition of a GIS is a computer based system used to capture, store, edit, analyze, display and plot geographically referenced data. However, this broad definition applies to three principal types of computer systems, each of which has distinctly different characteristics and applications: CADD, AM/MF and GIS. Computer Aided Design and Drafting (CADD) technology is widely used by many professionals to help them design and produce design drawings. However, CADD can also be used to produce maps. It is an effective replacement for the traditional manual cartographic process. CADD can greatly reduce map production time and money over the traditional cartographic process. CADD offers many other benefits over traditional mapping techniques. However, CADD is not suited for analyzing map data. Automatic Mapping/Facility Management (AM/FM) is used by utilities to manage mapping and attribute data regarding their physical plans. AM/FM uses graphic data elements to represent map features. The attributes of the utility system are also stored in a separate data table. A GIS is similar to CADD and AM/FM. Although, the GIS may divide the entire area being mapped in to separate files, it also stores attribute data. These are associated with the spatial data and provide further descriptive information.

Geographic Information System can also be defined as a set of integrated activities which provides tool to (i) integrate geographic data received from different sources such as maps, charts, tables, aerial photographs, satellite imagery, GPS in digital environment; (ii) attach thematic information to the geographic details; (iii) analyze results and build up queries or spatial information, (iv) get the results in a desired form.

DEVELOPMENT OF GIS

GIS has been developed due to combination of many disciplines - such as computer mapping, databases, computer science, geography, remote sensing, data processing, mathematics and statistics, Computer Aided Design (CAD), cartography etc. GIS was used in a few universities and organizations during 1960's. Today, GIS is a component of IT and used in diversified disciplines. The Romans first employed the concept of cadastral records i.e. land records. In India, the origin of organized land record system dates back to one thousand years when the Chola Kings initiated revenue surveys. During the 15th and 16th century, Raja Todermal under Akbar's regime is credited with the introduction of land management for revenue. In 1935, Municipal Committees of Nagpur after investigations found 'aerial survey' as the best solution and accordingly by 1936 completed Nagpur city maps on 16 inches to a meter scale. During 1970-71, under UNDP, Cadastral Survey Pilot Project was undertaken by the Survey of India, covering an area of 8000 hectares, constituting 16 villages. However, GIS origin dates back to 1940's and 1950's. Successful implementation of computer aided graphical data processing at Massachusetts Institute of Technology and data base management system by General Electric in 1965 paved the way for GIS development at a much faster pace.

Government agencies in USA, Canada, UK started using GIS for processing large amount of data. During 1960's, CGIS developed and regarded as first GIS used by Canada government agencies was used for land and resource management. USGS used Geographical Information Retrieval and Analysis System to analyze land use and land cover data. During 1970, Swedish Land Data Bank took steps to automate the land and property registration. Harvard Graphics Laboratory developed first vector GIS called as ODESSEY. Centre for Urban and Regional Analysis, University of Minnesota developed Minnesota Land Management Information System. During 1970's and 1980's, hundreds of packages related to GIS were developed. However, during 1990's, many types of software on GIS came into existence. During 1990 to 2000, GIS Technology was standardized and software were made available for various platforms. Since 2000, GIS is used in virtual reality through multimedia integration, mobile mapping and web based technology.

COMPONENTS OF GIS

There are four integrated components of GIS; data and database management systems and users. The data in a GIS are by nature geographic. Spatial data is the information pertaining to where the objects of interest are located. A fully functional GIS must have hardware to support data in-put, out-put, storage, retrieval, display and analysis. Some of the most popular GIS software are Arc Info, Arc GIS Map Info, Geo Media and TNT-MIPS. Each of these softwares offers different levels of functionality. Importantly, GIS is used by diverse professionals-from a cartographer to a commercial pizza dealer. Among the disciplines such as geology, hydrology and social sciences, GIS has become as indispensable a tool as word processing and spread sheet software such as MS Excel.

APPLICATIONS OF GIS

GIS is a tool that can be used in varied disciplines ranging from civil engineering to business. Remote sensing data is often brought into GIS to have a complete data set in many natural resources application areas. Remote sensing and GIS technology is useful in the important fields of protection of environment, water resources management, urban planning and transportation, watershed management, surveying, coastal zone management, natural disaster management, agriculture, land use planning, forestry, geosciences, demography, town and country planning, oil, water and soil resources, oceanography, tax assessment and physical and social environment.

Dataquest's market survey (1999) sub-divided GIS applications into the following nine categories:

- Base data includes the creation of vector data and vaster images representing physical features on earth's surface
- Land information includes the creation and maintenance of the data for land records, land planning and land use (21 per cent)
- Bio-logical uses include environmental, public health and safety, forestry, and agriculture (9 per cent)
- Geosciences applications includes oil, gas, and mineral exploration (16 per cent)
- Infrastructure management includes transportation, logistics, emergency services, and dispatch management (7 per cent)
- Utilities include water, sewer, storm water, electric, telephone, CATV, data communication, and stream systems (28 per cent)
- Business marketing and sales involves demographic, sales and location analysis (9 per cent)
- Geopolitics involves the military or other defense use (6 per cent).
- Cartography or map making (4 per cent)

GIS TECHNIQUES

Geographic Information System handles large volumes of data. GIS data is either spatial or aspatial. All locations on the earth's surface are spatial data. Spatial data consist of location; shape and size in earth, line point etc. Interestingly, remote sensing means acquiring information about objects without having physical contact with the object. Aerial Photography is the remote sensing data, providing visual imagery of landscape on films. Remote sensing satellites take images in the visible and infra-red regions Radar microwave data are long wave producing land and water information much different from that of the visual region of the spectrum. Vector data input is the process of converting paper map into digital data while Global Positioning System (GPS) are used for the calculation of latitude, longitude and altitude for many users.

Roughly two thirds of the total cost of implementing a GIS involves building the GIS database. Many GIS programmes start with editing digital map data because of its relatively low cost. Subsequently, plans may be implemented to improve data with more accuracy and detail. Digitizing is the process of tracing paper maps into a compute format. There are two most widely used types of GIS data structure, viz. vector format and vaster format. The vector and vaster models for storing geographic data have unique advantages and disadvantages both of which models can be handled by a full function GIS. Vector digital map data is recorded as distinct points, lines, or areas. Vaster data files consist of rows of uniform cells covered according to data values.

SELECTING AND IMPLEMENTING GIS

The benefits of GIS for government agencies and urban management are substantial and well documented. However, adoption of GIS technology requires thorough planning and vigilant control. The best way to begin a GIS programme is to carefully review the organization's needs, and then develop a strategic plan that will systematically guide the selection and implementation of the system. A GIS Plan includes (i) introduction and background of GIS, (ii) existing operation; (iii) existing needs and problems; (iv) general description of GIS; (v) GIS hardware and software; (vi) GIS database, (vii) GIS data maintenance, (viii) data communication; (ix) staffing and organization; (x) training, (xi) schedule; (xii) financial analysis.

There are eight key components of a successful GIS operation. These are:

- management support, leadership and vision
- data conversion and maintenance
- hardware and software
- user training
- data communication
- software customization
- user support
- funding

There are three general types of costs associated with the implementation of a GIS:

- Services
- Hardware and software purchases
- Database creation

These costs also include ancillary charges such as taxes, insurance, shipping, and installation. Data base creation is usually the largest cost component of a GIS programme. This category comprises of all costs required to create the GIS data base.

Importantly, ongoing cost of operations and the maintenance of the digital data base include:

- Data management
- Data maintenance
- User training
- System support
- User support
- System development
- Supplies

IMPLICATIONS FOR UTTAR PRADESH

Uttar Pradesh is the most populous State in the country which accounts for 16.4% of the country's population. It is also the fourth largest State in geographical area covering 9.0% of the country's geographical area. The pace of urbanization has been lower in the State, and the level of urbanization has been reported lower than most of the other States. In 2001, 20.78 per centof its population was found living in urban areas. During 1991-2001, its urban population grew by 2.84 percent per annum. The pace of urbanization has declined during 1991-2001 from 1981-91 due to creation of a new state- Uttaranchal. As per the 2001 Census, there are 670 towns and cities in the State. There are 628 urban local bodies, out of which 12 are Municipal Corporations, 193 Municipalities and 423 Town Panchayats.

Urban property taxation is an important source of municipal revenue in most of the urban local bodies, however, the system of property taxation is manual and filled with discrepancies. There is need to enhance the revenue base in a structured manner. The models to enhance the property tax system by introducing GIS in Mirzapur and Kanpur have shown potential for GIS application in municipal revenue administration.

In order to develop a pilot model city programme consistent with Uttar Pradesh realities, the Ganga Institutional and Community Development Project (ICDP) in Mirzapur was developed by Governments of the Netherlands, India and Uttar Pradesh. The project provided a platform to develop and test a Geographic and Management Information System for improving the municipal administration of a small city in the state of Uttar Pradesh. It was a remarkable achievement which improved basic municipal data base and computerized system of resource mapping. Thus, Mirzapur become the first city where G.I.S. was introduced, allowing testing of the full range of applications for identifying, diagnosing and resolving administrative problems that had been unresolved for decades. The initiative cleared the misconceptions about the required data base, development, operation and application of a geographic information system in India. In 1995, municipal staff could not provide basic financial or infrastructure information because of the break - down of administrative activities and the absence of any information management system. The city was bankrupt and conditions were getting worse with a widening gap between income and expenditure.

At the commencement of the ICDP programme, the municipality's current revenues were not sufficient to meet even the basic payroll, let alone to sustain the operation and maintenance of basic urban services. In order to address the situation, ICDP developed a successful intervention package that included immediate service improvements, property reassessment and environment planning. The primary objectives were the computerization of property tax records, and the proper enumeration and mapping of all properties and infrastructure. The first objective of the programme was to collect and computerize the critical property tax assessment registers for the 23,590 properties. The assessment registers are the only official property tax records and any changes in taxation should have reference to them. Even though the registers may be disorganized and have not been updated for some years, they contain at least partial records of most of urban property data base. Any change or the creation of any registration system would need to be linked to the existing entry 'khatas' to modern usable computer files. The municipal tax department firstly had to conduct property enumeration to register new properties. After existing records were computerized they were easily printed out to be used in the field as the basis of property enumeration. Municipal staff conducted the enumeration between April and December, 1996 under the supervision of consultants. At the start of the project, the only property maps available were out-dated and rough outline maps. From these, revenue ward maps were extracted by rough boundaries for use in the property enumeration. National ward maps were taken to the field and used along with the assessment printout to verify and update property information. Surveyors made current notations both on records and on maps in the field. A property survey was conducted along side the enumeration based on a simple questionnaire, which emphasized location and basic property characteristics likely to effect property values, Land use, type of construction, floor level of unit, neighbourhood area and front/back street access were the main contents of the questionnaire. At the end of every-day, enumeration survey information was checked, corrected and entered in computer files. Rough field notation maps were faired and fitted to the outline city map to create the first ever property tax maps for the city. The city property tax maps were scanned and digitized using maps into computer mapping software.

The methodology adopted was the representative neighbourhood approach where all the city's 610 Mohallas were classified into one of 7 neighbourhood types based on rental values. Once this coding was done, values for owner occupied properties were calculated. Mohalla and street coding formed the foundation of assessment of values. Property with values significantly higher or lower than surrounding properties were reviewed in the same way. After application of a computerized assessment programme property values were normally checked. The staff of Mirzapur Municipality were given technical and management training necessary to implement computerization and to supervise the field and office work.

Appreciation of geographical information system has increased revenues and improved services of municipality. The Mirzapur model has thus become the first initiative in improving the efficiency of municipal administration through implementation of GIS in India. The GIS tools are now available to increase municipal revenues and improving the urban basic services.

CONCLUSION

GIS offers solutions for data needs for both macro and micro level analysis of urban environment, development and governance to city planners. A comprehensive assessment of the efficacy of remote sensing and GIS techniques needs to be substantiated by a pragmatic and realistic evaluation of the emerging problems and opportunities in the urban sector. The local governments have been also empowered and strengthened through functional and financial devolution of powers in view of 74th constitutional amendment act. Accurate, reliable and comprehensive spatio-temporal information and GIS data on urban entities is a prerequisite for urban bodies and authorities to effectively perform the assigned functions. The GIS data-base provides an analytical framework for analyzing the emerging problems and constraints in urban development and governance as well as assessing the physical, social, and financial resources and effective management of urban services. Non-availability of reliable information base acts as one of the major constraints in preparing plans at local level where data base of physical features and resources are necessary. The conventional ground methods of obtaining the necessary data on physical, geographical, natural resources, land use and base maps are extremely slow and it is difficult to keep pace with the rapid changes in settlement and land use pattern. Moreover, there were inconsistencies in the statistical data obtained directly on the spatial phenomenon and the maps prepared therein. These inherent problems resulted in hurdles and constraints of severe nature at all levels of planning, implementation and monitoring. Therefore, application of remote sensing and GIS is imperative for holistic and planned development of the urban sector.

CASE STUDIES IN REMOTE SENSING OF INDIAN CITIES

City	*Year*	*Urban Themes*
Jaipur, Rajasthan	1983	Land use mapping Open space change detection; 1974-83
Coimbatore, Tamil Nadu	1984	Land use mapping and changes: 1979-84 Growth, distribution and morphology of slum during 1979-84 Residential area typology Estimation of population
Ujjain, Madhya Pradesh	1985	Land use inventory and changes Changes detection and growth 1983-95 Study of residential environment Development plan evaluation Population estimation Space use mapping in city centre
Hyderabad, A.P.	1986	Urban land use changes and its structure during 1984-86 Study of the residential environment, population estimation and housing density.

Contd...

City	*Year*	*Urban Themes*
		Urban spatial growth and change detection during 1979-86
Rohini, Delhi	1987	Monitoring urban growth. Study of residential area: Shalimar Bagh Land use inventory.Inventory of derelict land.
Kanpur, Uttar Pradesh	1988	Mapping of urban land use/land cover.Study of commercial and industrial Land use in City centre. Quantitative assessment and qualitative judgment of habitat and its refuse. Identification of disposal sites, their capacity and projections.
Narela, Delhi	1988	Study of unauthorized development
Ujjain, Madhya Pradesh	1989	Residential land use inventory. Population Estimation and environmental impact assessment
Dehradun, Uttar Pradesh	1989	Land use inventory, change detection and residential environment
Jaipur, Rajasthan	1989	Mapping and monitoring of urban sprawl and land use/land cover. Site suitability analysis for residential development
Delhi	1989	Mapping and monitoring of urban sprawl and land use/land cover
Lucknow, Uttar Pradesh	1989	Mapping and monitoring of urban sprawl and land use/land cover.
Bhubaneshwar, Orissa	1990	Study of residential structure, potential of open/vacant spaces and growth of industrial area.
Bardez, Goa	1991	Implementation of zonal plan, housing types and density and land use analysis in Calangute tourist site. Suitability analysis for urban development. Rural population estimation.
Saharanpur, Uttar Pradesh	1991	Land use/land cover mapping. Land use change detection. Analysis of urban amenities and facilities. Residential service level and accessibility to facilities and services. Study of potential areas for residential development.

Contd...

City	Year	Urban Themes
		Housing density and urban population estimation.
Saharanpur, Uttar Pradesh	1993	Identification of slums. Efficacy of remote sensing in census operations. Morphology of city. Suitability analysis of vacant lands for urban development
Dwarka, Delhi	1993	Inventory of built-up environment
Bangalore, Karnataka	1994	Quality of residential environment. Appraisal of development plan. Land use change detection. Study of open spaces.
Jammu, Jammu & Kashmir	1995	Land use/land cover mapping. Growth profile of city. Identification of slums and squatter settlements. Selection of new sites for residential development. Inventory of vacant lands. Urban land use change detection. Qualitative assessment and zonation of natural hazards
Mizapur, Uttar Pradesh	1997	Mapping properties for tax assessment.

REFERENCES

Abbasri, S.A., and K.B. Chari, (2005), Application of GIS and Remote Sensing in Environmental Management, Discovery Publishing House, Delhi.

Arnoff, S., ((1989),), Geographic Information System: A Management Perspective, WDC Publications, Ottawa.

Atenucci, T.C. (ed), (1995), Geographic Information Systems: A Guide to Technology, Van Nor stand Rain hold, New York.

Bernhardsen, T., (1999), Geographic Information's Systems: An Introduction, John, Wilby & Sons.

Brandon Plewe, (1997), GIS Online: Information Retrieval, Mapping and the Internet, Onward Press.

Burrough, P.A., (1986), Principles of Geographic Information System for Land Resources Assessment, OUP, Oxford.

Henk, J. et. al., (1990), Geographical Information Systems for Urban and Regional Planning, Kenwar Academic Publishers.

Huxcold, W.E., (1991), An Introduction To Urban Geographic Information Systems, Oxford, University Press, Oxford.

Korte, G.B., (2001), The GIS Book, On Word Press - Thomson Learning, Singapore.

LOCP and Yeung K.W., (2002), Concepts and Techniques of Geographic Information Systems, PHI, New Delhi.

Michael, N. Demers, (1996), Fundamentals of Geographic Information Systems, John Wiely & Sons.

Rao, P.S.N. (ed), (2006), Urban Governance and Management; Indian Initiatives, Kanishka Publishers Delhi.

Sokhi, B.S. and S.M. Rashid (ed) (1999), Remote Sensing of Urban Environment, Manak Publications, Pvt., Ltd., Delhi.

Star, J.L., and Estes, J.E., (1990), Geographic Information Systems: An Introduction, Prentice Hall, Englewood, Cliffs.

Welliam E. et. al., (1995), Managing Geographic Information Projects, OUP, Oxford.

Worrall L. (ed), (1990), Geographic Information Systems: Developments and Applications, Belhaven Press, London.

10

DISASTER MANAGEMENT

India is one of the world's major theaters of disasters and both natural and human made. Floods, droughts cyclones, and earthquakes pound it end to end every year. Communal riots, conflicts, fires, epidemics, and other disasters compound the country's chronic troubles. The social and economic progress achieved over decade by the people, and advances in physical development, can be significantly devastated and degraded by disasters. Urbanization, industrialization, globalization and liberalization of economy all have influenced human life. People are tend to live in disaster prone areas due to severe stress on land, high prices of land and construction of buildings, poverty, migration and non-regulation of urban housing constructions. Even, the natural protection measures are neglected to pave the way for economic development. The government of India through various stake-holding agencies has been making efforts to meet the exigencies as arisen by natural disasters. It is, however, experienced that all these efforts and contingency plans concentrate on the post disaster situation. A half backed approach is adopted for preventing the occurrence of disasters. There is need for fundamental change in national disaster policy itself. The community has to be associated at all levels of planning and implementation of the disaster management programmes.

HAZARDS AND DISASTERS

The term disaster owns its origin to the French World '*Desastre*" which refers to bad or evil star. A disaster can be defined as 'a serious disruption in the functioning of the community or a society causing wide spread material, economic, social or environmental losses which exceed the ability of the affected society to cope using its own resources.' A disaster is a result from the combination of hazard, vulnerability and insufficient capacity or measures to reduce the potential changes of risk. A disaster is the product of a hazard such as earthquake, flood or wind storm coinciding with a vulnerable situation which might include communities, cities or villages. A disaster happens when hazard impose on the vulnerable population and causes damage, casualties and disruption. Without vulnerability or hazard there is no disaster. A disaster occurs when hazards and vulnerability meet. Hazard may be defined as dangerous condition or event that threat or have the potential for causing injury to life or damage to property or the environment. Hazards can be grouped into two broad categories namely natural and manmade. Natural hazards are those hazards which are caused because of natural phenomenon. Cyclones, tsunamis, earthquake, and volcanic eruption are exclusively of natural origin. Landslides, floods drought, fires, are socio-natural hazards since their causes are both natural and manmade. Manmade hazards are hazards which are due to human negligence. Manmade hazards are associated with industries or energy generation facilities and include explosions, leakage of toxic waste, pollution, dam failure, wars or civil strife etc. (Table 1)

Table 1
Hazard Classification and Related Disaster Types

Water & Climate Related	*Geological Disasters*	*Chemical, Industrial & Nuclear Disasters*	*Accident Related Disasters*	*Biological Disasters*
Floods & Drainage Management**	Earthquakes**	Chemical and Industrial Disasters	Urban Fires**#	Biological Disasters** & Epidemics$

Contd...

Water & Climate Related	*Geological Disasters*	*Chemical, Industrial & Nuclear Disasters*	*Accident Related Disasters*	*Biological Disasters*
Cyclones**	Land Slides and Mudflows**	Nuclear Disasters**	Mine Flooding**#	Pest Attacks$
Tornadoes & Hurricanes**	Dam Failure and Dam Bursts**		Oil Spill**#	Cattle Epidemics$
Hail Storms**	Mine Fires**		Major Building Collapse**#	Food Poisoning$#
Cloud Bursts**			Electrical Disasters and Fires**#	
Snow Avalanches**			Air Road and Rail Accidents**#	
Heat & Cold Waves**			Festival Related**#	
Sea Erosion**			Boat Capsizing#	
Thunder & Lightening**			Village Fires#	
Droughts**			Forest Fires#	
			Serial Bomb Blasts#	

** Engineering related
# Accident/Terrorism related
$ Biological related

Vulnerability may be conceptualized as the extent to which a community structure, service, or geographic area is likely to be damaged or disrupted by the impact of particular hazard on account of their nature, construction and proximity to hazardous terrain or a disaster prone area. The vulnerable buildings and infrastructure are more prone to earthquake hazards. Hence structures should be built strong enough to resist maximum force exerted by any event or for combination of event. Social and economic conditions also determine the vulnerability of a society to an extent. Interestingly, risk is a measure of the expected losses (deaths, injuries, property, economic activity etc.) due to a hazard of a particular magnitude occurring in a given area over a specific time period. The level of risk depends upon (i) nature of the hazard; (ii) vulnerability of the elements which are affected; and (iii) economic value of those elements. Thus, disaster risk management includes measures which reduce disaster related losses of life, property or assets by either reducing the hazard or vulnerability of the elements at risk. Disaster management is conceptualized as the body of policy and administrative decisions and operational activities which pertain to the various stages of a disaster at all levels. Broadly disaster management can be divided into pre-disaster and post-disaster contexts. There are three key stages of activity that are taken up within disaster management. They are (i) pre-disaster - mitigation, prevention, preparedness, risk assessment; (ii) during a disaster - emergency response, relief distribution, search and rescue, shelter, medical and trauma care etc., (iii) post disaster-rehabilitation and reconstruction of disaster affected persons and areas.

NATURAL DISASTERS

There has been increase in the number of natural disasters over the past years, on account of urbanization and population growth; as a result impact of natural disasters is now felt to a larger extent. According to the United Nations, in 2001 alone, natural disasters of medium to high range caused at least 250,000 deaths around the world, more than double the previous year, and economic losses of around 836 billion. The natural disasters are not bound by political boundaries and have no social or economic considerations. They are borderless as they affect both developing and developed countries. Since 1991, two third of the victims of natural disasters were from developing countries, while just 2 per cent were from highly developed nations. Those living in developing countries and especially those with limited resources tend to be more adversely affected (Government of India, 2002). The continent of Asia is particularly vulnerable to disaster strikes.

SITUATION ANALYSIS

The Indian subcontinent is vulnerable to droughts, floods, cyclones and earthquakes. Land slides, avalanche and forest fires also occur frequently (Table 2).

Table 2
Major Disasters in India Since 1970

Disaster	*Impact*
Cyclone	
29 October 1971, Orissa	Cyclone and tidal waves killed 10,000 people
19 November 1977 Andhra Pradesh	Cyclone and tidal waves killed 20,000 people.
29 and 30 October 1999 Orissa	Cyclone and tidal waves killed 9,000 and 18 million people were affected
Earthquake	
20 October 1991 Uttarkashi	An earthquake of magnitude 6.6 killed 723 people
30 September 1993 Latur	Approximately 8000 people died and there was a heavy loss to infrastructure
22 May 1997 Jabalpur	39 people dead
29 March 1997, Chamoli	100 people dead
20 January 2001, Bhuj, Gujarat to infrastructure	More than 10,000 dead and heavy loss
Landslide	
July 1991, Assam	300 people killed, heavy loss to roads and infrastructure
August 1993, Nagaland	500 killed and more than 200 houses destroyed and about 5 kms. Road damaged
18 August 1998, Malpa, Uttarakhand	210 people killed. Villages were washed away
Floods	
1978 Floods in North East India	3,800 people killed and heavy loss to property
1994 Floods in Assam, Arunachal Pradesh, Jammu and Kashmir, Himachal Pradesh, Punjab, Uttar Pradesh, Goa, Kerala and Gujarat.	More than 2000 people killed and thousands affected
2004 Tsunami, Coastal areas of Tamil Nadu, Andhra Pradesh, Andaman Nicobar Islands and Pondicherry.	More than 10,000 people were killed and damage of $1068 million to properties.

Source: Natural Hazards and Disaster Management, Text Book in Geography for Class XI CBSC, Delhi.

Among the 32 states and Union Territories in the country, 22 are multi-disaster prone. About 40 million hectares of land in the country has been identified as flood prone and on an average 18.6 million hectare of land is flooded annually. About 57 per cent of area of the country is vulnerable to seismic activity. About 18 per cent of country's total area is drought prone, approximately 50 million people are annually affected by droughts and about 68 per cent of total sown area of the country is drought prone. India has a long coastline of 8040 km. which is exposed to tropical cyclones arising in the Bay of Bengal, the Arabian Sea and Indian Sea. The Indian Ocean is one of the six major cyclonic prone regions of the globe (Jain, 2004:61). The Coromandal coastline is more cyclones prone, with 80 per cent of the total cyclones generated in this region. Risk to the existing housing stock in various states and union-territories had been estimated by Expert Group Set up by the Ministry of Urban Affairs and Employment, Government of India. About 3.9 million houses are susceptible to earthquakes of very high intensity, about 20 million houses are susceptible to damage due to winds and about 9.3 million houses are susceptible to damage due to floods. Besides the risk of earth quakes, cyclones and floods are liable to very high damage and destruction of vulnerable houses under heavy rains. (Jain, 2004:61). Some 49 per cent of the total housing stock is liable to very high damage from natural hazards, while about 1 per cent of the total housing stock gets destroyed every year. It is to be noted that in earth quake, 80 per cent of the casualties are due to collapsing buildings. Brick and stone buildings without proper support are liable to collapse. Non-engineered buildings continue to be built in the areas prone to natural disasters. Unemployment, poverty backwardness, migration from rural areas and increasing price of land and construction, million of people are occupying disaster prone areas. Thus about 6 per cent increase in disaster affected population has been reported.

According to the World Bank assessment, the natural disasters alone accounted India whopping amount of $13 million during 1986-2001, depleting 2 per cent of the GDP and

12 per cent of national revenue. Compared to the loss of $13.4 billion during 1981-95 and $2.9 million during 1965-80, the present swelling in the volume of losses is certainly frightening and demands urgent attention of development planners (Kishore K. Singh, 2004:349). The dilapidated and poorly built houses in urban areas increase the risks of disasters. Lack of tenurial rights over the urban space and shortage of housing facilities have forced to urban poor to live in the most unsafe environment. The Indian sub-continent is highly prone to natural disasters. Floods, droughts, cyclones and earthquakes are a recurrent phenomenon in India. Between 1988 and 1997 disaster Killed 5116 people and affected 24-79 million every year (Table 3).

Table 3
Damage due to Natural Disasters in India

Year	*People Affected (lakh)*	*Houses & Buildings Damaged*	*Amount of Property Damage/Loss (Rs. crore)*
1985	595.6	2449878	40.6
1986	550.0	204927	30.74
1987	483.4	2919380	20.57
1988	101.5	242533	40.63
1989	30.1	782340	20.41
1990	31.7	1019930	10.71
1991	342.7	1190109	10.90
1992	190.9	570969	20.05
1993	262.4	1529916	50.80
1994	235.3	1051223	10.85
1995	543.5	2088355	40.73
1996	549.9	2376693	50.43
1997	443.9	1103549	N.A.
1998	521.7	1563405	0.72
1999	501.7	3104064	1020.97
2000	594.34	2736355	800.00
2001	788.19	846878	12000.00

Source: Annual Reports, NDM Division, Ministry of Agriculture, Government of India, Delhi.

The changing topography due to environmental degradation has also increased the vulnerability in the country. In 1988, 11.2 per cent of total land area was flood prone, but in

1998 floods inundated 37 per cent geographical area. Three major disasters that India have experienced in the recent past are the super cyclone in Orissa (1999), earthquake in Gujarat (2001) and Tsunami (2004) in Tamil Nadu, Pondicherry, Andaman Nicobar Islands and parts of other southern states. Frequent disasters lead to erosion of development gains and restricted options threatened by hazards.

The continent of Asia is particularly vulnerable to disasters strikes. Between the years 1991 to 2000 Asia has accounted for 83 per cent of the population affected by disasters globally. Within Asia, 24 per cent of deaths due to disasters occurred in India, on account of its size population and vulnerability. Floods and high winds account for 60 per cent of all disasters in India. Many parts of the Indian sub-continent are susceptible to different types of disasters owing to the unique topography and climatic characteristics. About 54 per cent of the sub continent's landmass is vulnerable to earthquakes while about 4 crore hectares is vulnerable to periodic floods. The country has suffered four major earthquakes in the span of last 50 years along-with a series of moderate intensity earthquakes that have occurred at regular intervals. Since 1988, six earth quakes have struck different parts of the country. Tsunami in India killed 10749 persons while $1068 million loss or damage to properties was reported.

The Indian sub-continent lies upon the Indian plate which is moving northward and collides with the Eurasian Plate. Due to this collision, the Himalayas are generated in the process. This is the main cause of earthquakes from Himalayas to the Arakan Yoma. The same process, results in earthquakes in Andaman and Nicobar Islands. Sometimes earthquakes of different magnitudes occur within the Indian Plate. As per the latest seismic zoning map of India, the country is divided into four Seismic Zones. Zone V marked in red shows the area of very high risk zone, Zone IV marked in orange shows the area of high risk zone, Zone III marked in yellow shows the region of moderate risk zone and Zone II marked in blue shows the region of low risk zone. Zone V is the most vulnerable to earth quakes, where historically some of the country's most powerful shock has occurred (Table 4).

Table 4
Significant Earthquakes in India

Date	Location	Magnitude M>6
1819 June 16	Kutch, Gujarat	8.0
1869 January 10	Near Cachar, Assam	7.5
1885 May 30	Sopor, J & K	7.0
1897 June 12	Shillong Plateau	8.7
1905 April 4	Kangra, Himachal Pradesh	8.0
1918 July 8	Srimangal, Assam	7.6
1930 July 2	Dhubri, Assam	7.1
1934 January 15	Bihar-Nepal Border	8.3
1941 June 26	Andaman Islands	8.1
1943 October 23	Assam	7.2
1950 August 15	Arunachal Pradesh-China Border	8.5
1956 July 21	Anjar, Gujarat	7.0
1967 December 10	Koyna, Maharashtra	6.5
1975 January 19	Kinnaur, Himachal Pradeh	6.2
1988 August 6	Manipur-Myanmar Border	6.6
1991 October 20	Uttarkashi, U.P. Hills	6.6
1993 September 30	Latur-Osmanabad, Maharashtra	6.3
1997 May 22	Jabalpur, Madhya Pradesh	6.0
1999 March 29	Chamoli District, Uttar Pradesh	6.8
2001 January 26	Bhuj, Gujarat	6.9
2005	Muzaffarabad Jammu & Kashmir	7.4

Source: http://www.ind.ernet.in/section/seismo/static/signif.htm

As per India's Seismic Vulnerability Atlas, 58 cities of India fall within seismic vulnerability Zones. Out of which 13 cities are located in Zone V, 16 Cities in Zone IV AND 29 cities are situated in Zone III (Table 5).

Table 5
Classification of Cities in Seismic Zones

Zone	No.	Cities
V	13	Aizwal, Bhuj, Chamoli, Dharamshala, Guwahati, Itanagar, Kohima, Kullu, Pithoragarh, Port Blair, Shillong, Srinagar
IV	16	Amritsar, Chandigarh, Darjeeling, Dehradun, Delhi, Gangtok, Gorakhpur, Gurgaon, Haridwar, Jammu, Jamnagar, Ratnagiri, Shimla, Meerut, Patna, Uttarkashi
III	29	Ahmedabad, Bhubaneshwar, Bikaner, Bokaro, Mumbai, Kolkata, Calicut, Coimbatore, Cochin, Cuttack, Gandhinagar, Gaya, Jabalpur, Kanpur, Lucknow, Pune, Puri, Mangalore, Nellore, Panaji, Patiala, Porbandar, Pune, Puri, Rajkot, Surat, Trivandrum, Vadodara, Vijayawada, Warangal

Source: Anup Karanth, GOI-UNDP-DRM Programme, December 2006.

Geographically, Zone V includes the Andamand and Nicobar Islands, all of North Eastern India, parts of north western Bihar, eastern parts of Uttaranchal, Kangra Valley in Himachal Pradesh, Srinagar area in Jammu and Kashmir and Rann of Kutchh in Gujarat. Earthquakes with magnitudes in excess of 7.0 have occurred in these areas, and have had intensities higher than IX. Most of the earthquakes which occurred were rated at 5-6 scale (60 per cent) while more than one third earthquakes were in between 6-7 Richter scale. Again, about half of the earth quakes have occurred in North East India alone (Table 6).

Table 6
Earthquake occurrence in India

Seismic Region	*No. of Earthquakes having M=*				*Max. MM Inten-sity*	*Average Return Period observed*	*Total*
Kashmir and Western Himalayas (J&K, Himachal Pradesh, Sub-mountain parts of Punjab)	25	7	2	1	X	2.5 -3 yrs.	35 (491)
Central-Himalayas (Uttarakhand, Nepal,Himalayas, North Bihar)	68	28	4	1	XI	1 yr.	101 (14.18)
North East India	200	130	15	4	>X	<4 months	349 (49.01)
Indo-Gangetic Basin & Rajasthan (Rajasthan, Punjab, Haryana, Delhi, Plains of U.P., Bihar and Bengal)	14	6	–	–	VIII	5 years	20 (2.81)
Cambay and Rann of Kutchh	6	5	3	1	X-X	7 years	15 (2.11)
Peninsular India	32	10	–	–	VIII	2.5-3 years	42 (5.89)
Andaman & Nicobar	80	68	1	1	>IX	<8 months	150 (21.06)
Whole in India	425	254	25	8	–	<2 months	712 (100.00)

Source: Dr. A.S. Arya Progress Towards Earthquake Risk Reduction in India, INCEDE Report

During the earthquakes, majority of losses is due to collapse of buildings and damage to infrastructure. More than half of the houses are built with stone walls and 35 per cent have burnt brick units which are highly vulnerable to sustain damage of seismic intensities namely VII, VIII and IX.

Tsunami Disaster in the Indian Ocean was one of the worst natural disasters in modern times. Over 200,000 people died and more than 1.5 million people lost their homes and their livelihoods. If the earthquake is under water and land movement is near the coast then tsunami may strike suddenly and if the earth movement is far in the sea then it may take few minutes to hours before striking the coast. The onset is extensive and often very destructive. The general causes of tsunamis are geological movements. Major tsunamis occurred in India are shown in Table 7.

Table 7
Tsunamis in India

Date	*Location*	*Impact*
1524	Near Dabhol, Maharashtra	Sufficient data not available
02 April 1762	Arakan Coast, Myanmar	Sufficient data not available
16 June 1819	Rann of Kutchh, Gujarat	Sufficient data not available
31 October 1847	Great Nicobar Island	Sufficient data not available
31 December 1881	An earthquake of 7.9 in the Richter scale in Car Nicobar Island	Entire east cost of India and Andaman & Nicobar Islands; 1 m tsunamis were recorded at Chennai
26 August 1883	Explosion of the Krakatoa volcano in Indonesian	East coast of India was affected ; 2 m tsunamis were recorded at Chennai
26 June 1941	An 8.1 Richter scale earthquake in the Andaman archipelago	East coast of India was affected but no estimates of height of the tsunami is available
27 November 1945	An 8.5 Richter scale earthquake at a distance of about 100 km south of Karachi	West coast of India from north to Karwar was affected; 12 m tsunami was felt at Kandla
26 December 2004	Banda Aceh, Indonesia; Tamil Nadu, Kerala, Andhra Pradesh, Andaman and Nicobar Islands, India; Sri Lanka, Thailand, Malaysia, Kenya, Tanzania	The East cost of India was affected. The waves measured around 10 m high killing more than 10,000 precious lives

Source: NDMD, MOH, Government of India, Delhi

The recent tsunami strike in December 2004 severely hit the coastal states of Tamil Nadu, Kerala, Andhra Pradesh and union territory of Andaman Nicobar Islands. According to Government reports, 10739 people in India lost their lives and 6913 were injured. It was reported that 5640 persons are still missing. The highest human losses were in the Andaman Nicobar Islands and the state of Tamil Nadu. Overall damages were estimated at about $660 million and losses to $410 million (UN, 2005).

Landslides are slippery masses of road, earth or debris which make by force of their own weight down mountain slopes or riverbanks. Though, they occur gradually, however, sudden failure can often bring toll and heavy losses to humankind and property. Erosion, intense rainfall, geological weak materials, human excavation, earthquake shaking and volcanic explosion are some of the factors for land sliding (Table 8).

Table 8
Major Landslides in India

October 1990	Nilgiris	36 people killed and several injured. Several buildings and communication network damaged
July 1991	Assam	300 people killed, road and buildings damaged.
November 1992	Nilgiris	Road network and buildings damaged, Rs. 5 million damage estimated
July 1993	Itanagar	25 people buried alive 2 km road damaged
August 1993	Kalimpong, West Bengal	200 houses destroyed, 500 people died, about 15 km road stretch was damaged
November 1993	Nilgris	40 people killed, property worth several lakhs damaged
January 1994	Kashmir	National Highway 1A severely damaged
June 1994	Varundh ghat, Konkan Coast	20 people killed, breaching of ghat road damaged to the extent of 1km at several places
May 1995	Aizwal, Mozoram	25 people killed. Road severely damaged
September 1995	Kullu, HP	22 persons killed and several injured. About 1 km road destroyed
14 August 1998	Okhimath	69 people killed

Contd...

18 August 1998	Malpa, Kali river	205 people killed. Road network to Mansarovar disrupted
August 2003		Uttarkashi Heavy loss of infrastructure

Source: Natural Hazards and Disaster Management, Text Book in Geography for Class XI CBSE, Delhi

Cyclonic disturbances of varying intensities originate in the Bay of Bengal and the Arabian Sea mainly during the April-December period. A scrutiny of cyclones in nearly 100 years (1891-1989) reveals that a few districts were hit by cyclones more often than other districts. These districts are Junagarh, 24 Parganas, Midnapur, Balasore, Cuttack, Puri, Srikakulam, Vizag. East Godavari, Krishna, Nellore and Tanjore while the coastal areas of Orissa and West Bengal were affected, by a large number of cyclonic storms during post 1949 period (Subhiah, 2004). The cyclone of 1977 caused death toll of over 14000 while recent cyclone in December 2000 severely hit three districts of Tamil Nadu (Table 9).

Table 9
Noteworthy Tropical Cyclones

Year	*Area*	*Death toll*
1971	Eastern Coast	9658
1972	Andhra Pradesh and Orissa	100
1977	Chennai, Kerala & Andhra Pradesh	14,204
1979	Andhra Pradesh	594
1981	Gujarat	470
1982	Gujarat & Maharashtra	500
1984	Tamil Nadu & Andhra Pradesh	512
1985	Andhra Pradesh	5,000
1990	Andhra Pradesh	957
1990	Orissa	250
1999	Orissa	8,913

Source: Office of the US Foreign Disaster Assistance

Major cyclones occurred in Indian ocean are shown in Table 10. The Bangladesh cyclone of 1991 hit India too and caused death of 1.32 lakh persons.

The coastal bet plantation (green belt plantation along the coastal line in a scientific interweaving pattern) can reduce the adverse impact of hazards of cyclone, tsunami, and flood.

However, the frequent cutting of plants, trees and clearance of forest and mangroves, the cyclone and tsunami waves trend freely in land. The lakh of productive forest cover allows water to immediate large areas and cause destruction. Thus, community based mitigation strategies are to be introduced.

Table 10
Recent Cyclones in Indian Region

Cyclone	*Peak wind Intensity m/s*	*OCS* M/S*	*MSDW** m/s*	*Size dia. of area of 17 m/s or more wind*	*Peak Surgem Lives*	*Loss of Human million*	*Loss of Property Rupees*
Chirala cyclone (1977)	70	28.5	31.0	750	5.2	10000	3500
Machilipatnam Cyclone (1979)	58	22.2	20.0	600	3.5	700	1700
Sriharikota Cyclone (1984)	58	11.5	12.2	300	3.2	604	4000
Bangladesh Cyclone (1985)	58	28.4	28.0	800	4.5	2500	1377
Kavali Cyclone (1989)	65	10.3	13.2	250	3.5	51	140
Machilipatnam Cyclone (1990)	65	23.2	23.9	550	3.5	967	22480
Bangladesh Cyclone (1991)	65	23.0	24.2	500	6.0	132000	–
Orissa Cyclone (1999)	72	42.0	20.0	10000	5.5	–	–

* Outer Core Strength
**Main Strength of Destructive Wing
Source: Bhandari, N.M. *et. al.*, Structural Damage due to Cyclones and their Retrofitting, World Congress on Disaster Management, WFEO'S Vol. II, 2004

Floods are a recurring phenomenon in chronically flood prone regions in India. Floods affect around 7.56 million hectares of area (2.30 per cent of country's area) and 3.3 million hectares of crop lands every year (4 per cent of the cropped area). Eastern India, comprising Uttar Pradesh, Bihar, West Bengal, Assam, and Orissa account for about 70 per cent of the flood impacts in the country. The death toll due to major floods in India is shown in Table 11.

Table 11
Major Floods of India

Year	*Number of people killed*	*Location*
1961	2,000	North
1968	4,892	(1) Rajasthan, Gujarat - (2) Noth-East, West Bengal, Assam
1971	4,023	North India
1978	8,800	North, Northeast
1980	1,600	Uttar Pradesh, Bihar, Gujarat, Kerala, Haryana
1989	1,591	Maharashtra, Andhra Pradesh, Gujarat
1994	2,001	Assam, Arunachal Pradesh, Jammu and Kashmir, Himachal, Punjab, Uttar Pradesh, Goa, Kerala, Gujarat states
1995	1,479	Bihar, Haryana, Jammu & Kashmir, Punjab, Uttar Pradesh, West Bengal, Mahrashtra
1997	1,442	Andhra Pradesh, Arunachal Pradesh, Assam, Bihar, Gujarat, Himachal Pradesh, Jammu and Kashmir, Karnataka, Kera, Maharashtra, Madhya Pradesh, Orissa, Punjab, Rajasthan, Sikkim, Uttar Pradesh, West Bengal states
1998	1,811	Assam, Arunachal, Bihar, Kerala, Meghalaya, Punjab, Sikkim, Uttar Pradesh, West Bengal states
2000	1,290	Gujarat, Andhra Pradesh, Assam, Arunachal Pradesh, Bihar, Himachal Pradesh, Kerala, Madhya Pradesh, Punjab, Uttar Pradesh, West Bengal

Source: NDMD, MOH, Government of India, Delhi

The flood of 2000 alone killed about 1300 persons in Gujarat, Andhra Pradesh, Assam, Arunachal Pradesh, Bihar, Himachal Pradesh, Kerala, Madhya Pradesh, Punjab, Uttar Pradesh and West Bengal. Even, floods have adversely affected economy and society of major metropolitan cities like Mumbai, Surat, Ahmadabad, Raipur, and Pune etc. in the recent past. The annual damage due to heavy rains landslides and floods is shown in Table 12.

In 2001, 122 districts were hit by floods and affected 21.110 million population. Mapping of flood prone areas; land use regulation and control; construction of engineered structures; flood management; and community based mitigation such as sedimentation clearance, reforestation, etc. may reduce the adverse impact of floods in vulnerable areas.

Table 12
Damage Due to Floods in India

Year	Districts affected	Villages affected (No)	Population affected (Lakh)	Crop Area affected (Lakh Ha.)	Houses Damaged (no.)	Human life loss (no.)	Cattle loss (No.)	Estimated value of loss to houses (Rs. in crore)	Estimated of value of Public Properties (Rs. in crore)
1999	202	33,158	328.12	8.45	884,823	1,375	3,861	0.72	
2000	200	29,964	416.24	34.79	2,736,355	3,048	102,121	631.25	389.72
2001	122	32,363	210.71	18.72	346,878	834	21,269	195.57	676.05

Source: Annual Reports, Natural Disaster Management Division, Ministry of Agriculture.

Drought is an insidious natural hazard that results from a departure of precipitation from expected or normal that is insufficient to meet the demands of human, plant and animal activities. Almost 35 per cent of the country's area, receiving annual average rainfall of less than 750 mm is prone to drought once in three years. In these areas, almost 200 million people are affected in varying degrees by drought (Table 13). In the arid and the semi arid regions, seasonal periodicities can affect the pattern of livelihood system of farmers.

Table 13
Losses due to Drought in India

Year	*Districts affected*	*Villages affected (No)*	*Population affected (Lakh)*	*Damage to crops area (Lakh Ha.)*	*Estimated value of damaged crops (Rs. crore)*	*Cattle population affected (in lakh)*
1999	125	–	369.88	134.22	6.44	345.60
2000	110	54,883	378.14	367.00	371.87	541.67
2001	103	22,255	88.19	67.44	NA	34.28
Total	338	77,138	836.21	568.66	378.31	921.55

Source: Annual Reports, Natural Disaster Management Division, Ministry of Agriculture

HUMAN INSTIGATED

In a society where gender, caste, religion, region, and class differentials are extremely predominated human made disasters tend to occur more frequently and often with great intensity. Communal riots, terrorism, militancy, ethnic conflicts, plight of refugees, internally, displaced persons, road and train accidents, forest and buildings fire, epedemics and industrial accidents etc. cause heavy toll of human lives and property. The natural disasters cannot be properly predicted and controlled while manmade disasters may be controlled through proper planning and preparedness.

Forest fires are a major cause of degradation of India's forests. About 90 per cent of the forest fires in India are created by humans. India witnessed the most severe forest fire in the recent time during the summer of 1945 in the hills of Uttarakhand and Himachal Pradesh. The fires were very severe and attracted the attention of whole nation. These affected 6.78 million hectares of forest land. About 3.75 million hectares of forests are affected by fire annually, as per Forest Protection Division, Ministry of Forests and Environment, Government of India.

Fires in Urban Structure - houses, buildings, and other structure also cause destruction to property and human lives. Heating sources, cooking accidents, electric short, combustible and hazardous materials etc. cause the fire in urban structures. In the event of fires, chemical leakages, or explosions occurring in industrial facilities, people are exposed to risks and hazards. Bhopal chemical gas leak disaster (1984) was the worst industrial disasters of India. The tragedy was a technological accident in which 45 towns of highly poisonous methyl iso-cyanide gas along with hydrogen cyanide and other reaction products leaked out of the pesticide factory of Union Carbide into the night air of Bhopal. The official death toll reached to 3,598 in 1989 and thousands still face a fate worse than death.

The nature and impact of disasters are changing. They need to be placed in the larger context of present day realities. Most experts refuse to include epidemics in their short list of disasters, costing the world dearly in terms of morbidity, mortality, and hence, the human capital. Today, aid and relief go largely to non-biological disasters while increasingly treatment immune and mutagenic bio-systems wreck havoc in the developing countries. The Surat plague outbreak in 1994 killed 56 people nationwide. This outbreak served as a chilling reminder of how rapid urbanization and deterioration of the urban environment can bring people into contact with forgotten disease factors. The scientific studies show that an increase in the temperature viz. 1-2 degrees would enable mosquitoes to extent their range to low geographical areas, leading to an increase in cases of malaria and several other infectious diseases especially in populations living at the periphery of the areas currently prone to these diseases. Tuberculosis, Malaria, Kalajar Dengue, plague, Japanese encephalitis, diarrhea diseases, including cholera, poliomyelitis, HIV/AIDS, etc. are some of the chronic diseases which have caused concern today.

India has one of the largest populations of people living with HIV/AIDS, second only to South Africa CVN-AIDS, 2003). An estimated 5.1 million individuals currently live with the HIV infection, across all states. The HIV prevalence rate among the adult population is 0.8 per cent, but the absolute number of people living with HIV/AIDS is very high and growing gradually. The endemic is challenging the development achievements of recent years and raising fundamental issues of human rights. In India, HIV/AIDS epidemic is characterized by heterogeneity; it seems to be following the type 4 pattern, where the epidemic shifts from the most vulnerable populations (including sex workers, injecting drug users, men who have sex with man) to bridge populations (client of sex workers, STD patients, partners of drug users) and then to the general population. The epidemic continues to shift towards woman and young people. Migrates both within and between states is a major source of transmission of infection. Srivastava and Sasikumar (2003) estimated that migrants account for 26.6 per cent of the country's population. This shows a declining trend, however, the absolute number of migrants grew from 67.7 million in 1971 to 231.9 million in 1991. Migration of semi skilled and unskilled labours to West Asia and OECD countries started in mid 1970; the growth in demand for foreign labour was triggered by the oil price boom. South Arabia and UAE were the principal destinations for Indian migrants during the past two decades (Table 14) State-wise distribution of emigration clearances granted during the period 1993-2001 shows that 16 states contributed to the process of emigration to the OECD countries. Three states - Kerala, Tamil Nadu, and Andhra Pradesh-together accounted for 60 per cent of those who obtained emigration clearance (Table 15). The returning migrant is often unaware of whichever has been infected with HIV and the potential risk of infection that his spouse and urban children face.

Trans-border migrants in India - especially Nepali, and Bangladesh migrants also face the high risk of HIV infection.

Nepalese women migrants are highly vulnerable to commercial and sexual exploitation (UNDP, 2004). Those who are engaged in commercial sex line in unhygienic and inhuman conditions, even those who work as domestic help are at risk of being physically and sexually abused by their employers. Bangladesh migrants are less vulnerable them Nepalese migrants however, their number in India is rapidly increasing which causes severe stress on civic services.

Table 14
Distribution of Indian Migrant Workers in West Asia

(%)

Country	*1979*	*1983*	*1987*	*1991*	*2000*
Bahrain	5.19	3.28	7.03	6.64	4.23
Iraq	3.99	5.46	3.19	–	–
Kuwait	12.97	12.55	9.12	5.85	9.12
Libya	2.00	4.37	2.28	0.80	–
Oman	11.98	10.92	16.79	14.62	11.07
Katar	5.99	4.37	4.56	4.98	3.91
Saudi Arabia	19.96	29.48	34.67	39.87	39.09
UAE	30.34	27.29	20.53	26.58	32.57
Others	7.58	2.29	1.82	0.66	–
Total	100.00	100.00	100.00	100.00	100.00

Source: Based on Data of Ministry of External Affairs, Government of India, UNDP, No Safety Signs Here, Delhi, 2004

Table 15
State-Wise Distribution of Emigration Clearances Granted

(%)

State	*1993*	*1994*	*1995*	*1996*	*1997*	*1998*	*1999*	*2000*	*2001*
Andhra Pradesh	8.12	8.11	7.29	7.24	9.19	8.62	9.58	12.47	13.64
Bihar	1.72	1.60	1.41	1.40	1.53	4.10	2.96	2.80	3.55
Gujarat	3.14	3.01	2.93	2.89	3.07	2.40	2.00	2.38	3.99
Goa	0.39	0.04	0.23	0.23	0.25	0.27	0.27	0.55	0.82
Haryana	0.19	0.18	0.19	0.22	0.22	0.48	0.15	0.02	0.06
Karnataka	7.84	7.58	0.06	8.15	9.70	3.25	2.67	4.54	3.60
Kerala	35.41	36.30	15.80	40.40	37.49	25.82	30.52	28.95	22.40
Madhya Pradesh	1.49	1.37	1.02	1.00	0.94	1.81	0.46	0.71	1.84
Maharastra	8.04	7.56	6.34	6.09	6.04	6.94	4.98	5.55	8.30
Orissa	0.80	0.85	0.89	0.83	0.84	0.58	0.28	0.24	1.10
Punjab	3.24	2.93	2.85	2.84	2.98	7.57	7.66	4.17	4.54
Rajasthan	5.76	6.45	6.83	4.40	6.78	5.58	4.95	4.23	5.48

Contd...

State	1993	1994	1995	1996	1997	1998	1999	2000	2001
Tamil Nadu	16.04	16.58	15.83	15.69	15.79	19.65	23.93	26.56	22.52
Uttar Pradesh	5.73	5.36	4.56	4.58	4.26	9.50	5.95	3.81	5.08
West Bengal	0.64	0.47	0.55	0.57	0.54	1.06	0.79	0.81	1.76
Delhi	0.99	0.90	0.79	0.70	0.60	1.56	1.80	1.32	1.16
Others	0.46	0.72	24.42	2.77	0.27	0.81	1.05	0.90	0.00
Total	100.00	100.00	100.00	100.00	100.00	100.00	100.00	100.00	100.00

Source: Based on data of Ministry of Labour, Government of India, UNDP,No Safety Signs Here, Delhi, 2004

The illegal immigration from Bangladesh has become a serious problem; it has changed the demographic landscape and affected Delhi, Rajasthan, Gujarat, Maharastra. In India, the quantum of immigration is small in relation to the total population of the country. There are about 8 to 10 million Bangladeshis nationals in India who are spread all over north India from West Bengal to Rajasthan (Week, December 5, 1993). The illegal immigration from Bangladesh has caused concern in Mizoram, Tripura, Assam, and West Bengal. Even, it caused to some extent the emergence of militancy and ethnic unrestness in North East region of India (Tewari and Singh, 1998). The militancy in North East region has caused concuss to the policy makers and development activists. The increasing trend of violence and destruction of property in the region has caused setback to development efforts (Table 16).

Table 16
Militancy in North East Region (2003)

Head	Assam	Tripura	Nagaland	Manipur	Meghalaya	Arunachal Pradesh	Mozoram
Incidents	358	394	199	243	85	50	03
Extremists Killed	207	50	70	128	37	31	–
Extremists Arrested	215	336	90	232	103	32	–
Security Forces killed	12	39	03	27	07	01	01
Arms Looted	02	36	15	03	02	02	–
Arms Recovered	186	76	64	29	53	34	-

Contd...

Head	*Assam*	*Tripura*	*Nagaland*	*Manipur*	*Meghalaya*	*Arunachal Pradesh*	*Mozoram*
Arms Surrendered	–	–	–	–	–	–	–
Extremists Surrendered	328	268	29	05	20	18	01
Civilians killed	182	207	13	50	35	07	–
No. of Persons Kidnapped	89	221	163	81	51	42	

Source: Annual Report, 2003-04, Ministry of Home, Government of India, Delhi

Though, scheme of rehabilitation of surrendered extremists in North East has checked insurgency, however, a large number of districts in Tripura, Mizoram, Assam, Manipur and Nagaland are affected with militancy. Similarly, the terrorism in Jammu & Kashmir and Punjab has derailed the development efforts for a long time. However, terrorism activities in Jammu & Kashmir, supported by neighbouring countries are causing tremendous loss to human lives and public property (Table 17).

Table 17
Terrorists activities in Jammu & Kashmir

Year	*No. of Incidents*	*Civilians killed*	*SFs killed*	*Terrorists killed*	*Foreign Terrorist killed*
1990	4158	461	155	550	14
1991	3765	382	173	844	12
1992	4817	634	189	819	14
1993	5247	747	198	1310	90
1994	5829	820	200	1596	122
1995	5938	1031	237	1332	85
1997	3420	971	193	1075	197
1998	2932	889	236	999	319
1999	3071	873	355	1002	305
2000	3074	847	397	1520	436
2001	4522	996	536	2020	625
2002	4038	1008	453	1707	508
2003	3401	795	314	1494	470
2004(upto March)	638	150	62	263	60
Total	59864	11945	3882	17820	3396

Source: Annual Report, 2003-04, Ministry of Home, Government of India, Delhi.

The increasing influence and incidence of violence by Naxalism in India is also causing concern. Naxalite extremism is spread over 9 states (Table 18).

Table 18
Incidents of violence by Naxalite - Extremists

State	*2001*	*2002*	*2003*	*2004 (upto March)*	*2006 (upto June)*
Andhra Pradesh	461 (180)	346 (96)	575 (139)	155 (50)	104 (18)
Bihar	169 (111)	239 (117)	249 (127)	79 (32)	63 (30)
Chhatisgarh	105 (37)	304 (55)	254 (74)	61 (14)	360 (244)
Jharkhand	355 (200)	353 (157)	341 (117)	80 (18)	169 (58)
Madhya Pradesh	21 (92)	17 (3)	13 (1)	2 (1)	6 (-)
Maharastra	34 (7)	83 (29)	74 (31)	10 (10)	56 (25)
Orissa	30 (11)	68 (11)	49 (15)	19 (4)	21 (4)
Uttar Pradesh	22 (12)	20 (6)	13 (8)	3 (3)	6 (2)
West Bengal	9 (4)	17 (7)	6 (1)	4 (8)	14 (11)
Other States	2 (-)	18 (1)	16 (-)	2 (1)	5 (-)
Total	1208 (564)	1465 (482)	1590 (513)	415 (132)	806 (392)

Source: Annual Report, 2003-04, Ministry of Home, Government of India, Rastriya Sahara, 6 March 2007, Lucknow

The extremism has its root cause in socio-economic backwardness of the region and development deprivation of weaker sections of society. The terrorist activities are being supported by neighbouring countries. These are being operated from Territory of Bangladesh, Pakistan, Myanmar, Bhutan and Nepal. There is marked increase in attacks on government and private properties by naxilites displacing a growing penchant for attacking railway property.

India like many other developing countries, is witnessing a spiraling increase in the number of vehicles clogging its roads.

Between 1970 and 2003, number of registered vehicles increased by about 48 times. During 2003, registered vehicles were reported to be 67.03 million. By 2050, there will be over 267 million vehicles on Indian roads (World Disaster Report, 1998). Of the world wide annual average of 0.7 million road accidents, 10 per cent occur in India. In 2003, number of road accidents was reported to be 406.73 million in which 85.99 million persons were killed. Number of accidents per ten thousand vehicles was reported to be 60.68 while number of persons killed per ten thousand vehicles was 12.88 (Table 19). Most of the road fatalities were reported in Andhra Pradesh, Mahrashtra, Rajasthan, Uttar Pradesh, Tamil Nadu, and Karnataka. The economic cost of road accidents is equivalent to about one per cent of Gross National Product.

Table 19
Road Accidents in India

Year	*Total No. of Road Accidents*	*Total No. of Persons killed*	*Total number of Registered Motor Vehicles (in '000)*	*No. of Accidents per '0000 Vehicles*	*No. of Persons killed per '0000 Vehicles*
1970	114100	14500	1401	814.42	103.50
1980	153200	24000	4521	338.86	53.09
1990	282600	54100	19152	147.56	28.25
1991	295131	56278	21374	138.08	26.33
1992	275541	60113	23507	117.22	25.57
1993	284646	60380	25505	111.60	23.67
1994	325864	64463	27660	117.81	23.31
1995	351999	70781	30295	116.19	23.36
1996	371204	74665	33786	109.87	22.10
1997	373671	76977	37332	100.09	20.62
1998	385018	79919	41368	93.07	19.32
1999	386456	81966	44875	86.12	18.27
2000	391449	78911	48857	80.12	16.15
2001	405637	80888	54991	73.76	14.71
2002	407497	84674	58924	69.16	14.37
2003	406726	85998	67033	60.68	12.83

Source: Ministry of Transport, Government of India.

India's Ariel skies and airports seem relatively safe an average of two accidents and 10 deaths a year, however, India's skies are a battleground of bad policies, civil military and technological obsolescence. The increased aircraft movement and number of private air lines have increased density with more vulnerability of air accidents.

India has the largest rail system which played by ad-hoc modernization, a bureaucratic outlook on some of the worst global accidents and an inadequately trained work force (Mathur, 2000). The increasing incidence of bomb blasts and explosions in trains has caused concern. There has been fluctuating trend in rail accidents and fatalities. During 1997-98, 420 rail accidents caused 316 fatalities (Table 20). During 2001-02, 413 rail accidents occurred in India. Number of train accidents per million km. has been reported to be 0.55 while number of casualties per million passengers carried was reported just 0.02 (Table 21).

Table 20
Railway Accidents in India

Year	*Total Railway Accidents*	*Total Fatalities in Railway Accidents*	*Accidents at Level Crossing*	*Fatalities in Level Crossing*	*Total in injuries in Railway Accidents*	*Injuries in level crossing accidents*
1988-89	545	231	55	52	736	134
1989-90	541	239	42	51	992	192
1990-91	532	322	37	75	88	175
1991-92	742	235	48	104	896	302
1992-93	746	282	71	116	908	222
1993-94	675	369	71	168	906	312
1994-95	604	296	74	187	676	159
1995-96	440	589	69	138	934	191
1996-97	426	353	66	221	610	264
1997-98	420	316	65	134	977	179

Source: Annual Report Indian Railways, New Delhi, 1998

Table 21
Details of Railway Accidents in India

Particulars	*1997-98*	*1998-99*	*1999-2000*	*2000-01*	*2001-02*
Collisions	35	24	20	20	30
Derailments	285	292	325	344	279
Level crossing accidents	66	67	93	83	88
Fire in trains	6	5	21	15	8
Misc. accidents	–	–	–	2	8

Contd...

Particulars	*1997-98*	*1998-99*	*1999-2000*	*2000-01*	*2001-02*
Total	392	388	459	464	413
Train accidents per million kilometre	0.58	0.56	0.64	0.64	0.55
No. of persons killed	171	280	338	55	85
No. of passengers injured	747	615	716	281	565
Casualties per million passengers carried	0.20	0.06	0.22	0.01	0.02
Compensation paid (Rs. lakhs)	240.89	489.65	110.95	88.07	482.46

Source: Year Book 2001, Indian Railways.

INSTITUTIONAL ARRANGEMENTS

India has integrated administrative machinery for management of disasters at national, state, district and sub-district levels. However, the basic responsibility of undertaking rescue, relief and rehabilitation measures is that of state government concerned. The Central Government supplements the efforts of the states by providing financial and logistic support.

The Contingency Action Plan identifies initiatives required to be taken by various Central Ministries and Public Departments in the wake of natural disasters. Ministry of Home Affairs is the nodal Ministry for coordination of relief and response and overall natural disaster management, and the Department of Agriculture and Cooperation is the nodal Ministry for drought management. Other Ministries are assigned the responsibility of providing emergency support in case of disasters that fall in their purview as indicated in the Table 22.

Table 22
Ministries responsive for Various Categories of Disasters

Disaster Type	*Nodal Ministry*
Natural Disaster & Management (Other than Drought)	Ministry of Home Affairs
Drought Relief	Ministry of Agriculture
Air Accidents	Ministry of Civil Aviation
Railway Accidents	Ministry of Railways
Chemical Disasters	Ministry of Environment & Forests
Biological Disasters	Ministry of Health
Nuclear Disasters	Department of Atomic Energy

The responsibility to cope with natural disasters is essentially that of the state Government. The Chief Secretary of the state heads a state level Committee which is in overall charge of the relief operations in the state and the Relief Commissioners who are in charge of the relief and rehabilitation measures in the wake of natural disasters in their states function under the overall direction and control of the state level Committee. In many states, Secretary, Department of Revenue is also in charge of relief (Government of India, 2003:195).

The district administration is the focal point for implementation of all governmental plans and activities. The administration of relief is the responsibility of the Collector/ District Magistrate who exercises coordinating and supervising powers over all departments at the district level.

The 73rd and 74th constitutional amendments gave the status of 'Institutions of self government' to Panchayati Raj Institutions. The constitutional amendments also laid down necessary guidelines for the structure of their composition, powers, functions, devolution of finances, regular holding of elections and reservation of seats for weaker sections and women. These local bodies may be effective instruments in tackling disasters through early warming system, relief distribution, providing shelter to the victims, medical assistant etc. The Eleventh Finance Commission too paid detailed attention to the issue of disaster management and came out with a number of recommendations, including expenditure on restoration of infrastructure and other capital assets as well as capacity building. Training and education are crucial for mitigating disasters and also for disaster response. Training is an integral part of the capacity building as trained personnel respond much better to different disasters. The multi sectoral and multi hazard prevention based approach to disaster management requires specific professional inputs. Similarly, preventive disaster management and development of a national ethos of prevention calls for awareness generation at all levels. Again, capacity building should not be limited to professionals and personnel involved in disaster management but should also focus on building the knowledge, attitude and skills of a community to cope with the effects of disasters.

The Yokohama Convention in May 1994 underlined the need for an emphatic shift in the strategy for disaster management. It was inter alia stressed that disaster prevention mitigation, preparedness and relief are four elements which contribute to and gain from the implementation of sustainable development policies. The Government of India has adopted mitigation and prevention as essential components of development strategy. In order to respond affectively to flood, Ministry of Home Affairs has initiated National Disaster Risk Management Programme in all the flood prone states. Elected representatives and officials of local bodies are being trained in flood disaster management under the programme. Bihar, Orissa, West Bengal, Assam and Uttar Pradesh are among 17 multi hazards prone states where this programme is being implemented with assistance from UNDP, USAID and European Commission.

A comprehensive programme has been taken up for earth quake risk mitigation. The building construction in urban and sub-urban areas is regulated by Town Country Planning Acts and Building Regulations. A National Core Group for Earthquake Risk Mitigation has been constituted consisting of experts in earthquake engineering and administration. Review of Building Bye-Laws and Adoption is being insured by the various state Governments. A National Programme for Capacity Building of Engineers and Architects in Earthquake Risk Mitigation has been implemented by the Central Government. Training for rural masons for construction of earthquake resistance buildings and houses is being provided under UNDP - Government of India, Disaster Management Programme in various States. Retrofitting of lifeline buildings is also been insured by the State Governments. An Earthquake Mitigation Project has been drawn with an estimated cost of Rs. 1132 crores. The programme includes training of masons in earthquake resistance constructions and adopting techno-legal regimes by state governments. Accelerated Urban Earthquake Vulnerability Reduction Programme has been taken in 38 cities in Seismic Zone III, IV and V in a population of half a million and above. Training Programmes have been organized for engineers and architects to impart knowledge about seismically safe construction and implementation of Bureau of Indian Standards Norms. A National Cyclone Mitigation Project with cost of Rs. 1050 crores has been drawn up in cyclone prone states. The project envisages construction of cyclone shelters, coastal shelter belt plantation, strengthening of warning systems, training and education etc. A Disaster Risk Management Programme has been taken in 169 districts in 17 multi hazards state prone with assistance from UNDP, USAID and European Union. Importantly, Disaster Management Faculties have already been created in Administrative Training Institutes located in 28 districts. Disaster Management as a subject in social sciences has been introduced in school curriculum for classes VIII and IX. Besides, 8 battalions of Disaster Risk Response have been created for providing prompt response during disasters. In order to provide training and knowledge for prevention, mitigation, response of disaster as well as rehabilitation and reconstruction of affected persons and areas, academic institutions have been established with financial assistance from government. However, disaster management required multi disciplinary and pro active approach.

DISASTER MANAGEMENT

Disaster risk management can be addressed in three ways: structural measures, non-structural measures and establishing communication networks. Structural measures would reduce the impact of disasters and non-structural measures would enhance the management skills and improve capacities of the community, local self governments, urban local bodies and the state authorities to prepare, prevent and respond effectively to disasters. Non-structural measures are more important and include vulnerability mapping, risk assessment analysis, hazard zoning, inventory of resources to meet the emergency etc.

The dynamics and machinery of urban development is complex. Therefore, careful attention is needed to find the best opportunities and effective routes to introduce safety measures. Many authorities fail to recognize the rich range of measures that need to be adopted and integrated into a viable and affordable programme. The expanding scale of urban pressures, problems, and risks in India is a daunting challenge. However, India has certain assets that many countries envy when it comes to reducing urban risks. There is strong and increasing government commitment to disaster protection, a vibrant civil society's network which provides base of community participation and high share of private sector in humanitarian aid to disaster's victims and reconstructions of disaster affected areas. However, there is lack of coordination and integrated approach for disaster response.

Chart 1 denotes elements of disaster management. There are mainly three elements of disaster mitigation viz. risk management, prevention and preparedness.

Chart 1
Main elements of Disaster Management

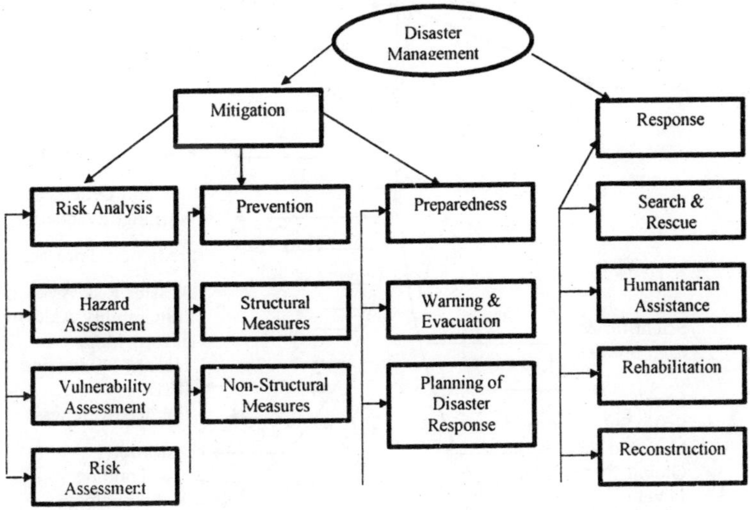

Source: Arya, A.S. (2004)

Chart-2 shows functional structure of natural disaster mitigation.The main three elements are rehabilitation, prevention and response. In responsive measures, relief, medical aid, shelter, food rescue, warning, evacuation, assessment of vulnerability and risks, public awareness, capacity building for livelihoods restoration etc. are included.

Chart 2
Functional Structure of Natural Disaster Mitigation

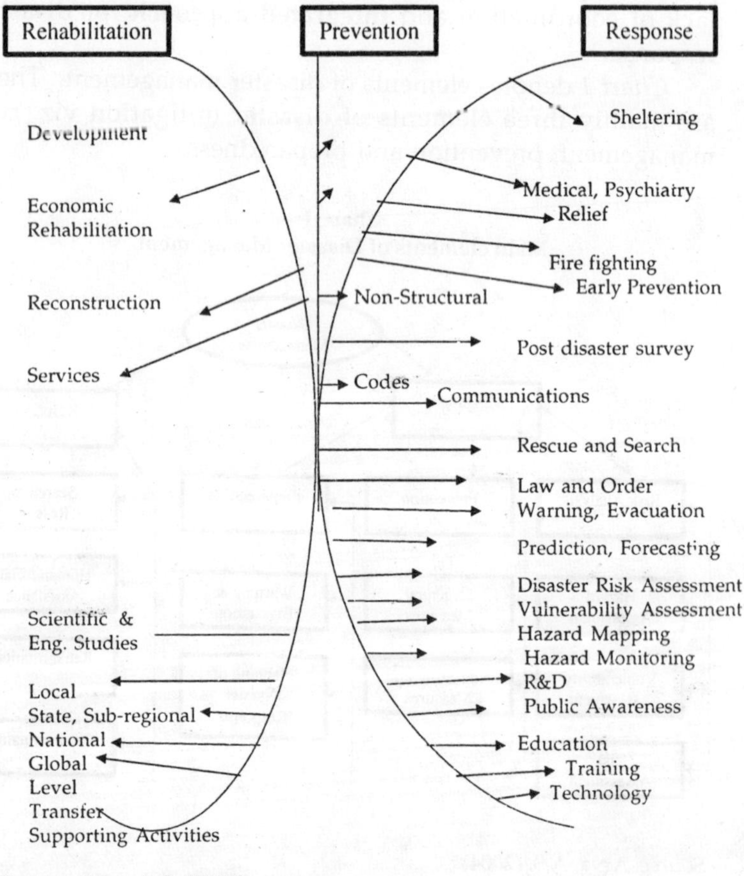

Source: Arya, A.S. (2004)

Disasters are the ultimate test of emergency response capability. The ability to effectively deal with disasters is becoming relevant because of the increasing risk factors. Increase in population density (Quarantell, 1981), population shifts and increasing technology are some of the important factors for increasing risks, leading to disasters. As areas become more densely populated, there are more potential victims when a disaster strikes. National disasters such as earthquakes, hurricanes, cyclones, Tsunami, and floods tend to result in greater losses due to densely populated areas in India. Another reason for increasing disaster losses are that population density in disaster prone areas is increasing. The increasing settlements development in high risk areas is the cause of concern. The pattern of settlement in high risk areas is reflected in the increasing mortality ratio in India. In the process of setting high risk areas, natural protection against environmental threats is removed. In India, the vegetative coverage and forests were destroyed in coastal areas for promoting shrimp farming, business, and tourism and housing colonies. This lead to damage of natural protection against hurricanes, and Tsunami and ultimately Tsunami affected to the large population in coastal areas in southern states recently. The vulnerability of people living in high risk areas is increasing because the habitations are often unaware of potential risks and how to deal with them. Even, the prices of land for house construction in high risk areas are lower which attract people for housing construction, even without proper approval of housing structures. People are living in structures that are not designed to resist the forces of local hazards. In India, earthquakes have affected severely due to lack of good design technology and inadequate earthquake resistance housing and building structures. The new technology is also adding to the list of disaster agents at an ever increasing rate. A large quantity of hazardous chemicals, wastes, bio-medical wastes, and dumping adds proliferation of high risk office buildings and hotels that subject their inhabitants to fire threats not experienced before. The society is also becoming more dependent on technology and specialization, making more vulnerable to disaster (Quarantell, 1985). Our dependence on computers is introducing a new form of disaster vulnerability (Drabek 1986: 375).

In the context of ever increasing risks of disaster losses, it is imperative to deal with these catastrophes with full preparedness and planning. In disasters there are often conditions that may make the traditional division of labour and resources, characteristics of routine emergency management, unsuitable for disaster response (Heide, E.A.). These are as follows:

- Disaster may put demands on organizations, requiring them to make internal changes in structure and delegation of responsibilities;
- Disasters may create demands that exceed the capacities of single organizations, requiring them to share tasks and resources with other organizations that use unfamiliar procedures;
- Disaster may attract the participation of organization and individual volunteers who usually do not respond to emergencies;
- Disasters may cross jurisdictional boundaries, resulting in multiple organizations being faced with overlapping responsibilities;
- Disasters may create new tasks for which no organization has traditional responsibility;
- Disasters may render unusable the normal tools and facilities used in emergency response;
- Disasters may result in the spontaneous formation of new organizations that did not exist before.

The typical response to a disaster includes multiple independent organizations from the private sector as well as from agencies of city, country, state, region and district governments. Disasters do not need to cover large geographical areas in order to cross multiple levels of government responsibility. However, disaster management is the only responsibility of government. Community based organizations and NGOs have to play a critical role in disaster management.

Disasters are characterized by great uncertainty. Often the character and extent of damage and the secondary threats are not immediately apparent and therefore the necessary counter measures not undertaken. Disasters often create the need for different organizations to share resources.Therefore, coordination of multi organizational task accomplishment is required. The needs such as fuel and maintenance for vehicles, sanitary facilities, food, shelter and rest facilities, relief and replacement, personnel and emergency message, contact arrangement also are to be included in the logistic support of an organization responding to a disaster (Kallsan 1983:28). In contrast to daily emergencies, disasters often call for large scale search and rescue operations. An important security task in disasters is keeping unauthorized persons out of the disaster area in order to prevent looting and decrease congestion hampering rescue efforts, and to prevent persons from being injured in the wreckage. Moreover, mass handling of the dead creates problems that may not have been faced in routine emergencies. Handling the dead poses different problems in disasters. The other tasks that are important in disaster response are:

- Warning and communicating with the public
- Shelter and feeding of displaced persons
- Evacuating neighbourhoods
- Evacuating hospitals, prisons, nursing homes and psychiatric facilities
- Coordinating volunteers
- Acquiring and allocating unusual resources
- Dealing with mass arrival carcasses
- Dealing with livestock or family pets that had to be left behind or sheltered (Drabek, 1986:116)
- Procedures for condemning damaged buildings
- Disposing of unclaimed valuable and merchandise found in the rubble at the scene (Moore, 1958:85)
- Control of air traffic (Drabek, 1981: 179)
- Disposing of large amounts of donations

- Controlling emergency vehicle traffic in order to avoid blockage of routes by emergency vehicles
- Checking the hospitals, nursing homes and day care centres that may need assistance
- Prioritizing of utility sources delivery

Adequate communication is a recurring challenge in disaster response. The importance of communication is its ability to get people to work together on a common task or toward a common goal to coordinate. It is the process by which each person understands that how his individual efforts intermesh with those of others. The information is required for need assessment and rescue operations. The most crucial types of information that need to be shared are related to (Brunacini, 1985:54):

(a) An ongoing assessment of what the disaster situation is and what disaster counter measures need to be undertaken;

(b) An ongoing determination of what resources are needed to undertake the counters measure. What resources are presently available and how they can be obtained;

(c) A determination of the priority of needed disaster counter measures;

(d) A determination of what persons and organizations will be responsible for the various tasks necessary to accomplish the counter measures (Sorensen, 1985:32)

Computers are not only useful for sharing and analyzing disaster information, but also for sharing it. The internet facility may provide strong base for efficient communications in the following measures (Wohlworth, 1987; Carroll 1983; Carroll, 1985, Wallace 1985).

- Sharing and collecting information about what agencies have responded and what resources they have dispatched.
- Locating and specifying procedures for obtaining special disaster resources;

- Sharing information about the location, scope, and character of the disaster and damage that has resulted;
- Sharing information about the status of transportation routes facilities, docking and landing sites;
- Generating and sharing predictions about weather and other expected conditions;
- Obtaining information on how to deal with a specific hazardous chemical;
- General electronic mail.

Thus, it is clear that the communication and equipments and procedures used by most emergency agencies are established primarily to deal with information flow within the organization. Disasters care for inter agency communication also. To some extent, it can be facilitated by the availability of inter-agency radio networks. However, the critical information requirements of the various organizations involved in disaster response need to be mutually understood and the responsibility for gathering and disseminating it needs to be made clear.

Significantly, disasters pose problems for resource management. A prerequisite to effective and efficient resource management is an accurate system for overall analysis of the disaster situation and the available resources (Dynes 1974; 77; Quarantelli, 1983:68). Overall, need, assessment, involves two major processes: (1) situation analysis; and (2) resource analysis. Situation analysis is the collection of information about the extent and character of the disaster itself and problems that have to be tackled. While resource analysis involves the collection of information about the resources needed to be handled. The source allocation of disaster resources depends on the task priorities already decided for the response of disaster.

In contrast to most routine emergencies, efficient response in disaster requires procedures for triage and casualty distribution. Triage has been called the key stone to mass casuality management (Bowers, 1960:59). The technique for assigning priorities for treatment of the injured when resources are limited is called triage. Generally, attention is given first to those with the most urgent conditions and to those who are the most salvageable (Silverstein, 1984:8). The triage is beneficial in disaster response due to the facts: (i) triage separates out those who need rapid medical care to some life or lives, (ii) by separating out the minor injuries; triage reduces the urgent burden on medical facilities and organizations, (iii) by providing for the equitable and rationale distribution of causalities among the available hospitals. Triage reduces the burden on each to a manageable level, often even to non-disaster level. In order to distribute casualties rationally among the hospitals, capacity assessment of the existing hospitals, dispensaries and clinics need to be examined.

It is to be noted that convincing the public to evacuate areas threatened by impending disaster is often challenging one (Mcluckie, 1970:2). In disasters, communication with the public assumes new dimensions not present in routine emergencies. Warning can be one of the most important types of disaster communication allowing the recipients to avoid the threat altogether or to significantly lesson its effects. However, people are often reluctant to evacuate the premises stricken by disaster (Quarantell, 1972:67). There are a number of reasons why persons hesitate to evacuate in the face of threatening disaster. They may not be convinced that they are actually at risk, they may wish to stay and protect their property, or they may want to assure the safety of other family members and property before leaving (Perry 1985; 60; Drabek, 1986:84). Those living in disaster threatened areas are more likely to evacuate if they are encouraged by invitations from relatives and friends outside.

In the impact area people prefer to seek shelter with friends or relatives rather than at public shelters. Importantly, the process of warning is complicated since it requires the accomplishment of a number of tasks. Jammed telephone lines and circuits as well as traffic congestion, make the process more difficult.

Disaster response and preparedness is most effective when it is built in to development programmes. In long run, disaster mitigation could be implemented at nominal cost by incorporating them into development programmes. The expenditure on disaster mitigation would reduce the potential losses that disaster cause. Significantly, urban planning urgently begs fundamental conceptual change, with a need for locating urban disaster management strategies in a holistic framework embracing issues like poverty, provision of institutional support for informal sector activities, over urbanization, environmental degradation and unchecked consumerism etc. A sound, effective and people centric urban disaster management strategy can emerge only in the context of a truly sustainable, and people centric development paradigm. Disaster management and mitigation be organized around local recovery efforts. In an integrated disaster risk management approach, activities from structural interventions to community based disaster management, which reduces hazard and vulnerability, should be coordinated. It is imperative to orient and train development agencies to integrate disaster risk management into the national and local planning process, thus mainstreaming disaster reduction into development collaboration among the stakeholders is a critical strategy in disaster reduction. It enhances complements the respective capabilities of concerned sectors and organizations in the pursuit of development objectives.

REFERENCES

Arya, A.S. (2004), Engineering Role in Earthquake Disaster Reduction in India, paper presented in World Congress on Natural Disaster Mitigation, by World Federation of Engineering Organization, at Delhi, 19-22, February.

Bowers, W.E. et.al. (1960), Surgical Philosophy in Mass Casualty Management, Springfield, IL, CC, Tharnao.

Brunacini, A.V. (1985), Fire Command, National Fire Protection Association, Quinty, MA.

Brunacini, A.V. (1998), Phoenix Fire Department Operation and Manual Vol. 2, Standard Operating Procedures, Unpublished, Phoenix, A2.

Carroll, J.M. (1983), Emergency Planning: Proceedings of the Conference or Emergency Planning, January 27-29, 1983, San

Diego, CA, Simulation Series, Vol.11(2), Society for Computer Formulation, Lactolla, CA.

Dheri S.K and Mishra, G.C. (2000), Fire: Blazing Questions, in India Disaster Report, OUP, Delhi.

Drabek, T.E. et.al. (1981), Managing Multi Organizational Emergency Responses: Emergent Search and Rescue Networks in Natural Disaster and Remote and Settings, Natural Hazards Information Centre, University of Colorado, Boulder.

Drabek, T.E. (1985), Emergency Management: The Human Factor, Federal Emergency Management Agency, National Emergency Training Centre, Emmetsburg, MD.

Drabek, T.E. (1986), Human System Responses to Disaster: An Inventory of Sociological Findings, Springer-Velar, New York.

Dynes, R.R. et. al. (1974), Organized Behaviour in Disaster, Disaster Research Centre, University of Delaware New York.

Dynes, R.R. et.al. (1977), Organizational Communications and Decision Making in Crises, Disaster Research Centre, University of Delware, New York.

Elegant, S. (2005), Resurrection, Time, April 4 .

Francis, C.M. et. al. (2000), Epidemics: Diseases as Disaster, in India Disaster Report, OUP, Delhi,

Government of India (2002), Disaster Management: Development Perspectives, National Disaster Management Division, Ministry of Home Affairs, Government of India, Delhi.

Government of India - Hazards, Disasters and Your Community: Primer for Parliamentarians, NDM Division, Ministry of Home Affairs, Government of India, Delhi

Government of India - Status of Disaster Management in India, Ministry of Home Affairs, Government of India, New Delhi.

Government of India Tenth Five Year Plan (2002 - 07), Government of India, Delhi.

Hamilton, R.V., et. al. (1985), Social Psychological Interpretation on the Udaukansas, Tornado, Unpublished Report, University of Wichita, October.

Hazarika S., (2000), Ethnic Conflicts in North East, in India Disaster Report, OUP, Delhi.

Heide, Erik Aderfder, Disaster Response: Principles of Preparation and Coordination, Disaster Research Centre, University Delaware, New York.

Jain, A.K., Emergency Planning for Natural Disasters, paper presented in World Congress on Nature Disaster Mitigation, organized by World Federation of Engineering Organization, at Delhi, dated 19-22 Feb. 244.

Kallsen, G. (1983), Collapse of Coalinga, Journal cf Emergency Medical Services 8(7).

Marshall, Andrao. (2005), Healing Hands, Time April 4 .

Mathur, Ranjeet, (2000), Railway Accidents, in India Disaster Report, OUP, Delhi.

Mcluckie, B. (1970), The Warning System in Disaster Situations: A Selective Analysis, Report Series No. 9, Disaster Research Centre, University of Delaware, New York.

Medury and Dhameja (2006), Rehabilitation of Cyclone in Orissa in Administrative Reforms (ed) Amita Singh in India, Sage Publications Delhi.

Moore, H.E. (1958), Tornadoes Over Texas: A Study of Waco and San Angelo in Disaster University of Texas Press, Austin, .

Nath Meenakshi, Sarangi S., (2000),. Industrial Disasters: Working Towards Oblivion Bhopal Gas Tragedy, in India Disaster Report, OUP, Delhi.

Parausraman, S. and Unnikrishnan, P.V. (ed) (2000), India Disaster Report, Oxford University Press, Delhi.

Perry, R.W. (1985), Comprehensive Emergency Management: Evacuating Threatened Populations, Greenwich, CT, JAI Press, Inc..

Quarantelli, E.L. (1981), Disaster Planning: Small and Large - Past, Present and Future, presented at American Red Cross, EFO Division Disaster Conference, Blacksburg, V.A., February 19-22, 1981, Disaster Research Centre, University of Delaware, New York.

Quarantelli, E.L.(1985), Organizational Behaviour in Disasters and Implications for Disaster Planning Report Series 18, Disaster Research Centre University of Delaware, New York .

Quarantelli, E.L. (1981), Socio-Behavioural Response to Chemical Hazards: Preparations for and Responses to Acute Chemical Emergencies at the Local Community Level, Disaster Research Centre, University of Delaware, New York .

Rai, N. and Singh, A.K., (2006), Disaster Response in India: With Special Reference to Tsunami Disaster, Urban Panorama, Vol. V (1), January-June.

Shashi Kumar S.K., (2002), Trends in International Migration from India- 1950-2000, Paper presented at Labour Mobility and Globalizing World, September 18-19, VVGNLI, ISLE, IHD, Noida.

Silver Mcein M.E. (1984), Triage Decision Trees and Triage Protocols: Changing Strategies for Medical Rescue in Civilian Mass Casualty Situations, U.S. Department of Commerce, Springfield, U.A.

Singh, K.K., (2004), Indian Policy, Legislation and Institutional Arrangements for Urban Risk Mitigation: An Argument for Right Based Approach, paper presented in World Congress on Natural Disaster Mitigation, by World Federation of Engineering Organization, at Delhi, dated 19-22, February.

Singh, U.B., and Singh A.K. (2004), Socio-Economic Dimensions of National Disasters in India: Suggested Strategies for Mitigation, paper presented in World Congress on Natural Disaster Mitigation by World Federation of Engineering Organizations at Delhi, February 19-22.

Sorensen, J.H., et.al. (1989), Inter and Intra Organizational Cohesion in Emergencies, Mass Emergencies and Disasters 3(3), November.

Srivastava R.S.and Sashikumar S.K. (2003), An Overview of Migration in India: Its Implications and Key Issues, JNU, VVGNLI, New Delhi.

Subbiah, A.R. (2004), Natural Disaster Management, Vol. 21, State of Indian Farmers, Academic Foundation, Delhi.

Thomas, V.J., (2000), Road Accidents in India, in India Disaster Report, OUP, Delhi.

Tiwari, B.K. and Singh, A.K., (1998), Bangladeshi Issue in Perspective: The Problem of Immigrants in India, Dynamics of Public Administration, Vol. III-IV (1-2), January, December.

UN Recovery Frame Work in Support of government of India for a Post Tsunami Rehabilitation and Reconstruction Programme, United States, March , 2005.

UNAIDS-Innovative Approaches to HIV Prevention, UNAIDS, Geneva, 2001

UNAIDS - Migrants: Right to Health, UNAIDS, Geneva, 2001

UNDP - HIV Vulnerability and Migration: South Asia Perspectives, UNDP, Delhi, 2002

UNDP - Recovery Framework in Support of Government of India for a Post Tsunami Rehabilitation and Reconstruction Programme, UNDP, Delhi, 2005

UNDP Disaster Risk Management Programme, (2002-07) MoHRD, Government of India, Delhi, 2003.

UNDP No Safety Signs Here, UNDP, Delhi 2004

Wallace, W.A., et.al. (1985), Decision Support Systems for Disaster Management, IW Petak W.J. Emergency Management: A Challenge for Public Administration, special issue, Public Administration Review, Jan .

Wohlworth, N., Putting (1987), Computer Technology to Work in Emergency Planning, Emergency Preparedness Digest, 14(2) April-June.

World Bank, World Bank in India, Newsletter, Vol. 4(3), November 2005.

11

MUNICIPAL FINANCE

Two decades ago, about 1.5 billion people lived in cities. The figure has mounted to 2.6 billion now. In another three decades, more than half of the world's population would become city dwellers. Moreover by 1995, over 45 percent of the world's populations were projected to be living in the urban areas. In India too, urban population has been growing almost twice as fast, and has in fact quadrupled from 50 million in 1947 to over 217 million in 1991. By the year 2001, it is expected to reach 301 million. The size of urban population as also the increase in it has serious repercussions on civic infrastructure and services.

In the recent years, most urban areas in the country have experienced deterioration in the standard and quality of life. In almost every city and town, the availability of basic services has either declined or remained inadequate and sizeable populations in them are without access to such services. Importantly, the new economic policy of the Government of India is aimed at stepping up of economic growth, improved market efficiency and competitiveness and integrating the Indian economy with global commodity markets. The likely increase in urban productivity and population will place a heavy demand on all types of urban infrastructure. Infrastructure bottlenecks in urban centers are likely to pose serious impediments in enhancing urban productivity. Municipal bodies are already under considerable pressure to cope up with the maintenance requirements of existing infrastructure and services. The revenue base of these urban local governments has been eroding consistently, while their responsibilities to augment existing services have been growing. Their dependence on the higher levels of governments for meeting the operation and maintenance requirements has increased phenomenally. Many of them have also accumulated debts.

During 1974-75 and 1986-87, revenue incomes of municipal bodies increased by 53 percent as against revenue expenditure accelerated by more than 420 percent. As a result, it is generally difficult for municipal bodies even to maintain the existing services. Augmentation of these services and provision of services in the rapidly growing urban areas, calls for lumpy investments that are beyond the means of these local governments. Importantly, most municipal bodies in India are financially sick to provide adequate services to their citizens. Again, the share of municipal governments in the total tax revenues of the country has come down to about 4.5 percent in 1980-81 from roughly 8 percent in 1960-61. This is despite the fact that in the same period urban population has increased from about 16 percent of total population in 1961 to approximately 24 percent in 1980-81. The situation has further deteriorated during the period 1980-81 and 1986-87, as the share of municipal tax incomes in the overall tax revenues of the centre, state and local governments has come down from about 4.5 in 1980-81 to almost 3.4 percent in 1986-87. It is estimated that urban share in NDP has steadily increased from 37.7 percent in 1971 to 42.8 percent in 1991 and expected to reach 47.3 percent in 2001.

FUNCTIONAL DOMAIN OF MUNICIPALITIES

The Constitution (74th Amendment) Act provides for three types of municipal bodies: Nagar Panchayats for transitional areas (in transition from rural to urban), Municipal Councils for smaller towns and Municipal Corporations for larger urban areas. There are 55 municipal corporations, 32 municipal councils, 1290 municipalities, 620 town committees, 453 town panchayats and 319 notified areas, as per information available from National Institute of Urban Affairs, Delhi, 1998. Thus, ULB's were numbered to be 3255 in India. As regards the functional domain of the local bodies, the Constitution Act envisages planning for economic development and social justice and performance of the functions as institutions of self-government. The Twelfth Schedule (Article 243-w) provides an illustrative list of functions that may be entrusted to the municipalities. These include:

- Urban planning including town planning;
- Regulation of land use and construction of building;
- Planning for economic and social development;
- Roads and bridges;
- Water supply for domestic, industrial and commercial purposes;
- Public health, sanitation, conservancy and solid waste management;
- Fire services;
- Urban forestry, protection of the environment and promotion of ecological aspects;
- Safeguarding the interests of weaker sections of society including the handicapped and the mentally retarded;
- Slum improvement and upgradation;
- Urban poverty alleviation;
- Provision of urban amenities and facilities such as parks, gardens, playgrounds;
- Promotion of cultural, education and aesthetic aspects;
- Burial and burial grounds; cremation ghats/grounds and electric crematoria;
- Cattle pounds, prevention of cruelty to animals;
- Vital statistics including registration of births and deaths;
- Public amenities including street lighting, parking plots, bus stops and public conveniences; and
- Regulation of slaughter houses and tanneries.

Conformity legislations enacted by the state governments indicate wide differences in the perception of the states regarding the obligatory and discretionary functions of the municipalities. Moreover, it is expected that functional domain of municipalities will increase with the process of functional devolution as per mandate of Amendment Act.

STRUCTURE OF MUNICIPAL FINANCES:

The structure of municipal revenues – mix of taxes, user charges and fees, transfer and loans varies considerably between countries. Differences are particularly significant between three tier (Central, State, Provincial and local) and two-tier (Central and local) federations. Cross-country comparison, however, indicates some broad patterns in municipal finances:

- **Vertical Imbalance:** Most of the urban local governments invariably suffer from inadequate 'own' resources which make them heavily dependent on transfers from the higher levels of government. Inter-governmental transfers often constitute the largest source of municipal revenues.
- **Horizontal Imbalance:** Municipalities often suffer from uneven access to resources. This gives rise to imbalances between municipalities of various population sizes and even within the same population size with similar tax base/rates, big and small cities, high and low-urbanized municipalities, etc.
- **Control by Higher Governments:** Generally, the higher levels of government control the municipal authority to levy taxes and user charges. Tax rates, grant exemptions, etc. and also determine the patterns of transfers to municipalities. High yielding sources of revenue are seldom assigned to local governments. Grants in-aid are often discretionary or negotiated.
- **Municipal Revenue Mix:** Taxes and transfers constitute the predominant sources of municipal revenues. Property tax is the most and often the single most important municipal tax. However, its relative importance has declined over a period of time in many countries. User charges, though

becoming increasingly popular, are yet to dominate the municipal scene. Borrowing constitutes a far more important sources in developed countries than in developing ones.

- **Systematic Inefficiency**: Municipalities generally suffer from under exploitation of 'own' revenue sources and high administrative and revenue collection costs.

SOURCES OF MUNICIPAL REVENUE

Municipal Taxes

The existing base of municipal taxes in India is extremely narrow and generally limited to property tax in the non-octroi states and octroi in the octroi levying states. Octroi, which is regarded as an obnoxious tax, is the most important source of municipal revenues in Maharashtra, Gujarat, Punjab, Rajasthan and Orissa. In the states which abolished octroi, compensations for the loss of octroi revenues over the years are found to be at precariously low levels. Other important municipal taxes comprise profession tax (taxes on profession, trade and calling), entertainment tax, advertisement tax and vehicles tax. These taxes too are under exploited. In some states, one or more of these taxes have been taken over by the state governments on the ground of inefficient collection by the local bodies. However, the devolution of revenues by way of compensation or sharing on this account has not kept pace over the years. In all the states, the Municipal Acts provide for levying a number of minor taxes, many of which have lost economic relevance over the years.

Shared Revenues

Some states in India share the motor vehicles tax, profession tax, entertainment tax and stamp duty/registration charges with the municipalities. In most states, tax sharing is in terms of a fixed amount, decided long time back and which has progressively declined in real terms.

User Charges and Fees

User charges appear to be grossly underutilized source of municipal revenues inspite of their inherent attractiveness as instruments of rationing public services, raising resources, facilitating the matching of demand for and supply of public services and ensuring accountability on the part of service provided.

Grants in-aid

The provision of grants-aid to the Municipalities in almost all the states is discretionary. States do not provide for divisible pools and formula based transfers to the municipalities. Grants are appropriate wherever services have benefits spill over and distributional consequences. Central and state governments in many countries place primary education, preventive health care, social assistance and environmental protection under the agency functions for which specific funds are given to the local bodies. They also provide equalizing grants to tackle the problems of fiscal imbalances between municipalities. In general, the grant systems operating in the various states in India are not based on decided principles. With the devolution of funds from centre to states, grants in aid have been replaced by devolution in some states.

Trends in Municipal Finances

The revenue structure of the municipalities shows that the relative share of own sources of revenue to transfers have declined. Although the share of tax income to total revenues declined substantially between 1974-75 and 1979-80, it went up from 15.39 percent in 1979-80 to 48 percent in 1997-98. The share of non tax revenue, however, has been declining over the years; it has declined from 22 percent in 1979-80 to 17 percent in 1997-98. Though, the Finance Commissions of many states have suggested that municipal authorities should utilize their properties for commercial purposes in big way. Studies show that cost recovery of the basic services is extremely low. Therefore, rationalization of user chargers for financing urban infrastructure and services is needed. The State Finance Commissions of many states have recommended effective pricing of municipal services with a view to balancing revenue and expenditure of ULBs. The Eleventh Finance Commission

(CFC) has recommended to consider the recommendations of State Finance Commissions and it has also looked into the following aspects of the ULBs in order to recommend grants to states for financing local governments:

- Powers of municipalities to raise financial resources including those by ways of raising additional taxes by municipalities;
- The powers, authority, and responsibility to municipalities under Article 243 W of the Constitution read with the 12th Schedule. Moreover, CFC has also recommended grants amounting to Rs. 10,000 crore to local bodies of the country during 2000-2005. Of this, Rs. 1600 crore are to go to rural panchayats and Rs. 400 crore to municipalities for each of the five years. Importantly, the Commission has recommended a special grant of Rs. 200 crore for development of a data base and maintenance of accounts.

Municipal bodies raised approximately Rs. 3900 crore on their own during the year 1991-92 which constituted a mere 4.7 percent of revenues by the Central Government and 8 percent of the revenues raised by state governments. This amount is estimated to be only 0.6 percent of the country's gross domestic product (GDP). In per capita terms, own sources of funds of municipal bodies works out to be nearly Rs. 205 per capita as against Rs. 987 per capita for the centre and Rs. 574 for the states. Although urban centres contribute nearly 60 percent of country's GDP but municipal bodies have not benefited from the economic activities that take place within their own jurisdiction. As per certain conservative estimates, the municipal bodies of country would require an additional investment of about Rs. 74000 crore to provide basic services by 2020. In addition, approximately Rs. 18,000 crore annually would be needed to operate and maintain these services at the barest minimum levels. However, it is expected that only two-third of the total operation and maintenance (O&M) requirements will be generated by the municipalities themselves.

The revenue income of ULBs shows that own sources of municipal income which comprise tax and non-tax revenue form an important part of the total revenue receipts of municipal bodies (Table 1 and 2). This is particularly true in the octroi levying states such as Gujarat (87.5 percent), Haryana (80.5 percent), Maharashtra (95.4 per cent), Punjab (89.0 percent) and Manipur (98.3 percent). Importantly, the share of tax revenues is higher than that of non-tax revenues. It varies from nearly 99 percent in Manipur to a slightly over 39 percent in Assam. Among the various taxes, property tax is the most common and stable source of income for the majority of municipalities in the country. Data shows that aggregate transfers constitute about 17 percent of total municipal revenue receipts. This proportion is very high in the case of Andhra Pradesh (48 percent), Assam (40 percent), Bihar (47 per cent), Himachal Pradesh (74 percent), Meghalaya (54 percent), Tripura (57 percent), Madhya Pradesh (52 percent), Tamil Nadu (56 percent) and Uttar Pradesh (80 percent).

Table 1
Source of Municipal Revenues (1997-98)

		Own Sources (%)			*Transfers (External Source) (%)*			
States	*Tax revenue (Rs. Crore)*	*Tax*	*Non-Tax*	*Both*	*Shared Taxes*	*Grants*	*Others*	*All*
Andhra Pradesh	13800.1	36.37	14.80	51.17	33.56	13.03	2.25	48.48
Assam	4721.4	23.24	35.84	59.08	–	23.37	17.55	40.92
Bihar	10,313.3	36.86	15.91	52.77	2.99	40.31	3.93	47.23
Gujarat	10,921.0	79.74	7.71	87.45	0.18	11.10	1.27	12.55
Haryana	5716.8	42.80	37.71	80.51	13.44	3.95	2.09	19.48
Karnataka	11,417.3	18.12	25.06	43.18	5.67	43.62	7.53	56.82
Kerala	7629.6	44.69	25.63	70.32	20.65	4.74	4.29	29.68
Madhya Pradesh	11,472.8	22.61	24.73	47.30	11.88	39.90	0.88	52.66
Maharashtra	21,721.1	65.44	29.66	95.40	0.53	3.84	0.23	4.60
Orissa	5046.7	46.92	20.20	67.12	0.93	28.59	3.36	32.88
Punjab	7,074.2	69.90	19.42	89.02	6.14	3.81	1.03	10.93
Rajasthan	8713.8	62.90	26.90	89.80	0.17	9.30	0.74	10.21
Tamil Nadu	13418.4	21.21	23.13	44.34	21.93	29.49	4.24	55.66
Uttar Pradesh	17478.1	13.50	5.95	19.44	0.36	79.14	1.06	80.56
West Bengal	9764.5\41	36.51	22.82	59.33	5.05	30.53	5.10	40.68
Himachal Pradesh	2117.6	15.27	10.59	25.86	–	72.04	2.09	74.13
Manipur	906.9	90.42	7.87	98.29	0.20	0.15	1.35	1.70
Meghalaya	947.5	37.66	8.62	46.27	–	40.09	13.63	53.72
Tripura	1130.3	27.31	15.61	42.92	–	33.74	23.34	57.08
All	1,63,413.49	56.40	26.38	82.38	4.05	11.99	1.19	17.23

Source: NIPFP (2000).

Table 2
Composition of Municipal Taxes (1997-98)

States	Tax revenues (Rs. Crore)	% Share to tax revenue									
		Property Tax	Advertise-ment Tax	Tax on vehicles and boats and animals	Betterment tax	Profession & callings	Trade tax	Enter-tainment tax	Octroi	Show tax	Others
AP	81.13	88.51	1.05	0.54	6.82	–	–	–	–	–	3.08
Assam	2.67	63.54	0.23	2.14	6.00	8.21	8.18	0.04	–	–	11.63
Kerala	42.90	53.01	0.66	–	Neg.	6.47	0.30	39.12	–	0.17	0.25
West Bengal	12.82	94.10	0.13	0.80	2.00	–	–	–	–	–	2.98
Gujarat	428.09	24.84	–	0.32	–	—	—	0.10	74.05	–	0.69
Maha-rashtra	982.87	21.59	0.01	0.33	0.97	Neg.	0.01	0.07	76.01	–	0.30
Punjab	105.63	12.06	0.05	0.38	–	0.02	0.29	86.06	–	0.75	

Source: NIPFP (2000).

The revenue base of municipalities in Indian states has shown little signs of change. Octroi as a major source of revenue for municipalities has been abolished and it has substantially shrunk the revenue base of municipalities in such states as Haryana, Orissa and Rajasthan. During 2001-2002, the size of municipal sector measured in terms of revenue that municipalities generated by way of levy of taxes, duties, fees and fines was estimated at Rs. 12748 crores. This accounted for 3.07 percent of publicly raised resources, the share of Central Government and all the state governments combined together reported to be 57.5 percent and 39.5 percent respectively. Over 1997-98 to 2001-2002, the size of municipal sector has registered a nominal increase. Municipal share in the total revenues of the three tiers of government rose from 2.84 percent in 1997-98 to 3.07 percent in 2001-2002, while relative to GSDP, its share increased from 0.61 to 0.63 percent during the same period (Table 3).

Table 3
Internal Resource Generation

States	*Resources Generated (Rs. Lac) 2001-2002*	*Per Capita (2001-2002)*	*AAGR (1997-98 to 2001-2002)*	*Percentage of GSDP*	
				1997-98	*2001-2002*
Andhra Pradesh	71745.7	386.8	14.5	0.42	0.48
Assam	3825.8	153.3	9.1	0.12	0.12
Bihar	3408.4	39.5	- 2.7	0.07	0.07
Gujarat	144849.2	809.4	5.1	1.3	1.16
Haryana	12106.9	207.8	3.6	0.27	0.20
Karnataka	56349.7	322.0	25.2	0.29	0.51
Kerala	22432.8	371.1	11.2	0.29	0.29
Madhya Pradesh	29437.0	188.7	- 4.1	0.44	0.36
Maharashtra	587058.3	1493.3	11.9	1.88	2.16
Orissa	10176.8	194.5	3.8	0.27	0.24
Punjab	75381.2	932.4	20.2	0.69	1.07
Rajasthan	10339.7	80.7	- 27.8	0.49	0.12
Tamil Nadu	92013.0	355.5	9.9	0.60	0.62
Uttar Pradesh	26551.0	79.5	11.2	0.12	0.14
West Bengal	42201.7	215.8	8.1	0.31	0.27
Himachal Pradesh	1978.9	335.6	14.5	0.13	0.15
Manipur	224.0	41.6	- 3.7	0.12	0.06
Tripura	217.7	58.9	19.6	0.03	0.04
Total	1209727.8	482.1	10.5	0.65	0.71

Source: India Infrastructure Report, 2006.

Table 4
Structure of Municipal Revenue

States	*Share in own revenues (%) 2001-2002*	*Transfer (Rs. Lac) 2001-2002*	*Percentage of transfer to total municipal revenue (2001-2002)*	*Per capita Transfers (Rs.) (2001-2002)*	*AAGR (1997-98 to 2001-2002)*
Andhra Pradesh	5.93	31784	30.7	171.4	12.4
Assam	0.32	1624	29.7	65.1	16.7
Bihar	0.28	5559	62.0	64.4	- 0.5
Gujarat	11.97	31395	17.8	175.1	14.6
Haryana	1.00	7892	39.5	135.5	18.6
Karnataka	4.66	60859	51.9	347.7	14.5
Kerala	1.85	17949	44.5	296.9	3.4
Madhya Pradesh	2.43	37663	54.8	241.4	- 2.1
Maharashtra	48.53	94177	13.8	239.6	22.8
Orissa	0.84	8047	44.2	153.8	22.4
Punjab	6.23	8489	10.1	105.1	9.7
Rajasthan	0.85	51703	83.3	403.5	38.6
Tamil Nadu	7.61	46770	33.7	180.7	- 2.8
Uttar Pradesh	2.19	77488	74.5	232.1	14.4
West Bengal	3.49	50203	54.3	256.7	14.1
Himachal Pradesh	0.16	2787	58.5	472.6	0.7
Manipur	0.02	195	46.5	36.1	33.1
Tripura	0.02	1100	83.5	297.8	5.6
Total	100.00	562958	31.7	224.4	13.5

Source: India Infrastructure Report, 2006.

Internal resource mobilization is the principal criterion for measuring the performance of municipalities. An analysis of internal resource generation shows a large variation across states in the performance of municipalities. Municipalities in Bihar having an annual per capita revenue generation of Rs. 39.5 compared with Rs. 1493 generated by municipalities in Maharashtra shows a contrast in municipal revenue generation. There are states like Goa, Gujarat, Maharashtra and Punjab whose per capita own revenue averages are close to or in access the country wide average of Rs. 482 per capita. Many states such as Andhra Pradesh, Karnataka, Kerala, Maharashtra, Punjab and Uttar Pradesh have witnessed high annual growth in own revenue generation. The per capita own revenues of municipalities in Bihar, Madhya Pradesh, Manipur and Rajasthan declined due to abolition of octroi, division of states and other exogenous reasons. It appears that in the states such as Assam, Bihar, Madhya Pradesh, Tamil Nadu, Uttar Pradesh and West Bengal, little efforts has been made to make use of charges, fees etc. Transfers in municipal finances accounted 31.7 percent during 2001-2002 at the national level, however, the share of transfers to municipal finances was reported as high as 83.7 percent in Jammu and Kashmir, 83.3 percent in Rajasthan, 83.5 in Tripura and 74.5 percent in Uttar Pradesh. Per capita transfer was reported Rs. 224.4 at the national level; however, it was recorded highest in Himachal Pradesh followed by Rajasthan, Karnataka, Chhatisgarh and Kerala (Table 4).

The analysis of municipal finances in India demonstrates that the present revenues are highly insufficient to meet the growing expenditure needs of urban areas. The present municipal expenditure levels are far from satisfaction, as per norms suggested by Zakaria Committee in 1963. Importantly, Municipal expenditure could be categorized into three main components; wages and salaries; operations and maintenance (O & M) and interest payments. Wages and salaries constitute nearly 60 percent of total municipal expenditure, followed by O & M (20 percent) and interest on payment (7.17 percent). Moreover, expenditure on O & M accounts for only one-fifth of the total expenditure of municipal services (Table 5). The components of wages and salaries was reported more pronouncing in Bihar followed by West Bengal, Manipur, Uttar Pradesh while it was reported least in Karnataka (20.93 percent). Similarly, proportion of expenditure on O & M was reported in Karnataka (78.11 percent), followed by Assam (54.14 percent) and Himachal Pradesh (52.32 percent) while it was recorded least 1.15 percent in Tripura. On an average, municipalities spend Rs. 747 per capita annually on various municipal activities (Table 6). Again, municipalities spent more than 58 percent on core municipal services. There has been rapid increase in per capita revenue from own sources during 1974-75 to 1997-98. However, per capital total revenue expenditure during the corresponding period has been reported much higher as compared to per capita revenue generation (Table 7).

Table 5
Composition of Revenue Expenditure (1997-98)

States	(%) of Total Revenue Expenditure			
	Wages and Salaries	O & M	Interest and Debt	Others
Andhra Pradesh	49.21	49.60	0.24	0.95
Assam	42.43	54.14	1.90	1.53
Bihar	77.21	21.13	1.03	0.63
Gujarat	53.20	30.02	6.30	10.48
Haryana	48.76	44.49	0.00	6.75
Karnataka	20.93	78.11	0.48	0.48
Kerala	55.04	34.57	5.19	5.20
Madhya Pradesh	51.01	37.67	0.61	10.71
Maharashtra	61.50	13.29	9.89	15.31
Orissa	38.30	21.61	0.00	40.09
Punjab	52.46	28.68	4.27	14.59
Rajasthan	–	–	–	–
Tamil Nadu	49.13	47.49	2.53	0.86
Uttar Pradesh	69.18	29.62	0.00	1.20
West Bengal	71.09	18.52	1.01	9.38
Himachal Pradesh	46.98	52.32	0.00	0.71
Manipur	70.69	8.73	0.00	20.58
Meghalaya	52.28	30.37	0.00	17.35
Tripura	56.64	1.15	2.26	39.95
Total	60.32	20.00	7.17	12.51

Source: NIPFP (2000).

An analysis of municipal expenditure shows a large variation across the states. Maharashtra, Punjab, Gujarat and Goa have higher per capita expenditure and higher expenditure ratios to the gross domestic product of the states. Other states such as Andhra Pradesh, Kerala, West Bengal and Tamil Nadu show medium level of expenditure. The low per capita expenditure was reported in the states such as Manipur, Bihar, Jharkhand, Assam and Uttar Pradesh (Table 8). Expenditure on establishment (salaries and wages) accounts for 54.2 percent of the total municipal expenditure. In several states, however, it is high in Madhya Pradesh (84.4 percent) Haryana (69.7 percent), Orissa (50.6 percent), West Bengal (65.0 percent), Rajasthan (63.2 percent), and Uttar Pradesh (60 percent).

Table 6
Per Capita Revenue Expenditure on Core Services (1997-98)

(Rs.)

States	Water Supply	Sewerage and Drainage	Conservancy and Sanitation	Municipal Road	Street Lighting	All Functions
Andhra Pradesh	50.52	55.12	63,37	102.53	13.19	313.38
Assam	2.98	7.46	12.60	24.17	2.49	81.77
Bihar	4.32	40.45	39.85	2.93	1.29	104.29
Gujarat	60.40	44.28	119.37	52.23	29.86	438.21
Haryana	191.84	89.99	108.56	57.77	30.74	598.22
Karnataka	62.56	42.91	74.19	46.46	25.92	321.05
Kerala	2.84	8.98	66.14	46.49	8.37	228.38
Madhya Pradesh	79.44	31.92	37.10	27.19	13.16	322.74
Maharashtra	230.00	155.58	195.87	117.35	43.08	1750.50
Orissa	9.66	42.58	67.91	16.29	13.08	248.29
Punjab	95.38	109.70	118.44	48.67	23.35	542.81
Rajasthan	–	165.07	–	12.28	5.40	497.24
Tamil Nadu	45.92	13.39	111.86	56.13	23.25	331.46
Uttar Pradesh	16.48	5.41	112.10	34.64	9.52	223.23
West Bengal	60.01	41.58	119.48	63.71	13.72	522.83
Himachal Pradesh	89.57	36.67	251.76	304.90	15.62	1112.85
Manipur	0.03	–	27.05	16.38	–	101.42
Meghalaya	46.57	16.66	55.98	47.32	23.03	272.10
Tripura	0.01	–	–	2.13	4.99	255.90
All	125.77	93.21	123.36	70.19	23.48	247.02

Source: NIPFP (2000).

Table 7
Trends in Municipal Finances in Selected States

(In Rs.)

	Per Capita Revenue from Own Sources				*Per Capita Total Revenue Expenditure*			
States	*1974-75*	*1979-80*	*1992-93*	*1997-98*	*1974-75*	*1979-80*	*1992-93*	*1997-98*
Gujarat	67.70	90.00	486.25	618.66	85.90	119.40	501.56	438.21
Maharashtra	103.40	149.00	275.80	1829.00	107.20	131.40	877.20	1750.50
Punjab	41.90	78.00	275.66	444.23	40.50	55.20	298.20	542.81
Andhra Pradesh	37.30	38.00	89.55	210.03	28.30	53.90	163.26	318.38
Assam	13.70	11.00	43.75	47.13	18.50	20.00	59.57	81.77
Kerala	28.30	46.00	146.62	193.70	22.30	37.00	190.95	228.38
West Bengal	33.40	28.00	44.74	337.23	41.00	54.60	121.88	522.83

Source: NIUA (1989) and NIPFP (2000).

Table 8
Per Capita Revenue Expenditure during 2001-2002

States	*Per Capita Revenue Expenditure (2001-2002)*	*Annual Growth (1997-98 to 2001-2002)*	*Percentage of GSDP (2001-2002)*
Andhra Pradesh	508.88	14.47	0.63
Assam	211.79	5.21	0.16
Bihar	87.20	5.53	0.15
Gujarat	865.12	7.11	1.24
Haryana	255.23	1.45	0.25
Karnataka	418.29	11.23	0.67
Kerala	493.17	10.65	0.39
Madhya Pradesh	427.66	- 2.59	0.82
Maharashtra	1253.71	6.51	1.82
Orissa	355.06	13.87	0.43
Punjab	1008.12	17.22	1.15
Rajasthan	390.36	7.30	0.56
Tamil Nadu	481.79	0.96	0.84
Uttar Pradesh	275.18	9.54	0.49
West Bengal	487.49	10.33	0.61
Himachal Pradesh	955.45	13.02	0.38
Manipur	81.03	4.90	0.22
Tripura	356.75	7.09	0.37
Total	576.71	7.36	0.85

Source: India Infrastructure Report, 2006.

MUNICIPAL FISCAL PROBLEMS

The problems of the municipalities in India are multifarious. Considering:

(a) The national priorities of economic reforms, stabilization, poverty alleviation and removal of inter-regional disparities;

(b) The structure of fiscal federation provided by the Constitution of India; and

(c) That the centre sharing bulk of the income tax with state governments, it is most unlikely that the municipalities will have an access to the direct income tax base in the near future. The increasing gap between required revenues and actual revenues has attracted our attention. This municipal fiscal gap van be redressed in the following broad ways:

- Reducing municipal responsibilities;
- Scaling down municipal services;
- Cutting costs and unnecessary expenditures;
- Enhancing municipal powers to raise revenues;
- Increasing transfers from higher levels of governments; and/or
- Stepping up local efforts to raise revenues.

Moreover, reforms to correct the municipal gas will have to address to down sizing and fiscal corrections.

IMPLICATIONS OF 74TH AMENDMENT FOR MUNICIPAL FINANCE

Article 243 (w) of the Constitution of India envisages the role of urban local bodies as Institutions of Self-Government. Article 243 (x) provides that a state legislature may, by law,

- Authorize a municipality to levy, collect and appropriate such taxes, duties, tolls and fees in accordance with such procedure and subject to such limit;
- Assign to a municipality such taxes, duties, tolls and fees levied and collected by the state government for such purposes and subject to such conditions and limits;
- Provide for making such grants-in-aid to the municipalities from the consolidated fund of the state; and
- Provide for the constitution of such funds for crediting all moneys received, respectively, by or on behalf of the municipalities and also for the withdrawal of such moneys there from; as may be prescribed by law.

Under Article 243 (y), it is mandatory for the State Finance Commission to review:

The principles that should govern:

(i) The distribution between the state and the municipalities of net proceeds of the taxes, duties, tolls and fees leviable by the state, which may be divided between them and the collection between the municipalities at all levels of their respective shares of such proceeds;

(ii) The determination of taxes, duties, tolls and fees which may be assigned to, or appropriate by the municipalities;

(iii) The grants-in-aid to the municipalities from the consolidated fund of the state;

- The measures needed to improve the financial position of the municipalities; and
- Any other matter referred to the Finance Commission by the Governor in the interest of sound financing of the municipalities.

EXPENDITURE PATTERN OF MUNICIPAL REVENUE

The performance of a local body in the discharge of its various functions tends to be judged by the ways its revenues are spent, the tendencies of increase or decrease in expenditure. It is also to be noted that in the present time, rapid urbanization has resulted in more stress on municipal bodies in terms of meeting out the raising expectations of urban dwellers. The civic services are gradually declining in their quality. The process of urbanization and the problems arising out of it has awaken a national consensus and quite a number of civic problems are being now tackled at local level as well as they have become a national phenomenon. Housing, education, water supply, environmental pollution, employment opportunities, industrialization etc. can be effectively dealt with at national level.

In respect of a number of services, therefore, the state is either taking upon itself the responsibility of implementing thee programmes by setting up its own statutory agencies or providing finances to local bodies for implementation by ways of loans and grants. This is another aspect, which has widened the scope of civic services and has considerably increased the expenditure of urban local bodies. Moreover, after execution of the capital projects, the burden of maintenance and operational cost and debt services gradually falls on local bodies thereby increasing expenditure.

FISCAL NEEDS DURING 2001-2005

For computing fiscal requirements for the upkeep and maintenance of core urban services at the barest minimum level, the following expenditure norms have been used by adjusting them at 1994-95 prices (using the All India Consumer Price Index for urban non-manual workers): (i) Zakaria Committee (1963, Augmentation of Financial Resources of Urban Local Bodies); the committee has laid down the desirable levels of expenditure on operation and maintenance of basic services as 1960 prices. These are adjusted to 1994-95 prices; and (ii) NIUA study (1989; Upgrading Municipal Services, Norms and Financial Implications, New Delhi).

It has been estimated that upto the year 2001, urban local bodies in India would require an investment in basic infrastructure of about Rs. 34512 crores if the deficiencies in the existing level of services are to be eliminated and all sections of the urban population are to be provided with access to a modicum of core services according to the norms proposed by Zakaria Committee. The financial investment requirements will, however, increase to Rs. 51,102 crores (about 148 percent), if municipal managers choose to raise the services according to the norms proposed by the Planning Commission, Government of India. On the other hand financial needs will dip to Rs. 38,890 crores, if the municipal governments opt for the lower level as standards laid down by the Planning Commission. In addition, approximately a total of Rs. 168,987 crores (or Rs. 16697 crores annually) will be needed to operate and maintain these services at the barest minimum level according to the Zakaria Committee norms. According to the NIUA Study (State averages), the cumulative operation and maintenance requirements will be Rs. 164,312 (on an average Rs. 16431 per annum) by the year 2001. At present rates of municipal taxation, user charges and efficiency, it is expected that more than one-third of these operation and maintenance requirements will be generated from the urban centres themselves, being a recurrent resource gap of about Rs. 10,624-10,891 crores per annum. Additional investments need for provision of core urban services by 2001 in Inia would be Rs.

29337 crore as per Zakaria Committee while Rs. 32776 crore and R.s 44138 crore at low and high estimates of Planning Commission. Against this, in the state of U.P. there will be need of Rs. 3848 crore as per Zakaria Commission and Rs. 4293 crore and Rs. 5790 crore at low and high estimates of Planning Commission. Again, financial needs for O & M of core municipal services for the period of 1996-2001 in the state of U.P. will be Rs. 39850 million (8.1 percent) against all India financial requirement of Rs. 489630 million. There will be estimated revenue generation of Rs. 22560 million, leaving resource gap of 76.64 percent. It is worth mentioning that resource gap in the state of Uttar Pradesh is higher than national average of 61.39 percent.

As per report of Rakesh Mohan Committee (1996) on Infrastructure, it is estimated that urban local bodies of India will require Rs. 9792 crore per year for O & M during the period 2001-2006. Out of this amount, 75 percent has to be mobilized by the urban local governments and 12.5 percent is to be met by the State Finance Commission transfers and the remaining gap of 12.5 percent requires to be filled through the Finance Commission.

ISSUES OF FINANCIAL MANAGEMENT

It is clear that given the present situation of a low resource base and poor services levels, most municipal bodies of the country would find it difficult to raise the necessary finances to meet the growing demand for urban services. They are suffering from poor administration of property taxes, inelasticity of most of the tax revenues, except octroi which is going to be abolished everywhere as per the policy decision taken by the National Government, poor cost recovery of services rendered, mismatch between functions and sources of revenue developed to them; defective grants-in-aid and tax sharing principles; lack of access to financial institutions; and insufficient resource mobilization and ineffective use of available man power and equipments to improve delivery of services. Following responsible for the fiscal stress of urban local bodies:

- Poor tax administration;
- Inelasticity of tax revenue;
- Inadequate and ineffective cost recovery mechanism;
- Insufficient devolution of funds and powers from the state to local government;
- Managerial inefficiency;
- High establishment cost.

The options to improve the situation include:

- Effective fiscal management;
- Efficient tax administration;
- Rationalization;
- Fiscal discipline;
- Fiscal transfers;
- Resource mobilization through tapping new sources of revenue;
- Privatization of services and cutting revenue expenditure; and
- Additional government grants.

CONSTITUTION OF 11TH FINANCE COMMISSION

In pursuance of the provisions of the Article 280 of the Constitution of India and the Finance Commission Act, 1951, the 11th Finance Commission has been constituted consisting of Prof. A.M. Khusro as chairman and four other members. The terms of reference define the tasks of the EFC. The Commission shall make the following recommendations in case of local bodies: (a) the Commission shall take into account the recommendations of the State Finance Commissions; and (b) where that State Finance Commission have not been constituted as yet, or have not submitted their report giving recommendations, the Commission will make its own assessment about the manner and extent of augmentation of consolidated fund of the state to supplement the resources of the panchayats and municipalities in the state. While making such assessment, the Commission: (i) shall take into account the provision required to be made for the emoluments and terminal benefits of the employees of local bodies including those of teachers; (ii) shall take into account the existing powers of the panchayats and municipalities to raise financial resources including those by way of raising additional taxes by the panchayats and municipalities; and (iii) the powers, authority and responsibility transferred to panchayats and municipalities under Article 243 (G) and 243 (W) of the Constitution read with Schedules Eleven and Twelve.

The Eleventh Finance Commission (EFC), unlike its predecessors, had to take into account the responsibilities cast upon it by the 73rd and 74 Constitutional Amendments. Importantly, EFC had to make recommendations regarding the measures needed to augment the Consolidated fund of a state to supplement the resources of the panchayats and municipalities in the state and that these had to be on the basis of the recommendations made by the Finance Commission of the State. These are Constitutional mandates. Since only 19 State Finance Commission (SFC's) have submitted their reports, this mandate can not be fully honoured. There is another hitch because the period of recommendations of most of the SFCs covers the period of 1996-97 to 2000-01 whereas the EFC covers a period from 2000-05. However, EFC can legitimately base its recommendations on the first round of SFC's and cover period, from 2000-05. Moreover, two problems emerge from this situation: (a) how to evaluate the SFC reports, and (b) how to assess the states which have no reports. In both cases, the purpose of the assessment is to help the Commission in regard to the manner and extent of augmentation of the consolidated fund of the states to supplement the resources of the local bodies. Significantly, SFC has to formulate clear ideas regarding the functional domain of the state on the one hand and that of the urban local bodies on the other. The size of the divisible poor, other things being equal depends on prudent housekeeping by the state. Most SFC's have done some review of the State Finances although none of them could be considered as normative evaluation.

Importantly, the design of transfers from the state's divisible pool to the urban local bodies and PRI's envisaged by each SFC necessarily will have to take into the principles of tax assignments, expenditure assignments and the grants-in-aid/tax sharing regime recommended. Furthermore, EFC had to investigate the matter that how far the SFC's have done this exercise with wisdom, faithfulness to the Constitution, efficiency and equity. To sum up, the Eleventh Finance Commission had a crucial task in working towards a national system of federal public finance taking into account the need for building the financial foundation of third tier of governance in the country. The 10th Finance Commission transfers to states and local bodies constituted 24.7 percent of the total central non-plan revenue receipts, of which 22.3 percent as shares and 2.2 percent as total grants. The share of grants to local bodies (ad hoc arrangement) constituted only 0.6 percent(0.1 percent to urban local bodies) in the total transfers and 24.2 percent in total grants. After meeting the non-revenue expenditure and 10th Finance Commission transfers, there is still revenue surplus to the extent of 4.3 percent, which can be transferred to capital and plan investments.

The 11th Finance Commission has recommended grants amounting to Rs. 10,000 crore to local bodies, out of which Rs. 2000 crore are to go to municipalities for 2001-2005. The 12th Finance Commission has recommended for 2005-2010, a sum of Rs. 5000 crore for municipalities. Recently, Government of India has launched Jawaharlal Nehru Urban Renewal Mission in 63 selected cities of India and Rs. 50000 crore as a central share has been allocated under the scheme. It is expected that the same amount will be mobilized from the state governments and the concerned local bodies for implementing the project. The project is aimed at improving municipal governance and development of infrastructure. The other two major schemes such as Urban Infrastructure Development Scheme for Small and Medium Towns, and Integrated Housing and Slum Development Programme also have provision of higher budgetary allocation as central share. These schemes also focus on development of infrastructure and strengthening local bodies for delivery of municipal services.

FINANCING URBAN BASIC SERVICES

Urban basic services in general and urban water supply and sanitation sector in particular have shown growing deficit in terms of availability to the larger popular of the city. The urban services are found to be not only inadequate but the quality of such services is also deteriorating. Thus, substantial amount of investment is needed to augment the facilities related to environmental services in order to meet out the emerging demand in the urban centres. Financing of basic amenities in India has largely remained within the purview of public sector. Though, the state governments largely made the required capital investment in projects related to basic amenities, the maintenance of the utilities were the responsibility of city governments. The analysis of trends and patters in expenditure on urban development and services shows interesting facts. Out of 17 states, 8 states have experienced declined in the growth rate of per capita expenditure on urban water supply in post-decentralized period i.e. since 1994. Tamil Nadu, West Bengal, Rajasthan and Assam have registered significant declined in the growth rate in this period. On the other hand, states of Andhra Pradesh, Goa, Gujarat and Orissa have recorded an increase in per capita expenditure on urban water supply during the period. Per capita expenditure on urban development by 11 of the 17 states has shown higher growth during the post-decentralization period. Among them, the increases have been substantial for the states like BIhar, Gujarat, Kerala, Orissa, Punjab, Rajasthan and West Bengal. In the post-decentralization period, Rajasthan and Kerala have increased their expenditure on urban development. However, states like Andhra Pradesh, Assam, Karnataka, Maharashtra and Tamil Nadu have recorded a declined in per capita expenditure on urban development during the period (Table 9).

The growth in state expenditure on urban water supply and urban development is shown in Table 10. During 1991-1994, growth in per capita expenditure on urban water supply was recorded highest in Haryana followed by Tamil Nadu, West Bengal, Bihar and Rajasthan. However, the negative

Table 9
State Government Expenditure on Urban Development & Urban Services

	PC Expenditure on UWS			*PC Expenditure on UD*			*PC Expenditure on Assistance to LBs*			*PC Expenditure on UWSS*		
States	*1990-91*	*1995-96*	*1999-00*	*1990-91*	*1995-96*	*1999-00*	*1990-91*	*1995-96*	*1999-00*	*1990-91*	*1995-96*	*1999-00*
Andhra Pradesh	9.03	8.57	8.46	21.88	10.79	5.14	0.13	2.60	2.11	9.88	13.64	15.20
Assam	4.51	5.12	3.63	16.61	29.72	21.33	0.00	0.00	0.00	27.89	14.44	16.0
Bihar	7.80	11.18	15.36	9.44	7.17	21.68	0.33	0.42	1.26	8.93	6.67	6.4
Goa	222.42	216.50	226.81	38.97	41.76	35.88	0.00	0.00	0.00	64.03	106.14	138.4
Gujarat	1.45	2.42	4.00	16.14	18.30	39.31	0.00	0.00	0.00	12.42	13.23	38.8
Haryana	0.00	14.64	0.00	11.74	22.82	27.54	0.00	0.00	0.00	17.85	34.30	31.0
Himachal Pradesh	188.81	237.98	0.00	34.98	53.17	48.66	4.50	23.10	0.00	80.89	101.93	0.0
Karnataka	0.00	0.00	0.00	8.12	30.60	16.25	21.84	41.85	50.32	8.48	17.67	19.9
Kerala	0.00	0.00	0.00	4.60	6.58	50.98	0.00	0.00	0.00	14.12	13.00	14.7
Madhya Pradesh	9.82	6.34	6.76	22.63	16.12	20.96	1.51	2.62	2.52	15.66	17.42	18.0
Maharashtra	1.00	0.22	0.21	17.67	30.04	22.88	12.32	3.58	29.37	16.85	14.83	21.6
Orissa	21.30	18.04	34.48	23.37	20.92	35.61	2.26	12.16	6.80	9.67	15.19	19.2
Punjab	0.00	0.00	0.00	- 2.85	13.13	14.20	0.00	0.00	0.00	12.03	17.81	13.9
Rajasthan	74.95	114.57	93.80	10.82	17.45	86.16	1.28	2.23	1.98	37.08	54.70	49.3
Tamil Nadu	21.29	19.06	6.18	22.81	12.50	16.32	1.82	2.82	2.20	16.50	17.27	14.7
Uttar Pradesh	5.84	7.45	0.00	4.85	4.12	6.18	2.38	0.16	0.00	9.28	6.44	0.00
West Bengal	2.24	2.19	1.13	57.67	41.71	104.36	0.00	0.00	0.00	6.44	6.84	11.7
India	0.03	0.69	0.80	3.31	0.73	2.02	0.09	0.00	0.03	0.77	1.78	2.0

Source: State Finance Accounts for Corresponding years.

Table 10
Pre and Post-Decentralization Growth in State Expenditure

States	PCE on UWS		PCE on UD		PCE on Asst. to LBs		PCE on UWSS	
	90-91 & 94-95	*95-96 & 99-00*	*90-91 & 94-95*	*95-96 & 99-00*	*90-91 & 94-95*	*95-96 & 99-00*	*90-91 & 94-95*	*95-96 & 99-00*
Andhra Pradesh	5.13	10.01	- 7.49	- 8.59	155.27	5.17	15.61	8.44
Assam	0.82	- 11.94	4.61	- 8.97	0	0	- 17.38	2.75
Bihar	19.8	8.51	- 9.34	24.1	- 30.02	34.59	- 7.27	- 1.52
Goa	- 2.48	1.38	- 4.43	- 2.37			9.03	8
Gujarat	- 2.37	11.03	- 8.34	23.21			15.78	33.66
Haryana	167.3	8.07	0.75	4.17			29.72	- 4.15
Himachal Pradesh	2.97	0	- 1.2	0.84	68.66	0	2.92	
Karnataka	0	0	3.84	- 18.02	15.32	5.23	15.56	1.4
Kerala	0	0	5.48	56.31			- 2.61	2.6
Madhya Pradesh	- 0.06	- 0.24	- 11.85	3.64	7.03	- 7.83	5.71	0.8
Maharashtra	- 0.87	- 4.59	- 0.16	- 5.4	- 14.3	63.31	- 4.39	10.13
Orissa	- 3.24	20.12	- 4.7	12.84	23.53	- 8.34	7.19	8.37
Punjab	0	0	- 16.8	10.74			0.57	- 4.54
Rajasthan	11.79	- 1.33	- 2.52	71.4	5.73	- 3.82	7.88	- 0.28
Tamil Nadu	18.47	- 34.99	- 18.38	- 2.41	14.13	- 6.93	10.57	- 6.95
Uttar Pradesh	0	0	- 10.59	0	- 37.05	0	- 8.19	
West Bengal	14.39	- 15.82	- 2.3	22.41			8.8	16.22

Source: State Finance Accounts for Corresponding Years.

growth rate was reported in Orissa, Goa, Gujarat, Madhya Pradesh and Maharashtra. During 1995-06 to 1999-2000, growth in per capita expenditure on urban water supply was recorded highest in the state of Orissa followed by Gujarat and Andhra Pradesh. However, negative growth rate was recorded in Tamil Nadu, West Bengal, Assam, Madhya Pradesh and Maharashta. Growth in per capita expenditure during 1990-91 to 1994-95, the significant growth in per capita expenditure on urban development was recorded in Kerala, Karnataka and Assam while other states recorded negative growth rate. During the post-decentralization period, highest growth in per capita expenditure on the sector was reported in Kerala, Gujarat, Bihar, Rajasthan and West Bengal. During post-decentralization period, growth in per capita expenditure in urban water supply and sanitation was recorded significant in the state of Gujarat, West Bengal and Maharashtra.

Table 11 provides the sector-wise disbursement of HUDCO loan for urban infrastructure at the All India and the state level during the 1990s. The less developed states like Orissa, Rajasthan, West Bengal, Himachal Pradesh, Bihar and Assam received major HUDCO loans for water supply scheme. However, it is not the case for sewerage schemes. States like Tamil Nadu, Karnataka, Gujarat and Maharashtra received major HUDCO loans for other infrastructure projects as well as sewerage schemes. Gujarat, Maharashtra, Karnataka and Tamil Nadu accounted for about 40 per cent of the total loans sanctioned by HUDCO. However, the share of these states in number of schemes for urban infrastructure projects range between 12 and 26 per cent during 1970s to 1996. The backward states such as Bihar, Orissa, Rajasthan, Madhya Pradesh and Uttar Pradesh accounted for about 25 per cent share during 1970s and 1996.

Per capita HUDCO loans sanctioned and corresponding growth rate has experienced an increase in the post-decentralization period. Per capita HUDCO loan assistance for the developed states like Gujarat, Maharashtra, Tamil Nadu and Karnataka increased over the years during the 1990s. However, most of the backward states have registered a decline

Table 11
Spatial & Sectoral Distribution of HUDCO Loans

	Share of Loans for Water Supply			*Share of Loans for Sewerage and Sanitation*			*Share of Loans for other Infrastructure*		
States	*199-91*	*1995-96*	*1999-00*	*199-91*	*1995-96*	*1999-00*	*199-91*	*1995-96*	*1999-00*
Andhra Pradesh	0.00	90.38	0.00	0.00	9.62	0.00	100.00	0.00	100.00
Assam	72.65	100.00	0.00	0.00	0.00	100.00	27.35	0.00	0.00
Bihar	0.00	100.00	0.00	0.00	0.00	0.00	0.00	0.00	0.00
Goa	0.00	0.00	100.00	0.00	0.00	0.00	0.00	0.00	0.00
Gujarat	0.00	0.00	42.39	62.10	0.00	0.00	37.90	100.00	57.61
Haryana	0.00	0.00	0.00	0.00	0.00	0.00	0.00	0.00	100.00
Himachal Pradesh	0.00	0.00	0.00	0.00	0.00	0.00	0.00	0.00	0.00
Karnataka	0.00	10.10	5.02	0.00	0.00	10.45	0.00	100.00	84.53
Kerala	100.00	0.00	0.00	0.00	0.00	5.96	0.00	27.10	94.04
Madhya Pradesh	0.00	0.00	19.71	0.00	0.00	0.00	0.00	100.00	80.29
Maharashtra	9.29	0.00	1.40	5.75	0.00	0.00	84.96	100.00	98.60
Orissa	0.00	0.00	0.00	0.00	0.00	0.00	0.00	0.00	0.00
Punjab	0.00	80.70	0.00	0.00	60.35	0.00	100.00	31.30	0.00
Rajasthan	0.00	49.17	0.00	0.00	4.60	0.00	0.00	52.85	100.00
Tamil Nadu	100.00	0.00	45.26	0.00	19.72	0.00	0.00	68.89	54.74
Uttar Pradesh	0.00	0.00	0.00	0.00	0.00	0.00	100.00	100.00	100.00
West Bengal	100.00	0.00	0.00	0.00	0.00	98.47	0.00	0.00	1.53
India	45.48	12.55	13.13	3.65	8.89	20.36	50.87	61.52	66.51

Source: HUDCO.

in the growth of loans sanctioned by HUDCO for urban infrastructure (Table 12).

From 1980 onwards, external assistance mainly from World Bank and other foreign agencies have been coming in for the urban infrastructure in general and urban basic services in particular. A substantial portion of this assistance i.e. more than 50 per cent has been for the urban water supply and sanitation programme. However, the developed states received a major chunk of the assistance. Out of 15 completed externally aided projects, 9 of them were found located in the developed states. There are 18 ongoing projects in different stages of implementation. 6 of them are located in the developed states.

Table 12
Pre and Post-Decentralization Growth of HUDCO Loan Sanction

	PC Loans for UIPs		*Growth*	*PC Loans for UIPs*		*Growth*
States	*1990-91*	*1994-95*	*Pre Decent.*	*1995-96*	*1999-00*	*Post Decent.*
Andhra Pradesh	4.5	2.24	0	17.05	2.83	- 37.63
Assam	26.82	9.13	- 44.92	7.53	58.87	0
Bihar	0	0	0	2.5	0	0
Goa	NA	0	0	0	124.98	0
Gujarat	1.92	4.94	0	2.84	32.91	100.91
Haryana	0	0	0	0	88.9	0
Himachal Pradesh	0	0	0	0	0	0
Karnataka	0	86.95	0	7.28	90.23	82.81
Kerala	12.48	82.32	92.75	33.43	78.64	24.48
Madhya Pradesh	0	0	0	0.01	15.48	588.65
Maha-rashtra	18.25	0	0	1.37	32.4	138.78
Orissa	0	0	0	0	0	0
Punjab	2.75	9.36	0	18.94	0	0
Rajasthan	0	16.68	0	27.99	45.86	18.81
Tamil Nadu	11.8	14.23	16.52	22.28	58.57	48.59
Uttar Pradesh	2.99	1.42	0	9.8	4.56	- 18.45
West Bengal	10.09	0	0	0	66.2	0

UIPs: Urban Infrastructure Projects
Source: NIPFP (2000).

Private sector involvement in infrastructure services in general and water and sewerage projects in particular have become a focal point in the era of liberalized economy. The public-private initiatives have largely remained confined to the maintenance of urban basic services through service contract and management contract. These initiatives have to larger extent remained confined to the developed states like Maharashtra, Gujarat, Karnataka and Tamil Nadu. The involvement of private investment for financing capital investment in urban services like water supply and sewerage has remained limited. Even the issuing of the municipal bonds for mobilizing the public money for development and maintenance of urban infrastructure is confined to a few municipal corporations. There are 28 water and sanitation related projects in which private-public partnership has been initiated. Out of them, 20 projects are located in developed states. Similarly, out of 44 projects in solid waste management, about half of them are found in the developed states. 30 of these 44 projects are in the big cities. Thus, the advantages of external financing of urban infrastructure projects and resource mobilization are confined to the developed states and particularly to the metropolitan cities.

It is clear from the above analysis that the present institutional arrangements for the provision of urban services is unlikely to sustain in the face of mounting fiscal pressures on municipal bodies and the rapid demand for urban services. The new economic policies, oriented towards market based economy led growth objectives, would also entail a significant contribution of the urban sector and efforts would be needed to reduce infrastructure bottlenecks and increase urban productivity and employment. The growing fiscal stress on municipal bodies will require fiscal corrections, effective fiscal management, and resources mobilization through initiating financing reforms. Moreover, legislative exercises to precisely define the functions and finances of municipal bodies especially after functional devolution as per 74th Amendment Act are needed. Again, there should be re-assessments of finances of municipal bodies after complete functional devolution. Introduction of administrative reforms to develop an accountable municipal bureaucracy with suitably design policies regarding staff recruitment, incentives and penalties to ensure results, results, performance contracting etc. is also called for. Training of newly elected municipal representatives and municipal officials regarding the Constitutional mandates and especially effective fiscal management/ administration is also needed. As per fiscal needs of municipal bodies, State Governments should make serious efforts for resource mobilization through enlarging fiscal domain of local bodies and its resource base.

FINANCIAL INVESTMENTI IN INFRASTRUCTURE AND SERVICES

In the context of growing cities and urbanization, there is need for effective governance. Urban governance is no more limited to the provision of infrastructure and operation of civic services. The traditional approaches of urban governance are proved to be inappropriate and restrictive. Good urban governance is called for which is characterized by sustainability, equity, efficiency, transparency, accountability, civic engagement, security development of partnerships, etc. There is a need for prudent and efficient financial and asset management to increase their capacity to facilitate market borrowings for investment in urban development. In view of the emerging challenges of urban development, Government of India launched JNNURM with three interrelated and complimentary components i.e. governance, infrastructure development and provision of basic services to poor. Implementation of governance reforms like enactment of community participation and public disclosure laws, earmarking of funds for poverty alleviation by local bodies, levy and collection of user charges, simplification of procedures etc. in identified areas is a precondition for accessing funds under JNNURM.

It is estimated that over a seven year period (2005-12), the urban local bodies would require a total investment of Rs. 120536 crores. This includes investment in basic infrastructure and services i.e. annual fund requirements in the tune of Rs. 17219.5 crores. The larger amount of funding is required for larger cities above one million populations (Table 13).

Table 13
Urban Sector Investment Requirement

(Rs. Crores)

Category	*Number of Cities*	*Investment Requirement (Over 7 Years Starting 2005-06)*	*Annual Funds Requirement*
Cities with over 4 million Population	*7 (11.11)*	*57,143 (47.41)*	*8163.3 (47.41)*
Cities with 1-4 million Population	28 (44.44)	57,143 (47.41)	8613.3 (47.41)
Selected cities with less than one million Population	28 (44.44)	6,250 (5.18)	892.9 (5.18)
Total	63 (100.00)	1,20,536 (100.00)	17,219.5 (100.00)

Source: Ministry of Urban Development, Government of India, Delhi, 2007

The Government of India has proposed substantial assistance through JNNURM over the seven years period. During the period, funds will be provided for proposals that would meet the Mission's requirements. Under JNNURM financial assistance will be made available to the urban local bodies and parastatal agencies, which could deploy these funds for implementing the projects themselves or through the special purpose vehicles that may be expected to be set up. Assistance under the Mission is additional central assistance, which would be provided as grant to the implementing agencies. Further, assistance from JNNURM is expected to facilitate further investment in the urban sector.

One of the objectives of Mission is to facilitate and ensure participatory urban development to contribute to sustainability. The community development programmes by the cities are the result of stakeholder consultations. One of the mandatory reforms for the participation of the community of stakeholders is decision making and governance at ward and sub-ward level. The projects under Community Participation Fund are eligible to a maximum funding of Rs. 10 lakhs and there should be a community contribution of 10 per cent which may be relaxed to 5 per cent in case of projects involving the poor.

In view of increasing demand of urban services and infrastructure, National Commission on urbanization recognized the role and importance of the urban sector for the national economy. The estimates of the Expert Group on Commercialization of Infrastructure Projects for annual investment need for urban infrastructure are most recent. The annual investment need urban water supply, sanitation, and roads, stood at Rs. 280 billion for the period of 1995-2005. Another estimate made for the Ninth Five Year Plan had estimated the investment requirement for urban housing at Rs. 526 billion. The Central Public Health Engineering has estimated the requirements of funds for 100 per cent coverage of the urban population with safe water supply and sanitation services by the year 2021 at Rs. 1729 billion. Estimates by RITES indicate that the investment required for urban transport infrastructure in one lakh plus cities during the next 20 years would be of the order of Rs. 2070 billion. Traditionally, the provision of urban infrastructure and services has been the primary functions of government; however, most of municipalities face problems of resources and these are effectively dependent on their respective state governments for allocating or transfer resources to them. In absence of resources, fragmentation of schemes, and increasing stress on services, the quality of basic services is declining. Even the increasing coverage of infrastructure is not matched by improvement in the service levels. The failures in urban service delivery are caused by overlapping of policy, regulation and operational roles; fragmentation and duplication; limited autonomy to ULBs; weak links with citizens; lack of capacity; lack of incentives; etc.

Solid waste management is one of the important essential urban services provided by municipalities. Urban India produces about 48 million towns solid waste annually. It is estimated that by year 2047, waste generation will increase to 200 million tonnes, five times to present level. Cities with one lakh and above population contribute 72.5 per cent waste generated in the country as compared to 3955 urban centres that produce only 17.5 per cent of the total waste. The collection, segregation, storage, transportation, treatment, and disposal arrangements of waste are not proper and scientific. It leads to health hazards, and inefficiency in solid waste management. The bio-medical waste is also not properly managed in most of towns and cities. A study was conducted to ascertain the status of compliance of MSW Rules, 2000 by class one cities in India. The study shows that there is insignificant progress in the matter of processing of waste and construction of sanitary land fills.

Water supply and sanitation hold very important place in urban services. India's urban water supply and sanitation (UWSS) sector focus many problems and require a huge investment for revamping. Many service providers are not financially viable and are unable to maintain services without extensive subsidies. The services fall short of full coverage of the population and are often of low quality due to insufficient funding of operation and management. Environmental degradation has also deteriorated the quality of services. The latest data provided by the 58th round of the National Sample Survey (2002) specify the level of disparities in the modes of access for water supply across states. The states performing poorly in providing tap water to urban households are Bihar (35 per cent), Assam (35.5 per cent, Kerala (40 per cent), U.P. (50 per cent) and Orissa (50 per cent). In nine other states including large states such as Maharashtra, Andhra Pradesh and Gujarat, 90 per cent of the urban population receives tap water. Data on sanitation services, from the 54th round of NSS (1998) also indicate considerable state wise variations. Sanitary standards are abysmally low in the urban areas of Bihar and Madhya Pradesh where more than 45 per cent of the population has no access to any type of latrine. The septic tank is the most common mode of sanitation in use with more than one third of the urban population relying on them. Sewerage is virtually non-existence in Bihar, Madhya Pradesh, Orissa, and Assam. Punjab, Mahrashtra, Gujarat and Tamil Nadu are placed better.

The official statistics show that service coverage of water supply is quite high. However, low pressures and intermittent supplies allow back symphonize resulting in contamination of water in distribution network. The metering of domestic consumers in most of the cities is rarely taken seriously. Only 70 per cent of India's urban population has adequate excreta disposal facilities. There has been government policy not to build sewerage systems in towns of less than 10 million people. Thus due to inadequate sewerage and lack of waste water treatment facilities, river water and other sources for drinking water supply are excessively polluted. The uncollected solid waste creates hurdles in drainage system in most cities and causing flooding and water lagging in monsoon rains.

The increasing population in urban India has led to the growth of variety of economic activities which demand for a variety of transport modes and travel operators. A study carried out in 21 cities suggests that more than 75 per cent of the trips in a city are on account of either employment or education. However, the congestions in urban transport is gradually increasing due to increase in vehicles and inadequate expansion of road network. The increase in vehicles has caused air pollution and road accidents. Though India has developed an extensive public delivery system for the provision of health care and education, however, role of public sector in delivery of health and education services is gradually reducing. Only one third schools are managed by local bodies (35.6 per cent). The quality of infrastructure in schools run by local bodies is found to be poor. Though municipal hospitals exist in most Indian cities but generally public hospitals are quite inadequate for rapidly expanding urban population. Most of the health centres do not cover the slum populations. The access of poor to health care services managed by government is also declining.

URBAN REFORM INCENTIVE FUND (URIF)

The Tenth Plan underlined the need for broad based reforms to overcome the impediments of urban growth and stipulated that conformity to the reform agenda through the URIF will be made obligatory for the Central assistance. URIF called upon the States to repeal the Urban Land (Ceilings and Regulation)

Act 1976, reform Rent Control Acts, strengthen property tax system, reduce stamp duty, introduce double entry accounting system, and revise user charges to cover operations and maintenance costs. An allocation of Rs 300 crore was made under URIF for allocation to different States for implementing the reform agenda. The scheme was later subsumed in JNNURM.

An Urban Reform Incentive Fund (URIF) with an initial allocation of Rs.500 crores is to set up to provide reform-linked assistance to states. The process of release of funds would be initiated by states individually entering into a memorandum of agreement with this ministry. The planning commission has decided that in the initial phase following actions be taken:

- Repeal of Urban Land Ceiling and Regulation Act at the state level by resolution
- Rationalization of Stamp Duty in phases to bring it down to no more than 5 per cent by the end of the tenth plan period
- Reform of Rent Control Laws to remove rent control so as to stimulate private investment in rental housing
- Introduction of computerized process of registration
- Reform of property tax so that it may become a major source of revenue of urban local bodies and arrangement for its effective implementation so that its collection efficiency goes up by atleast 85 per cent by the end of tenth plan
- Levy of reasonable user charges by urban local bodies with the objective that full cost of operation and maintenance is collected by the end of tenth period
- Introduction of double entry system of accounting

CITY CHALLENGE FUND

Citywide reforms and restructuring will result in significant transaction costs. These may include the cost of preparing the reforms, implementing regulatory bodies, financing gradual phasing of tariff rebalancing, financing safety nets for the poor, financing shares for workers communities in municipal bodies and other costs. Leaving cities to finance these costs by themselves will delay and make it difficult to implement city reforms. It is, therefore proposed to set up a City Challenge Fund as an incentive based facility that will support cities to fund transitional costs of moving towards sustainable and credit worthy institutional system of municipal management and service delivery. It will assist in partial financing of the cost developing an economic reform programme and financially viable projects to be undertaken by local bodies. During the tenth plan a tentative provision of Rs.500 crores have been provided.

The overarching goal of the City Challenge Fund therefore, is to create economically productive, efficient and equitable urban centers in India. City productivity cannot be sustainable improved through a project-based approach to service delivery investments. A comprehensive program for addressing the challenges faced by cities in needed which focuses on reforms to institutions and practices. This requires:

- A strategic approach to transforming cities into vital centers for economic growth.
- A recognition that citizens – poor and rich, contribute to the cities growth and prosperity and have a right to basic services
- The development of empowered urban leadership and institutions, able to generate the political consensus and implementation capacity necessary to undertake critical reforms required for improved service delivery.
- Improvements in the creditworthiness of city governments and related municipal entities in order to facilitate the development of innovative infrastructure financing and delivery models for cities to overcome their infrastructure backlogs and management challenges.

The City Challenge Fund is intended as a catalyst for a new generation of such urban reform activities that focus on the large-scale restructuring of urban governance arrangements, fiscal systems and management practices, across a range of urban centers, in support of national growth and development priorities. It is intended that the reforms will result in the creation of well governed, managed and functioning cities that are able to finance and manage the delivery of basic service to all.

STATE POOLED FINANCE DEVELOPMENT SCHEME

The budget has also proposed to set up a pooled finance development scheme to provide credit enhancement to assist local bodies to access the capital markets on a creditworthy basis. The scheme would be meant for small and medium sized local bodies.

A group of small and medium sized urban local bodies could identify bankable/viable projects/ schemes and finance it by the way of issue of bonds of a state entity. Funds from the market would be raised without state government guarantee and based on credit rating of a group of municipalities and urban local bodies.

The scheme would promote reform in urban local bodies and usher in an era where user would pay for the services. This would also reduce dependency on state for subsidized funds. During the tenth plan Rs.400 crores have been allotted to the scheme.

Accessing the capital markets by the cities has therefore brought about perceptible change in the mindset of policy makers. In addition the central government has provided several fiscal incentives to help in the mobilization of resources for urban infrastructure. These include permitting the issuance of Tax-Free municipal bonds, broadening the definition of water supply, sanitation, removing restrictions on Foreign Direct Investment in Urban Infrastructure and encouraging externally assisted projects. However many more of such steps are needed and the implementation of the reforms needs to be expedited by the various levels of the government to meet the financial requirement.

MEGA CITY

A CSS for infrastructure development in the mega cities was introduced in 1993–94 to cover a wide range of projects on water supply and sewerage, roads and bridges, city transport, solid waste management, etc. The Central share released during Tenth Plan amounts to Rs 908.69 crore (anticipated expenditure) against an allocation of Rs 1050 crore. The scheme has since been subsumed in JNNURM.

INTEGRATED DEVELOPMENT OF SMALL AND MEDIUM TOWNS (IDSMT)

IDSMT was launched in 1979–80 to improve the economic and physical infrastructure and to provide essential facilities and services in small and medium towns. Since inception, upto 31 March 2007, a total of 1854 towns, out of 5092 small and medium towns (2001 Census), were covered under the scheme. Out of an approved outlay of Rs 1304.65 crore for the Urban Infrastructure, Housing, Basic Services, and Poverty Alleviation 397 Tenth Plan, the anticipated expenditure is Rs 566.43 crore (43.4 per cent). As the performance of the scheme was not satisfactory, an evaluation was carried out in 2002which showed that the scheme suffered from (i) lack of capacity for implementation, (ii) non-availability of matching States share, and (iii) non-availability of unencumbered land for the projects. The scheme has since been subsumed in JNNURM as Urban Infrastructure Development Scheme for Small and Medium Towns (UIDSSMT).

ACCELERATED URBAN WATER SUPPLY PROGRAMME (AUWSP)

AUWSP was launched in March 1994 to provide safe and adequate water supply to towns having population less than 20000 (as per 1991 Census), to improve environment and quality of life, and to bring about better socio-economic conditions to sustain the economy. Since its inception, 1244 towns have been covered and 639 projects have been completed at an estimated cost of Rs 1822.38 crore, including Central funds of Rs 828.06 crore. Against the approved outlay of Rs 900 crore for the Tenth Plan, an expenditure of Rs 406.50 crore was incurred which is about 45.2 per cent. Concurrent evaluation of the scheme was made in November 2003 for 62 towns in 24 States. Major recommendations of the study included handing over of the scheme to ULBs, timely release of State funds, periodic review of tariff, and training to field engineers for effective implementation. The scheme has since been subsumed under JNNURM. However, for completion of ongoing projects, Rs 32.50 crore has been provided for 2007–08.

PILOT PROJECT ON SWM

A Central sector scheme on solid waste management in 10 selected air field towns was approved in 2003 as 100 per cent grant from the Government of India towards capital cost and was to be completed in three years. Subsequent to the completion of the project, the scheme was to be handed over to the concerned ULBs for day-to-day O&M. While eight projects, viz., Sirsa, Jodhpur, Pune, Gwalior, Tezpur, Adampur, Dindigul, and Ambala are being executed by National Building Construction Corporation (NBCC), projects for Hindon and Bareilly are being executed by Uttar Pradesh Jal Nigam. The approved cost of the project is Rs 99.34 crore. The projects are under various stages of execution.

POOLED FINANCE DEVELOPMENT FUND (PFDF)

The government had approved on 29 September 2006 a proposal for setting up of a PFDF to provide credit enhancement to the ULBs to access market borrowings based on their credit worthiness through State-level Pooled Finance mechanism. The broad objectives of PFDF are:

- Facilitate implementation of bankable urban infrastructure projects through appropriate capacity building measures and financial structuring of projects.
- Facilitate the ULBs to access capital and financial markets for investment in critical urban infrastructure by providing credit enhancement grants to State-

pooled Finance Entities for accessing capital markets through Pooled Financing Bonds on behalf of one or more identified ULBs for investment in the urban infrastructure projects.

- Reduce the cost of borrowing to local bodies with appropriate credit enhancement measures and through restructuring of existing costly debts.
- Facilitate development of Municipal Bond Market.

All State/UT governments have been requested to take necessary preparatory action for operationalization of the scheme to avail benefit from this financial year. In this connection, to sensitize the State Governments and all stakeholders for implementation of the scheme in a time-bound manner, a National Workshop was organized in Chennai on 20 November 2006 and the scheme was formally launched. During 2006–07, Rs 50.00 crore has been provided for the scheme. An amount of Rs 100 crore has been provided to the Ministry of Urban Development for 2007–08 for PFDF. For the Eleventh Plan period, a provision of Rs 2500 crore has been made.

NATIONAL URBAN INFRASTRUCTURE FUND (NUIF)

The NUIF is proposed to be set up as a trust to provide source of funding for bankable projects/schemes pertaining to the ULBs. The commercial 398 Eleventh Five Year Plan banks are hesitant to lend to ULBs due to apparent lack of capacity of the ULBs to meet their debt service obligations on the one hand and lack of expertise amongst financial institutions to lend for viable urban infrastructure projects on the other. NUIF will serve as an SPV that will create necessary comfort level amongst financial institutions with respect to repayments by avoiding direct exposure of commercial banks to the ULBs. The process of consultation for setting up of NUIF is presently in the advanced stage.

DEVELOPMENT OF SATELLITE CITIES

Metros and mega cities, which have become the centre of trade and commerce, have to cope with their own problems along with unabated in-migration from small and medium towns and vast rural hinterland. These have to be planned beyond the municipal limits and due importance may be given to integrated transport and communication. The other settlements located in the vicinity of the mother city are to be developed as satellite/counter magnets to reduce and to redistribute the population and population influx. To cope with the above problem, the government has proposed a new scheme for development of satellite towns/counter magnet cities. This will help in the development of metropolitan regions. Token provision for the scheme has been made in the Budget of the Ministry of Urban Development for 2007–08.

E-GOVERNANCE IN MUNICIPALITIES

The key objectives of the Mission are to introduce e-governance in the municipalities to provide single window services to the citizens, to increase efficiency and productivity of the ULBs, to provide timely and reliable management information, etc.

The scheme envisages covering all ULBs in Class I cities (423 in total having population of one lakh or more) during 2007–08 to 2011–12. A total of 35 cities with million plus population are proposed to be covered as part of JNNURM. However, a new CSS Scheme for other cities and towns other than 35 cities would wait for the present till the implementation is watched in 35 cities as a part of JNNURM. Eight services relating to birth and death certificates, property tax, building plan approval, health programme, solid waste management, accounting system, etc., will be covered under the programme.

INVESTMENT NEEDS

The total fund requirement for the implementation of the Eleventh Five Year Plan schemes in respect of urban water supply, sewerage and sanitation, drainage, and solid waste management is estimated as given in Table 14

In order to improve the infrastructure relating to water supply and sanitation in the urban centres, the government is assisting the ULBs and the State Governments through various schemes and special Central assistance (SCA). Under

JNNURM, water supply and sanitation have been accorded highest priority among the eligible components and almost 40 per cent of the outlay would be spent on water supply and sanitation sector leaving a gap of Rs 89237 crore.

Table 14
Funds Requirement for Urban Basic Services

Sub-Sector	*EstimatedAmount (Rs in Crore)*
Urban water supply 53666	53666
Urban sewerage and sewage treatment 53168	53168
3. Urban drainage 20173	20173
4. Solid waste management 2212	2212
MIS 8	8
R&D and PHE training 10	10
Total	129237

Source: Ministry of Urban Development, GoI.

In order to bridging the gap, the following possible sources are identified. Table 15 gives the proposed flow of funds.

Table 15
Proposed Flow of Funds

Source of Funding Amount	*Amount (Rs in Crore)*
Central sector outlay	70000*
State sector outlay	35000
Institutional financing	10000
Assistance from external support agencies	10000
MIS 8	4237
FDI and private sector	10
Total	129237

Source: Ministry of Urban Development, Government of India.

During the Eleventh Five Year Plan, integrated efforts are to be made by the Central and State/UT governments to create an integrated and holistic approach on human settlements which adequately address issues of land, finance, legal, and regulatory framework, technology support, and PPP. However, it has to be understood that there can be no one solution and various options and initiatives would be needed based on national and local priorities.

With the introduction of reforms in the banking sector, considerable improvement has been made in enlarging access to finance for housing by individual families and also through co-operatives as well as private developers.

The 11th Fiver Year Plan has made the provision of estimated requirement for urban infrastructure in the tune of Rs. 186619 crores (USD 20.7 billion), based on the additional population growth excepted by 2012 and augmentation of existing facilities to achieve 100 percent coverage. For individual sectors broad estimates of require investments are shown in Table 16.

Table 16
Estimates for Urban Sector during 11th Five Year Plan

Description	*Rs. Crores*
Urban Transport	57,400
Urban Water Supply	53,666
Sewerage & Sanitation	53,168
Drainage	20,173
Solid Waste Management*	2,212
Total Investment Required in 11th FYP	186,619

* Additional investments of Rs. 2,445 crores will be made from allocations under 12th Finance Commission
Source: Planning Commission.

Due to the rise in urban population, RITES (1998) estimated that the travel demand would grow 3.5 times between 1991 and 2021. Based on this rising demand scenario, the Report of the 11th Five Year Plan Working Group on Urban Transport estimates that total investment requirements for the Urban Transport Infrastructure to be nearly Rs. 57,400 cores (USD 12.8 billion). Out of this, nearly 56 per cent or Rs. 32,000 crores in proposed for mass rapid transport system only. The working group recommends that funds to be channeled towards road infrastructure and facilities for pedestrians will have to come from the public budget. It suggests that only city bypasses may be constructed on a BOT basis, as toll collection in such cases is possible. Further, investments in parking facilities, terminals, bus operations, and high cost public transport system (such as the MRTS/BRTS) may be encouraged through the PPP route.

The investment requirements for water supply and sanitation (including sewerage, low cost sanitation and drainage) assuming the population of 36.5 crores and 100 per cent coverage by the end of 2012 is estimated at Rs. 127,007 crores (USD 28.2 billion). Of this investments in water supply would be Rs. 53,600 crores and sanitation (including sewerage) facilities would be Rs. 53,168 crores. Thus, investments in water supply are in between Rs. 69,500-107,000 crores.

Similarly, based on standard cost estimates for modernization of solid waste management practices in various city categories a waste management scheme for 423 Class I cities indicating a need of approximately Rs. 2,445 corres. This along with Planning Commission estimated to address the needs of increased urban population in class I towns and to cover the population in other towns would some of Rs.4,600 crores.

MISMATCH IN INVESTMENT REQUIREMENTS

The MOUD had estimated that around Rs. 1,20,536 cores would be the investment requirements for the identified 63 cities over 7 years and that Rs. 50,000 crores would be made available as central assistance. However, based on the CDPs submitted, the investment likely to increase. This figure would cross the MOUD estimates if the remaining cities were added. As a response to meeting this gap in the envisaged investment requirements between MOUD estimates and CDP estimates, the centre may want to increase the corpus availability from Rs. 50,000 crores to a higher amount. But even with the existing estimates, will the ULBs be in a position to garner their own share component given their financial health should be assessed.

Most of the ULBs will not have the financial sustainability for such large investment estimates. As release of funds is linked to physical progress of the project and improvements in service delivery, investments should happen in line with the absorption capacity of the ULBs. It would be worthwhile to revisit the estimates and prepare projects in line with the ability of the ULBs to sustain such investments.

A proactive approach wherein the ULBs prepare their revenue mobilization measures over the long term (not restricting only to the mission period) is required in order to assess the capacity to bear the investments. For instance, a progressive city with a population of around 1.2 million is in the process of preparing a DPR for a mass rapid transport system in its city and the rough estimates reveal that around Rs. 900 crores is required as its own contribution to the project cost. Therefore, it is imperative that the urban local bodies quickly identify other revenue streams and puts in concerted efforts to improve its existing revenue streams.

FINANCIAL ASSISTANCE UNDER UPA PROGRAMMES

With a view to provide gainful employment to the urban unemployed through encouraging the setting up of self employment ventures or provision of wage employment – Swarn Jayanti Shahari Rojgar Yojana (SJSRY) was launched in 1997 after subsuming the earlier three schemes of UBSP, NRY and PMIUPEP. SJSRY is funded on a basis of 75:25 between the Centre and states. The scheme rests on a foundation of community empowerment towards this ends, community organizations like Neighbourhood Groups (NHG's), Neighbourhood Committees (NHC's) and Community Development Societies (CDS's) are to be set up in the target areas. These CDS's may also self themselves up as thrift and credit societies to encourage community savings and also other group activities. The scheme has two major components. One is related with urban self employment programme which envisages setting up micro enterprises and skill development, training and infrastructure support, and Development of Women and Children in Urban Areas (DWCUA). The second component is concerned with urban wage employment programme. Funds released under the different poverty alleviation programmes are shown in Table 17.

There has been increasing trend in funds release except in case of National Scheme for Liberation and Rehabilitation of Scavengers. Funds allocation under SJSRY in the selected states is shown in Table 18.

Table 17
Central Release Under SJSRY, VAMBAY, NSDP, NSLRS

(Rs. Crores)

Year	*SJSRY*	*VAMBAY (Allocation)*	*NSDP*	*NSLRS*
1997-98	98.63	–	290.99	90.0
1998-99	158.47	–	351.63	5.90
1999-2000	118.77	–	384.96	70.0
2000-2001	85.13	–	247.34	60.92
2001-2002	38.31	69.0	282.40	9.20
2002-2003	100.92	256.85	333.44	40.95
2003-2004	100.74	238.50	335.08	21.41
2004-2005	122.01	280.58	613.77	13.56
2005-2006	155.88	249.00	–	–

Source: Ministry of Housing & Urban Poverty Alleviation, Govt. of India, New Delhi.

Table 18
Budget Allocation Under SJSRY In India

(Rs. Lakh)

Year	*Bihar*	*Jhar-khand*	*Chhatis-garh*	*MP*	*Orissa*	*UP*	*Uttara-khand*
1997-98	506.09	–	–	927.18	223.11	1181.03	–
1998-99	779.22	–	–	1511.77	360.44	1988.42	–
1999-2000	872.36	–	–	1692.17	403.63	2202.09	–
2000-01	606.30	422.69	202.10	1143.05	375.11	1956.43	102.97
2001-02	606.30	422.69	202.10	1143.05	375.11	1956.43	102.97
2002-03	427.02	236.41	213.37	813.93	330.94	1450.29	76.18
2003-04	425.38	235.88	212.31	818.32	329.69	1453.55	76.49
2004-05	468.09	278.58	156.02	753.15	322.65	1422.61	74.82
2005-06	681.66	405.67	227.16	1096.76	469.86	2071.43	109.14
2006-07	1173.65	698.46	391.11	1888.35	808.97	3566.49	187.91
Total	6146.07	2700.38	1604.17	11787.73	3909.51	19248.77	730.48

Source: Ministry of Housing & Urban Poverty Alleviation, Govt. of India, New Delhi.

During 1997-98 to 2006-2007, largest fund were allocated in the states of Uttar Pradesh, Madhya Pradesh and Bihar. However, there are discrepancies in funds allocated and funds released to the states. In Uttar Pradesh higher funds were released as against also cited funds while Bihar received fewer amounts of allocated funds (Table 19).

Table 19
Year-wise Fund Released Under SJSRY

Year	*Bihar*	*Jhar-khand*	*Chhattis-garh*	*MP*	*Orissa*	*Uttara-khand*	*U.P.*
1997-98	350.84	155.25	–	927.18	223.11	–	1181.03
1998-99	540.18	239.04	–	1511.77	360.44	–	1988.42
1999-2000	283.29	125.34	–	1836.21	460.83	–	2344.02
2000-01	–	202.10	422.69	888.59	69.24	102.97	1340.78
2001-02	–	66.64	128.44	304.02	300.00	27.88	733.07
2002-03	–	–	236.41	683.93	381.48	16.33	1671.76
2003-04	425.38	–	229.65	818.32	–	46.27	1571.74
2004-05	468.09	–	119.31	931.49	48.91	160.31	2622.61
2005-06	681.66	–	405.67	1596.76	469.86	309.14	3071.43
2006-07	586.83	–	698.46	2388.35	808.97	93.96	4566.49
Total	3436.27	788.37	2240.63	11886.62	3122.84	756.86	21091.35

Source: Ministry of Housing & Urban Poverty Alleviation, Govt. of India, New Delhi.

The financial progress of scheme is shown in Table 20 Expenditure as percentage of funds available was recorded highest in Uttar Pradesh (94.45 per cent) followed by Bihar (79.53 per cent), Orissa (78.15 per cent) and Madhya Pradesh (77.80 per cent).

Table 20
Financial Progress Under SJSRY
(From 1997-98 till Now)

(Rs. Lakh)

State	*Funds Released*	*Funds Available*	*Expenditure*
Bihar	4260.58	7346.31	5842.77 (79.53)
Chhatisgarh	3356.00	3356.00	2012.09 (59.96)
Jharkhand	886.71	2311.18	0.00
Madhya Pradesh	18968.99	22022.94	17134.46 (77.80)
Orissa	4592.30	5708.64	4461.57 (78.15)
Uttarakhand	1184.43	1184.43	623.40 (52.63)
Uttar Pradesh	29871.01	37634.44	35547.50 (94.45)
Total	59285.72	25763.94	61606.79

Source: Ministry of Housing & Urban Poverty Alleviation, Govt. of India, New Delhi.

FINANCING URBAN INFRASTRUCTURE

The traditional system of funding based on plan and budgetary allocations have to be minimized and withdrawn gradually, soft options for financing urban infrastructure and services available in the past will have to give way to new fiscal instruments which envisage reduction in subsidies, reduction in plan allocation and improved pricing and cost recovery mechanism. Developing commercially viable infrastructure projects, financing through access to capital markets, credit rating of municipal and urban infrastructure entities, forging Public Private Partnerships in the provision of urban infrastructure are some of the new approaches that need to be adopted by the city planners to improve the urban situation in the country.

PUBLIC PRIVATE PARTNERSHIPS IN URBAN INFRASTRUCTURE:

Public Private Partnership provides an opportunity for private sector participation in financing, designing, construction and operations and maintenance of public sector programmes and projects. This is high time to forge a greater interface between the public and private sector in a wide range of activities in the country. The overwhelming response of private sector, including civil societies in the Tsunami earth quake in India was an outstanding example of public-private partnership.

Most of the public services have been traditionally provided through in house facilities of governments, financed, and managed directly by them. Public Private Partnership is an approach under which services are delivered by the private sector while the responsibility for providing the services rests with the governments. This arrangement requires the government to either enter into a 'contract' with the private partner or pay for the services rendered by the private sector. Contracting prompts a new activity when neither the public sector nor the private sector existed to provide the service. Three things distinguished Public Private Partnership from direct provision of services by governments are (i) a partnership based on well articulated contact; (ii) a long term relationship between the public and private sector; and (iii) flexibility and responsiveness in decision making. The involvement of private sector participation for financing urban infrastructure and services, particularly water supply and environmental sanitation has not been very encouraging in India till recently. However, some private sector initiatives for financing long term capital investments in urban basic services, particularly water supply and solid waste management in recent years have indicated the potential of public-private partnership in delivery of services in urban sector. However, the basic hindrance towards the successful private sector participation in financing urban basic services is mainly, the failure of the governance system to create the conducive atmosphere in this regard rather than the failure of the initiative in itself. In order to derive the advantage inherent in public sector as well as private sector enterprises, the role of public-private partnership is considered to have great potential in some important areas in delivery of municipal services. The partnership fall into five main categories viz. - (i) contract services; (ii) privatization of services; (iii) designing, construction and operation of facilities; (iv) project financing and; (v) merchant facilities. The partnership in municipal services is expected to reduce cost of maintenance, increase efficiency and timely completion of new projects while community participation in operation and maintenance of services is expected to be of great importance. Government of India is committed to remove the roadblocks in delivery of services and creating infrastructure in collaboration with private sector under Jawaharlal Nehru Urban Renewal Mission. The Mission will have two main components, focusing on infrastructure and governance and services to the urban poor respectively. The government now recognizes that greater accountability for service delivery performance is a pre-requisite for improvement in the coverage and quality of services.

Public Private Partnership is being advocated in recent years in the municipal sector due to several spin offs of the partnership. It facilities the financing of urban services, augments the level of services, enhances efficiency of service delivery systems and brings in new technology. Public Private Partnership ranges between full privatization to simply contracting out services to private operators and providers. In order to enhance the efficiency and effectiveness of the system, the municipal governments and the urban infrastructure agencies are experimenting with various options. However, privatization has not yet materialized on a scale as required in the sector. Some of the factors responsible for this situation are:

- Lack of clarity in scope and framework for PSP (many of the initiatives in the sector are for the Build-Operate-Transfer (BOT) type projects for source development without adequate concern for management improvements for distribution systems and customer service);
- Lack of rigorous project and contract development, including risk management and lack of adequate concern for financial viability;
- Lack of policy support and appropriate regulatory framework at higher levels of government;
- Lack of participation and capacity of a wide variety of stakeholders;
- Lack of continuity of champion for the projects (leaders get transferred or defeated in elections);

DEVELOPMENT OF THE MUNICIPAL BOND MARKET IN INDIA

One of the key developments in the arena of infrastructure financing in the country has been the emergence of a nascent municipal bond market in the country. The concept of municipal bonds as an additional mechanism for raising resources for urban infrastructure projects was first presented in 1995 at a national seminar sponsored by USAID in December 1995. Later, the Rakesh Mohan Committee on the Commercialization of Infrastructure Projects in India also recommended such a system as well. Internationally, municipal bonds have played a key role in the creation of urban infrastructure assets in United States and Canada. Therefore, it was envisaged that adapting this model to the Indian context would open new vistas for attracting private capital to the urban infrastructure sector (Table 21).

Table 21
Municipal Bonds in India

City	*Amount (Rs. Million)*	*Interest (Per cent)*	*Guarantee*	*Purpose*
Ahmadabad	1000	14	No	Water supply and sanitation
Bangalore	1250	13	State Governments	City roads, Street, drainage
Ludhiana	100	13.5 - 14	No	Water supply and Sanitation
Nagpur	500	13	No	Water supply
Nashik	1000	14.75	No	–
Indore	100	NA	Yes	City road
Madurai	300	12.25	No	Water supply and sanitation
Ahmadabad (Tax Free)	1000	9	No	Road construction and widening
Hyderabad (Tax Free)	825	8.5	No	Water supply and sanitation
Tamil Nadu (Pooled Financing)	110	9.20	USAID Provided backup guarantee of 50 per cent of the bonds	–

Source: India Infrastructure Report, Oxford University Press, 2006.

HUDCO loans sanctioned and corresponding growth rate has experienced an increase in the post-decentralization period. Per capita HUDCO loan assistance for the developed states like Gujarat, Maharashtra, Tamil Nadu and Karnataka increased over the years during the 1990s. However, most of the backward states have registered a decline in the growth of loans sanctioned by HUDCO for urban infrastructure. From 1980 onwards, external assistance mainly from World Bank and other foreign agencies have been coming in for the urban infrastructure in general and urban basic services in particular. A substantial portion of this assistance i.e. more than 50 per cent has been for the urban water supply and sanitation programme. However, the developed states received a major chunk of the assistance. Out of 15 completed externally aided projects, 9 of them were found located in the developed states. There are 18 ongoing projects in different stages of implementation. 6 of them are located in the developed states.Private sector involvement in infrastructure services in general and water and sewerage projects in particular have become a focal point in the era of liberalized economy. The public-private initiatives have largely remained confined to the maintenance of urban basic services through service contract and management contract. These initiatives have to larger extent remained confined to the developed states like Maharashtra, Gujarat, Karnataka and Tamil Nadu. The involvement of private investment for financing capital investment in urban services like water supply and sewerage has remained limited. Even the issuing of the municipal bonds for mobilizing the public money for development and maintenance of urban infrastructure is confined to a few municipal corporations. There are 28 water and sanitation related projects in which private-public partnership has been initiated. Out of them, 20 projects are located in developed states. Similarly, out of 44 projects in solid waste management, about half of them are found in the developed states. 30 of these 44 projects are in the big cities. Thus, the advantages of external financing of urban infrastructure projects and resource mobilization are confined to the developed states and particularly to the metropolitan cities.

ROLE OF HUDCO

Housing and Urban Development Corporation, a 100 per cent central government owned non-banking finance company, is a specialized financial institution to fund state government, their specialized agencies like Housing Boards, Urban Development Corporations etc and municipal bodies for their urban infrastructure projects. HUDCO has been financing urban infrastructure projects in water and sewerage, roads, area development and housing in a big way.

HUDCO averaged new sanctions for three year period 1999-2002 at Rs.8000 crore ($1.8 billion) per annum. New sanctions dramatically soared to Rs.15627 crore ($3.5 billion) in 2002-03. A major part of the new loans and other investments were in the area classified as urban infrastructure at Rs.11134 crore. HUDCO has sanctioned total assistance amounting to Rs.29032 crores classified as urban infrastructure up to 2002-03 as per the details presented in Table 22

Table 22
Financing by HUDCO

	No. of Projects		*HUDCO Assistance*	
Infrastructure Segments	*2002-03*	*Cumulative*	*2002-03*	*Cumulative*
Water Supply	35	367	2714.31	8827.07
Sewerage, Drainage and solid waste management	11	88	263.00	1572.14
Transportation/Roads	36	160	42.16.70	8858.83
Area Development	3	101	105.28	1195.82
Social Infrastructure	31	131	713.51	1998.77
Others, including commercial	33	154	3120.07	6022 46
Sanitation	5	1034	1.41	512.86
Total	154	2035	11134.28	29032.95

Source: Annual Report, HUDCO, 2005.

HUDCO has primarily financed state government agencies like housing board and municipalities on the strength of the state government guarantees. As much as Rs.17154.60 crore of loans outstanding on 31st March, 2003 out of total outstanding loans of Rs.21535.82 crore were given for various projects against state governments/banks guarantees. Going by the anecdotal evidence, most of these projects were financially non-viable and the state governments would need to provide for their servicing from their budgets in time to come. In addition, HUDCO has lent Rs.1428.93 crores to the state government departments directly. HUDCO was fully secured by way of mortgage for loans outstanding amount of Rs.2599.51 crore by mortgages.

ROLE OF EXTERNAL AGENCIES

World Bank, Asian Development Bank, JBIC, French international development agency and some other bilateral aid agencies have funded several urban infrastructure projects especially in the urban water supply and sanitation schemes in Chennai, Bangalore and Mumbai. Recently, the Bank has adopted an urban reform based funding approach. Such programmes have been taken up in Karnataka and Tamil Nadu. Karnataka programme seeks to develop a long-term vision for the urban water sector into high quality, sustainable services in all urban local bodies. The strategy is to achieve this vision is to implement a phased program towards full service coverage, and quality service provision in sustainable services in all urban local bodies. The strategy is to achieve this vision is to implement a phased program towards full service coverage, and quality service provision in a sustainable manner. The Karnataka Urban Water sector Improvement Project components are: a) assist the State Government in finalizing its policy reform agenda, and carry out initial implementation steps of staged sector reforms; and, to prepare business model, and private sector participation processes for service provision in Karnataka. The second component seeks to improve the service provision, and attain continuous service in selected demonstration zones; generate credibility in the overall program and learn lessons on the challenges faced in the demonstration zones for scaling up continuous service provision; and, simultaneously improve the efficiency of bulk supply operations, and distribution networks, attaining initial improvements in water service provision to all State residents. The third component finances the project's incremental operational costs, and studies related to project management and implementation, including incremental, short term consultants for the Karnataka Urban Infrastructure Development and Finance Corporation (KUIDFC); the preparation and establishment of a monitoring and evaluation system; the costs related to the financial management systems within KUIDFC; staff training within KUIDFC, including supervision costs. Orientation of Bank programme in increasingly becoming reform oriented in urban sector. Implementation of externally aided projects in urban water supply and sanitation sector are shown in Table 23

Table 23
Externally Aided Projects

Scheme	*Cost (Rs. Crores)*	*External Assistance (US$M)*	*Agency*	*Year of Completion*
Bombay Water Supply & Sanitation Project Phase-I	185	55	World Bank	1981
Maharashtra Water Supply & Sanitation Project	86	48	World Bank	1985
Punjab Water Supply & Sanitation Project	67	38	World Bank	1988
Uttar Pradesh Water Supply & Sanitation Project	60	40	World Bank	1983
II Bombay Water Supply & Sanitation Project	640	196	World Bank	1988
Rajasthan Water Supply & Sanitation Project	137.76	80	World Bank	1988
Gujarat Water Supply & Sanitation Project	207.33	72	World Bank	1991
Tamil Nadu Water Supply & Sanitation Project	321.66	73	World Bank	1994
Kerala Water Supply & Sanitation Project	127.88	30.11	World Bank	1994
Madras Water Supply & Sanitation Project	255.95	69	World Bank	1996
III Bombay Water Supply & Sanitation Project	915	145	WB	1996
Gujarat Urban Development Water Supply & Sanitation Project	208	62	WB	1995
Uttar Pradesh Urban Development	463.86	150	WB	1996
Hyderabad Water Supply & Sanitation Project	337.8	311.5	WB	1998
Integrated Packed Water Treatment kiosk for high grade drinking water at Kangchup, Imphal, Manipur	4.75	FF 7.145	French Assistance	1998

Source: Indian Statistics.com.

COMMUNITY BASED URBAN INFRASTRUCTURE FINANCING

Community Led Infrastructure Finance Facility (CLIFF), a financial mechanism, created with the funding from DFID, SIDA and Homeless International, is providing venture capital in India through CLIFF-I for helping communities of urban poor to seek and avail finance from banks to carry out community driven infrastructure, housing and other urban services. CLIFF-I is working with Banks and regulatory authorities to bring about necessary changes in the mindset and the processes of the formal banking system to finance infrastructure projects undertaken by communities of poor people directly. If this succeeds, municipal bodies may join with such community organizations to help them complete the projects and also raise finances from banks for undertaking capital expenditure which the municipalities have to incur.

The Indo-USAID programme on Financial Institutions Reform and Expansion (FIRE (D) for developing a long-term debt market for viable urban infrastructure projects was launched in1994. The programme envisages development of a viable urban infrastructure finance system that could support development of debt market in India by using the Urban and Environmental Credit Guaranty Funds (earlier known as Housing Guaranty Funds) for contemplating the issuing of debt instruments to finance urban infrastructure projects. The mission of FIRE (D) programme is to institutionalize the delivery of commercially viable urban environmental infrastructure services to urban residents with particular focus on the urban poor.

Besides providing Technical Assistance, The USAID also facilitates access of Urban and Environmental Credit Guaranty Funds for a period of 30 years to develop and urban infrastructure finance system. HUDCO and IL&FS act as the financial intermediaries to channel the funds along with a matching amount of locally raised funds to municipalities or private sector entities to finance selected commercially viable urban infrastructure projects relating to water supply, sewerage, solid waste management and area development.

FIRE (D) Project demonstrated novel ways of financing by accessing the debt market, credit rating of municipal and urban infrastructure entities, and private participation for the provision of urban infrastructure projects. Initiatives have been taken to develop projects, in a number of cities, which are now in progress. Positive spin-offs of FIRE (D) have been substantial even in the non-project cities. The most important impact is the motivation and interest created in other cities in different states to think of alternative ways of financing urban infrastructure other than the traditional methods of plan and budgetary allocations which have built-in aberrations hindering effective and efficient management. Equally important impact of the programme is the interest created amongst the financial institutions for funding urban infrastructure projects. The programme has also led to innovative urban management practices in some of the cities in terms of public-private partnerships (PPP), accessing the capital market and sprucing up of financial management practices.

SUGGESTIVE APPROACH

The model for progressive improvement of infrastructure takes the form of a series of principles. The finance, institutional arrangements, technology and political constrains are central to these principles. Similarly, the concepts are self-help, decentralization of decision making and progressive improvements are important. The principles emerge from the critical appreciator of literature pertaining infrastructure development. These are:

- It must be recognized that within all cities and towns, two inter dependent circuits exist - the formal and informal. The urban poor cater the emerging needs of services of urban dwellers and need basic services for their own survival. The infrastructure services of water, sanitation, drainage, solid waste management and transport facilities may be divided into formal and informal facilities.

- Infrastructure system should be operated by municipal authority directly or in association with parastatal agencies on recovery basis. In order to maintain the infrastructure, user charges are necessary that can ensure recovery of cost also.
- Irregular land tenure issues should be resolved within the informal sectors of the city. The resolution of land tenure issues would seem to be an absolute prerequisite of any system of progressive improvement.
- Informal infrastructure should be designed and built using external technical assistance as required; however, technical assistance from government or non-governmental organizations may be required to facilitate its use.
- Informal infrastructure built by the local community should be under its control. The facilitating agency must act as a supporter of the community, not as the owner or manager of the programme. Without the involvement of the community, the infrastructural needs of the poor will never be met.
- The technology adopted for informal sector infrastructure must be maintainable by the community. It is necessary for municipalities to realize that standards and regulations must be minimized in order to allow the incorporation of alternative technology that can be maintained by the community.
- The informal sector must be affordable by its low income users.
- Informal sector infrastructure must be socially acceptable to the community involved.
- In order to achieve city-wide coverage of infrastructure, including within the informal residential sector; it is necessary that government adopt the role of facilitator and enable rather than merely as provider.

- The NGOs can play a key role in assisting communities to develop infrastructure systems. The non-governmental organizations can play an important role in the infrastructure development process. NGOs are useful in organizing communities and strengthening community based organizations.

Municipalities or local bodies are entrusted with a set of responsibilities of providing basic urban amenities and services to the people. They are dependent on states and centre for grant in aid and loans. Efforts at micro level are not effectively and efficiently made to mobilize additional resources due to several factors like political interference, lack of expert/professionals, legal framework bottlenecks etc. Recovery of taxes is also very poor. There is wide gap between commitment and resources. Thus, it is necessary to reduce dependence of local bodies on government budgetary support. They should effectively exploit the revenue potential through rationalization of assessment norms, simplification of procedures; rebate on timely payment, revision of old levies and taxes. Municipal governments may be allowed to enjoy fiscal autonomy with freedom of choice in regard to imposing new taxes and revising tax rates. It is argued that municipal bodies are not financially strong enough to tap capital market for undertaking infrastructure works which involve huge capital investment, long gestation period. But the provision of marketing borrowing will certainly motivate the municipal bodies to revamp their financial strength to mobilize resources from market. There is also need to encourage private sector involvement in the development, strengthening and creator of urban infrastructure. The conducive investment climate has to be created for encouraging the greater participation of private sector through introduction of suitable package of incentives. The concept of commercialization of urban infrastructure is very successful in developed countries. It can be also adopted in India with judicious mix. Similarly, contracting out of urban services has been quite common in the western countries. In this system, local authority contracts with private firm or public agency to take responsibility for operation and maintenance of a service or specific tasks. These arrangements can be based on profit sharing arrangement. It is also suggested that in effective public-private partnership should be developed in respect of each major urban services as well as at all the stages of activities from planning to resource mobilization, construction, management and maintenance.

Financial markets can contribute to improving the well being of low income households. This contribution is not inevitable but is achieved through a careful reflective design process that takes account of the particular circumstances of the target group and the vulnerabilities that they face. Lending to the poor does not have to threaten the stability of financial markets but can help to strengthen economics through encouraging savings and developing good lending practices. Financial intermediation, which appeared to be adding to the achievement of well being and prosperity by providing additional capital to markets, may have encouraged lenders to take excessive risks. Access to financial services is important to low income households, helping them to increase their development options and reduce future vulnerabilities. Core financial services are savings and loans. Savings reduce vulnerabilities by providing resources that can be used in emergencies; they also help households to spread income across productive and less productive periods. Saving is also a preparation for borrowing in several ways, they help accumulate required deposits, they enable households to see what they can afford to set aside for loan repayments and they build up solidarity between members of a collective finance scheme. Loan helps households to accumulate assets, paying for goods at the same time as they benefit from the services that they secure through ownership.

Local government severely lack the capacity for planning for local economic development and capital investments, preparation and management of projects, financial management and maintaining appropriate accounting and information systems which are crucial to efficient provision of urban infrastructure. Strengthening of local governments in these areas is imperative.

BEST PRACTICES

Pimpri-Chinchwad (Pune)

Pimpri-Chinchwad is a major industrial centre of the Pune region and also the entire country. It has witnessed a high population growth rate of around 100 per cent in the last two decades. With a current estimated population of about 1.2 million which is fast growing, the city is focused on providing quality services to its citizens. Traditionally, the city fo Pimpri-Chinchwad has been the place of work for people living in neighbouring Pune. However, in the last few years, this city has started gaining its own recognition due to its citizen-friendly approach to administration. Pimpri-Chinchwad Municipal Corporation (PCMC) is the Urban Local Body of the city.

JNNURM has enabled large scales investments towards development of infrastructure facilities in the city. From being one of the first ULBs to sign the MoA for the Mission, PCMC has been working towards meeting the requirements of the Mission in order to apply for funds for its projects.

So far, projects amounting to about Rs. 1,665 crores have been sanctioned by the Centre under JnNURM, and Rs. 170 crores have been disbursed (including PCMC's contribution). These projects are in the sectors of Water Supply and Sewerage, Municipal solid Waste, Slum Rehabilitation, Urban Transport and EWS. PCMC is also working towards implementation of reforms which form part of the Mission and has made good progress in the last one year. This has also helped PCMC in getting second installments for its Slum Rehabilitation projects. PCMC has also been the recipient of the ward-"Improvement in Municipal Financial Management" for the year 2007 - from the Ministry for its efforts towards reforms implementation.

It is one of the few Mission cities to have set-up a Project Implementation Unit (PIU) to assist it in the overall implementation of Mission objectives. The PIU is assisting PCMC in monitoring the implementation of JnNURM projects, implementing of reform commitments in the Memorandum of Agreement (MoA), coordination activities of PCMC with the various agencies involved in the Mission, and supporting PCMC in all JNNURM related activities. By driving the reforms implementation process, the PIU has ensured steady flows of funds for implementation of projects. The PIU has completed its one year with PCMC and has played a very important and active role in the progress made by the ULB in the mission. The guidelines suggested by Centre for smooth implementation of reforms have been tried out by PCMC and found to be successful to a large extent.

Dharavi Redevelopment Project (Mumbai)

Dharavi Redevelopment Project of Mumbai has attracted many developers. Many real estate developers have joined hands with reputed town planners of Singapore and China who have experience of integrated large urban projects. The big draw of the project is the high floor space index (FSI) of 4, which will allow companies to develop more area in Dharavi. Mumbai, barring some places, has an FSI of 1.33. The developers will provide 30 million sq. ft. of space, including housing, schools, parks, and roads. In return, they will be allowed to build 40 million sq ft of home and office space for sale. The Slum Rehabilitation Authority (SRA) of Maharashtra had received twenty-six bids from various consortiums, including seventy-eight real estate firms, many with considerable experience in township construction.

The 57,000 families that live in Dharavi will be rehabilitated in 225 sq ft multi-storeyed tenements, which will be maintained by the developer for fifteen years. The entire area has been divided into five sectors of about 1.5 crore sq. ft. each on an average. The projects is expected to generate close to Rs. 25,000 crore in revenue for the Maharashtra government.

Out of the total consortiums who had submitted the bids, nineteen consortiums have been short-listed by Maharashtra government. The selected consortiums will submit financial proposals, of which five will be selected for project implementation. The final selection and development work to start in 2008.

Bangalore (Karnataka)

The Bangalore Water Supply and Sewerage Board (BWSSB) responsible for the supply of drinking water, conveying, treating and disposal of sewage to the silicon valley of India "Bangalore city", has achieved 99 per cent bill collection efficiency with the adoption of latest technologies. The board had successfully leveraged Information Technology for the last five years such as implementation of SCADA and Telemetry, developing Geographic Information System (GIS) of Water Supply pipelines and Sewerage lines of the entire city, maintenance and updating of the same by an independent management system, Computerization of Revenue Billing and Collection, spot billing system with hand held computers, Payment of Water Bills through unmanned 'KIOSK' working 24 x 7 hours, Water Auditing to control Leaks, computerized and consolidated all accounts in Central Office, usage of LAN-WAN to facilitate transfer of data pertaining to revenue billing, connections to the poor through effective communication strategy. These initiatives resulted in significant cost savings and also enhanced the bill collection efficiency to 99 per cent.

Nagpur (Maharashtra)

As part of its effort to achieve cost recovery, Nagpur Municipal Corporation (NMC) has developed several innovative measures to reduce unaccounted for water. Motivated by the requirement to augment revenues, NMC came out with innovative idea of unearthing illegal water connections by using the same plumbers who fixed these in the first place. The corporation declared a time-bound programme aimed both at regularizing illegal water connections and also applying a universal metering policy. The incentive of Rs 100 for every illegal connection motivated about 200 plumbers. With insignificant expenses of about Rs 0.2 million as incentives for plumbers and a minimum amount spent on publicity drive, the programme achieved regularization of about 25,000 (71 per cent) connections within a short period of four months. There was significant and evident increase in revenue generation. The simplified and rationalized procedures, transparency, accountability of the corporation and the participatory mechanisms adopted have generated enormous citizen co-operation and revenue to the corporation.

Mumbai (Maharashtra)

Brihan Mumbai Municipal corporation has implemented a variety of strategies to achieve cost recovery, including targeted efforts to reduce non-revenue water by adopting various water conservation measures, strong management policies governing operations and maintenance, strong accounting and financial statements and public outreach programs to stay informed of both community and business needs. The corporation has also adjusted the tariff structure in order to meet the rising cost of water provision, although it retains the historically complex pricing regime. Since 1995 -1996, the total revenue income has doubled while the expenditure has increased by 1.5 times. In order to improve the cost of recovery (today: 80 per cent), the centralized computerized billing is being decentralized at the ward level. These measures ultimately increased transparency and accountability of the corporation to their customers.

Andhra Pradesh

Compared to other cities, Indian cities do not enjoy high levels of access to both water supply and sanitation. Central to the issue of affordability are high connection charges and low willingness to pay for water services. Connection charges often represent the greatest barrier to affordability of water services for the unconnected poor, while customer willingness to pay remains low in areas with intermittent water supply and poor water quality. To tackle these affordability issues, the government of Andhra Pradesh decided to extend individual connection to BPL families at Rs.1200 with the option to pay the cost in twelve equal installments. About one lakh eligible BPL households applied for individual connections under the scheme and over two-thirds of the applications were sanctioned by the local bodies and four-fifth got installed. This initiative has enhanced image of the local body, less scope for pilferage and illegal connections, improved operational efficiency, reduced expenditure on *adhoc* arrangements and more importantly increased the revenue of the local bodies.

Alandur (Tamil Nadu)

Alandur, a municipality in a residential suburb of Chennai, had initiated underground sewerage system through Public Private partnership. This is first of its kind in Asia with 100 per cent cost recovery. Though the concept had faced resistance in its initial phases due to lack of adequate public awareness and other bureaucratic problems, it achieved its target through extensive awareness campaigns and newspaper advertisements. The residents, who essentially belong to the middle class and slum dwellers, contributed to the cause in the form of payments for getting individual sewerage connections. Of the total cost of Rs. 34 crores, the public contribution amounted to about Rs. 11 crores (about 32 per cent). At the heart of the project's success lies a well-planned communications strategy that has evoked a strong and positive community response. This unconventional project, financially supported by the beneficiaries, emphasized the fact that the services can be improved where there is strong political commitment coupled with effective communications, transparency and partnership with community based organizations.

Ahmedabad (Gujarat)

Realizing the importance of and benefits from cleanliness, Ahmedabad Municipal Corporation (AMC) and the government officials determined to clean up the city and ensure better living conditions for the citizens. To accomplish this task, AMC took several precautionary and curative steps, as required and also encouraged private participation. As per the Mandatory Directions under Municipal Solid Waste rules 2000, the corporation has taken seven cost cutting steps such as prohibition of littering of waste from the streets, primary collection of waste from the doorstep, daily street sweeping, abolition of open waste storage sites, transportation of waste in covered vehicles, processing of waste by composting or power generation and disposal of non-biodegradable waste at the engineered landfills. These initiatives led to 50 per cent cost saving to the corporation.

Rudrapur (Uttaranchal)

Rudrapur Nagar Palika, marked by rapid industrial and commercial growth started contracting out solid waste management services. This PPP initiative enabled the local body in providing better services to the citizens and at the same time made considerable savings through cost-cutting mechanisms. This is a service contract between the municipality and the private contractor. Local body provides all the logistics required for the waste disposal and collection. After experimenting with PPP strategy the results unearthed the potential of the private player in providing public services and the citizens are much more delighted then ever before. It has also resulted in the savings of up to Rs. 1.2 lakhs per month for the ULB, as each permanent employee salary was about Rs. 5000 per month. Moreover, the private contractor does not have to make any investment and he would continuously provide the services.

Suryapet (Andhra Pradesh)

The effective implementation of Municipal Solid waste Management Rules, 2000 by the Suryapet Municipality, the first grade municipality in Andhra Pradesh, has emerged as a sustainable model for the smaller and medium towns and had earned revenue to the municipality. The critical factors to the success of this initiative are complete implementation of door to door collections and penalizing those who litter waste on roads and drains. The third has been removal of all community bins thus making the town dustbin free. These cost cutting measures has laid a path to the project's success. The micro level planning, training imparted for motivation of staff, public awareness, participation programmes gave exemplary results. Moreover, the enforcement of levying fine on commercial establishment throwing garbage on streets and drains has been the most critical factor and is equally responsible for success of the initiative. It is probably the only municipality, which earns money by selling the recyclable materials and has been able to provide additional employment to the urban poor women.

Alandur (Tamil Nadu)

Alandur municipality falls under the purview of Kanchipuram district of Tamil Nadu State. To deliver better utility services Mr. R.S. Bharati, Chairman of Alandur municipality, in 1996 has initiated a project based on public private partnership model. The project was carried out in two phases. The concession agreement signed between municipality and private contractor was based on BOT. Willingness to pay survey was conducted to assess financial viability and social acceptability of the proposed project. The financial incapability of the municipality and the increasing pressure on the city's infrastructure became the cause of initiative. Land for the pumping station and STP was acquired by the Municipality. Scheme was explained in detail to the office bearers of the various residents' associations. The residents were also motivated through advertisements in local cable TV network, and newspapers.

The following results were achieved from the initiatives:

- The city now has a proper wastewater disposal and treatment system.
- Underground drainage network has considerably improved the hygienic conditions
- Direct involvement of citizens gives them a status of stakeholders of the project.
- Citizens' involvement helped to develop a rapport between the urban local body and the citizens being the partners of the same initiative.

Tirupur (Tamil Nadu)

Tirupur, a city in Coimbatore District is located in the South West part of Tamil Nadu. Tirupur faced problems associated with shortage of water supply and wastewater treatment. To address the acute shortage of water supply and to facilitate wastewater treatment a project was started in the year 2002 through PPP. It is the first of its kind in the water sector in India. The project aims at providing efficient living environment to the citizens of Tirupur and an infrastructural support to the textile industry.

The project is the first public-private partnership in the water and sanitation sector in South Asia. A Special Purpose Vehicle (SPV) was formed to shoulder the responsibility of augmenting funds and implement the project on a Build-Own-Operate-Transfer (BOOT) basis.

The following results were achieved from the project:

- Improved living standards of about 800,000 residents including 80,000 slum inhabitants.
- More than 600 textile firms in and around Tirupur are relieved of tanker dependency.
- Increased the supply of water to domestic consumers.
- Provided the town with its first sewerage system.

Pune (Maharashta)

Pune city is the Cultural capital of Maharashtra having a population of 36.20 lakhs. Around two-fifth of the total population of Pune lives in slums and providing toilets to them is a responsibility of various local government bodies and Pune Municipal Corporation (PMC) is one among them and the most responsible authority for the same. Inadequate planning, poor sanitation facility, and open defecation problem forced PMC to involve NGOs for facilitating effective services. In 1999-2000, it entered into a contract with SPARC, other NGOs and CBOs for building community/public toilets. This partnership between the Pune Municipal Corporation, NGOs and community-based organizations has built more than 400 community toilet blocks. They have demonstrated the potential of municipal community partnerships to improve conditions for low-income groups. PMC would permit SPARC to maintain the complex at their own cost for a period of thirty years. The following results were achieved from the initiatives:

- Improved living standards of about 800,000 residents including 80,000 slum inhabitants
- The partnership has improved sanitation facilities for about 5, 00,000.
- In the first phase of the program, about half the toilet blocks were built by slum communities and in the other phase this rose to three quarters.
- The actual cost of the toilet blocks was 5 per cent less than the municipal corporation's costing.
- The participation of women/community groups helped in building the skills of these groups and eventually increasing their employability and livelihoods.
- Unlike previously constructed toilet blocks the one constructed during this project are well ventilated, spacious and thereby made it easier for the caretakers to take up cleaning process.

Surat (Gujarat)

Surat is the second largest city of Gujarat and is the second cleanest city of India. The urban local body of Surat city faced lot of problems for provisioning and facilitating sanitary facilities to the citizens during the outbreak of the epidemic-Plague. Even before, the sanitation facilities were not that satisfactory. Realizing the importance of and benefits form cleanliness Surat Municipal Corporation (SMC) and the government officials determined to clean up the city and ensure better living conditions for the citizens. To accomplish this task in 1995, SMC took several precautionary and curative steps, as required and also encouraged private participation.

SMC has opted for service contract with regard to cleaning the city program. SMC has deployed private contractors for garbage collection (cleaning at busy streets), transportation and its treatment and disposal. The contract for collection and transportation is one-year period, for treatment and disposal the concession period is 30 years. However, it can be terminated giving 30 days notice, if the contractor fails to operate effectively. The private contractors transport about 40 per cent of the total garbage. The following results were achieved from the project:

- Played an instrumental role in improving the sanitation condition in the city.
- It is now identified as one of the cleanest cities in the country.
- With micro privatization, determined efforts and an additional 10 per cent investment of funds SMC is able to collect and dispose of about 93 per cent of solid waste of which 40 per cent is done by private contractors, clean 95 per cent of streets everyday, clean market areas, major roads & litter prone areas twice a day.

Jaipur (Rajasthan)

Jaipur is the capital of Rajasthan state, known as the 'Pink City' of India and famous for its arts & crafts. For improving the level of illumination in the city, Jaipur Municipal Corporation decided to privatize the maintenance of streetlights. The initiative in its first phase was experimented in six municipal wards only. As a result of privatization the municipal corporation is now able to provide a better level of service using less of its internal resources.The following results were achieved from the project:

- The efficiency level in the maintenance of the tube lights and sodium lights has increased from 70 to 99 per cent, while expenditure has reduced by more than 50 per cent.
- After the success of the pilot testing in the first phase, further privatization of maintenance of streetlights was undertaken in phases and given on contract. Twenty contractors were involved in maintenance of streetlights. Taking these efforts ahead, a street light policy is also under formulation for other cities of Rajasthan State.

REFERENCES

Agrawal, Amba, (2005), Fiscal Decentralization in India: An Inter-State Analysis of Panchayat Finances, Serials Publications, New Delhi.

Bahl, R.W. & J.F. Linn, (1992), "Urban Public Finance in Developing Countries", World Bank Report, OUP, New York.

Basu, Amitava, (2001), Road Map for Municipal Reforms, in Good Urban Government Campaign India Launch Learning from one another, VNCHSC habitat, September 4-6, New Delhi.

Bhusan, B., (2002), Urban Infrastructure and Financing: An Indian Perspective, in Financing, Pricing and Cost Recovery of Urban Infrastructure, by (Ed) Sehgal, R.L. and R. Asthana, Bookwell, New Delhi.

CGG, JNNURM - RTP Training Module, Centre for Good Governance, Hyderabad, 2008.

Choguil, C.L., (2002), Ten Steps to Sustainable Infrastructure, in Financing, Pricing and Cost Recovery of Urban Infrastructure, by (Ed) Sehgal, R.L. and R. Asthana, Bookwell, New Delhi.

CRISIL, (2008), Urban Development Through JNNURM - From Definition to Delivery, FICCI – CRISIL Infrastructure Advisory, New Delhi, April.

Das, A.K. and Benjamen S., (1999), Implications of 74th C.A. on Urban Management and Planning in Three South India States: Karnataka, Kerala and Andhra Pradesh, September.

DFID, Practitioner's Conference on Mobilizing Urban Infrastructure Finance in a Responsible Fiscal Framework, Seminar Proceedings, 6-8, Jan., 2006, Jaipur.

GOI, "Report of 11th Finance Commission, Govt. of India, New Delhi.

GOI, "Report of 12th Finance Commission, Govt. of India, New Delhi.

Jayal, Nirza Gopal et.al., (2007), Local Governance in India, Oxford University Press, New Delhi.

Karnik, A. et.al., (2007), Developing Quantitative Framework for Determining Devolution of Funds from the State Government to Local Bodies in Local Governance in India by (ed) Jayal, N.G. et.al., OUP, New Delhi.

Kundu Amitabh, (2001), Urban Development Infrastructure Financing and Emerging System of Governance in India: A Perspective, UNESCO, New Delhi, April.

Kundu, Amitabh, et.al., (1999), "Regional Distribution of Infrastructure and Basic Amenities in Urban India: Issues Concerning Empowerment of Local Governments", Economic and Political Weekly, Vol. 34, No. 28.

Kundu, Amitabh, (2006), Trends and Patterns of Urbanization and Their Economic Implications, India Infrastructure Report, OUP, Delhi.

Mathur, M.P., (2006), Finances and Functioning of Urban Local Bodies: A Situation Report, India Infrastructure Report, OUP, New Delhi.

Mathur, O.P. & S. Ray, (2003), "Financing Municipal Services: Reaching Out to Capital Markets", National Institute of Public Finance and Policy, New Delhi.

Mathur, O.P., (1996), "Property Tax Policy and Local Governance", In Parthsarthy Som (Ed.), Fiscal Policy, Public Policy and Governance, National Institute of Public Finance and Policy, New Delhi.

Mathur, O.P., (2006), "Urban Finance", India Infrastructure Report, 2006, OUP, New Delhi.

Miltin, Diana, Editorial: (2008), Finance and Shelter Improvements, Environment & Urbanization, Vol. 20, No. 1, April.

Pinto, M.R., (2007), People-Centered Development and Participatory Urban Governance: The Mumbai Experience, in Local Governance in India by (ed) Jayal N.G. et. al., OUP, New Delhi.

Planning Commission, Eleventh Five Year Plan, 2007-12, Academic Foundation, New Delhi, 2008.

Rai, Nishith & Singh, A.K., (2007), Decentralized Urban Governance in India, Regional Centre for Urban & Environmental Studies, Lucknow.

Rai, Nishith & Singh, A.K., (2007), Restructuring of Municipal Services in India, Regional Centre for Urban & Environmental Studies, Lucknow.

Rai, Nishith & Singh, A.K., (2007), Strategic Issues for Urban Infrastructure Development: A Case Study of Lucknow City, Regional Centre for Urban & Environmental Studies, Lucknow.

Rai, Nishith & Singh, A.K.,(2007), Urban Water Supply & Tariff Structure, Regional Centre for Urban & Environmental Studies, Lucknow.

Ramanathan, Tara, (2006), Urban Poverty Reduction Strategies: Past, Present and Future, National Institute of Urban Affairs, New Delhi, Dec.

Rastogi, Anupam, (2008), The Infrastructure Sector in India, 2007, Indian Infrastructure Report, OUP, Delhi.

Savage, David & Shushegata Dasgupta, (2006), Governance Framework for Delivery of Urban Services, India Infrastructure Report.

Sehgal, R.L. & R. Ashthana (Ed.), (2002), Financing, Pricing and Cost Recovery of Urban Infrastructure, Bookwell, New Delhi.

Sen, Ruchira, (2006), Urban Poverty Alleviation Initiatives: The JNNURM: A Critical Assessment, National Institute of Urban Affairs, New Delhi, Nov.

Sharma, Savita, (2004), Poverty Estimates in India: Some Key Issues, Perspective Planning Division, Planning Commission, Govt. of India, May.

Singh, A.K., (2006), "Municipal Finances in India: Functional Realities and Prospects", In Urban Management By (Ed.) Nishith Rai & Urmila Bagga, New Royal Book Company .

Singh, K., (2000), Trends in Decentralization and Urban Governance, Paper Presented at the Seminar on Emerging Perspectives on Urban Governance, Institute for Human Development, New Delhi.

Singh, Kulwant & Behnam, Tai (Ed), (2000), Financing and Pricing of Urban Infrastructure, New Age International, Delhi.

World Bank, Devolution of Resources to Local Bodies, its Occasional Paper Series, 21, World Bank, New Delhi,1998.

World Bank, India Synthesis Study of Public Financial Management and Accountability in Urban Local Bodies, Financial Management Unit, World Bank, New Delhi, March, 2007.

World Bank, India Urban Sector Strategy, Urban and Infrastructure Unit, South Asia, Regional Office, World Bank, New Delhi, 2002.

Yesudian, CAK, Poverty Alleviation Programmes in India: A Social Audit, Indian Journal of Medical Research, Vol. 26,'O

INDEX

Q

R

S